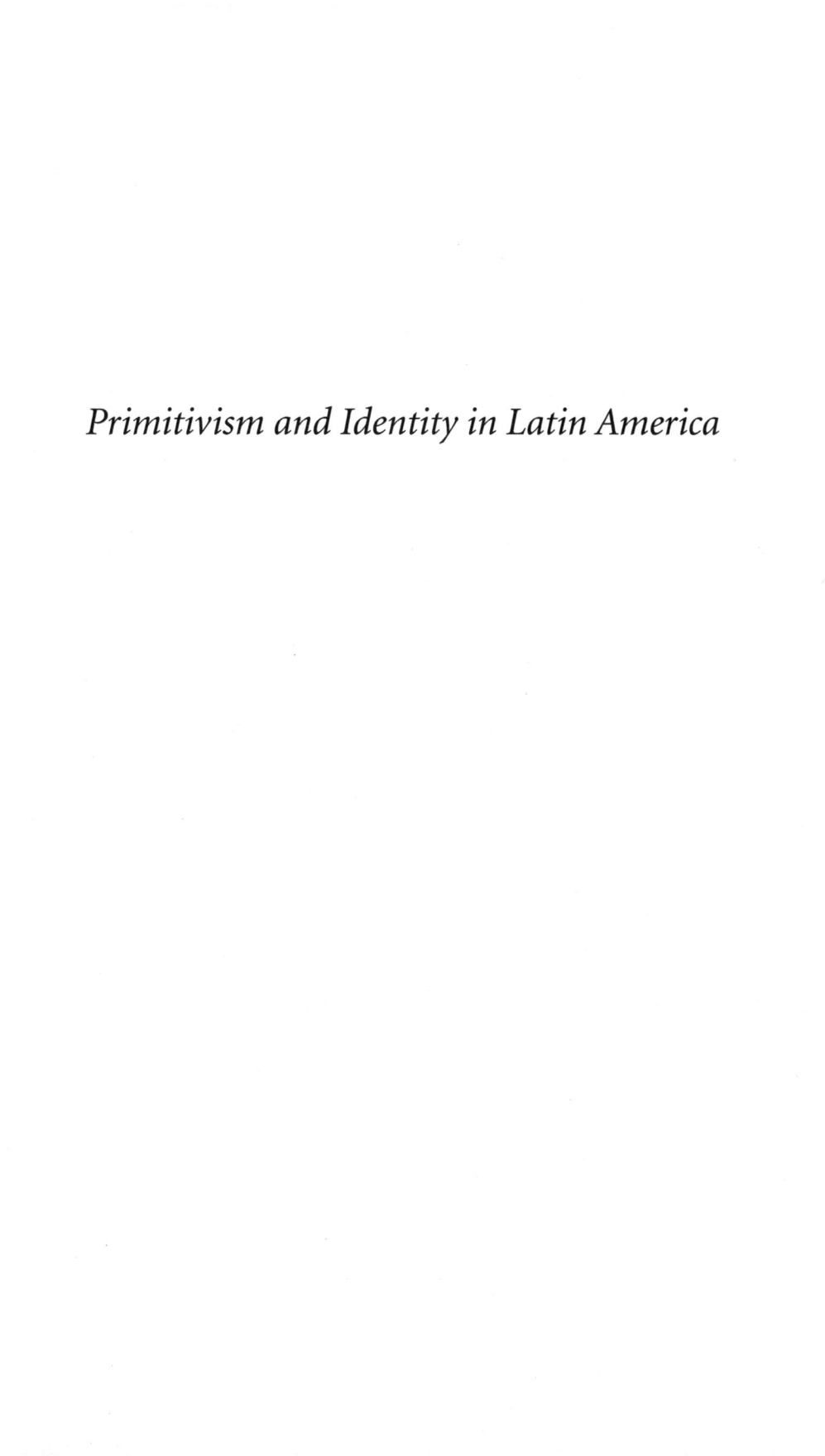

Primitivism and Identity in Latin America

Primitivism and Identity in Latin America

Essays on Art, Literature, and Culture

EDITED BY

Erik Camayd-Freixas

AND

José Eduardo González

The University of Arizona Press   Tucson

First printing

The University of Arizona Press

© 2000 The Arizona Board of Regents
⊚ This book is printed on acid-free, archival-quality paper.

Manufactured in the United States of America

05   04   03   02   01   00   6   5   4   3   2   1

Library of Congress Cataloging-in-Publication Data

Primitivism and identity in Latin America: essays on art, literature, and
culture / edited by Erik Camayd-Freixas and José Eduardo González.
p. cm.
Includes bibliographical references (p.) and index.
ISBN 0-8165-2045-3 (alk. paper)
1. Spanish American fiction—20th century—History and
criticism.   2. Primitivism in literature.   3. Latin America—
Civilization.   4. Primitivism—Latin America.   I. Camayd-Freixas,
Erik.   II. González, José Eduardo.
PQ7082.N7 P755 2000
863'.60911—dc21   00-008340

British Library Cataloguing-in-Publication Data
A catalogue record for this book is available from the British Library.

Contents

Introduction

The Returning Gaze

ERIK CAMAYD-FREIXAS

The present volume seeks to focus attention on the concept of primitivism and its implications for contemporary debates on Latin American culture, literature, and arts. Given the multidisciplinary nature of such implications and of primitivism itself, the essays here included touch upon several areas of interest pertaining to Latin American literature, art history, cultural policy, anthropology, and folklore, with several essays additionally oriented to the field of women's studies.

In recent years, the discourse of primitivism has begun to receive renewed international attention, but inquiry has been scant and overdue with respect to Latin America. The spark that reignited the debate was the 1984 landmark exhibition at the Museum of Modern Art in New York, "'Primitivism' in 20th Century Art," with a handsome two-volume catalog of the same title, edited by William Rubin. This event promoted the reprinting of older classics such as Arthur Lovejoy and George Boas's *A Documentary History of Primitivism and Related Ideas in Antiquity* (1935; 1997), Robert Goldwater's *Primitivism in Modern Art* (1938; 1967; 1986) and George Boas's *Primitivism and Related Ideas in the Middle Ages* (1946; 1997), together with several new studies (Barkan and Bush, Gombrich, Napier, Price, Rhodes, Torgovnick, Wassermann—see the Selected Bibliography) that expand the topic to touch upon interdisciplinary and cultural studies while challenging many previous assumptions. New theoretical approaches emerging in the 1980s and 1990s, particularly in critical theory and symbolic anthropology, are providing ways to analyze primitivism in relation to such important issues as the representation of the Other; the space of hybridity and cultural frontiers; the Western inventions of exoticism and Orientalism; the social construction of the body, gender, race, and sex; pop culture and outsider art; colonialism and postcolonialism, to mention a few.

These studies have thus far concentrated on how Western subjects have used the rhetoric of primitivism to justify ideologically either their exaltation of non-Western cultures, and concomitant critique of the West, or their often implicit discrimination against their cultural out-groups. The present volume takes a different approach. It seeks to produce a critical view of primitivism in which the center of analysis is how Latin American subjects employ a Western construct to look at themselves and appropriate it for their own purposes. The essays in this collection investigate both positive and negative effects of primitivism on Latin American culture, stemming as much from the Westerner's gaze as from Latin America's own versions of primitive.

Modern inquiry on primitivism begins with a seminal work of 1935 by Arthur O. Lovejoy and George Boas, *A Documentary History of Primitivism and Related Ideas in Antiquity.* Lovejoy and Boas established the distinction between "chronological" and "cultural" primitivisms. The first is a philosophy of history which theorizes that humanity's golden age was in the beginnings; that history is not marked by progress but by a tendency toward decline. The second is a cultural ideology, the dissatisfaction of the civilized with complex civilization, of the modern with sophisticated modernity, the attitude that a more natural and elementary life offers greater freedom and moral plenitude. Cultural primitivists need not deny the reality or the value of progress, as long as they are granted the opportunity for evasion, for a refuge, real or imagined, where they might recapture the simple life of old. They seek this ideal in the present, often in the way of life of exotic or primitive peoples who still survive in a "state of nature" preserved by remote isolation.

As I have suggested in my essay on narrative primitivism (see Camayd-Freixas in this volume), I believe it would be necessary to add an "aesthetic" primitivism to this typology, a plain and simple matter of "taste" for primitive forms and archaic sensibilities, as distinguished from the "ethical" value judgment implied by the other two. The signs of aesthetic primitivism can be seen most clearly in the plastic arts since the Avant-garde, among artists who otherwise feel quite at home in their modern urban habitat. Distinctions, however, can quickly become blurred. Chronological, cultural, and aesthetic primitivisms, though discernible, are rarely if ever found in such pure theoretical form. Every work, author, and period shows a different combination and predominance of these very relative categories. What is the real distance, after all—as Gombrich asks—among the chronological idea of a golden age, the nostalgia for one's own lost youth, and the longing for a more plentiful and innocent life than the present one?

To complicate this typology, the three attitudes I have outlined are subject to diverse approaches. Each period seeks this feeling for the archaic in different preferred themes: the "bucolic" of the Renaissance; the "prodigious and portentous" (*bizarro y peregrino*) of the Spanish Baroque; the "exotic" of Romanticism; the "odd" (*los raros*) of Spanish American *modernismo;* and the "formal primitivism" of the Avant-garde. Goldwater points out three tendencies in modern artistic primitivism: the "vital-romantic" of Gauguin and the Fauves, the "emotional" of the Expressionists, and the "intellectual or formal" of the Cubists and Surrealists. James Baird distinguished between an "academic" primitivism, presumed to be studied and contrived, and an "authentic" primitivism, more spontaneous and intuitive (though hardly believed in today). The distinction may also be drawn between what might be called an "idyllic" primitivism, which idealizes Arcadian serenity, beauty, and innocence, and a "morbid" primitivism, which values the grotesque, the monstrous, and the brutal, as part of the liberating "expressive force" of primitive forms. In *Totem and Taboo* and *Civilization and Its Discontents,* Freud popularized the idea that the primitive instincts of the id (which descended to the animal scale) were part of the subconscious organ of modern man, lurking repressed under layers of morality and civilization. On the other hand, ethnology had long been pointing out the presence of atavisms and vestiges of primitive myths and rites that survive at the base of modern values and social institutions. Hence, another contrast may be drawn: between "psychological" primitivism, whose field of inquiry is the individual and the species, and "social" primitivism, oriented toward the anthropological, the communal, the cultural, the tribal—both levels of course being interrelated.

Each essay in this collection explores various aspects of primitivism as they impact particular areas of Latin American culture and identity. They are organized thematically in sequential clusters. The first two essays, devoted to cultural criticism in Mexico from an anthropological standpoint, establish a dialogue with the next two pieces, on Mexican Colonial and folk art, surrounding the issue of national identity. In focusing on art's relationship with social issues and popular culture, they set the stage for the following two essays, which focus on questions of ethnic identity, racial politics, and conflictive modernity in different Latin American contexts. The last essay in this group, devoted to Angel Rama's concept of *transculturación narrativa,* leads in turn to a cluster on primitivism in narrative (essays 7 through 10), which respectively study narrative theory, Julio Cortázar's primitivist short fiction, the cycle of novels of the Amazon rain forest, and the oral narrative of the Tupi Indians of northern Brazil. Essays 11 and 12 are devoted to stage arts; the first of these to the representation of Indian bodies in narrative film, and the second to shamanistic ritual's potential for a body-centered dramaturgy in modern theater. This focus on the body paves the way for a final cluster constructed around women's issues: essay 13 treats the relation between the body and female identity in Frida Kahlo's primitivist self-portraits and self-fashioning; and essay 14 studies the importance of women's labor in César Vallejo's indigenist poetry.

Given the breadth of the topic, I would like to frame these essays in the broader context of Latin American primitivism and its historical relevance. Even though contemporary reflections on primitivism were inspired in large measure by the artistic revolution of the Avant-garde, where Picasso's *Demoiselles d'Avignon* (1907) is generally remarked as a turning point, it would be nearsighted to consider Latin American primitivism a mechanical influence of the European Avant-garde, or even an exclusively twentieth-century phenomenon. "Primitive" is of course a relative term, since every epoch and culture has had its primitives, at times admired or rejected. As a philosophy of history, as a cultural ideology, or as a radical aesthetics, primitivism has always been a part of the Latin American experience. Yet, by virtue of the historical effects of colonization that continue to operate at multiple levels, Latin American primitivism includes a tenor distinct from that of its metropolitan counterpart. It posits itself as the returning gaze of the colonized, a reappropriation of identity that lays claim to the rhizomorphous continuity of multiple cultural origins. While the foundational work by Lovejoy and Boas identified the roots of primitivism in Greek antiquity, today we recognize that "advanced" pre-Columbian cultures also had their golden age—Tula for the Aztecs, Tahuantinsuyu for the Incas—and that the globally diffuse practice of ancestor worship should alert us to the possibility of a primitivism among primitives. Modern testimonial peoples, perhaps most of all, are susceptible to that nostalgic, idealizing, backward gaze. Ivete Walty's essay documents just that in the modern descendants of the Brazilian Tupi, whose stories divide history before and after the arrival of the white man.

Medieval and Renaissance brands of primitivism took root in the New World from the moment of the Encounter. The European gaze revealed this in many ways, from utopian and religious thought to the hard primitivism of Montaigne's *Of Cannibals* and Bartolomé de Las Casas's defense of human sacrifice. In the imaginary of many sixteenth-century Europeans, America and her native inhabitants existed in an uncorrupted "state of nature"; for others they were hopelessly savage. Both images have coexisted and competed until the present day. Spanish missionaries, too, were split on this issue: most considered Indian idolatry the work of the devil, but some "religious primitivists," as it were, found this "uncorrupted nature" ideal for creating new Christians without European vices and were ready to translate Christian teachings into remotely similar Indian images. One notorious theory attempting to reconcile Indian origins with the Bible identified the civilizing deity Quetzalcoatl as the Apostle Thomas. Often, thus, religious syncretism combining Christian and Indian imagery placed primitivism at the service of evangelization and quickly found its way into Hispanic American art. Delia Cosentino's essay documents this process in early Colonial painting.

Creole primitivism flourished with the Colonial Baroque, first in an architecture whose *structure* remained Arabic and European while the *ornamentation* that overpowered it was decidedly syncretic, not only in its motifs but also in its affinity with indigenous principles of composition. Baroque allegory became primitivist in refined literary works such as Sor Juana's *Loa to The Divine Narcissus* (1690), which metaphorically reconciled Aztec, ancient Greek, and Christian mysteries and religious symbols, and Sigüenza y Góngora's *Teatro de virtudes políticas* (1680), which favorably compared the pre-Hispanic rulers of Mexico with the great statesmen of Roman antiquity, presenting them as models of virtue to be emulated by the Spanish viceroys. Neoclassicism, in turn, adapted the rustic ideal from Virgil's *Georgics* to America in long-winded poems like Rafael Landívar's *Rusticatio mexicana* (1781) and Andrés Bello's *Agriculture in the Torrid Zone* (1826). In another of Bello's post-Independence poems, *Allocution to Poesy* (1823), as well as in his essays, Latin American identity was constructed as *difference* by means of a lasting binarism: "the cultured Europe" versus "the primitive America." On the one hand, Latin American primitivism became a gesture of self-affirmation in the face of the unreachable modernity of the European Enlightenment and industrial revolution. On the other hand, ancient Indian nobility became a symbol of that difference, appropriated by the white creole elite for political aims. Independence leaders even entertained the project of a continental state united under the decorative figure of a legitimate Inca emperor, while José Joaquín de Olmedo's ode *The Victory at Junín* (1825) brought the ghost of Inca emperor Huaina Capac to lecture the new republican ruling class on the art of government and unity.

Rousseau's primitivism, with its idealized "state of nature" and its "noble savage," became a major influence in politics through *The Social Contract*, as well as in literature through *Emile*. Latin American Romanticism learned to seek the exotic at home, finding in *indianismo* (not to be confused with the Marxist-leaning *indigenismo* of the 1930s) a common expression for a trend with many national variations. After the 1880s, the *modernistas* sought a remote exotic in refined Orientalism, in the literary eccentric, and even in the occult. One way in which the modernistas, led by Rubén Darío, sought to renew poetic expression was by reviving forgotten metric forms of the Spanish fourteenth and fifteenth centuries. As the movement matured, the "second" modernismo of the early twentieth century abandoned the earlier exoticism in which it had honed its "modern" technical skills, merging with nativist movements such as *regionalismo*, *mundonovismo*, and *indigenismo*, and applying its refined technique to themes of autochthonous tradition.

Part of the current critical reexamination of Spanish American modernismo (which had been too easily dismissed as exoticist, bourgeois, and un-American) questions the unqualified view that considers the Avantgarde as a complete break with the past and as the true usher of artistic modernity emanating from Europe to Latin America. The case of César Vallejo is a pertinent example of a poet's successful transition from modernismo to the Avant-garde. Hedrick's essay on Vallejo shows that this transition was in many ways a refashioning, given that in modernismo—as Roger Shattuck's *The Banquet Years* showed of the European *belle époque*— archaism and modernity had already coincided *before* the Avant-garde. Similarly, José Eduardo González's essay shows that Angel Rama's influential theory of "narrative transculturation" in Latin America was based on a notion of modernity as the technification of the archaic, which originated in Rama's own reevaluations of modernismo.

Yet, even in its exoticist vein, romantic and *modernista* irrationalism was still self-affirming in that it remained largely immune to the scientific faith of the times. Gaining momentum since the eighteenth century and culminating with nineteenth-century positivist and evolutionary thought, the Western *philosophy of progress* compromised its scientific and material basis by association with a distorted idealism and social organicism, which yielded pseudoscientific and racist concepts of history and cultural development. Accordingly, in an increasingly globalized world, Western countries, which possessed an evolved "national soul," were justified, even obliged, to assume a paternalistic, patronizing role toward "inferior (less than white) societies." Colonial expansion was again disguised as philanthropy. In Latin America, where even abolitionist thought had frequently been allied with a demographic policy of social "whitening" and notions of a secular struggle between "civilization and barbarism," the dominant scientific discourse produced a turn-of-the-century social thought marked by racial self-prejudice and historical pessimism. In the early 1900s, Creole positivists and naturalists often saw the "sick continent" as doomed by a "social pathology" that was racial in nature. The rise of Lombrosian "criminal ethnology" in Latin America reflected the generalized preoccupation with suppressing cultural difference in unassimilated, nonwhite groups, stigmatized as possessing a "primitive" psychology and morality. Valerio-Holguín's essay on the Dominican massacre of Haitians in 1937 shows the prevalence of these sentiments well into the twentieth century.

Far from being a new import, modern primitivism in Latin America is, then, mutatis mutandis, a resurgence, a broad reevaluation of culture, prompted by several factors: an overdue reaction against positivism; a rise in nationalist sentiments after the Mexican Revolution; a disillusionment with Western civilization after World War I; the rise of ethnology and humanistic anthropology; major archaeological discoveries in the Americas; and, certainly, the influence of artistic primitivism as propelled by the European Avant-garde. Tribal art became particularly influential in the main Avant-garde movements: Cubism, Expressionism, and Surrealism. Realistic depiction was abandoned in favor of primitive angularity and geometric design. Form and technique were simplified, gaining expressive, emotional force through distortion and stylization. The resultant freedom from the laws of proportion and the limits of visual perception was taken as a statement of psychic, spiritual, and cultural liberation. The affinity between primitive and modern art became so widely recognized that by the 1920s the artistic circles of Paris had become the world trade center of tribal art objects. It was an environment in which young Latin American artists were received with admiration and curiosity. Encouraged by European primitivism, they soon turned their gazes home, seeking a more authentic primitive in their own countries' indigenous traditions. Thus, the same primitivism that in the West remained a countercultural movement soon became, for Latin American artists, a form of cultural affirmation and a reformulation of identity starting from non-Western autochthony.

Ancestral American art offered them a long and diverse tradition to emulate. Tribal painting had flourished before the ninth century in the Maya civilization, in pottery, codices, and murals such as those preserved at Bonampak. Aztec, Inca, and many other ancient civilizations of Central and South America produced great painting, pottery, sculpture, weaving, and feather work, whose patterns have influenced modern primitivists. Their descendants still practice some traditional techniques, including body painting, an art form in itself. Thus, modern artistic primitivism in Latin America soon became independent of its European sources. Diego Rivera (1886–1957), who started as a Cubist in Paris, returned home after the Mexican Revolution to celebrate the national past in murals inspired by pre-Columbian art. Among Mexican muralists, José Clemente Orozco (1883–1949) mixed primitive traditions with modern expressionism; David Alfaro Siqueiros (1898–1974) oriented his painting more directly toward political metaphor and protest within the international indigenista movement. Rufino Tamayo (1899–1991), of Zapotec Indian ancestry, followed the belief in the *nahual,* using animals to reflect human behavior. Frida Kahlo (1907–1954) extended her primitivism beyond her paintings, to her artistic persona, becoming a cultural icon for female identity and natural power, as Wendy Faris's essay explains. María Izquierdo (1902–1955) mixed avant-garde primitivism with pop art. Alejandro Colunga (b. 1948) and Rocío Maldonado (b. 1951) have continued this Mexican tradition in original ways.

In Peru, the indigenista movement found early expression in the "Incaism" of José Sabogal (1888–1956), which grew under the intellectual leadership of José Carlos Mariátegui and the *Amauta* group. Osvaldo Guayasamín (b. 1919), Ecuadorian of Indian-mestizo family, embodies indigenista painting with its typical mixture of social realism and pre-Columbian motifs. The Quechua-titled paintings of Fernando de Szyszlo (b. 1925), inspired by Tihuanaco culture monoliths, gave a new dimension to Abstract Expressionism. Tilsa Tsuchiya (1932–1984) depicted pre-Columbian Peruvian myths and iconography with highly stylized renditions of Chavín culture motifs. Armando Villegas (b. 1928) applies primitivist stylization to his images of the Conquest and colonization.

Among the foundational figures of Latin American primitivism, Uruguayan Joaquín Torres García (1874–1949) mixed pre-Columbian and abstract art in a Constructivist, geometrical style of metaphysical intent. Argentine Alejandro Xul Solar (1888–1963), working within the *Martín Fierro* group, developed the influence of Dada and Surrealism in American themes. Chilean Surrealist Roberto Matta (b. 1912) drew from Mexican codices, as well as Eskimo, Kwakiutl, and other American tribal objects to create abstract, multidimensional, and dynamic spaces fixed on canvas. Influenced by Matisse and Leger, Brazilian Tarsila do Amaral (1886–1973) composed images of cultural cannibalism in simplified shapes and primary colors, as a pictorial response to poet Oswald de Andrade's 1928 *Anthropophagite Manifesto.* Brazilian Teresa D'Amico (1914–1965) emulated ancient maps in her *Enchanted Landscapes,* featuring a collage of seeds for land and the neo-African mermaid deity Yemanjá swimming the oceans as a replacement for the mythological sea creatures of old European cartography. Cândido Portinari (1903–1962) marks a return to social realism with his depictions of rural poverty in the Brazilian Northeast.

In Cuba, Wifredo Lam (1902–1982), of black and Chinese parents, influenced by Surrealism in Paris, developed after 1940 a powerful style that mixed Afro-Cuban and varied tribal traditions with the shapes of the tropical jungle, to produce a spiritlike fusion of animal, plant, and human forms. Many white creole painters, such as Mario Carreño, began at that time to draw direct inspiration from Abakuá and other Afro-Cuban religious sects, following the "Negroid poetry" movement that had been flourishing in Cuba and Puerto Rico since the late 1920s. René Portocarrero (1912–1986) superimposed Baroque ornamentation on simplified primitive forms. Cundo Bermúdez (b. 1914) treated typical everyday scenes of popular and country life from a naive *guajiro* perspective.

Among postmodern primitivists, Argentine Antonio Berni (1905–1981) marked the passage from Surrealism back to social critique and parody with his *Juanito Laguna* series. Colombian Fernando Botero (b. 1932) equally parodies Renaissance masters and Latin American institutions, from the Church to the military. His rotund childlike figures, reminiscent of Olmec sculpture, exemplify another trait of primitivist art: the uniformity of facial traits. Individualized only by their dress, his chubby characters, even their pets, all bear variations of the same face, like members of a single clan. Uruguayan José Gamarra (b. 1934) offers a naive tropicalism in his lush scenes of the Amazon jungle, interrupted by a small airplane or helicopter where one would expect a bird. Argentine César Paternosto (b. 1931) draws abstract geometric designs inspired by Indian textiles. Argentine Luis Felipe Noé (b.

1933) parodies primitivism itself in his abstract social painting *To Flee like Gauguin or to Dream like Rousseau* (1985).

Primitivism thus pervaded all modern schools and styles, including Impressionism, before the Avant-garde. Gauguin, the first modern primitivist, was after all an Impressionist. Uruguayan Pedro Figari (1867–1938) brought naive post-Impressionism to social themes, while Dominican Cándido Bidó (b. 1940) re-created it with a lighter, more decorative tenor and brighter tropical colors, a Caribbean Van Gogh. Then again, Camille Pissarro, a father of French Impressionism, was actually from the Antilles. Thus, primitivism is not a style but an orientation, an evolving sensibility, and, for Latin American heritage, a matter of national and continental identity.

In contrast to sophisticated, highly stylized primitivism, naive or folk art is said to be produced by amateurs, without commercial intent, solely for the artist's satisfaction. Some critics have claimed that it resembles children's art in its lack of formal discipline and technique, and its disregard for perspective, proportion, and volume. It seeks realism through minute detail, like painting a tree leaf by leaf. The classic example of naive artist was the French customs officer Henri Rousseau. Valued for its charm, naive art often becomes studied and contrived, while sophisticated primitivism may also conceal a false naivete: no sharp boundary exists. Latin America's most important naive school is the Haitian Centre d'Art. Hector Hyppolite (1894–1948) and the barber Philomé Obin (1892–1985) are among its pioneers. Musician, shoemaker, and taxi driver Rigaud Benoit (1911–1986), who became an internationally acclaimed painter, used a magnifying glass to render minute detail. Their subject matter is everyday Haitian life and landscape, often with religious themes, both Christian and Voodoo. Since colonial rule in the Americas forbade slaves to make images of any kind, the great West African sculptural tradition was severed, but ritual, mythology, music, and dance survived. Characteristic visual forms developed in isolation, resulting in Haitian art's distinctive style.

Better known for its poetry, the Solentiname peasant group organized in Nicaragua by Ernesto Cardenal also produced folk painting, though not of the importance of the Haitian school. Yet, independent folk painters have been recognized throughout Latin America, including the sophisticated Brazilian Emiliano di Cavalcanti (1897–1976), Brazilian rural worker José Antônio da Silva (b. 1909), Nicaraguan Asilia Guillén (1887–1964), Honduran José Antonio Velásquez (1906–1983), Colombian Noé León (1907–1978), Colombian Sofía Urrutia (b. 1912), Venezuelan Feliciano Carvallo (b. 1920), and a newer generation: Mexican Zapotec Indian Francisco Toledo (b. 1940), Brazilian Dircen Carvalho (b. 1942), Nicaraguan Julio Sequeira (b. 1947), and Venezuelan Neké Alamo (b. 1948). Contrary to modernist primitivism—Marta Traba once claimed—naive art is a static art that permits no evolution. Eli Bartra's essay in this volume dispels this and other myths regarding its production, consumption, and definition.

Finally, outsider art is oblivious by choice or circumstances to academies and prevailing artistic and social trends. Often occurring in urban industrial societies, it does not qualify as folk art, though no sharp boundaries exist. Since Latin American art fundamentally seeks identity affirmation, outsider art, decidedly countercultural, is scarcer than in the developed West. There are exceptions, however, like the untrained Venezuelan artist Apolinar (Pablo Livinalli Santaella; b. 1928), who started painting in 1965 and achieved notoriety for his bizarre book-objects.

Beyond the plastic arts, modern primitivism has influenced music, dance, theater, literature, and film. As the essays by Restrepo, Weisz, and Faris will show, primitivism in visual and stage arts privileges the human body itself, over the outward signification of words, as the central object of interpretation, an elementary text to be read with the awareness that it has been historically and ideologically inscribed. In literature, the domain of words, the struggle to return to the image, to the primordial unity when word and thing were not yet divorced, is also apparent. From the Amazonian heartland, taken as continental synecdoche, poetic imagination has posited a primitive Latin American space, giving rise to an interartistic tendency often referred to as "tropicalism," as well as to a novelistic cycle whose historical, political, and ecological complexities are explored here in Jorge Marcone's essay. In one way or another, primitivism has continued to touch major Latin American writers, sometimes with defining force. It can be variously found in main works by Asturias, Carpentier, Borges, Cortázar, Vallejo, Mistral, Neruda, Paz, Arguedas, Roa Bastos, Rulfo, García Márquez, Donoso, Fuentes, Vargas Llosa, Valenzuela, and many others. One of the most salient signs of this influence is the contemporary fusion of literary and anthropological discourses. The varieties and implications of that fusion are the subject of several essays in this collection, particularly those by Roger Bartra, Chanady, Kauffmann, and Camayd-Freixas.

In short, primitivism has not only affected cultural policy and patterns of consumption; beyond the social surface, it has also been a hidden actor in the drama of national and continental identity formation, from the early twentieth-century contest among the myths of *latinidad, indigenismo,* and *negritud,* to the latest versions of transculturation, *mestizaje,* and hybridity, jading every concept of modernity and postmodernity applied to Latin America.

Even though modern primitivism acquired a new meaning in Latin America, many European misrepresentations inherent in the concept were transmitted along with it. Since the Avant-garde, for example, primitivism has been consistently characterized along racial or ethnic lines as related to the nonwhite, despite the recognition that the "prescientific" period of European civilization has also been considered "primitive." Particularly problematic is the association of neo-African cultures with primitiveness that we find in Fernando Ortiz, Alejo Carpentier, and Caribbean *negrismo* in general. At bottom, primitivism, as a product of Western conventions, domestication, and misconceptions about the Other, remains a representation based on pastiche and simulacra. To use it for examining *self*-representation in Latin America is immediately to expose the contradictions of cultural myths and to deconstruct the instrumental concepts of identity construction.

Often enough, *contradiction* is the operant word. While the primitivist enterprise has been predominantly associated with anticolonialism and cultural democratization, the idealization and recuperation of pure cultural archetypes has also been an underlying aspiration of fascism. After rescuing the formerly marginalized and often despised ethnic aspects of culture and making them a source of pride and national value, it also made them available to officialdom, whether in the form of tourist market trinkets or of venerable cultural artifacts appropriated once again by the dominant culture's patron institutions, and even by the state itself, as a means of self-legitimation by repressive structures of power. A central issue here is the distance, widespread in Latin America, between nation and state: whereas the concept of nation is primitivistic in that it seeks its identity in a foundational past, and its fervor in ancestry, the state is progressivist insofar as it posits its very justification in the future and argues policy on the basis of promise— while at the same time maintaining the pretense of representing the nation, or appropriating it altogether by claiming their identity, if not at the least their coincidence. Still reactive to the flawed Western developmental models unevenly imposed on Latin America, primitivism often becomes a melancholic expression of disillusionment, a compensatory search for the ideal values lost to modernity, but also a sublimation of its very own unconfessed fetishism of progress.

Noting that cultural inquiry from the standpoint of primitivism has been conspicuously absent from critical discourse on Latin America, the present anthology has attempted to bring together for the first time the views of investigators who, in diverse fashion, are currently engaging the concept and its related ideas to address relevant and varied aspects of Latin American cultural production, consumption, and policy. To the extent that "primitive" remains an ethnocentric term belonging to the monologue of modernity for what it considers "backward" or "rudimentary," we must admit that what is primitive are not the cultures to which it is customarily applied so much as our understanding of them, the cannibalistic image that we have created for our own consumption. Thus, this volume seeks to contribute to our understanding of the constructs of identity and counter-identity, in the desire that our concepts of self and cultural other may someday become less rudimentary.

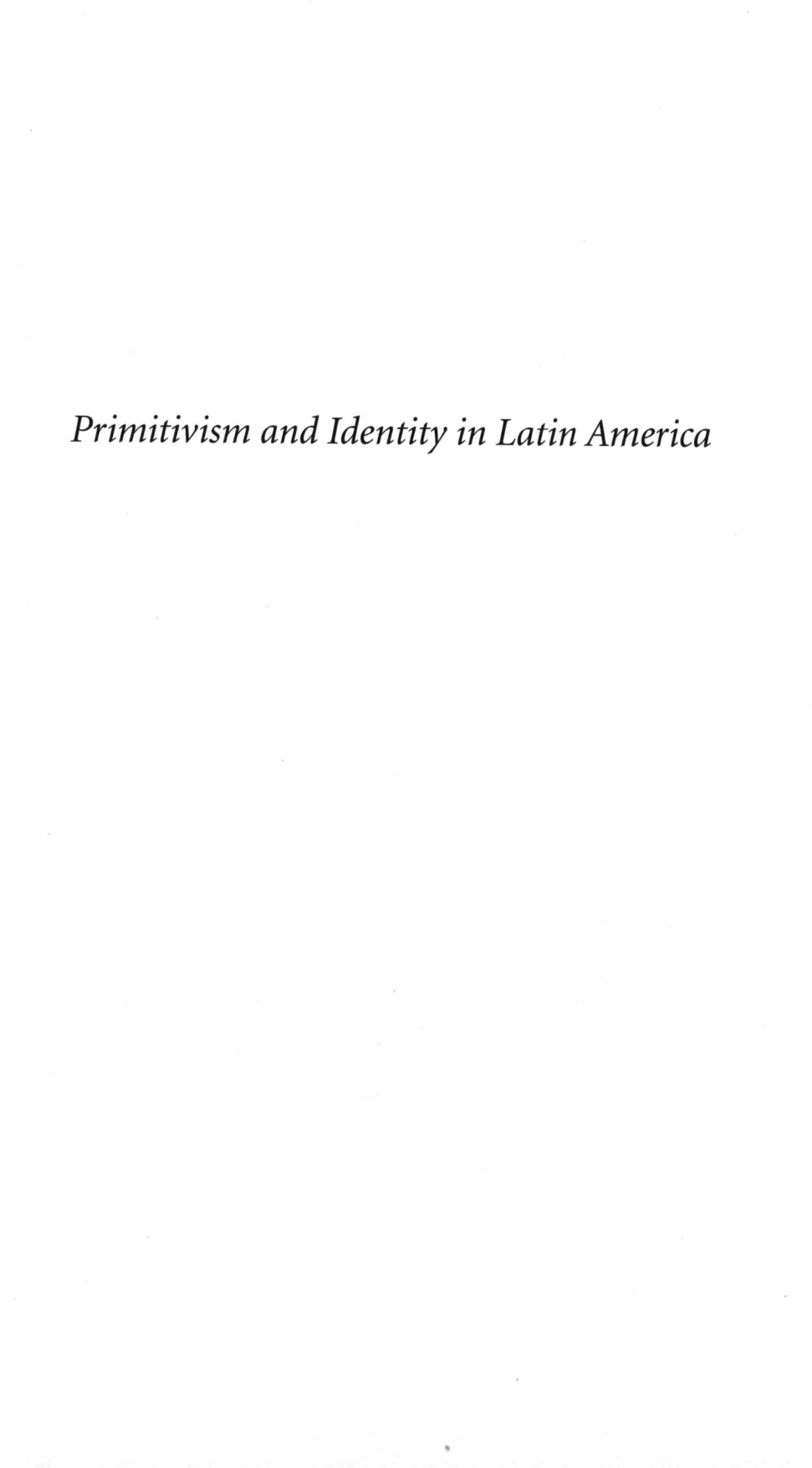

Primitivism and Identity in Latin America

Paradise Subverted

The Invention of the Mexican Character

ROGER BARTRA

TRANSLATED BY CHRISTOPHER J. HALL

Peasants are in the habit of casting a long shadow of nostalgia and melancholy over modern society. They are the survivors of a period that must never return. Although its memory awakens a heartfelt sadness, it is nevertheless capable of being expanded by society into a cultural and political phenomenon, that "reactionary heartfelt sadness" of which Ramón López Velarde spoke in the poem "El retorno maléfico" (The Ill-Fated Return), which begins:

> Better not to return to the village,
> to the subverted paradise which remains silent
> in the laceration of the shrapnel.

It is not my intention to propose a return to paradise subverted or an investigation into the nature of the rural world. I wish, instead, to reflect on the form in which modern culture creates or invents its own paradise lost; I want to make clear the way in which, as a *reaction* to its own contradictions, capitalist industrial society searches insistently for a mythical level at which primitive innocence and the original order were supposedly lost.

In Mexico, as in many countries, the re-creation of agrarian history is an essential ingredient in any characterization of the national culture; it is, I believe, the keystone without which the coherence of the cultural edifice would tumble down. But I am not merely confirming the truism that the national culture is nourished by the preindustrial history of the country and the ashes of the peasantry. What I wish to emphasize, on the contrary, is a process through which is *invented* a mythical paradise, one that is indispensable not only in order to fuel the sentiments of guilt occasioned by its destruction, but also in order to trace the outline of cohesive nationality; it is indispensable, likewise, for the imposition of order in a society convulsed by the abrupt arrival of the modern age and rocked by the contradictions of the new industrial lifestyle.[1] From the perspective of the city and modern culture these peasants are, like Pedro Páramo, the ghosts of blurred recollections in the collective memory. This paradisiacal space created by the national culture is a true anti-Utopia: its function is the delimitation of the national establishment, the definition of the "authentic" national being through opposition in any Utopia intending to revolutionize (or contaminate) it.

In this sense, the subverted paradise can be defined as an *archaeotopia;* that is, the contemporary image of an earlier place in which happiness reigned. But it is a past and faded happiness that reposes at a deep, mythical level, buried by the avalanche of the Mexican Revolution, through which we can feel only melancholy. It is a place in which present and past are confused in order to exclude the future. Without a doubt, the work of Juan Rulfo best reveals and describes this pristine state of trampled happiness; the deep insight of Carlos Fuentes reveals in Rulfo's work the existence of the old postcosmogonic myth "in which the original unity is lost on the intervention of history." Fuentes adds: "This historic battle can be manifested in epic fashion, as a celebration of human power, or tragically, as a lament on the loss of unity preceding that power."[2] It seems to me that this can be applied also to a considerable portion of contemporary culture.

Nevertheless, I believe that the cultural gestation of an imaginary subverted paradise does not just pay tribute to the original postcosmogonic myth to which Carlos Fuentes refers. We are also dealing with the creation of a new mythical space that is modern and endowed with powers remaining, in large part, unknown and unexplored. Therefore, rather than turn back to its primitive origins, I shall try to follow the guiding thread in the other direction, toward its function in modern society.

It should be emphasized in this light that the mythological force of paradise lost, of the noble savage destroyed, is rooted not only in the depths of history, but also in the fact that it forms part of a modern network of cultural and political mediations; this network has its own dynamism, relatively distinct from that which characterizes the original set of myths. The principal difference lies in the fact that the present-day elaboration of the myth of paradise subverted is part of an extensive system of political legitimation, which I have described elsewhere as an imaginary network of political power.[3] Thus, this image distinguishes two major cadences: original primitive time and historical time. The reconstruction of a mythical rural past faces the real horror of industrial society. Clearly we are witnessing here the well-known Jungian archetype of Janus: the opposition of past and future, of what is behind and what is ahead. This polarity permeates Western thought; but when it is developed in the limited situations of "Third World" societies, the polarity acquires a strange and nebulous form that even, at times, borders on the realm of madness.[4]

The wound is still open that the revolutionary shrapnel of modern society, guided by the symbols of future and progress, inflicted on the rural, indigenous past. Through this wound the political culture wheezes; and in the name of pain for the shattered past it devises a profile of contemporary man that corresponds, point by point, with the myth of paradise subverted. Thus, the Mexicans resulting from the immense tragedy begun with the Conquest and ending with the Revolution are imaginary and mythical inhabitants of a violated limbo. Backwardness and underdevelopment have come to be seen as manifestations of a perennial static infancy that has lost its primitive innocence.

The myth of paradise subverted is the inexhaustible spring at which Mexican culture quenches its thirst. The present-day definition of nationality owes its intimate structure to this myth. It is therefore a commonplace to think that the Mexicans resulting from the coming of history are archaic souls whose tragic relationship with the modern age obliges them to reproduce their primitivism permanently. In this paradox we can locate Alfonso Reyes's metaphor about Mexicans as the amphibian variety of mestizo: they endure all the sins of the modern epoch, but still live immersed in the golden age.[5] The subverted paradise in which they find themselves is an eternal instant trapped between two mythical fissures: *after* the original sin, when women and men have already tasted the fruit of the tree of knowledge, but *before* their expulsion from paradise. In this tragic and marvelous moment, man is already burdened by sin and guilt but still possesses the natural goodness of his first infancy.

The myth of paradise subverted is destined to become securely anchored in the history of industrial societies; it is no transient myth. To study it in the present-day reality of Mexico is, for this reason, highly interesting. Moreover, we can still see on the historical horizon the very "trauma" that stimulated it: the Mexican Revolution and consequent industrialization. In Mexico the myth acquires epic proportions, for two main reasons: first, because of the antiquity of the process, rooted as it is in the Conquest and acquiring its form from the clash and fusion of two different cultures; second, in paradoxical and dramatic fashion, because the end of the peasant world is precipitated by one of the biggest peasant revolts of the twentieth century.

The hero of this imaginary epic is a singular character, because he belongs to a suffering, wronged species. He is an extremely sensitive, timorous, suspicious, susceptible being.[6] This peasant hero has been held captive in a prison of logic, confined between a past of savage misery and a future of barbaric riches. He has been the starting point for the definition of the twentieth-century Mexican: a definition that has been imprisoning the imaginary melancholic being in a mythology permanently fed by poets, philosophers, psychologists, novelists, and sociologists. In the name of that Mexican of the final stages of the second millennium, all of them feel a "nostalgia for death." The creator of this metaphor, the great poet Xavier Villaurrutia, has described that ancient death which precedes us in these melancholy words:

> To return to a distant fatherland,
> to return to a forgotten fatherland,
> obscurely deformed
> by exile in this land.
> —("To Return . . .")

We accept the invitation and set out on a journey around that mythical fatherland, that foundered paradise which has been invoked as the source of the Mexican nation.

Primordial Mourning

Mexican culture has spun the myth of the peasant hero with a yarn of nostalgia. Inevitably, the national imagery has converted the peasants into dramatic characters, victims of history, suffocated in their own land after the great disaster of the Mexican Revolution. The literary reconstruction of the peasant is a dueling ceremony, a rending of garments before the sacrificed body on the altar of the modern age and progress.

El luto humano (Human Mourning), a novel by José Revueltas, is one of the most transparent examples of this myth. It is the story of a group of peasants who are trapped by a great flood while keeping vigil over the body of a little girl; they are drowned and attacked by buzzards, as though they were the carrion of the Mexican Revolution. Significantly, the central character is called Adán (Adam); his life story is told as his body floats on the water. The image of the rural world that slowly develops is that of the past which it has been necessary to sacrifice; for this reason, the image is constructed in parallel with and in very similar fashion to that omnipresent Western archetype to which both psychology and literature owe so much: melancholy.

In fact, the catalog of classic symptoms of melancholy is extraordinarily similar to the features that the sociological and anthropological traditions assign to the peasant. The parallel between the melancholy/mania duality of psychiatrists and the rural/urban polarity of anthropologists is amazing. The Janus archetype is deeply ingrained in both paradigms: the opposition between a past that founders and a future that explodes is what separates the agrarian from the industrial world. From the modern perspective, the peasants are passive, indifferent to change, pessimistic, resigned, timorous, and independent.[7] Classic psychiatry has defined melancholiacs by their slowness, their dismal stupor, their sadness, their bitterness, and their lassitude, as well as by their fear and intense desire for solitude. It is enough to look through the pages dealing with melancholy in a history of mental illnesses to recognize immediately the misty world of Comala, as Rulfo has described it in *Pedro Páramo*.

The stereotype of the peasant as melancholy figure has become one of the most important constituents of the so-called Mexican character and national culture. It is essential to recognize that a good part of what is called the *ser del mexicano* (essence of the Mexican) is no more than the transposition to the cultural domain of a series of commonplaces and formative ideas that Western culture has for a long time forced on its rural and peasant substrate. As in Revueltas's novel, the body of the peasant floats for a long time on the national conscience. One ends up believing firmly that, under the turmoil of the modern age, exacerbated by the Revolution, runs a mythical level, a flooded paradise with which we can have only a melancholic relationship; only by way of deep nostalgia can we make contact with it and communicate with those beings who populate it. For those paradisiacal figures are also melancholic beings with whom it is impossible to relate materially, even though they are the Mexican's raison d'être.

I shall tear out, woman, the impossible
love of melancholy prayer,
and even though the soul remains solitary,
the faith of my ludicrous passion will be free.
　　—("To an Impossible")

López Velarde wrote this around 1905; in some way, the melancholic ideal was already anchored as a firm stereotype of the Mexican intelligentsia of that period. In 1901, in a truly enjoyable, as well as pioneering, study of the "social psychiatry" of the Mexican, the features of the Mexican character were established with academic forcefulness and solemnity. Many of the features cited in this study by Julio Guerrero were taken up again some decades later by various writers (from Samuel Ramos and Emilio Uranga to Jorge Carrión, Octavio Paz, and Santiago Ramírez) in order to develop the so-called philosophy of Mexicanness. Here I should like to quote Guerrero's reflection on melancholy:

> And so the Mexican who has no alcohol, even though he is not by nature sad, suffers lengthy attacks of melancholy, as can be seen in the elegiac, spontaneous tone of their poets, starting with Nezahualcóyotl ... the unending series of modern romantics; popular Mexican music, written in a minor key; those dances, full of melancholy, which the military bands in public parks hurl into the twilight breezes, pregnant with whispers and wailings; and those popular songs which, to the sound of the guitar on moonlit nights, are intoned in the houses of the neighborhood. . . . The medium in which we live is wont to transform the gravity of the Indian and the solemnity of the Castilian into melancholy tendencies.[8]

In this manner of thinking Guerrero begins to develop the mythology of the diverse facets or masks of the Mexican, that singular being in which ferocity and misanthropy, mockery and stoicism, caprice and sloth, bestiality and lack of aspirations serve as counterpoints.[9]

It should be noted that in the process of formulating and inventing the nation (and, therefore, the national character), we always run up against a paradoxical confrontation with "the Other." In this confrontation, conscience itself becomes peopled with stereotypes and dominant ideas that, in turn, exercise an influence on the behavior of the inhabitants of a particular nation. Let us consider an example: it is not difficult to track down the origin of the opinion that Mexicans are spineless and idle (in Europe, this idea is applied as much to Latins as to Slavs); but even recognizing the colonialist and racist roots of this idea, there can be no doubt that, in some measure, it is taken, elaborated, and revalued by the nationalist conscience in order to set it with patriotic pride against the pragmatic values that are attributed to Anglo-Saxons. This nationalist intention takes very clear form in the "dance symphony" *H.P.* (Horsepower) of Carlos Chávez, in which the music contrasts tropical exuberance with the powerful industrial rhythms of the North. Diego Rivera, who influenced the composition of this symphony, represented the same idea in murals.

Thus, we find that in the invention of the Mexican national character, there is a search for that barbaric Other which we carry within us as our ancestor, our father; it fertilizes the natural mother country, the land, but at the same time stains it with its primordial savagery. Hence springs that melancholic ingredient that we observe, in greater or lesser proportion, in every nationalist sentiment. It is curious to find here a parallel with certain facets of the formation of religious sentiment. How can one avoid thinking of the typical medieval Castilian compulsion to "seek martyrdom among the unbelievers" in order to define the realm of faith? This was the first impulse of St. Teresa, who at an early age felt an intense desire to confront the torment that the Moors, the Others, could inflict upon her. In the end, however, she plunged within herself in search of the castle of God.

But in melancholy the will, too, is oriented toward martyrology: the conscience is confronted with barbaric ancestors, those unbelievers of the soul, and is obliged to hate them, but to vaunt them nevertheless as terrible scars and deformities. Perhaps for this reason the mythical character that has been set up in Mexico as the symbol of the whole nation is the *pelado*,[10] a kind of urban peasant (if I may employ such a paradox), half-asphyxiated by the city, who has lost the rural paradise and has not found the promised land. In the pelado is restored the horrendous image of the *lépero*, from the Porfirian era.[11] That mob, the *leperaje*, which was seen by the scientists of the nineteenth century as a bottomless well of vice, bestiality, and cruel atavisms, reemerges in the eyes of the post-Revolution intelligentsia in the person of the pelado, who is clearly dominated by a feeling of inferiority (according to Ramos and Paz) but in whom abides, hidden, the complex tragedy of human solitude. Or rather, according to Agustín Yáñez, the lépero reappears as the Mexican in his natural state, a contradictory being in whom "realist primitivism," violence, and distrust nonetheless reveal a "libertarian will" and a "proud misery."[12] By now these brief images depict a vague silhouette of the down-and-out hero, the first imaginary inhabitant of the great paradisiacal theater of cruelty.

Since the nineteenth century, the Mexican intelligentsia has frequently summoned up this ancestral character via the incense of melancholy. They have believed that only melancholic rapture could facilitate communication between Mexicans and the ancient, profound strata of a native land that has been built outside history, at the wrong moment, and with the use of scrap materials. For this reason, so many Mexican intellectuals have chosen to use the ink of melancholy in their depictions of the national culture. If we pause a moment to examine the problem, we see that it is not a phenomenon concerned only with Mexican culture, but rather a theme that has enormous historical dimensions. In fact, everywhere in modern Latin American literature we find traces of the melancholy attitude, and we need not search far to come across Rubén Darío:

> And in the uncertainty of courage and agony,
> I am burdened with griefs I can hardly bear.
> Can you not hear my melancholy tears fall?
>   —("Melancholy")

This sad weeping was heard in many places. In Mexico, for example, Luis G. Urbina resurrected it in 1909 in his poem "Vieja lágrima" (Old Tear), in which he says:

> Today I'm not crying . . . My life is dry
> and my soul serene.
> Why, then, do I feel cascading
> tear after tear,
> such an inexhaustible fountain of affection,
> such a vein of sorrow which does not cease?
> Who knows? It is not I: it is those who were;
> my sad progenitors; it is my race;
> the distressed spirits,
> the flagellated flesh;
> impossible millennial yearnings,
> mystical hopes,

abrupt, savage melancholies,
impotent, sylvan rages.[13]

In these lines we see the Mexican version of that melancholy madness with which Don Quijote was diagnosed, and which has flowed through four centuries of Spanish poetry[14] up to the modern solitudes of, for example, Antonio Machado: "I do not know legends of ancient joy, / But only old stories of melancholy" (*Solitudes VI*, "It Was a Bright Afternoon").

And yes, it is a very ancient story. When we talk of melancholy, we are immersing ourselves in a torrent of ideas and images that have traversed a great part of European history. I would go so far as to assert that the idea of melancholy constitutes one of the fundamental axes of Western culture; quite astonishingly, it spans the millennia from Aristotelian and Hippocratic thought to contemporary modernism, on its way passing through medieval Christianity, illuminating the spirit of the Renaissance, and clouding the view of the Romantics. When Mexican culture adopts melancholy as one of its distinctive, special symbols, it is in fact connecting itself with and diluting itself in the huge whirlpool of Western history.

The history of melancholy has many sources, two of them quite interesting to us. One takes us to the tragedy of the Fall and, as I have already suggested, to martyrology, where the soul is driven mad by unparalleled anguish and grief caused by a feeling of guilt for bygone sins. The other leads to the drama of the hero or genius who has to bear melancholy's heavy load in exchange for the lucidity with which he can observe the world and create things: this is the terrible price paid for knowledge and power. Both sources find expression in modern Mexican culture.

In the full turbulence of the Revolution, one writer who exercised a formative influence on the institutionalization of the modern national conscience, Martín Luis Guzmán, anxiously sought (like so many intellectuals before and after him) the original causes of the Mexican tragedy. With great precision he identified two painful factors. In the first place, of course, there are the "sad progenitors": "Since the Conquest or since precolonial times," he tells us, "the Indian is there, prostrate and submissive, indifferent to good and bad, without any conscience, his soul a primitive bud, incapable even of hope." In the second place, however, the systematic immorality of Mexican politics must, according to Guzmán, be governed by a "congenital evil." In fact, "In the drawing of our autonomy, enshrined in the beliefs for which the

War of Independence was fought, there lies a real, and unfortunately inevitable, defect in the constitution of the nation: *we Mexicans had to build a fatherland before conceiving it as an ideal and feeling it as a noble impulse; that is, before deserving it.*"[15] All modern Mexicans must, in some way, pay for those original sins.

But the other source of the history of melancholy leads us to contemplate a less obvious dimension in the structure of the Mexican national conscience, one that is linked to one of the oldest concerns of the intelligentsia. Through melancholy the artist or writer, and the politician (who is unaware of the solitude of the president?), establish a connection with the dark forces of society and the soul, and make noble contact with the tragedy of the original sin. Melancholy stimulates the genius to elevate himself, in his ecstasy, above the rest of humanity. This ecstasy permits the soul to distance itself from the body, stimulated by a profound nostalgia for the very worldliness it abandons. In this manner love, sexual climax, drunkenness, and bravery on the battlefield have all been considered forms of ecstasy. We witness in the melancholic state a dangerous meeting of genius and stupidity, the exceptional man and the beast, the civilized man and the peasant.

The intellectual finds that, despite everything, there is a connection which unites his anguish with the terrifying miseries of society's underworld. The dregs of society, the poorest peasants, the starving in the countryside—all have something in common with the man of letters: solitude. A solitude that "is a yearning for the body we were wrested from," as Octavio Paz has put it.[16] Sprung from a paradisiacal but earthly womb, the soul roams in search of a new golden age, a new native land. In this journey most become lost in the labyrinth of a gloomy delirium; but some will reach a melancholic ecstasy enabling them to guide their people toward the new promised land.

Time without Meaning

Rousseau placed man in his natural state outside of history and the world of events. In such a situation, "which does not exist now, which perhaps did not exist then, which probably will never exist," man would find himself happy in his immobility, living an endless life that would pass slowly and indifferently. This image of mythical time has a long, branching history in Western thought and manifests innumerable and contradictory facets. Typically, it has been the idea forged by the city dweller about rural barbarism, or the idea the "civilized man" has imposed on the lifestyle of the "savages" of

Africa and America. Western thought came to establish its notions of space and time in terms of its ideas of historical progress. Thus a Eurocentric cultural stereotype was shaped which came to consider, let us say, that the temporal coordinate ran from east to west; this axis was crossed by another (vertical) coordinate according to which in the north there are always barbarians and, in the south, savages. Thus, point 0, where the Cartesian coordinates crossed, represented the here and now of the "civilized" observer. Progress had to pass dangerously between the barbarians of the north and the savages of the south, always in a westerly direction. Progress was seen as being threatened even from within, from a "deep south" in the metropolis itself.

For Voltaire, for example, primitive men were not to be found only in Africa or the New World. "There are such savages all over Europe," he said, explaining: "rustics who live in their huts with their women and a few animals, constantly exposed to the inclemency of the seasons; who know no more than the land that feeds them and the market they visit occasionally to sell their wares in order to buy coarse garments; who speak a dialect not heard in the cities; who have few ideas and, consequently, seldom express themselves."[17] This is not the place to pause for an account of how such ideas have survived to the present day. However, at the beginning of the twentieth century, an illustrious French academic, Lucien Lévy-Bruhl, took up this tradition and dedicated the better part of his efforts to explaining "mental functions in lower societies." His book *Primitive Mentality* is now unused and rejected by anthropologists, but many of the ideas expressed there form part of the current political culture and modern mythology. Anthropologists would do well, therefore, to reread Lévy-Bruhl. I wish now to turn to a single aspect of the problem: the notion of time ascribed to primitive men.

Lévy-Bruhl establishes that the "primitive prelogical mentality" is generally unaware of the causal connections that unite phenomena in time and space; instead, the idea of a "mystical immediate causality" based on the existence of occult powers and dark forces predominates. Lévy-Bruhl claims as logical the Kantian notion of a universal network of cause and effect: "Time seems to us . . . a homogeneous quantum, divisible into identical parts that occur with perfect regularity. But for spirits who are indifferent to these regular series of spatial phenomena . . . who pay no attention to, nor reflect upon, the irreversible succession of causes and effects, what is their representation of time? Without support, it can only be indistinct and badly defined."[18] In the mind of Lévy-Bruhl, the Kantian idea of time and space prevails; according to this conception, which dominates everyday life, there is no relationship between space and time. Space is a stationary notion and, according to Kant, an intuitive form of our sense of the *external;* in contrast, time is an intuitive form of our sense of the *internal.* In the Kantian civilized perception, time *flows* independently of space and is an absolute concept. It is clear that the Kantian conceptualization is in turn a primitive and savage idea from the point of view of modern physics. Since Albert Einstein developed his theory of relativity, we have understood that it is impossible to separate time from space.

In his concern with spatiotemporal notions, Einstein decided to consult Jean Piaget on the issue of the child's subjective ideas about time. He wanted to know whether the child started with relativist or Newtonian absolutist ideas: Was the child's subjective intuition of time immediate or derived? As we know, according to Newtonian physics, velocity is derived from absolute notions of time and distance. For Einstein, in contrast, it is the other way round: velocity has a primary character, and time is derived. Piaget's studies led him to reply that velocity and distance are primary intuitions in children, and that the idea of time only gradually becomes clear to them. Time, for the child, is not an absolute notion.[19]

But it is precisely the idea of absolute time, without any connection to space, flowing *forward* at a regular speed, that permits the attribution of a vital, gentle, slow rhythm to the primitive mind. It is for this reason that the European is so surprised at the notions held by certain Nigerian tribes. Lévy-Bruhl quotes Major A. G. Leonard, who explains that "What we Europeans call the past is linked to the present, which is, in turn, linked to the future. But for these people, believing as they do in an irreparable dual existence, in which one life is submerged in the other, time actually lacks the divisions it has for us. Therefore it has neither value nor purpose, and so they treat it with a disdain and indifference entirely inexplicable to the European."[20]

The idea of a homogeneous vision of the sense of time shared by all primitive men stems neither from the reality of non-European peoples nor from the barbarians who live immersed in the heart of Western civilization. This supposed homogeneity is the imaginary construct of a mechanical rationalism anchored in the notion of progress: only thus can we explain how civilized men everywhere contemplate their predecessors and primitive contemporaries in such a similar way. Incapable of understanding the new mythology in which they find themselves immersed, many civilized men see the rural primitive world as a space that dwells outside of time or within a mythical time. "On top of indigenous mythical time," says Carlos Fuentes, "the time of the Western calendar, the time of progress, lineal time, was superimposed."[21] It is indeed so, with one important exception: *Western time is mythical time, too;* its myths, different from those of pre-Hispanic culture, are concerned with linearity, progress, the future, the Gregorian calendar. And one of its central myths is precisely the devising of another mythical time linked to the primitive paradise rather than to modern notions of historical fact.

To the civilized mind, primitive man treats time with disdain and indifference; the savage and the barbarian are defined by their natural slowness and apathy. From this stems the notion of their disdain for death: "The Mexican's indifference to death," says Octavio Paz, "is fed by his indifference to life."[22] So, to the extent that the value of life is measured in terms of Western time—a quantum or homogeneous fluid, measurable and divisible into equal parts according to Lévy-Bruhl's definition—it is clear that a lebensraum which seems immobile and crossed by qualitatively distinct time lines will lack value for the modern Western mind.

The variety of notions of time among peoples categorized as primitive is enormous. The Cree Indians of North America ignored those days on which they could not see the moon. The inhabitants of the Trobriand Islands were accustomed to classifying past events, both mythical and real, as if in a universal present or, rather, in an entirely different type of time (which was not considered to be previous to the present). In the Luapula Valley, in northern Zimbabwe, time was split into two types, depending on whether the events were tied to the history of a particular person or to general history.[23] All such forms of marking out and measuring time, however strange they might appear to us, are coherent within the cultural worlds that create them in accord with their different needs: from the simplest tasks, related to the regularity of agricultural and pastoral work, to complex cosmogonic notions. And, in reality, they are not so far removed from our Western society. Need we recall that there were mass riots, demanding the eleven lost days, when England adopted the Gregorian calendar and September 3, 1752, became September 14? Have we not noticed that there is one time for the office, one for the street, and another for the home—all different? Is not the notion of "free time" completely ignored in the world of industry? Does one not agree with the Freudians that the events stored in our unconscious belong to an eternal present, outside of time? Modern culture, too, has its myths. . . .

Western political culture has generated the myth of two times: paradisiacal time, not measurable in terms of industrial rationality; and the progressive, dynamic time of civilized man. This polarity embraces the great diversity of subjective expressions of time, which have extraordinarily rich cultural forms of expression. One need only take an impartial glance at ethnographic studies to appreciate that the large diversity of conscious forms of time exhibited by so-called primitive peoples cannot be homogenized. Any apparent homogeneity is created by the Western eye, through a process of exclusion: any manifestation that eludes the "common sense" of industrial society is considered to be part of a unique, ancestral mythical time. It is equally false to try to reduce to a unique form the awareness of events that crystallizes in industrial societies—like those overseers of the spirit who seek to measure out in organized fashion the course of life according to the rhythms of the office and the factory. But what should be emphasized here is not the falseness of the bipolar conception of time: rather, it seems more interesting to posit a modern myth about primeval time that employs the time of the modern age as counterpoint.

That myth is the source of one of the features ascribed to the Mexican character with greatest insistence. The sense of time (and distance) attributed to the Mexican is, as we have seen, the same as that attributed to the peasant and the primitive by the city dweller. "Only time is in Mexico docile and gentle," according to Jorge Carrión, author of a well-known essay on the Mexican character. He continues: "He has no landmarks and can only differentiate day from night. We know the seasons by the pages of the calendar rather than by the leaves of the trees. Each day is followed by another in exactly the same way, and even the night falls calmly as if afraid to alter the gentle rhythm of time." Urban man contemplates the rural world with sorrow; since he perceives neither changes nor movements, he believes that time is not passing. It is obvious that the peasant perceives the seasons of the year very clearly, but it is of no concern to him that farther to the north the leaves fall in autumn: what concerns him is the form the seasons take in his own part of the world. However, the stereotype must prevail: "The Mexican is adapted to this imperceptible flow of time. He does not feel time. He does not feel the need to do today what he can do an identical tomorrow, and he is not punctual because nothing in nature urges him to be so. Because of this, and because of the transparency of the air, the Mexican measures distances in terms of 'just over the hill.' Just over the hill is the *sociological equation of an easygoing time,* constituting a clear perspective, free of obstacles."[24]

A psychologist has summarized the idea thus: "Mexicans perceive time in such a way as to believe that it passes more slowly for themselves than for those of other nationalities." The same author notes that Mexicans are traditionally considered to be "idle," in contrast to North Americans, who are "active" and "efficient": "What happens," he explains, "is that Mexicans are characterized by *passive* methods of dealing with stress."[25]

The Spanish writer José Moreno Villa has noticed that gesture of the hand which indicates delay: by signaling with the fingers that it is necessary to wait a *momentito* (short moment) or a *tantito* (little bit), "the Mexican crumbles up the time, he makes crumbs of it, so that it will not pressure or compromise him."[26] The immensity of time which fits into that little space between thumb and index finger is a mystery which drives the European, the civilized man, to despair. Modern Western man (another myth) does not tolerate delay. He cannot understand what happens during the (for him) very long interval between the agreed time to begin and the actual beginning, the agreed time to meet and the actual meeting. What happens during that delay? Is it really a delay? What lies hidden in that inaccessible period?

There is no doubt in Moreno Villa's mind that the Mexican attitude qualifies as "Asian passivity"; whereas European civilization is imbued with a desire to live at perpetual top speed, the Mexican, in contrast, is a man "curled up" (referring to the peculiar indigenous way of sitting or squatting), and this suggests to Moreno Villa an Asian image, connected with calmness, passivity, and self-absorption. This reminds us of the old European vision of the Asian as a barbaric or savage being, the *Homo asiaticus* of Linnaeus: "luridus, melancholicus, rigidus, pilis nigricantibus, oculis fuscis, reverus, fastuosus, avarus." That is just the way "cultured" Europe viewed those northern barbarians, the Slavs, the true representatives of Asianism within civilization: "What we call the fatalism and resignation of the Russian people seems to be at base nothing other than a lack of concern about the future. They tend to think: why worry? Nothing is about to change the ills of the *present,* and what does *tomorrow* matter?"[27] In the same breath one speaks of their "melancholy," "natural apathy," "passive resignation," "indolence," and "lack of energy and willpower." Samuel Ramos dedicates a chapter of his famous book on Mexican culture to this indigenous "Egyptianism," discussing the rigidity of death, which is expressed in pre-Hispanic art as the hardness of rock conquering the fluidity of life. In Mexico, therefore, life "slips by with a slowness similar to the immutability of the Asian peoples." This peculiarity is, for Ramos, a transcendent phenomenon that remains unexplained by the centuries of colonial domination: "We do not believe the passiveness of the Indian to be the unique result of the slavery into which he fell after being conquered. He let himself be conquered perhaps because his spirit was already disposed to passivity."[28]

Man in modern capitalist society believes that peasants and primitive peoples live immersed in passivity; this belief stems from a simple psychological mechanism that determines man's subjective estimation of time. It has been formulated most precisely by Paul Fraisse: the greater the number of changes observed, the longer the apparent duration.[29] The city dweller perceives few changes in country life and, for this reason, believes that in the country, time is interminably drawn out. A European who is unable to interpret the social and cultural meaning of a non-Western society will believe that time moves slowly there. Moreover, on recalling his experiences in rural or non-Western situations, it is easy for him to minimize and considerably reduce the importance of the temporal space in which history runs its course (or even to deny that there is any history there at all).

In European culture there is an ancient tradition, reinforced by Descartes, Kant, and even Bergson, that seeks to understand the passing of time in terms of internal states of consciousness. In fact, the notion of boredom becomes a synonym for time (the German *Langeweile* means "long time," especially boredom in the face of an unavoidable situation). So time ends up as the obstacle that hinders the termination of a task. This is the tragedy of Western man: the absolute time that he has conceived as the measure of all things is actually boredom and tiresomeness. "In its pure form," says Levelle, "consciousness of time is boredom; it is the consciousness of an interval traversed by nothing and filled by nothing."[30] Gaston Bachelard confirms this perception: "We recognize *duration* in time only when we recognize it as *too long.*"[31]

We find a curious identification being made in Western thought: to the savage, who supposedly lives without consciousness of the flow of time, is attributed that peculiar melancholy which is, in fact, an emanation of Western man. For the latter, clock time occasionally flows slowly compared with the uncontrolled rhythm of the nostalgic thoughts his consciousness exudes, despite the fact that (as is often observed) they often concern a nostalgia for the future, a Utopian feeling. In contrast to Rousseau's contention that the original immobility was an idyllic, happy state of affairs, passivity in Mexico is acted out in tragic fashion. In his *Análisis del ser del mexicano* (1952), Emilio Uranga talks of an "ontological wound," oozing melancholy, and considers that all the elements of the Mexican character (inactivity, melancholy, emotivity) are found in four lines by López Velarde:

Rainy afternoon, in which together
with an inner sadness, both
a quiet disdain for things
and a subtle, contrite praying emotion grow.
  —("The Weaver")

It is impossible not to recognize the profound stamp of nationalist romanticism in this plunge into the primordial fountains of the Mexican character. To create the myth of the modern man, it is necessary to reconstruct the primordial original, to generate a tragic sense of the opposition between the barbarian and the civilized man, and to create for modern man a mythical past, so that this modernity can, apparently, shed such myths and rationally confront the construction of the future. I should emphasize that the romantic tradition which is observed so clearly in Mexican literature and thought (José Vasconcelos being the best example) is not merely an expression of the influence of German irrationalism: the romantic ideas reproduce and re-create a very diffuse cultural and political process that goes far beyond the historical framework in which romantic literature was developed.

The cultural-political process involved is related to the creation of tragic scenarios in which modern society, like that of ancient times, projects its heroes and myths. The influence of Max Weber's ideas has led us to believe that modern society constitutes a rational, functional, disillusioned world in which myths and magic no longer hold sway. This is a grave error: capitalist industrial society, just like socialism, constantly generates ceremonies, rites, cults, and symbols. For example, the ideas of such scientists as Auguste Comte and Johann Bachofen, even though frustrated, are indicative of a desire to found new religions. The dialogues of the Comtian positivist catechism invite the foundation of a religious cult of the Invariable Laws of Positivist Reason; Bachofen proposed the adoration of the trinity of Earth-Mother-Death in his project to exalt the mythic consciousness, because for him myths are spiritual powers rooted not only in primitive times but also in fundamental forces.

The culture of modern man requires myths: it inherits them, it re-creates them, it invents them. One of them is the myth of the primordial man, which fortifies national culture and at the same time serves as a contrast in order to stimulate modernity and progress in the nation. As we have seen, one of the fundamental characteristics of the primordial being is that he inhabits a peculiar melancholy dimension in which time passes slowly and gently.

Notes

This chapter is adapted from *The Cage of Melancholy* (Rutgers University Press, 1992).

1. In Mexico a peasant tradition has been *invented;* but this is not exceptional. See Eric Hobsbawm and Terence Ranger, eds., *The Invention of Tradition* (Cambridge: Cambridge University Press, 1983), where similar processes are explored with regard to Africa, Europe, and India.

2. Carlos Fuentes, "Rulfo, el tiempo del mito," in *Juan Rulfo, homenaje nacional* (Mexico City: INBA/SEP, 1980), 24.

3. Roger Bartra, *The Imaginary Networks of Political Power* (New Brunswick, NJ: Rutgers University Press, 1992).

4. This polarity is expressed in the duality Paradise/Utopia, which is one form of the contrast between melancholy and metamorphosis. A good summary of these myths can be found in Louis Rougier, *Del paraíso a la utopía* (Mexico City: Fondo de Cultura Económica, 1984).

5. See Alfonso Reyes, *La x en la frente* (Mexico City: Porrúa y Obregón, 1952).

6. Many modern phenomena, including nationalism, can be interpreted as a search for community lost. In this regard, see R. A. Nisbet, *The Quest for Community* (Oxford: Oxford University Press, 1953).

7. These commonplaces are summarized in Everett Rogers and Lynne Svenning, *La modernización entre los campesinos* (Mexico City: Fondo de Cultura Económica, 1973), 33–46. Raymond Williams, *The Country and the City* (New York: Oxford University Press, 1973), is an excellent study of the country/city duality in English literature. Note also the thesis that there is an almost eternal "peasant culture," according to E. K. L. Francis, "The Personality Type of the Peasant According to Hesiod's *Works and Days,* a Culture Case Study," *Rural Sociology* 10 (1945): 275–295; and Peter Walcot, *Greek Peasants, Ancient and Modern: A Comparison of Social and Moral Values* (New York: Barnes and Noble, 1970). Robert Redfield, *Peasant Society and Culture* (Chicago: University of Chicago Press, 1956), took from Francis the idea that Hesiod's Greeks, the Mayas of modern Yucatan, and nineteenth-century inhabitants of the English countryside could be assimilated into a single group. This type of study has contributed to the establishment of the peasant stereotype.

8. Julio Guerrero, *La génesis del crimen en México: Estudio de psiquiatría social* (Paris: Charles Bouret, 1901; Mexico City: Editorial Porrúa, 1977), 23–24. It is not difficult to identify the origin of these evaluations. Humboldt wrote: "The indigenous Mexican is grave, melancholy, silent, and liquor does not get him worked up. ... The Mexican likes to make a mystery out of his most indifferent acts: not even the most violent passions are registered in his physiognomy; he represents a frightful *je ne sais quoi* when suddenly he passes from absolute repose to violent and uncontrolled agitation." *Ensayo político sobre el reino de la Nueva España,* vol. 2 (Mexico City: P. Robredo, 1941), 86.

9. For the ideas cited, see Guerrero, *La génesis*, 11, 24, 34, 139, 231ff., and 321.

10. Translator's note: *pelado* (shorn, broke) refers to a Mexican social type from the working class noted for his coarse, uneducated, uncouth language and behavior.

11. Guerrero, *La génesis*, 159ff. Translator's note: *lépero* refers to a historical Mexican social type roughly equivalent to the nineteenth-century notion of "guttersnipe."

12. Samuel Ramos, *El perfil del hombre y la cultura en México* (Mexico City: Espasa-Calpe, 1977); Octavio Paz, *El laberinto de la soledad* (Mexico City: Fondo de Cultura Económica, 1964); Agustín Yáñez, "Estudio preliminar," in José Joaquín Fernández de Lizardi, *El pensador mexicano* (Mexico City: UNAM, 1960).

13. Luis G. Urbina, *Poesías completas*, vol. 2 (Mexico City: Porrúa, 1946), 12–13. Stereotypes of indigenous melancholy are also expressed in clumsy and obvious form in a book by the Colombian Armando Solano, *La melancolía de la raza indígena* (Bogotá: Librería Colombia, 1929).

14. See Guillermo Díaz-Plaja, *Tratado de las melancolías españolas* (Madrid: Sala, 1975).

15. Martín Luis Guzmán, "La querella de México," in his *Obras completas*, vol. 1 (Mexico City: Compañía General de Ediciones, 1961), 13–15.

16. Paz, *El laberinto* 172.

17. Quoted in Michèle Duchet, *Antropología e historia en el siglo de las luces* (Mexico City: Siglo XXI, 1975), 265–66.

18. Lucien Lévy-Bruhl, *La mentalidad primitiva* (Buenos Aires: Leviatán, 1957), 84–85. One need only study the phenomenon of rhythm in "primitive" music, or the knowledge of natural phenomena connected with agriculture, in order to appreciate the absurdity of Lévy-Bruhl's conclusions.

19. Jean Piaget, *Le développement de la notion de temps chez l'enfant* (Paris: Presses Universitaires de France, 1946).

20. A. G. Leonard, *The Lower Niger and Its Tribes*, 181; quoted in Lévy-Bruhl *La mentalidid primitiva*, 85.

21. Carlos Fuentes, *Tiempo mexicano* (Mexico City: Joaquín Mortiz, 1971), 26.

22. Paz, *El laberinto*, 48.

23. John Cohen, *Psychological Time in Health and Disease* (Springfield, IL: Charles C. Thomas, 1967).

24. Jorge Carrión, *Mito y magia del mexicano* (Mexico City: Nuestro Tiempo, 1975).

25. Rogelio Díaz Guerrero, *Psicología del mexicano* (Mexico City: Trillas, 1982), 15, 155.

26. José Moreno Villa, *Cornucopia de México* no. 5 (Mexico City: Porrúa, 1952), 30.

27. Alfred Fouillée, *Bosquejo psicológico de los pueblos europeos* (Madrid: Daniel Jorro, 1903), 502.

28. Ramos, *El perfil*, 36. For a summary of stereotypes of the Mexican, and their "translation" into the codes of U.S. culture, see Alan Riding, *Distant Neighbors: A Portrait of the Mexicans* (New York: Knopf, 1985).

29. Paul Fraisse, *The Psychology of Time* (New York: Harper & Row, 1963).

30. L. Levelle, *Du temps et de l'éternité,* quoted in ibid., 203.

31. Gaston Bachelard, *La dialectique de la durée* (Paris: Boivin, 1936), 48.

2

Between Sade and the Savage

Octavio Paz's Aztecs

AMARYLL CHANADY

In his essay collection *Posdata,* the Mexican poet, critic, and essayist Octavio Paz paints a surprisingly negative portrait of the Aztecs as assassins and barbarians. Considering the importance of the official revalorization of indigenous heritage in Mexico after the Revolution of 1910, and the increasing criticism by Western intellectuals since the 1960s of the conquest of America and its disastrous consequences for native peoples, Paz's demonization of the Aztecs is at first difficult to explain. Since I believe that it would be simplistic to attribute it to mere prejudice or Eurocentrism, I would like to examine in some detail the way in which Paz introduces and develops his views on the Aztecs in the context of his other essays. His comments on Mexican politics and on the global situation at the time he was writing *Posdata* provide an important key to understanding this puzzling depiction. Rather than a demonization of the "savage" before the Conquest, Paz's description appears to be a somewhat contradictory allegory of the modern Mexican government.

Toward the end of his *The Labyrinth of Solitude,*[1] in which Paz analyzes his country's "national character," the essayist reflects melancholically on the nature of what he describes as the universal crisis affecting the contemporary world. He argues that Mexico's situation is not different from that of other countries; that all societies, including Europe and the United States, have become peripheral because there are no longer any centers; and that the crisis of Mexican culture is that of humanity in general. He even considers Latin American intellectual alienation, produced by the imaginary construction of the "New World" by Europe, as a universal predicament. Echoing the pessimistic conclusion of Claude Lévi-Strauss's *Tristes tropiques,*[2] Paz refers to the dissolution of the world's former cultural plurality in the wake of universal Westernization. The Mexican labyrinth of solitude, characterized by an irremediably lost past and an uncertain future, is that of all human beings. Consequently, Mexican philosophy should simply be considered as philosophy, without any essentialist national definition and limitation.

In the last chapter of *The Labyrinth of Solitude,* Paz returns to the particular predicament of Mexico as an underdeveloped nation. In spite of its ambitious projects, the Mexican Revolution could not succeed in eliminating the distance between Mexico and the industrialized nations, which were able to modernize gradually, with the help of riches obtained from the colonies. Mexico, on the other hand, was hampered not only by its industrial belatedness but also by its neocolonial situation, which Paz compares to that of most Latin American, African, and Asian nations. He considers the increasing chasm between developed and underdeveloped nations to be an insoluble problem. The direct intervention of the Mexican state in the modernization of the country was not sufficient, since it had to start "before the beginning."

Communism, briefly considered by Paz as the only possible solution to economic disparities, is immediately rejected for what he sees as its inevitable defects: concentration camps, forced labor, the violation of workers' rights, and the creation of stifling bureaucracies. Although it may transform the economy, it cannot liberate humankind. Contrary to the Mexican Revolution, which lacked "organized terror," the Soviet Union is described as a conjunction of revolutionary measures, such as the abolition of private property, and "archaic" traits, such as the sacred nature of the state and the deification of leaders: "Past, present and future: technical progress and inferior forms of political magic, economic development and union slavery, science and state theology" (170). Instead of the fulfillment of utopian dreams of universal equality, the world has seen the rise of what Paz calls "barbarous regression" (Nazism, for example), as well as the emergence of the Party, which combines the values of discipline and hierarchy characterizing the Church and the Army.

Paz's portrait of the Communist state provides an essential key to his condemnation of the Aztec empire in his later essay "Critique of the Pyramid."[3] Contrary to many Marxist thinkers, who also established parallels between indigenous societies and communism,[4] Paz situates the parallel not on the level of communal property but on that of the conjunction of different "historical temporalities" (*tiempos históricos;* 170). It is not modernity in itself, based on reason and progress, that is the object of his criticism; neither is it the mere resurgence of irrational behavior, theology, and magic (see the quotation above). Rather, it is the mingling of the two. Stalinism, according to Paz, is not rational, but a rationalization of certain obsessions— the rationalization of the irrational. Furthermore, the disillusionment with twentieth-century utopian systems explains Paz's distinctly "primitivist turn" in the appendix to *The Labyrinth of Solitude.*

In spite of the ostensibly optimistic closing statements of the eighth chapter, in which he mentions the possibility of concerted action in the periphery, the preceding pessimistic description of global inequalities prepares the reader for Paz's final reflections. At the end of the essay, solitude is no longer the particular condition of Mexicans, or of New World societies in general. Neither is it only a result of the singular failings of modern civilization. In the appendix "The Dialectics of Solitude," Paz affirms that solitude is the basis of the human condition. Having constructed itself in opposition to nature, and nostalgic for the security of life in the womb, humanity is afflicted with a profound feeling of solitude, which results in a permanent quest for communion and belonging. The solitude of separation is seen as punishment and exile, generally interpreted as the consequence of a transgression of communal or divine laws. Certain stages of life, such as adolescence, or certain vocations, such as that of the hero or the saint, exacerbate the condition of solitude.

However, Paz rapidly returns to the particular predicament of modern society, which constitutes an extreme manifestation of universal human solitude. According to Paz, our contemporaries (and not only adolescents) suffer more acutely from the feeling of solitude than our predecessors. Life in modern society has no "finality," since it is no longer seen as a temporary purgatory or a trial that hardens the individual in preparation for a renewed participation in the group. The "promiscuous solitude of hotels, offices, workshops and cinemas" is a "total condemnation, mirror of a world without escape" (184). At this point Paz introduces the theme of primitive society, quoting from Lucien Lévy-Bruhl's *La Mentalité primitive* (1922), Gerardus van der Leeuw's *L'Homme primitif et la religion* (1940), and other scholars. He explains that "ancient societies" or "archaic culture" developed complex systems of prohibitions, rules, and rituals in order to preserve the members of the community from solitude by limiting individual action and fostering a sense of cohesion. In spite of all precautions, however, the equilibrium of what Paz calls the "closed society" is a precarious one, since war, internal strife, or rapid transformation threatens it with disintegration and dispersal.

This leads to the emergence of the idea of a golden age in the remote past, to which the new "open society" wishes to return. Solitude is constructed as the result of sin or degradation, while communion, frequently based on the image of an ideal community in the past, is seen as salvation.

The concept of the golden age has an ambiguous status in Paz's description of primitive society. On one hand, he postulates an archaic "closed society" in which communion and a sense of belonging actually existed, and which he contrasts with an "open society" of exiles. Orphic and Dionysian cults, for example, are seen as evidence of a transition from closed to open societies. Furthermore, Paz argues that moribund and sterile societies create redemption myths, thus implying that there are (or were) societies which lack these defects. On the other hand, his comments that no group is safe from disintegration and that the golden age is situated in a remote past even in archaic society, suggest that the organic society characterized by communion has always been a construct, and not a memory of an actual state preceding a particular social calamity. This is corroborated by the statement that sacrifice and communion in an "open society" (where they are accompanied by the idea of redemption, the existence of purification and initiation rites, and the emergence of theology, mysticism, and asceticism) are no longer a totemic celebration, "if they were ever really that at any time" (186). Not only does Paz's skepticism concerning totemism echo the widespread opinion among ethnologists at the beginning of the twentieth century that previous constructions of totemism were inaccurate (according to Robert Lowie, for example, whose books *Primitive Society* and *Primitive Religion* appeared in 1920 and 1924 respectively, totemism was a fantasy).[5] It also suggests that Paz recognizes the constructed nature of "primitive society" as an organic and fully integrated community. His discussion of the trauma of birth and separation at the beginning of the appendix allows us to interpret his remarks on the golden age as a description of a universal phenomenon of nostalgia that has little to do with the supposed harmony of past societies. Even primitive society as constructed by ethnologists created versions of an imaginary archaic society.

The treatment of the theme of sacrifice in *The Labyrinth of Solitude* is interesting in light of Paz's later writing on the subject. Sacrifice (including that of a divinity) and communion are described as a means of achieving cohesion in the new, "open" society, and of "prefiguring" the ideal society of the future, identified with a return to the golden age. Sacrifice is not equated with cruelty or barbarism, but with rituals having an important spiritual function. Paz's comments on the Aztecs in this work are very different from his virulent condemnation of the pre-Columbian "assassins" in "Critique of the Pyramid."

In the appendix of *The Labyrinth of Solitude,* Paz refers to the Aztecs' belief in Mictlán, a mythical place situated in the north, from which they had emigrated and to which the dead return. He also comments on the Aztecs' conception of mythical and cyclical time, opposed to our "homogeneous and empty" time that proceeds chronologically. Like most religious festivals, even including the Catholic Mass, Aztec rites constitute a repetition of a past event that transforms this past into an eternal present. Myth, religion, love, theater, and poetry enable us to glimpse an "original time" far removed from the modern conception of chronological time, which makes us into "prisoners of succession." The festival, whether religious or secular, combats solitude, brings about communion, and re-creates the golden age from which humanity was violently removed and to which it yearns to return. In this sense, Aztec society is no different from our own.

However, the utopian dreams of Western modernity are explicitly linked to those of a "sterile" society. Rational systems constitute a "sinuous nightmare, in which the mirrors of reason reproduce torture chambers" (191). Since these constructions are the result of "dreaming with open eyes," Paz ends with the hope that we will again learn to dream with our eyes closed. Even though all societies believe in a golden age, it is those of the past which are closest to achieving this state.

Paz's comment, on the last page of his essay, that the sterility of modern bourgeois society can only lead to suicide or new forms of "creative participation," strikes an interesting parallel with his description of Aztec society in the fifth chapter. Abandoned by their gods, the Aztecs, according to Paz, committed suicide, as Rome and Byzantium had done. Contrary to the "old empires," however, which self-destructed at the end of a period of decadence, the Aztec state committed suicide in its youth. Suicide thus links Paz's construction of the Aztec state, Rome, Byzantium, and modern "sterile" society. In spite of the Aztecs' conception of cyclical time, they are not portrayed as "primitives" living in an organic, integrated society. The Aztec empire is described as a vigorous and efficient state in which a priestly caste at the "pinnacle of the social pyramid" (84) indulged in incessant theological speculation in its systematization of older belief systems and imposed a certain degree of homogenization on the heterogeneous indigenous groups—without, however, destroying "primitive beliefs."

Paz's comments on human sacrifice are significant in this regard. He refuses to see this practice as an "isolated expression of cruelty without relation to the rest of their civilization: the extraction of hearts and monumental pyramids, sculpture and ritual cannibalism, poetry and ritual warfare,
theocracy and grandiose myths are an indissoluble whole. To deny this is as
childish as disregarding Gothic art or the poetry of Provence because of the
condition of medieval serfs, or disowning Aeschylus because there were slaves
in Athens" (94). Aztec society is thus as contradictory as any other relatively
"evolved" civilization. Paz's hope, expressed in the last sentence of *The Labyrinth of Solitude*—that we will once again be able to dream with our eyes
closed—certainly does not take the Aztec state as a model. But neither does
he condemn it, as he does the totalitarian regimes created by the lucubra-
tions of modern rationality.

The penultimate sentence of "Critique of the Pyramid" constitutes a reply to this exhortation to dream with closed eyes. Here Paz affirms that,
instead of dreaming, we must "learn to destroy idols." Whereas communion
was a major theme in *The Labyrinth of Solitude* (Paz praised Catholicism for
providing the indigenous population with a sense of belonging and a place
in the universe after the upheaval of the Conquest), and led to reflections on
organic, closed communities based largely on ethnographic accounts of
primitive societies, critical distance and lucidity are the major themes of
"Critique of the Pyramid." In a very interesting analysis of what we may call
the narrative structure of the arrangement of indigenous art in the Museum
of Anthropology in Mexico City, Paz criticizes the representation of the extremely diverse and complex indigenous cultural development during two
thousand years as the "prologue to the final act, the apotheosis-apocalypse
of Mexico-Tenochtitlan" (152). He argues that this version is false, and that
the Aztecs in no way represent the culmination of the preceding cultures.
On the contrary, Paz describes them as the "assassins of the pre-Hispanic
world" (153). The glorification of the Aztec empire transforms the museum
into a temple in which the cult based on the pyramid with its sacrificial
platform corresponds to an archetype lying at the basis of the modern Mexican state, which Paz sees as the continuation of Mexico-Tenochtitlan.

The cult celebrated in the "temple" of anthropology thus bears no resemblance to the ritual communion of primitive societies or the Catholic religion that Paz had praised at the end of *The Labyrinth of Solitude*. Paz's negative portrayal of the Aztecs is largely due to his reaction toward, and
explanation of, particular circumstances in modern Mexico. "Crítica de la

pirámide" is the third and final essay of *Posdata,* a volume that starts with a pessimistic statement concerning Eastern and Western contemporary models of development, described as a compendium of horrors. He refers to his country's predicament as an underdeveloped nation living in the "shanty towns of history" *(suburbios de la historia)* and wonders whether Mexicans can develop their own models of modernity leading neither to the "frigid police paradises of the East" nor to the "explosions of nausea and hatred that interrupt the Western feast" (113–114). Essential to this quest is a thorough critique of his country, which can be carried out only by elucidating what is hidden underneath the mask of the Mexican "national character." In the first essay, "Olimpiada y Tlatelolco," Paz criticizes progress for stifling essential aspects of humanity, such as pleasure and enjoyment of the present, in favor of working for gain in a distant future. According to Paz, the definition of "Man" as a being that works should be replaced by that of a being that desires. Although he explains that dissatisfaction with modernity does not imply a hatred of reason or a nostalgia for the Neolithic period, it is significant that he adds that this period was, "according to Lévi-Strauss and other anthropologists, probably the only happy period that human beings have known" (28). As in *The Labyrinth of Solitude,* dissatisfaction with certain aspects of modernity and with the peripheral situation of Mexico in the global system precedes references to primitive society and positive traits associated with it: communion and a sense of belonging in *The Labyrinth,* and pleasure in *Posdata.*

The main object of critique in "Olimpiada y Tlatelolco," however, is the Mexican government's quelling of the student rebellion in Tlatelolco in 1968, in which the army opened fire on the student demonstrators, resulting in several hundred deaths. The two terms of the title refer to what Paz describes as the contradictory elements of modern Mexico: the relative state of the country's economic development, which enabled it to host the Olympic Games in 1968, and the violent reaction toward the student uprising. Paz's explanation of the massacre is highly significant in the light of his subsequent analysis of the Aztec heritage. He compares the government to a neurotic person who is incapable of facing new situations without committing irrational acts and reverting to "instinctive, infantile or animal behavior" (40). According to Paz, the government regressed to earlier periods in the country's history, especially that of the Aztec empire, in an instinctive repetition that took the form of a rite of expiation.

This explanation, in its emphasis on the return of a repressed past, and in view of the explicit parallels established by Paz between the events at Tlatelolco and the Aztec state characterized by human sacrifice, bears certain resemblances to Freud's theory of sacrifice in *Totem and Taboo*,[6] in which sacrifice is considered an instinctive reliving of a murder in the past that unifies the group around the ritual killing of a totem which functions as a substitute for the father of the primitive horde. However, the reference in Paz's text on vengeance and expiation acquires an entirely different signification in the light of a theory of sacrifice that was published three years after the appearance of *Posdata* and that reinterprets certain aspects of Freud's theory. In René Girard's *Violence and the Sacred,* sacrifice (including human ritual murder—Girard insists that there is no essential difference between the sacrifice of animals and that of humans) is defined as "an instrument of prevention in the struggle against violence,"[7] since it quells violence within the primitive community by deflecting it onto innocent victims. Since violence is inevitable, it would rapidly destroy the community if not effectively channeled into a strictly controlled and structured ritual that prevents the interminable chain reaction of violence and vengeance by the aggrieved party, which can only lead to new acts of revenge. The purpose of sacrifice is thus to "restore harmony to the community, to reinforce the social fabric" (8). Girard argues that instead of considering sacrifice as the ritual reliving of an actual murder in the past, as in Freud's theory, we should understand it as an outlet of destructive impulses that would otherwise be turned against members of the community.

The surrogate victim must in no way be connected to the original crime or transgression, in order to prevent a chain reaction of reprisal and further violence. This explains why sacrificial victims are chosen from a category of individuals lacking strong social bonds within the group that could lead to revenge. This category includes slaves, unmarried adolescents, and prisoners of war. Although there are obvious differences between the students killed at Tlatelolco and the category of sacrificial victims identified by Girard, we can see a fascinating superficial parallel between Girard's victims lacking strong social links and Paz's students, who are described as segregated from collective life and absent from the "mechanical circuit of production and consumption"[8] to the point where their actions cannot change society.

There is, however, an essential difference between the killing at Tlatelolco and the human sacrifice existing in primitive societies according to Girard's theory. Because of the threat of self-destructive violence, primitive society strives to eliminate revenge through preventive measures destined to provide an outlet for violence: "As I see it, the relationship between the potential victim and the actual victim cannot be defined in terms of innocence or guilt. There is no question of 'expiation.' Rather, society is seeking to deflect upon a relatively indifferent victim, a 'sacrificeable' victim, the violence that would otherwise be vented on its own members, the people it most desires to protect" (4). Paz, on the contrary, explicitly describes the events at Tlatelolco as an act of "destruction" and "vengeance" and a "ritual of expiation." The students are not "innocent" sacrificial victims, since they are considered as an aggrieving party. Since vengeance is absent from functional primitive societies, according to Girard's theory, Tlatelolco cannot be described as a ritual sacrifice as defined in *Violence and the Sacred*.

The theme of vengeance, however, returns in Girard's portrait of "civilized" society, characterized by the presence of a judicial system that does not suppress vengeance, but "limits it to a single act of reprisal, enacted by a sovereign authority specializing in this particular function," and whose decisions are "presented as the final word on vengeance" (15): "Instead of following the example of religion and attempting to forestall acts of revenge, . . . our judicial system *rationalizes* revenge and succeeds in limiting and isolating its effects in accordance with social demands" (22). Human sacrifice, according to Girard, exists in societies without firmly established judicial systems. Although Girard presents the progression from preventive measures to the "curative procedures" of "civilized" societies as an evolution "in ascending order of effectiveness" (21), he argues that sacrifice and the judicial system both have as their main purpose the general security of the community. Abstract notions of justice are secondary. However, he stresses that the judiciary is "at the disposal of everyone, and it is universally respected" (23). The quelling of the student rebellion at Tlatelolco obviously does not enter Girard's category of "civilized" forms of limited vengeance based on a respected judiciary because it is perpetrated by soldiers outside the judicial framework. Paz's repressed Aztec heritage, which emerges in the events of 1968, thus combines two different elements according to the distinction established by Girard between primitive and civilized societies: the violent elimination of what to Paz are innocent victims (sacrifice) and revenge against individuals who have transgressed the established order, although this revenge is not based on generally recognized principles of justice.

In the second essay of *Posdata*, "El desarrollo y otros espejismos" (Development and Other Mirages), Paz claims that the ruling political party in Mexico, the Partido Revolucionario Institucional (PRI), has political domination as its main goal and that in certain respects it resembles the Communist parties of the East. He adds that it is undemocratic in its internal functioning and that it is dominated by a "group of hierarchs who, in turn, show blind obedience to the president of the moment" (51), whom Paz compares to the Aztec emperor. On several occasions in the essay, Paz describes the PRI as based on a pyramidal power structure. As in *The Labyrinth of Solitude,* Paz also refers to Mexico's difficult passage to modernity. He mentions the country's "disconcerting modernity" and "scandalous inequalities," which lead him to introduce the expression "the two Mexicos," the developed and the underdeveloped: "half of Mexico, half naked and hungry, has been contemplating for several years the progress of the other half" (86–87). The only way to prevent the "strangulation" of the developed sector by the underdeveloped one is absorption and integration of the latter, accompanied by democratic reform. But, again as in *The Labyrinth of Solitude,* Paz expresses profound skepticism concerning modernity. He refers to "the destruction of the ecological balance, the pollution of spirit and lungs, the agglomerations and miasmas in hellish shanty towns, the psychic havoc in adolescents,"[9] and other evils of modern society, including the degradation of love and the explosion of hatred. According to Paz, all models of development, Eastern and Western, lead to disaster, and thus to the necessity of finding new models.

Inevitably, pessimism leads him to contemplate primitivism, but only as a temporary respite in his melancholic description of his country's predicament, not as a solution. He refers at this point in *Posdata* to the Neolithic period as "that happy age which hardly knew the monarch and the priest" (88). After referring to Zapata's aversion to the presidential chair, he affirms that Zapata was right and that we should burn all chairs and thrones. But the poor peasants, who are explicitly associated with primitive man and described as our "only link" with the Neolithic age, are incapable and unwilling to acquire power and overthrow a corrupt state; the latter has always been linked with the city. Nevertheless, Paz ends "Development and Other Mirages" with his version of political utopia: "A plural society, without majorities and minorities" (101), in which not everyone is happy, but in which everyone is responsible.

In the final chapter, "Crítica de la pirámide," Paz brings together the two main themes of the preceding chapters: state repression and economic inequality (Tlatelolco and the "two Mexicos"). Echoing a large number of Latin American intellectuals, he criticizes the modernized sectors of Mexican society for blindly imitating foreign models that do not correspond to the country's "true historical, psychic and cultural reality" (107). His dichotomization of Mexican society into developed and undeveloped sectors (the "two Mexicos") is no longer based solely on economic factors, but also on cultural differences. His "other Mexico" does not simply constitute a "culture of poverty," but a culture that is radically *other*. He argues that the "other Mexico" is the largely unconscious heritage of the Aztecs which has left its mark on most of Mexican society. It is a "complex of unconscious attitudes and structures that, far from being vestiges of an extinguished past, are surviving elements constitutive of our contemporary culture" (109).

This "submerged and repressed" Other—which, Paz specifies, should not be considered an ahistoric essence or Jungian archetype but a set of beliefs, images, and concepts that "history has deposited in the basement of the social psyche," and that he associates with the Freudian notion of the subconscious as well as the Marxian concept of ideology—is part of every Mexican. Paz adds that these two concepts do not, however, completely explain the existence in each society of certain complexes, presuppositions, and generally unconscious mental structures that resist the erosion of history. Dumezil's concept of ideology, in the sense of a "particular predisposition of the mind in the face of and toward objective reality" (110), may be more pertinent. Otherness thus exists in ourselves, and not in a particular sector of society considered as other (peasants or people living in extreme poverty). He calls this hidden otherness, consisting of relatively invariable elements, "real history," as opposed to the superficial history of "what happened" that is contained in history books. This "real history" must be deciphered, since the meaning of the "play" in which we have particular parts is not immediately visible.

Paz's depiction of this internal Other is unambiguously negative, since it constitutes the main catalyst for injustice and repression. Paz considers the violent quelling of the student rebellion at Tlatelolco in 1968, as well as the "permanent usurpation of power" by the PRI, to be the result of the presence of the repressed Other, which leads to perpetual violence and destruction. He explains that the unconscious foundation of the history of violence since the fourteenth century is to be traced to the "politico-religious archetype of the ancient Mexicans: the pyramid, their implacable hierarchies, with, at the top, the chief priest and the platform for sacrifice" (123). The killing at Tlatelolco is in fact explicitly described as "a ritual act: a sacrifice," and thus as a "symbolic representation of our subterranean or invisible history" (114).

Paz explicitly establishes a link between the political model at the base of the repressed Other and Mexican geography, in accordance with the belief widely held in the past (including among ethnographers) that a culture is determined by geographic and climatic conditions. He explains that Mexico has a pyramidal form, "as if there existed a secret but obvious relation between natural space and symbolic geometry and between the latter and what I have called our invisible history" (117).

In a curious reversal, the "other Mexico"—that underdeveloped sector of the country which is left behind in the process of unequal modernization—becomes the opposite: the principle of authoritarian government and violent repression that he traces back to the Aztec state. The contradictory equation is quite explicit when Paz asserts that "the other Mexico is poor and miserable; furthermore, it is actually *other*" (108). He later describes this Other as the unconscious heritage of authoritarian government, repression, and violence. How can we reconcile the identification of the "poor and miserable" Mexico with the ruling party in the light of Paz's previous association of peasants with the Neolithic age, "the only happy period of our history in which there were neither monarchs nor priests"? This contradiction, however, seems to dissolve in the explanation that the division of Mexico into two parts, developed and underdeveloped, "is scientific and corresponds to the economic and social reality of our country. At the same time, in a different stratum, there is *another* Mexico" (109). The "other Mexico" thus corresponds to two different "Others," the underdeveloped sector and the repressed heritage that Paz associates with Aztec society. The two "Others" are obviously linked, not in a relation of similarity but in one of causality.

In order to understand Paz's condemnation of the Aztec state, it does not suffice to invoke the widespread practice of human sacrifice, since this existed in Mesoamerica before the arrival of the Aztecs. As for the existence of cruelty toward sacrificial victims, one need only read the detailed descriptions of Iroquois practices by French missionaries in what is now Canada to realize that the torments invented by the indigenous people in the far North may even surpass those of the Aztecs. A closer examination of Paz's description of the Aztecs may provide some answers. The pyramid corresponds to the Aztec image of the world, in which the gods participate in games of destruction (sometimes self-destruction) and creation that end in sacrifice, considered as a "productive" or "creative destruction." The bloody dance of the gods is projected onto society in the forms of ritual warfare and the sacrifice of prisoners, thus establishing a connection between religious rites and political domination based on the hierarchical model of the pyramid. According to Paz, this model was taken over by the Spanish viceroys and Mexican presidents, who thus became the successors of the Aztec emperors; Mexico City was the continuation of the Aztec metropolis. Since independence, Mexico's "sentimental identification" with the pre-Hispanic world is limited to the Aztec worldview based on sacrifice and the pyramid.

Aztec culture in no way represents the culmination of indigenous civilization. Paz considers the "period of the great theocracies," which ended in the ninth century, as the "creative phase" of Mesoamerica. He attributes the "extraordinary artistic and intellectual fecundity" of the period to the absence of a hegemonic state, to the area's cultural heterogeneity, and to its genuine "diversity and confrontation, that interplay of influences and reactions" (127) which is at the base of creativity. Mesoamerica was thus an "assembly of pyramids." The following "period of the great hegemonies," starting with Toltec domination and ending with the consolidation of the Aztec state, put an end to what Paz considers the Mesoamerican golden age, even though he admitted the existence of human sacrifice and cannibalism before the Aztec conquest. The Aztecs are described as "wandering nomads" (128) and stereotypical barbarians, belonging to uncultured tribes from the north who invade previously established centers of civilization. Paz also compares Aztec society to medieval Europe, the "Dark Ages" in which Greco-Roman civilization is forgotten in a long-lasting regression to more primitive ways of life and general ignorance. What is even more interesting is that he extends this comparison to what he considers to be the Latin American lack of enlightenment with respect to Paris, London, and New York! The model of degeneration and degradation, which frequently inspired metropolitan portrayals of the colonies, is obvious here.

Although this model of the Aztec as the barbarian is widespread, it is instructive to compare Paz's version with that of Miguel León-Portilla. In his introduction to *The Broken Spears: The Aztec Account of the Conquest of Mexico*, the Mexican scholar explains that the Aztecs, or "northern barbarians—like the Germanic tribes in the Roman world—were a constant threat to established cultures." He describes them as "a poor band of outcasts"; "a mere band of nomads"; "almost totally uncultured"; and adds that the "only heritage they brought with them, besides the Nahuatl tongue, was an indomitable will." However, this "destitute tribe" rapidly assimilated various cultural traditions and succeeded, in only two centuries, in building a city of such splendor that Bernal Díaz del Castillo "thought that the wonders he

beheld must be a dream." The "life of Tenochtitlan was that of a true metropolis."[10] Although León-Portilla describes the Aztecs' mystical conception of warfare based on human sacrifice, adding that sacrifice was more
widespread among the Aztecs than elsewhere, he also emphasizes the importance of schooling, writing, and calendars. His avoidance of negative judgment is entirely consistent with the purpose of his edited volume: to provide
an insight into Aztec versions of the Conquest. It is interesting in this regard
to read René Girard's comments on religious "aberrations" (the term is also
used by Paz, who, however, unambiguously condemns practices designated
by it), which seem appropriate to the Aztec cult of human sacrifice: "Even
the wildest aberrations of religious thought still manage to bear witness to
the fact that evil and the violent measures taken to combat evil are essentially the same" (37). A hypothetical Girardian explanation of Aztec ritual
warfare and sacrifice would possibly point out that violence was strictly controlled, and that the neighboring Tlaxcaltecs, for example, were never anni-
hilated, so they could provide a perpetual source of sacrificial victims. Paz,
however, condemns this "Aztec peace" and calls proponents of this concept
"contemporary idolatrous scholars" (130).

Paz describes the Aztecs in the following dichotomous terms: "Solar religion and expansionist ideology, superhuman heroism and inhuman political realism, sacred madness and cold astuteness, sacrifice and pillage" (131).
To these dichotomies he adds those of nomadic and sedentary societies, and
of solar and agricultural religions. The terms he uses in this passage—amal-
gam, syncretism, duplicity, and hybrid (132)—suggest that one of the main
reasons for condemning the Aztec state may be related to the *scandal of hybridity.* It is not the uncultured barbarians who are on the lowest rung of
humanity, but those cultures characterized by the mingling of barbarism
and civilization, reason and the irrational—a mixture that reminds us of
Paz's criticism of the Soviet state in *The Labyrinth of Solitude.* It is not violence in itself that is intolerable, but the *combination* of the senseless destruction of life and petrified reason, of delirium and rationality.

However, the conjunction of what are generally constructed as dichotomous elements, superstition and reason, is one of the defining characteristics of the primitive society that practices sacrifice, according to René Girard.
With respect to the fear of pollution and impurity, Girard argues that while
"Frazer and his disciples tend to view this fear of infection by the 'impure' as
a prime example of the 'irrational' and 'superstitious' element of religious
thought, other observers regard it as an anticipation of sound scientific prin-

ciples. They point out the striking resemblance between the precautions that modern medicine takes against bacterial infection and the ritualistic avoidance of pollution" (29). In the same way, sacrifice, as constructed by Girard, is seen as the conjunction of ritual murder and superstition on the one hand, with a rational strategy for controlling destructive violence, on the other. The dichotomy between superstition and reason is replaced by the differentiation between types of violence: preventive and destructive, sacrificial and vengeful.

In León-Portilla, the conjunction in Aztec society of what are considered contradictory traits is in no way portrayed in a negative manner. On the contrary, the "indomitable will" of the northern barbarian is implicitly represented as a rejuvenating force that is essential to the creation of a thriving empire which assimilates the cultural traditions of the older civilizations. An analogous construction of the uncultured individual as invigorating element and catalyst for social renewal characterizes descriptions of the Mexican Revolution of 1910. In *The Cage of Melancholy*, Roger Bartra argues that the Mexican Revolution has contributed to the transformation of the stereotype of the passive, melancholy peasant into that of the underprivileged urban Mexican (the *pelado*), evicted from his pastoral world and living on the edge of modern industrial society as a violent, rebellious, emotional, and uprooted marginal. This newer construct, however, is not entirely negative, since it presents the marginal as a rejuvenating and revolutionary force, a symbol of the new nation. Bartra considers it indispensable for the founding and consolidation of the new state of the Mexican Revolution.[11]

Paz's Aztecs, however, are described in radically different terms. Paz compares the ceremonies of the indigenous conquerors of Mexico to the torments imagined by the Marquis de Sade, and attributes to the obfuscation of our intellect the inability to admit that "the Aztec world is one of the aberrations of history" (133). The Aztec thus becomes a symbol of barbarism, in what appears to be a pejorative reductionism redolent of the negative portrayal of the New World native that persisted (concurrently with more positive depictions) throughout the period of conquest and colonization. But when Paz concludes that contemporary Mexicans, the "real inheritors of the assassins of the pre-Hispanic world" (153), must engage in a process of self-criticism resembling therapeutic psychoanalysis in order to extirpate this heritage, it is obvious that the repressed internal Other, the Aztec heritage, has become the sign of a negatively constructed national identity.

However, Paz also deconstructs the specificity of the internal Other when he argues that "the emulators of the Aztecs are to be found not in Asia, but in the West, since only amongst ourselves has the alliance between politics and metaphysical reason been so intimate, exacerbated, and lethal: the Inquisition, religious wars, and, above all, the totalitarian societies of the twentieth century" (134). Not only are the Aztecs reduced to their negative qualities, and the heterogeneous native population of Mexico reduced to the Aztec heritage, but the Mexican native is equated with the worst tyrants of European history. Having lost all specificity in order to merge into the general category of reprehensible specimens of the human race, Paz's Amerindians can no longer be considered as markers of a specifically Mexican identity, as is the case with other symbolic constructions of Mexico based on specific elements of the indigenous heritage. His Aztecs correspond, at least in certain respects, to the archetypal barbarian, which Western societies supposedly left behind on their long march to civilization. At the same time, his "other Mexico" conforms to the more recent "psychologization" of "primitive" impulses like the id, which the "civilized" person must continually strive to control. But his construction of the internal Other diverges from that of the primitive and the barbarian when he equates the Aztecs' mentality with the calculating *ratio* of Western tyrants. The "other Mexico" becomes an integral part not only of the dual nation but also of the modernized West. A conjunction of the primitive and the modern, instinct and reason, his paradoxical Other finally stands for everything he considers negative in humankind—in short, the universally abject.

In *Violence and the Sacred,* Girard suggests that literature has a function analogous to that of sacrifice: to provide an outlet for violent impulses that would otherwise lead to the destruction of the community.[12] The suffering heroes of Greek tragedy are thus surrogate victims of the spectators' aggressive instincts. In an analogous manner, we can surmise that Paz's Aztecs, whom he condemns in such virulent terms, stand in place of the modern Mexican state, which is criticized as well, but less aggressively. In fact, Paz adduces certain mitigating circumstances to his explicit criticism of the ruling party, such as the difficulty of bringing about economic development in an underdeveloped country and the necessity of a strong government to ensure stability after the revolutionary upheaval of 1910. His abject Aztec state thus functions as a scapegoat, as well as a perfect object for an ethnographic allegory in which the construction of the primitive (or, in this case, barbarian) "Other" is a displaced representation of the Self. Only as an allegory can we understand the contradictions of Paz's essay, in which Mexico's poverty-stricken peasants are associated with the repressed heritage of the murderous Aztecs, while the Inquisition and the East European totalitarian regimes are described as emulations of the Aztec state.

Notes

1. Octavio Paz, *El laberinto de la soledad* (Mexico City: Fondo de Cultura Económica, 1959), 152–155. All subsequent citations of this work refer to this edition. Page numbers are indicated parenthetically in the text. All translations from this work are my own.

2. Claude Lévi-Strauss, *Tristes tropiques* (Paris: Plon, 1955), 417.

3. Octavio Paz, "Crítica de la pirámide," in his *Posdata* (Mexico City: Siglo XXI, 1970), 103–155. All subsequent citations of this work refer to this edition. Page numbers are indicated parenthetically in the text. All translations from *Posdata* are my own.

4. For example, José Carlos Mariátegui, *Siete ensayos de interpretación de la realidad peruana* (Mexico City: Fondo de Cultura Económica, 1979).

5. For a discussion of the debates concerning totemism since the nineteenth century, see Adam Kuper, *The Invention of Primitive Society: Transformations of an Illusion* (London: Routledge, 1988).

6. Sigmund Freud, *Totem and Taboo* (London: Hogarth Press, 1918).

7. René Girard, *Violence and the Sacred,* trans. Patrick Gregory (Baltimore: Johns Hopkins University Press, 1977), 17. All subsequent citations of this work refer to this edition. Page numbers are indicated parenthetically in the text.

8. Paz, "Olimpiada y Tlatelolco," in his *Posdata,* 24.

9. *Posdata,* 74–75.

10. Miguel León-Portilla, *The Broken Spears: The Aztec Account of the Conquest of Mexico,* trans. Lysander Kemp (Boston: Beacon Press, 1962), xi–xxiii.

11. Roger Bartra, *La jaula de la melancolía* (Mexico City: Grijalbo, 1987), 127–134. See also his "Paradise Subverted: The Invention of the Mexican Character," Bartra in this volume. Bartra examines the way in which the Mexican national character is constructed in the social imaginary and thematized in various intellectual, fictional, and political discourses. The internal Other in question is not the unmitigatedly abject rational barbarian of Paz's essay, but the rural inhabitant as constructed by the Western urban elite as well as by sociologists and anthropologists.

12. "*Totem and Taboo* and the Incest Prohibition," in Girard, *Violence and the Sacred,* 193–222.

3

Under the Shadow of God

Roots of Primitivism in Early Colonial Mexico

DELIA ANNUNZIATA COSENTINO

Before the contemporary resurgence of discussions on primitivism, when the term "primitive" was conjured in association with premodern Mexican art, it was usually used by early critics to classify pre-Columbian forms (their "childish freshness," as Benjamin Peret put it in 1947) and later the modernist reverence of those forms. A different definition of the term now surfaces in conjunction with early Colonial art, which was produced in a complex context of discovery, confrontation, confusion, expectation, and deep-rooted fear. The "primitivism" that has only recently been used in regard to Colonial art and times has generally given a name to the imposition of a constructed identity on non-European people by the Western world. Studies have cited this type of primitivism, for instance, in early representations of indigenous Americans that circulated in Europe during the first age of exploration, usually revealing highly distorted understandings of their subjects. Often inspired by travel accounts and executed by Europeans with little or no direct knowledge of their subjects, the pictures generally focus on what their creators perceive as their subjects' savage nature. Emphasizing, for instance, disheveled appearances or wild behavior, like the practice of cannibalism, these pictorial constructions imply native irrationality, aggression, and mystery—characterizations that generally succeed in coaxing fear and loathing and that really only speak volumes about the European beast within.

In contrast, this study looks to a different genre of Colonial art whose implications are more elusive because in these representations there is generally no native dressed (or not) as the savage he was sometimes understood to be. Considered here are more implicitly primitivist representations created in the context of the evangelical mission in the New World, as part of the program of the "spiritual conquest" of Mexico. In this context, paradisiacal imagery presents an idealized environment that, upon analysis, reveals hybrid origins and therefore requires a reassessment of what might have been understood as a purely European construct. In this study, primitivism is not simply Western projection but also native contribution to the construction of a space and identity for indigenous Mexicans. At the center of this analysis is an Indo-Christian tree that lends tangible and symbolic form to the construct, offering an excellent opportunity to examine its framework and the position of the colonized subject in relation to it. It is here, under the shadow of God, that we find the roots to a special kind of primitivism in early Colonial Mexico.

At the start of "Signs Taken for Wonder," Homi K. Bhabha relates the experience of an early Indian catechist who witnessed "500 people, men, women and children, seated under the shade of the trees" in the countryside of northern India, marveling over the wonders of Christianity in the early nineteenth century.[1] Bhabha is so clearly struck by the account of that scene of shaded converts that he incorporates the tree, apparently as a metaphor for colonial presence, into the subtitle of the essay, "Questions of Ambivalence and Authority Under a Tree Outside Delhi, May 1817." In a parallel universe—that is, in sixteenth-century Mexico—a similar, if distant, vision of conversion, ambivalence, and wonder—again, under a highly symbolic tree—is conjured by a painted image and related text never before examined together. This essay presents a snapshot of life under the shadow of the Christian God in early Conquest Mexico that is first located within a broader tradition of Colonial religious imagery on formerly Nahua (Aztec) soil. Not only reflecting the dreamy hopes of Spanish mendicant friars in search of paradise, this imagery might also be understood to reveal some nascent roots of primitivism in the New World.

In this essay, the term "primitivism" is used in reference to the imposition of a constructed identity on non-Westerners, in this case in the context of Spanish-Nahua interaction in early Colonial Mexico. This imposition, however, is not simply a European one; examples suggest its heavy dependence on indigenous contributions. In this place and time, forms, concepts, words, and imagery of Nahua origin mingle with mendicant projection to redefine the space of this new world and to create an identity for its indigenous inhabitants within that space. An imposed framework is therefore enhanced and fleshed out by an infrastructure of ambivalent origin. The construct is further complicated by the fact that the very people who would (and did) suffer from its limitations literally end up singing its praises in their own terms.

The religious assault on a captivated sixteenth-century Mexico was something fantastic—or at least that was the way the mendicant forces sent to cover the job intended it to be. Arriving on the heels of the conquistadors, Franciscans, Dominicans, and Augustinians descended upon the land with a determination to bring special significance to their mission. An image originally from a detailed European woodcut that was evidently transmitted to central Mexico, where it was reproduced in a somewhat rougher form, suggests that on both sides of the Atlantic, audiences were provided with a visual sense of just how special that mission might be (fig. 3.1). Though now damaged with time, we can still make out the early representation located in the sixteenth-century monastery of Actopan (Hidalgo), which shows a large wooden ship, with billowed sails and oars cocked, arriving on the crowded shore of the new territory. In this solid vessel, mitered mendicants and haloed figures pack the decks, their eyes fixed on the fantastic visions of their destination, and with reason; like a sharpened index finger, the bow of their ship points to the paramount symbol of Christianity awaiting them right at their landing point—the crucified Christ. Appropriate to the setting, his living cross is a palm tree, around which tonsured friars, evidently earlier arrivals, kneel and pray in reverence. Nearby, classicized figures react to the apparently simultaneous apocalyptic apparition of Christ in the foreground. Beneath the head of God the Father, which looms with the Holy Spirit at the top of the painted scene, the word "Paradisus" is inscribed. A special mission, indeed.

Henri Baudet observes at the end of his short history of European longings for paradise that the more people are "historical orientated, the less inclined [they are] to seek Paradise beyond the horizon."[2] While he emphasizes a "protesting attitude toward the whole of history" from the eighteenth century, that protest started centuries earlier for the devoted group that spearheaded the anticipated spiritual conquest of Mexico. As shiploads of friars disembarked, they had plenty to keep in mind and enough to leave behind. Few would have been free, for instance, of Erasmus of Rotterdam's criticisms of widespread corruption in the Catholic Church at the beginning of the sixteenth century. His brand of sentiment inspired, for one, a serious attempt at the realization of Thomas More's utopia by the Dominican Bartolomé de Las Casas and others, such as Bishop Vasco de Quiroga, during their American tenure.[3] Besides humanist pressures, European Catholicism was falling on hard times as the Protestant campaign strengthened and the Eastern centers were becoming increasingly Muslim. Motivation for a

FIGURE 3.1. A sixteenth-century mural at a monastery in Actopan, Hidalgo (top), and a counterpart European woodcut.

grand escape among Franciscans, in particular, was further fueled by teachings revered in their order, like those of Joachim of Fiore in the twelfth century. Joachim's work encouraged the adoption of an apocalyptic perspective by the spiritual church of the friars, which he predicted would replace the material church before the Second Coming.[4] Within a century, Joachim's ideas had seduced Saint Francis, becoming the perpetual cause of Franciscan conservatives who struggled to retain the order's original vision. Fifteenth-century Spain was a hotbed of such traditionalist reform and Joachimist apocalyptic views, which coincided nicely with that country's unanticipated discovery of a "new" world.

Given their historical send-off, it is hardly surprising that outward-bound mendicants would hold great hopes for the new Spanish territory; some accounts reveal plans to unleash there a pristine form of Christianity, the kind known to the "primitive Church" of the past.[5] The writings of Spanish friars in Mexico, including Martín de la Coruña, Gerónimo de Mendieta, and Juan Torquemada, betray such ambitions; they conjure visions of a "New Jerusalem" that the mendicant mission would help to secure in Mexico. Mendieta, whose *Historia ecclesiástica indiana* of the late sixteenth century is recognized by John L. Phelan as "one of the last flowerings of medieval Franciscan mysticism,"[6] predicted the enactment of a millennial kingdom for which he and his spiritual brothers were busy laying the foundations.

Those foundations were in large part tangible—a quantity of monasteries in settlements big and small, which often dominated the local landscape and set the visual environment for the mendicants' special mission. As if to realize Mendieta's dream to make it seem "as if the whole province were a monastery,"[7] the building program included the incorporation of enclosed churches and open chapels (for outdoor Masses), walled gardens, and tree-lined atria into enormous constructions that tended to radically overwhelm the one or two friars who actually lived in them. To further establish the ambiance, the monasteries were embellished with painting and sculpture that helped to transport the material constructions to a spiritual realm which would match the anticipations of mendicants—hence, for instance, the painted scene of divine apparitions on the American shores at Actopan. One of the more elaborate visual translations of this utopian spirit is the Augustinian monastery in Malinalco, where Jeanette Peterson has surveyed the extensive iconography to identify the rabbits nibbling pomegranates, monkeys hanging from leafy trees, and a variety of blooming flowers that transform the painted garden into "a terrestrial paradise ... perfectly suited to the

FIGURE 3.2. Detail of paradisiacal garden frescoes from the cloister walls of an Augustinian monastery in Malinalco.

utopian ideas that profoundly shaped mendicant thinking on arrival in the New World" (fig. 3.2).[8]

This primitivist construct is a familiar one and seems basic enough: the New World paradise is timeless—a nature haven that eludes history as a space of primal existence. It also seems to elude human occupation; in this visual realm, elaborate flora and fauna are effective substitutes for the would-be inhabitants of this Garden of Eden, leaving the subjects of the spiritual mission glaringly absent. Mendieta suggests, if somewhat vaguely, that indigenous people were indeed an important part of the construct as he considers how, through proper organization, the native population could "live virtuously and peacefully serving God, as in a terrestrial paradise."[9] Not surprisingly, their great promise was, for Mendieta, at least partially a function of the fact that they were outwardly simple *gente de tan pocos quilates y de tan bajo talento* (people so unpolished and so poor in talent), whose angelic potential would be revealed through mendicant guidance.[10] In this way, far from the complicated circumstances of European life, the unforgiving problems of history found solutions in an eternal lyricism that, in the visual realm, often excluded the very subjects whose primitive identity was so well suited for the idealized landscape.

But essential elements of the painted utopia at Malinalco, for one, also begin to suggest a complexity to the paradise construct that takes it out of the realm of straightforward European projection and into a world of hybrid idealism. At the most basic and general level, the art and architecture of sixteenth-century Mexico is the product of native workers, and Malinalco was no exception. Peterson's analysis shows that, despite the presence of some distinctly European qualities, the style of line, space, and form in the garden murals betrays a pervasive native approach to pictorial space. In terms of content, the flora and fauna so carefully depicted not only are overwhelmingly native but also are exclusive to the New World, each species carrying with it important cultural (indigenous) associations that were surely not forgotten as the monastery was decorated by local hands. These iconographic details take on an even greater layer of significance when juxtaposed, as Peterson shows, with chroniclers' reports of purely native concepts of a paradise very similar to the Christian one—verdant, fecund, and a promised land for good people. This apparent point of cultural convergence is verified by the presence of distinctly indigenous symbols embedded in the pictorial program, one of which Peterson identifies as a "precious green stone" bee that, according to Aztec myth, is the form taken by a sacred soul destined "to suck [honey] from all the varied flowers" of this suddenly pre-Hispanic paradise.[11] What once seemed pure imposition now seems a complex mix of Western projection and native contribution held together by some culturally converging, idealized concepts.

It is in this context that the shadow of a grand arbor is cast in central Mexico, more than half a decade after the Spanish siege of the Aztec capital of Tenochtitlan. We catch a partial glimpse of its trunk and crown at the monastery of San Miguel in Zinacantepec (Toluca Valley) where *El árbol de San Francisco* was painted with other nature images on a heavy wall of the open chapel in the 1580s (fig. 3.3). The colorful mural shows a reclining Saint Francis from whose chest emerges a tree with blooming branches. Each blossom gives way to a member of the Franciscan order, generally unidentifiable, male, tonsured, and clutching a simple wooden cross. The composition is immediately reminiscent of the Tree of Jesse, a twelfth-century Christian motif based on a biblical description of Christ's mundane family with Jesse as its "root." The painted flowers also reflect a clear formal parallel to a Spanish illustration of the living cross or *arbor vitae,* known to be circulating in the religious libraries of mendicant Mexico. Despite these influences, which suggest a straightforward European provenance, this particular composition was, in fact, unprecedented in Europe, whereas unexpected parallels appear in pre-Columbian art. I have demonstrated elsewhere the existence of a temporally and geographically widespread precontact Mesoamerican tradition of depicting figures in repose with trees that emerge from their upper torsos.[12] The other components of this native pattern include a mountain on which the figure generally reclines, and the nourishment of the leafy growth through sacrificial blood, a substance revered for its powers of regeneration and often obtained through heart extraction. In *El árbol de San Francisco,* native influence first seems present in the brown peak that supports the horizontal Saint Francis. More striking still is the fact that the tree grows not from the saint's groin, as one would expect after the Jesse model, but from his heart. These details suggest that this sprawling arbor, Franciscan as it may seem, actually has its roots in two different but converging cultural traditions.

An additional view of this ambivalent tree comes from an equally hybrid text that contains some more tangible evidence of the indigenous contribution to the motif and its setting while offering a rare glimpse of the animated performance by natives in the mendicant drama that subsumes it. The source is the *Psalmodia christiana y sermonario de los sanctos del año,* a 1583 book of songs for Church festivals written under the direction of the leading Franciscan chronicler of the time, Fray Bernardino de Sahagún.[13] Despite these orthodox qualifications, in reality the text is overwhelmingly indigenous in style and thrust. Actually written by four Indian scholars in Nahuatl, the language of the Aztecs, the book's entries are characterized by writing patterns and symbolism that are unmistakably native. The first few lines of the song for the festival of Saint Bernardino of Siena introduce Saint Francis as

the cypress tree of quetzal feathers,
the silk cotton tree of trogon feather,
which our lord God caused to bud . . .

The allusion to a common metaphor used to express the protective nature of an authority in Aztec courtly speech is undeniably direct: a mid-sixteenth-century Spanish guidebook to Nahuatl records, under the heading "Author-

FIGURE 3.3. *The Tree of Saint Francis,* a mural in the open chapel of the monastery of San Miguel in Zinacantepec, Toluca.

ity as Protector," registers the indigenous idea that "A mother, a father is as a foundation, and a covering like the silk cotton tree, the cypress tree."[14]

The entire book and the aforementioned song have been associated by Louise Burkhart with the "flowery world" complex of the Uto-Aztecan language family, in which a verbally evoked garden of native flora and fauna becomes the "consummate manifestation of holiness," according to Nahua sensibilities.[15] Burkhart suggests that the writing of such rhetoric was encouraged by friars who sought convincing parallels between Christian ideas and indigenous constructs. Indeed, in the song examined here, we see how a Christian paradise becomes "Nahuatlized" in the description of the tree's surroundings, which read like a verbal reiteration of the painted haven at the Malinalco monastery. Enumerated are not only "all the various precious stones" that "lie massed, . . . gleaming there," but also "all the various heavenly flowers" that "spread [perfume] on [the tree]," like "the heart flower, the godly popcorn flower, the cacao flower, the Indian corn flower, the cup flower, the red bone flower," which "are all arched, fragrant; scattered widely," and "shine like the golden dew."

It is in the midst of these heavenly words and the images they conjure that the presence of the colonized natives is finally inserted into the bicultural paradise, with their positions established in relation to the sheltering crown of arboreal authority. Creating the image of a now towering form representing the central and unifying pillar of the entire faith, the song asserts that

> everywhere in the world, [this tree]
> shades all the children of the Holy Church.

This line suggests an interesting parallel with modernist primitivism. Sally Price has termed this popular twentieth-century type of construct the "universality principle," a myth of brotherly equality that was theorized by Roland Barthes in his analysis of the Museum of Modern Art's 1955 "Family of Man" photographic exhibition.[16] Barthes lays bare that exhibition's dependence on an extraction of history and its focus on nature for an effective celebration of the human condition, which he claims "serves as an alibi to a large part of our humanism."[17] The lesson taken from the Christian brotherhood of man by the show's curator seems to be expressed in the divine words that introduced the photographs: "let there be light (Genesis 1:3)." The reality of the universality myth, even for devoted believers of the Colonial period, seems thinly rooted. Mendieta, for one, suggests his own uncertainty about the native race while commenting about the native subjects: *si no fuera porque tenemos por fe que todos descendemos de Adán y Eva, diríamos que es otra especie* (would we not hold in faith that we all descend from Adam and Eve, we would say it is another species).[18] Under the equalizing shadow of the tree, however, native alterity appears normalized as the colonized subjects become another batch of children in the family of God.

But these native "children" do not simply sit in silence under the tree, in what Homi Bhabha might call their "place of difference and otherness." On the contrary—the song for Saint Bernardino's Church festival cuts through the quiet of history, giving Nahua converts a voice that forcefully activates their presence while raising questions about the nature of their involvement in the spiritual program. Proclaiming their emotional reaction to the environment of which they are a part at so many different levels, the words out of the mouths of the converts continue:

> And in its shade, in its protection,
> We the people of New Spain
> are here happy, rejoicing greatly . . .

With these lyrics, we suddenly face the uncomfortable idea that the idealized habitat has indeed found its ideal inhabitants in the colonized Nahua, now a community of joyful Christians who gladly embrace their sheltered existence as they sing its praises. Not only is it an image that seems to undermine the troubling truths of the Conquest (enormous loss of life and cultural disorientation, to mention a couple), but it also challenges us to consider the degree to which the paradise construct is an unwelcome fantasy, since the language, metaphors, images, and accepting voices that shape it are decidedly Nahua. As one imagines these sounds of paradise complementing the built and decorated foundations of the spiritual enterprise, the vision that was beheld in northern India is foreshadowed centuries earlier in central Mexico. Across the new Spanish territory, groups of native converts surely gathered in the shade of trees, both actual and pictorial (sculpted and painted trees exist in countless places in and around central Mexico, including Charo, Cuernavaca, Cuilapan, Mazapa, Metztitlan, Oaxaca, and Tlamanalco, not to mention the sites of churches that feature stone crosses which meet the ground in a snarl of roots), to croon over the wonders of Christianity.

An early primitivism with ramifications for the present reigned strong in early Colonial Mexico in a mendicant-Nahua paradise, and it was no simple construct. With a sacred tree of ambivalent origins at its center, the darker aspects of the nature haven have been obscured by the attractive but ominous shade cast soon after the fall of the Aztec empire. As Nahua peoples in the first century of colonization helped to create and animate the idealized environment, they joined Spanish mendicants in fixing a space and identity that they have since been challenged to live with. What started as lofty fantasy has been invested with generations of theory and practice that have only served to complicate the basic questions of when, why, and how identities are constructed to begin with.

Notes

1. Homi K. Bhabha, "Signs Taken for Wonders: Questions of Ambivalence and Authority Under a Tree Outside Delhi, May 1817," *Critical Inquiry* 12 (1985): 144–165.

2. Henri Baudet, *Paradise on Earth: Some Thoughts on European Images of Non-European Man,* trans. Elizabeth Wentholt (New Haven, CT: Yale University Press, 1965), 75.

3. See Victor N. Baptiste, *Bartolomé de Las Casas and Thomas More's Utopia: Connections and Similarities. A Translation and Study* (Culver City, CA: Labyrinthos,

1990), for a discussion of Las Casas's independent utopian ideas in his *Memorial de remedios para las Indias* (1516).

4. Georges Baudot, *Utopia and History in Mexico: The First Chroniclers of Mexican Civilization (1520–1569)*, trans. Bernard R. Ortiz de Montellano and Thelma Ortiz de Montellano (Niwot: University Press of Colorado, 1995), 78–82. For an extensive discussion of Joachim of Fiore, see George Boas's *Primitivism and Related Ideas in the Middle Ages* (Baltimore: Johns Hopkins University Press, 1997).

5. José Antonio Maravall, "La utopía político-religiosa de los franciscanos en Nueva España," *Estudios Americanos* 1, no. 2 (1949): 207.

6. John Leddy Phelan, *Millennial Kingdom of the Franciscans in the New World* (Berkeley: University of California Press, 1970), 1.

7. In ibid., 69.

8. Jeanette Favrot Peterson, *The Paradise Garden Murals of Malinalco: Utopia and Empire in Sixteenth-Century Mexico* (Austin: University of Texas Press, 1993), 138.

9. In Phelan, *Millennial Kingdom,* 69.

10. Joaquín García Icazbalceta, *Cartas de religiosos de Nueva España, 1539–1594,* Nueva Colección de Documentos para la Historia de México, vol. 1 (Mexico City: Editorial S. Chavez Hayhoe, 1941), 8.

11. Peterson quotes a belief recorded in Fray Bernardino de Sahagún's *Florentine Codex: General History of the Things of New Spain,* trans. Arthur J. O. Anderson and Charles Dibble (Salt Lake City: University of Utah Press, 1950–1982), vol. 3, 47–48; see Peterson, *Paradise Garden Murals,* 133.

12. Delia A. Cosentino, "Zinacantepec's Tree of Saint Francis: Cross-Cultural Roots and Colonial Blossoms in a Sixteenth-Century Mexican Mural" (Master's thesis, UCLA, 1996).

13. Fray Bernardino de Sahagún, *Psalmodia christiana y sermonario de los sanctos del año* [1583], trans. Arthur J. O. Anderson (Salt Lake City: University of Utah Press, 1993). A complete translation of the song examined here is found also in Arthur J. O. Anderson, "The 'San Bernardino' of Sahagún's Psalmodia," *Indiana* 9 (1984).

14. Judith M. Maxwell and Craig A. Hanson, *Of the Manners of Speaking That the Old Ones Had: The Metaphors of Andrés de Olmos in the TULAL Manuscript, Arte para Aprender la Lengua Mexicana, 1547* (Salt Lake City: University of Utah Press, 1992), 169.

15. Louise Burkhart, "Flowery Heaven: The Aesthetic of Paradise in Nahuatl Devotional Literature," *Res* 21 (1992): 91.

16. Chapter 2 of Sally Price's *Primitive Art in Civilized Places* (Chicago: University of Chicago Press, 1989) captures the phenomenon noted earlier in Roland Barthes's *Mythologies,* trans. Annette Lavers (New York: Hill and Wang, 1972), which takes on *The Family of Man* (New York: Museum of Modern Art, 1955).

17. Barthes, *Mythologies,* 100.

18. Icazbalceta, *Cartas de religiosos,* 7.

4

Of Alebrijes *and* Ocumichos

Some Myths about Folk Art and Mexican Identity

ELI BARTRA

TRANSLATED BY JOHN MRAZ

Folk art, the art that all peoples of the world produce, is an inexhaustible source of surprises. Defining it is part of a larger, eternal question: deciding what is (and is not) art. Among laymen as well as critics there is a tendency to place handicrafts and folk art into the same bag. For example, the well-known Latin American art critic Marta Traba believed folk art to be made up of handicrafts, folklore, and primitive painting.[1] I think, rather, that handicrafts are something quite different from the folk arts, among which I would include primitive painting. All folk art is made by artisans, but not all that artisans make is folk art. For example, chairs of palm fronds or clay pots, while handmade and often decorated, are not what I consider folk art. Although the distinction does not always hold true, as we shall see, handicrafts are generally produced in series and often collectively; they tend to be utilitarian and repetitive, the result more of manual dexterity than of creative imagination. Folk art seems unique, more personal, more imaginative, more . . . art. Folklore, on the other hand, is something apart, made up mostly of oral and musical expression: stories, songs, legends, dances. It is another kind of artistic production entirely. In my opinion, these are three distinct fields: folk art, handicrafts, and folklore.

It is often said that folk art is created by "the people" *(el pueblo)*. But who are they? We might ask William of Baskerville, one of the characters in Umberto Eco's *The Name of the Rose*, to help us define "folk": "By the term 'people'—he said—it would be best to signify all citizens, but since among citizens children must be included, as well as idiots, malefactors, and women, perhaps it would be possible to arrive reasonably at a definition of the people as the better part of the citizens, though he himself at the moment did not consider it opportune to assert who actually belonged to that part."[2]

There are those who define "the people" in a very different way, as a heterogeneous grouping "composed of all those who are in a subaltern position with respect to the different relations of power, which are polymorphous."[3] But if that is the definition of "folk," then all women (as a subaltern social group) would be "folk," something we know is not so. The fact is that although we might prefer to characterize "folk" in a more elegant and sophisticated way, what it really refers to is the poor. Not all the marginalized and oppressed are folk, not all women nor all blacks, yellow-skinned, and brown; only the poor.

Folk art is then, in my opinion, poor art; moreover, it is the art of the poor. Its creators are poor, and the materials they use are generally inexpensive. Because they are poor, they have little or no formal education; and because of this lack they are often called primitive, like the art they produce. Of course, there is always someone who, with the best of intentions, wants to romanticize poverty: "Folk art is the art of the poor, that is, of the immense majority of humanity, but folk art is not a poor art, it has the immense wealth that can only be afforded by humility and love."[4] Poor, popular, and cheap, whenever this art is called primitive, it is in contrast to elite or high art, which is supposed to be refined, sophisticated, erudite, expensive, and civilized. This poverty of origins is one of the reasons it has been systematically excluded from the traditional historiography of art, which focuses on great artists and their works. This exclusion also reflects the perception that folk artists are generally anonymous to people outside their community or to periods removed in time, although exceptionally some have achieved international recognition.[5] Some texts have begun to appear that confront these biases, addressing the issue of class in the categorization of art, but they do not mention generic division, for they fail to realize that folk art itself is undergoing a hierarchical segmentation of genre.[6]

An eminently traditional form of expression, folk art is often conceived of as unchanging and static. Nothing is farther from the truth. Though it changes in ways distinct from those of elite art, it is in constant transformation, a result both of artists perfecting their techniques and of adaptation to market demands. Although it does change, folk art tends to be conservative both in form and in content. Elite art always wants to be innovative and vanguardist, original and unique, but folk art conserves styles, motifs, symbols, forms, and techniques. Votive paintings and Judas figures illustrate some of the ways in which folk arts change. Votive paintings (ex-votos) are representations of "miracles"—extraordinary cures of illnesses, rescues from seemingly impossible situations—that are generally painted on thin sheets of metal to thank saints for their intervention. Although the form of votive painting has been maintained, the content has changed because it reflects an ever-changing social reality. A transformation of a different sort is represented by the fact that votive paintings are disappearing from the walls of today's churches. Judas figures, the papier mâché effigies that are burned on Holy Saturday, are another folk art form that seems to be disappearing. These figures represent the traitor of traitors, Judas Iscariot, but the specific forms they take can be anything from politicians to cartoon characters (see fig. 4.1). Thus, the particular beings represented, reproduced from daily life, are constantly changing.

It is important as well to note how new folk art forms are incessantly appearing. Consider the *amates,* paintings of flowers, animals, and scenes of daily life on bark paper. Amates, which began to be painted in the 1950s, incorporated previously existing plastic elements of the ceramics from the state of Guerrero. Another new creation is the *Friditas,* reproductions of Frida Kahlo paintings in clay made in Ocotlán de Morelos, Oaxaca. The involvement of women in the weaving of serapes in Teotitlán del Valle, Oaxaca, is also a relatively recent occurrence.[7] The *ocumichos* and the *alebrijes,* too, are novel creations that will be considered below; despite their recent origin they have already undergone complex transformations.

Simplicity, freshness, and innocence are characteristics invariably associated with folk art, a reason why it is often referred to as "naive" or primitive. But does this mean that it is somehow anterior, an art that existed at the dawn of humankind or, at the very least, prior to the Renaissance? It is thought to be little refined, poorly made, unsophisticated, clumsy, simple: the art of the folk, of the pueblo, and not of the elite. Why not call "savage" this art considered to be without cultivation, like wild nature? "Savage art" would immediately make people think of natives in feathers, and so the word used is "primitive."

Ernst Gombrich has argued that, contrary to common assumptions, primitive art does not resemble children's art; they are diametrically opposed.[8] Children's art is spontaneous. According to Gombrich, the latter contains all the elements of the artistic process but in an underdeveloped state, because children lack dexterity. Primitive artists, on the contrary, demonstrate much control over their tools and materials, a result of long and disciplined practice. Primitive art may lack a particular technical element—for example, perspective—but it does not lack dexterity or technical mastery, as is characteristic of children's art.

One could compare folk art to walking, and elite art to driving (a comparison which does not imply that primitive art is more pedestrian, rudimentary, or underdeveloped). They could be seen simply as two distinct ways of expression, as walking and driving are two different forms of transportation. If one wants to go from the kitchen to the bedroom, it is most probable that the best way to get there is on foot, but no one would dream of considering this a primitive form of locomotion. However, if one wants to go from New York to Mérida, a car or airplane would be better suited. Likewise, folk art and elite art use different means to achieve different ends.

For centuries folk art has been both admired and rejected in the Western world. At the end of the eighteenth century it became popular. Goethe, for example, considered it to be the only real art, while the Romantics generally regarded it as an expression of the national soul, a matter of identity and pride. Later, painters like Paul Gauguin and Pablo Picasso became great admirers of primitive art and incorporated many of its elements in their work. Folk art was appreciated for representing an ideal of purity; it was considered superior, but given that its superiority was seen to derive from its innocence and honesty, it took the form of a moral issue rather than a reference to mastery over the materials. Its forms were considered elemental but expressive of an enormous vitality. An international cult of primitivism has developed, which idealizes everything produced outside the so-called civilized world; similarly folk art, as we shall see, is often idealized at the national level. Part of this myth is the notion that folk art must have a utilitarian or functional character (beyond frivolous aesthetics) that is either immediate and practical or religious and ceremonial. Nonetheless, there are many examples of folk art that are fundamentally aesthetic, including the amates, the alebrijes, the ocumichos, ornamental ceramics, and many others. This of course calls into question the romantic-patriotic conception of all things folk.

The search for national identity has been, and continues to be, very important for Latin America, especially for Mexico. Central to that quest has been the attempt to slowly concoct what has been called a national culture, one of whose main ingredients has been folk art. That is, the characterization of popular culture in general, and of folk art in particular, has been intimately linked, in Mexico, to the issue of national culture and identity. If national culture is that great unifying myth conceived for the domination of people enclosed within political frontiers, then folk art is located within that culture as a fundamental element. In constructing a national culture, expressions of the Mexican pueblo are differentiated from those of other peoples or countries, and at the same time conceived in themselves as a unity. Folk art and handicrafts in general are held as the historical and cultural symbol of the pre-Hispanic roots of the modern Mexican nation. The great irony in this myth of nationality is that often those roots are not pre-Hispanic at all. In fact, a substantial part of those popular expressions have their origin in Spain: votive paintings, Judas figures, foot-driven textile looms, several kinds of pottery. The list could very well be endless.

National culture holds itself to be above social class and ethnicity (despite its appropriation of popular class and indigenous cultural production). By definition it represents all ethnic groups, making them automatically Mexican and national. In the same way, within national culture there are no genders; men and women cease to exist as differentiated subjects of history.

"Folk art" is one of the frequent responses given to the question about which is the *true* Mexican art. Within this myth, folk art is glorified as the authentic expression of our people, while elite and vanguardist art is rejected as a mere aping of the Western metropolis. For example, the vanguard attitude of Latin American artists is said to be a way of disguising their creative impotence, inertia, and laziness. This sort of nationalist purism reflects the colonizer's way of thinking, which has been internalized by the colonized. This becomes apparent when we consider that the attempt to explain cultural subalternity as a product of impotence or laziness is only one step removed from asserting the belief in the natural incapacity of certain peoples (usually dark) or social groups (often women).

Inasmuch as artistic creation is a product of social beings, and these beings have been subjected to conquests, reconquests, colonizations, and neocolonizations, and as development itself, in all aspects of life, has been determined or conditioned by the historical circumstances of colonization, what is *Mexican* in art can only be the result of this situation. If the search for *Mexicanness* or *Latin Americanness* in art is to be accorded such importance, it might be appropriate to begin by recognizing the reality of the colonized. Colonization implies imposition, violent and pacific, obvious and subtle, of the cultural patterns of the colonizer, which leads to a rapid or slow, greater or lesser, destruction of cultural and social forms in the subjugated societies. The result of the colonizing process is colonized culture. For that reason it seems to me foolish to look for the authentically Mexican in the Indian leftovers of the Conquest. To close one's eyes to reality and deny the "Westernness" of the Mexican is to negate a part of ourselves. From this point of view, kinetic art is as Mexican as Huichol art.

Still, we are told that there are two kinds of art in Mexico: high art and folk art. The former is said to be that produced by a minority for a minority, cast in the language of the elites and representing their interests. Characterizing folk art production and consumption, on the other hand, is not so simple. Some people think it is art produced by the majority for the majority. Yet it is obvious that folk artists constitute a minority within their own communities, and even where almost an entire community is devoted to an artistic activity, they are still a minority within the abstract majority of "the people." It may be argued that their creation ultimately expresses the desires, feelings, and tastes which make up the culture of the majority, but this results in a claim (much like that of elite populist art) whereby the creation of a few is supposed to represent the interests of the many. If we consider consumption, we find that while the poor cannot buy paintings or sculptures of the elite, they nevertheless consume them through printed reproductions or television. On the other hand, if we define consumption only as purchase, we increasingly find folk art being produced exclusively for consumption external to the community through the national and international markets, while the general tendency is for "the people" to consume it less and less. Thus, persons from all sectors of society consume folk art: some is now produced expressly for an elite, although most is consumed by a middle-class minority. Consumers outside the community may use it in diverse ways, but principally in aesthetic ways.

At the base of the merchandising process, both the state and private enterprise at times remove this artistic creation from its context, stripping it of its original meanings. "Authentic" pieces of folk art are converted into cheap merchandise and placed in stores, galleries, exhibition halls, and even museums; there they lose the meaning they had when and where, for what and for whom, they were produced.[9] This has been a common fate for many forms of Mexican folk art, resulting in much of it now being produced as merchandise. Thus, the meaning of a work, as derived from satisfying the needs of its original producers-consumers, is constantly modified by the demands of extracommunity consumption. The creators often find themselves needing to sell (and now having the demand and opportunity to do so) works whose original meaning may have been magic-religious, but whose new purpose is only to be sold. Such is the case of the Huichol votive boards (nearikas) made of colored string and wax, a good part of which, though not all, are produced to be sold, although their original purpose was (and to a limited extent continues to be) giving thanks to the gods. For a long time, capitalism has imposed its laws on the production of folk art: contents and forms are in constant transformation in response to an external market.

It could be said, then, that folk art manifests a curious irony: on one hand, it is undervalued and not considered true art, while, on the other hand, it is overvalued as the unique, authentic, and true artistic creation of the Mexican people—or, better still, of the Mexican nation. There have, of course, been moments in the history of Mexican art during which folk art has been considered the most authentic form of representation. One of the most significant periods was that of muralism, in the 1920s and 1930s. Diego Rivera, in particular, was one of the greatest defenders of folk art, although populism often lurked behind his stance. It is thus necessary to distinguish folk or popular art, in its conception as the artistic creation of the people, from what I would call "populist art." The latter is produced by elite artists who are conscious of social inequalities and wish to utilize artistic communication to denounce them, thus raising themselves to spokesmen of the pueblo. Based upon their supposed or actual ability to understand social reality and express it in art, they assume the privilege of speaking for others. These are artists who are not part of the pueblo, but who believe that they know what the people feel, want, and need.

Though "populist art" is directed toward the people, it is not evident that the majority receive it. At times the language used is not the artist's own but one which attempts to imitate that of the working class or the campesinos. While it gathers certain aspects of the pueblo's problems and expresses them in works, it also transmits the ideology of those in power, a criticism that could be made of a good part of Diego Rivera's work, as well as of that of other Mexican muralists. When a cultural elite believes itself to be knowledgeable about the problems, sensibilities, and interests of the people, and claims to be producing folk or popular art, another myth is created.

Are Alebrijes Primitive?

The alebrijes made by the Linares family of Mexico City are strange, fantastic animal-like creatures of cardboard and wire, painted in bright colors, and lacquered (fig. 4.2). They come in sizes from fifteen centimeters to a meter. Alebrijes are also made in Oaxaca, though these are simpler, made of wood, painted in colors less lively and varied, and not glossy (fig. 4.3). Don Pedro Linares claims to have invented both the concept and the figure of the alebrijes.[10] However, exceptionally monstrous zoomorphic figures have ex-

FIGURE 4.1. Anonymous, *Judas*. (Photo by John Mraz)

isted in very different cultures throughout history, essentially as representations of evil. The Minotaur of Greek mythology is an obvious example; Scylla
is another. The gargoyles found by the dozen on Gothic churches represent
many different kinds of monsters. The *dracs* of Catalonian folk festivals are
giant dragons of painted cardboard that look like huge alebrijes. The history
of monstrous figures in world art would be extensive.

The birth of the alebrijes was a humble one. They were born where many
Judas figures had been born before, from the hands of the Linareses. I imagine that the increasing prohibition of Judas burning, and the concomitant
decline in sales, led Pedro Linares to try something new. Giving free rein to
his imagination, he invented the alebrijes, which appear to be improvisa-
tions, created without previous sketches and perhaps without even a finished image in the artist's mind; as the hands work, the figures evolve.

Today these fantastic creatures are made almost always by men. In families of lesser resources, the labor is divided in such a way that women make

FIGURE 4.2. Alebrijes in papier mâché. The dragonlike figure below is in the style of the Linares family. (Photos by John Mraz)

FIGURE 4.3. Anonymous, alebrijes in wood. Oaxaca. (Photos by Marta López)

the small Judas figures while the men devote themselves to the big Judases and the alebrijes. They are apparently sexless monsters, though to me they are very masculine. I see them as macho monsters, perhaps because many of their elements belong to male animals or because of their aggressive poses, though it is possible that they have been created with no intention of having a gender.

The alebrijes are a form of folk art that has no immediate practical function. However magical they look—and there are those who ascribe to them a magical power—they are born to be purely and simply aesthetic objects, something they share with elite art. These multicolored monsters can be bought in Mexican handicraft stores as well as in some places outside the country. They are relatively expensive: the production is limited because they are labor-intensive and, as always, middlemen raise the price. The very large alebrijes are usually in museums and institutions, because their size makes it difficult to display them in private homes.

The alebrijes, like the ocumichos, are surreal and fantastic. While I might not describe the alebrijes as primitive, that would be the perfect word for the ocumichos.

Ocumichos: Indian Folk Art

The ocumichos are the most fantastic and surreal pieces of Mexican folk art. Their name derives from their provenance: they are made in Ocumicho, a Purépecha Indian town of some five hundred families, located 150 kilometers northwest of Morelia, the capital of Michoacán. There it is said that a Marcelino Vicente "invented" them, though a different story traces their creation to outside influences; some people state that the ideas for the erotic pieces are taken from foreign magazines. Saying that folk arts are influenced by more developed areas is a common practice; in this case, because it is an art made by women, it may seem important to certain individuals to cast doubt on the makers' imaginativeness.

Among the great variety of pieces made in Ocumicho are whistles, piggy banks, virgins, women in their traditional dress *(huares)*, scenes of daily life, carousels, suns, moons, animals, sirens, Last Suppers, births, and devils. The size of the pieces ranges from a few centimeters to half a meter. Often the themes overlap and intertwine. There are Last Suppers peopled by devils, and others where Jesus appears with twelve sirens. There are devils that are piggy banks and many others that are not. There are also clay masks representing typical Michoacán folk dance characters, such as devils, *negritos* (little black men) and *viejitos* (little old men).

In re-creating scenes of daily life—weddings, births, surgeries, peasants working in the field—the artists make pieces that may appear surrealist but are in fact quite realist; an expression, perchance, of the very surreality in their lives. For example, one piece depicts a peasant seated in a field with a dead burro whose belly has been opened up and the innards exposed, next to the disemboweled burro is a pumpkin with holes in it; both have enormous worms crawling out of them. Although it may seem difficult to believe, this piece is not an attempt to represent a dream or create a deliberately surrealist work.

For me, the most interesting of all the ocumichos are the devils. In their scenes from real, imaginary, and religious life, anything is possible: devils drive Coca-Cola trucks, ride buses, fly airplanes, and dash about on bicycles; they sing, dance, and play instruments; they eat and drink voluminously, devouring corn and fish beneath black suns. In imitation of what can only broadly be described as everyday life, they saddle burros, perform cesarean sections in operating rooms, and make love, but, most of all, they laugh—all

FIGURE 4.4. Anonymous, "Diablito riding a donkey" (photo by John Mraz), "Diablita with baby," and "Diablito in a helicopter" (photos by Marta López). Ocumicho, Michoacán. (*cont.*)

the time. It is fabulous. These devils who, dying of laughter, devote themselves to doing mischief all over the world are inspired by real dancers who disguise themselves as devils, hermits, and negritos during Christmas celebrations, and go out into the town's dusty streets to enjoy themselves, constantly laughing (fig. 4.4).

The devils incarnate and exude eros. Figures often have phallic elements in their mouths—eating bananas, corn on the cob, or fish, or playing flutes and trumpets, all the while grinning from ear to ear. They are frequently found in loving embraces or mounted on other figures, such as turtles, bulls, and sirens. A number of pieces are explicitly erotic: fantastic zoomorphic figures, roundish and multicolored, are covers that can be lifted to reveal couples, and often trios, of persons or devils making love in every position imaginable. These figures are generally pink-skinned white women and bearded men, though in some cases they are mestizo. Called *tapados* (covered) or *eróticos,* these pieces are usually made to order, often during the night, and hidden under the bed until collected by the buyer (fig. 4.5).

It seems incredible that this art which is so dynamic, so colorful, so entertaining, and so erotic is created by women in the moments they can spare from making tortillas, day and night, amid their numerous children. There

FIGURE 4.4.

is a clear division of labor in Ocumicho. The women are the artists and the males (children and mates) sometimes "help" when they are around. They bring the clay, which is found some kilometers from the town, paint the figures, and sell them. Nonetheless, there were and are male potters, beginning with the mythical Marcelino Vicente. In my opinion, the inordinate amount of recognition the male potters have received gives a distorted image of ocumicho-making. Though men are becoming involved in creating the pieces, they learn as adults, because boys are not apprenticed into the process as girls are.

Eduardo Galeano offers us truth and poetry when he writes:

Like the Chilean *arpilleras,* the little clay devils of the Mexican village of Ocumicho are the creations of women. These devils make love, in pairs or in groups, go to school, drive motorcycles or airplanes, sneak into Noah's Ark, hide among the rays of the moon-loving sun, and intrude into Christmas nativity scenes. They lie in waiting under the table at the Last Supper, while Jesus Christ, nailed to the cross, shares a meal of Patzcuaro lake fish with his Indian disciples. Eating, Christ laughs from ear to ear as if he had suddenly discovered that this world is more easily redeemed by pleasure than by pain. In dark windowless houses the Ocumicho potters model these luminous figures. Women tied to an endless chain of children, prisoners of drunken husbands

FIGURE 4.5. Anonymous, tapados, or erotic pieces. Ocumicho, Michoacán. (Photos by John Mraz)

who beat them, practice a new free-style art. Condemned to submission, destined for sadness, they create each day a new rebellion.[11]

The devils and the majority of the pieces are made by hand, although molds are used for the piggy banks and whistles. Formerly, pieces were made only with molds, but, according to one woman, "now we make them purely from sense." They are fired in the ovens that each woman has at home. At one time, there was a collective kiln, but no longer. The clay is fired at low temperatures, so the pieces are extremely fragile. Some figures are more skillfully made than others, since some artists are more capable and imaginative.

It is said in Ocumicho that there are individuals who do not work through the whole process: they buy pieces already made, paint them, and sell them; but this is not well thought of. After being fired in the ovens, they are taken out, painted, and varnished. In general, the women would rather not varnish the pieces, but buyers prefer them varnished, so the women often comply. The paints they use are anilines with lime, as well as vinyl and oil paints. They use pure, unmixed colors, as bright as the women's dresses.

Today some of the women sign their pieces. It is clear that they are conscious of the importance a signature has in the market; that is why they sign their names, and when they do so, it is with pride. However, they generally sign only if they are asked to, so the majority continue to leave their pieces unsigned. Although the potters' labor generally tends to be collective and anonymous, the Casa de las Artesanías of Morelia will sometimes place a tag with the author's name on unsigned pieces.

The ocumichos can be bought cheaply in the town itself or at the fairs of nearby towns. They are available at higher prices in handicraft stores in Morelia, Mexico City, and Monterrey. Often, the women grab their boxes full of devils and other figures; cram onto buses, sometimes with their children, sometimes without; and travel long distances in order to sell, cheaply, those pieces which arrive intact. They frequently make pieces to order. Someone sees the virgins, for example, and orders 150 units. Generally these persons are middlemen who resell to folk art stores.

One should not imagine that all is peace and harmony in this "simple" Indian town removed from capitalist ferocity. Competition, capitalist and otherwise, is in the very guts of the community. There are great rivalries among the potters, which can take many forms, including political disputes between members and nonmembers of the National Union of Campesino Artisans; ethical or aesthetic differences among those who carry out the entire process and those who do not; and envy of those who are famous, on the part of those who are not.

The Syncretism of High Art and Primitive Art in Ocumicho

In 1989 and 1992, Mercedes Iturbide, then director of the Casa de México in Paris, organized two exhibitions of Ocumicho pottery. She commissioned women artists to create representations of the French Revolution and the conquest of Mexico from models she provided. The first exhibit, in 1989, was to commemorate the bicentennial of the French Revolution, whose images served to inspire the women's pieces.

In 1992, Iturbide repeated the experiment for the five hundredth anniversary of Columbus's landing in America (although the theme she chose was the conquest of Mexico, an event that, in fact, occurred some thirty years later). The potters were shown reproductions of Mexican and European images: paintings and lithographs made in Europe during the sixteenth, seventeenth, and eighteenth centuries; reproductions from the Florentine, Yauhuitlan, and Durán codices; fragments of murals painted by José Clemente Orozco and Diego Rivera. They were commissioned to "copy" them, using them as inspiration in making their figures. In March 1993, the exhibit opened in Barcelona's Ethnographic Museum under the title "Rage of the Discovery" *(Arrebato del encuentro)*, a euphemistic way of referring to the Conquest and colonization.[12]

The author of each piece was clearly identified, which distinguished this exhibit from many folk art expositions in which the artists remain anonymous. These figures are a wonderful expression of cultural syncretism. Given "models," the Ocumicho artists translated this information into clay. It is a process similar to that followed in the reproduction of Frida Kahlo's paintings in clay by women in Ocotlán de Morelos, or in the use of famous paintings as the source of designs in the serapes of Teotitlán del Valle.

One of the curious aspects of *Arrebato del encuentro* is the women's interpretation of history. Despite the fact that they are Mexican, the Conquest must be as abstract an event to them as the French Revolution. In fact, their "copies" are the result of a *multiple* reinterpretation. The models they were given are graphic renderings of written interpretations of the Conquest, a historical event about which no direct visual evidence exists. Thus, it is important to take into account how removed the Ocumicho artists were from the history they pictured—theirs being only the latest in a succession of interpretations—as well as to see how they incorporated the conquest of Mexico into their own very particular style.

The representation of skin color offers a fascinating panorama. Artist María Luisa Basilio made a *Virgin of Guadalupe with Personifications of America and Europe,* copied from a Colonial oil painting (112–113). In Basilio's version, the Virgin's skin is white, although the Virgin of Guadalupe, Mexico's patroness, is as dark-skinned as most Mexicans. Perhaps Basilio felt that making the Virgin dark would be degrading or render her less sacred.

FIGURE 4.6. Carmela Martínez, *Virgen de Guadalupe*. Ocumicho, Michoacán. (Photo by Lourdes Grobet)

America, personified as an Indian, stands to one side of the Virgin; in the original painting, America is a light-skinned Indian, but Basilio's America has black skin. The Virgin of Guadalupe made by Carmela Martínez (fig. 4.6) is white and, moreover, the artist has added a Mexican flag that is not in the original painting (114–115). The combination of Guadalupism and nationalism is well represented in this work of folk fantasy. Magdalena Martínez's Virgin of Guadalupe is brown, but Juan Diego, the Indian boy to whom the Virgin first appeared, is depicted as very white (116–117). Indians with extremely white skin are also found in the works of Guadalupe Alvarez (92–93) and Bárbara Jiménez (100–101) (fig. 4.7). This may be due to the fact that some of the models they used show Indians who are blond and white-skinned, such as in the rendition by the painter Antonio Solís (84).

Some artists took great liberties in their interpretations. Virginia Pascual

FIGURE 4.7. Guadalupe Alvarez, *Slaughter of Indians at the Fiesta*. Ocumicho, Michoacán.
(Photo by Lourdes Grobet)

gave her Indians dark skins, but she also placed farm animals in the center
of her figure that were not in the model painting, *First Encounter of Cortés
with Moctezuma's Envoys* (84–85). Carmela Martínez reproduced the god
Huitzilopochtli with the head of a devil, though the original etching has a
human face (62–63). Although it might be an accurate representation of this
bloodthirsty Aztec god, I would nonetheless imagine that she has little idea
what Huitzilopochtli represented. An artist who signs herself "Sabina" copied a seventeenth-century statue of the Virgin of Guadalupe made of white
marble (118–119). However, she took the liberty not only of making the Virgin dark but also of turning an angel carrying the Virgin into an Indian.
Moreover, Sabina added lilies to the scene, a fad that has penetrated the most
diverse forms of Mexican folk art, and has arrived even in remote Ocumicho.

In a "baptism" made by Rutilia Martínez, the priest is represented as a
smiling devil (106–107). Four people appear in the detail of the model paint-

ing by Miguel González: the priest, a man, and two others whose gender is unclear. Rutilia converts them into three devils and a kneeling woman who is to be baptized. In another piece, she re-creates Cortés's ship, sporting what appears to be a Mexican flag (red, white, and green) rather than the Spanish flag, and depicts the Spaniards as dark, bearded, and wearing Mexican sombreros (76–77).

Paulina Nicolás copied a Florentine Codex page on which Moctezuma is bearded (74–75). She left the Spanish beardless. In the original image, La Malinche wears her hair in braids on top of her head, in such a way that they could be taken to be little horns. For the artists of Ocumicho, accustomed to making devils, it was no trouble to create a Malinche with devil horns. It is difficult to know if this artist conceives of La Malinche as a traitor, as most Mexicans do, but her representation provides another interesting facet.

Two artists based their imagery on a fragment of an Orozco mural in which Cortés and La Malinche have an Indian at their feet. In the piece by María de Jesús Basilio, the Indian is white, but he is very dark in the figure made by Antonia Martínez (cover and 66–67). The Indians look like Europeans and are as white as Cortés in a nineteenth-century Italian lithograph of the conqueror with Indians. Paulina Nicolás used this image as a model but made the Indians dark (78–79). Moreover, in the original a female nude appears with her back to us; Paulina, apparently deeming this improper, dressed her in underwear.

María Luisa Basilio reproduced a scene from the Florentine Codex in which Cortés receives presents in Tepozotlán, accompanied by a Spaniard in armor (80–81). Basilio made an absolutely otherworldly creature of the armored Spaniard, giving it the face of a fish, a green head, white scarf, and red blouse, accompanied by a small skirt and a "feather" that appears to grow out of its head. It is not clear whether it was the artist's intention to create such a personage or whether it was the result of an accident. I tend to think that it was intentional because the other figures, Cortés and some Indians, are realistic and perfectly identifiable.

It is particularly interesting to find in one piece the rape of a woman by a Spaniard, a scene that was not in the original but was created by the artist.[13] The woman is tied to a tree and gagged; she has long, black hair and her skin is white. The rapist has a beard and a large penis. On the other side, a white, half-naked Indian woman lies with a club in her hand. Representing rape in scenes of the Conquest is unusual, above all in such a crude manner. I suppose that this has to do with the women's sensitivity to sexual violence.

Although the Ocumicho artists were given visual information about the Conquest, the pieces are essentially variants of what they commonly create; moreover, they employ the same colors that they use in the rest of their work. The famous devils with their enormous smiles now sail in caravels, baptize Indians, fight against the Spanish, stick out their tongues, eat, play music, or simply observe the various scenes. Even historical figures are often given a devil's head. The syncretism of "high" art and folk art in these figures from Ocumicho amalgamates the themes of the models with the habitual forms of the women's pieces. In place of a sun with devils eating fish, they make a caravel with a bearded man, supposedly Cortés, and many devils eating bananas. The result is quite funny. Seeing these pieces, a smile is quick to appear on the face of the onlooker, like that of the devils from Ocumicho who run around the four corners of the world, spreading their good humor while their makers cannot leave their alebrije and ocumicho misery in the dust of their small Purépecha town.

The alebrijes and the ocumichos would probably be considered primitive, because they are folk art. However, while this concept may not be entirely applicable to the alebrijes, it is clear that the daily life of the Ocumicho artists is primitive, as is the town where they live, a forgotten corner of an underdeveloped country in the backyard of the most powerful nation on earth. The way in which they make their art is primitive, and the figures are clumsy, but the scenes they represent are often very sophisticated. This is another of the innumerable contradictions that permeate the universe of artistic creation, be it folk art or otherwise.

Notes

1. Marta Traba, "Relaciones actuales entre arte popular y arte culto," in *La dicotomía entre arte culto y arte popular: Coloquio Internacional de Zacatecas* (Mexico City: UNAM, 1979), 62.

2. Umberto Eco, *The Name of the Rose,* trans. William Weaver (New York: Warner Books, 1983), 424.

3. Ana Sojo, *Mujer y política* (San José, Costa Rica: Eduménico de Investigaciones, 1985), 21.

4. Juan Ramírez de Lucas, *Arte popular: El arte que hace el pueblo de todos los pueblos de la tierra* (Madrid: Más Actual, 1976), 152.

5. For example, the ornamental ceramics of Teodora Blanco and the Friditas of the Aguilar sisters are produced in Oaxaca and prized in many corners of the world.

6. See, for example, Montserrat Galí, "La historia del arte frente al arte popular," *La expresión artística popular* (Mexico City: Museo Nacional de Culturas Populares, 1982), 9–26.

7. For a discussion of the Friditas and the serapes of Teotitlán del Valle, see Eli Bartra, "Más allá de la tradición: Sincretismo, género y arte popular en México," in *Cultura Visual en América Latina: Estudios Interdisciplinarios de América Latina y el Caribe* 9, no. 1 (1998): 75–93.

8. Ernst Gombrich, *The Primitive and Its Value in Art* (London: BBC, 1979). Videocassette.

9. The poet Marge Piercy wrote:

The work of the world is common as mud.
Botched, it smears the hands, crumbles to dust.
But the thing worth doing well done
has a shape that satisfies, clean and evident.
Greek amphoras for wine or oil,
Hopi vases that held corn, are put in museums
but you know they were made to be used.
The pitcher cries for water to carry
and a person for work that is real.
—(*To Be of Use* (New York: Doubleday, 1969), 50)

10. See the videocassette by Judith Bronowski and Robert Grant, *Pedro Linares: Folk Artist* (Santa Monica, CA: Production Centre West, 1980/1989), which contains a long interview with him. See as well Susan Masuoka, *En Calavera: The Papier-Mâché Art of the Linares Family* (Los Angeles: UCLA Fowler Museum of Cultural History, 1994).

11. Eduardo Galeano, *Century of the Wind*, trans. Cedric Belfrage (New York: Pantheon Books, 1988), 227.

12. Some months later an exhibition bearing the same title, but featuring many more pieces, opened at the Museum of Modern Art in Mexico City. It was documented with the catalog *Ocumicho: Arrebato del encuentro* (Mexico City: Consejo Nacional para la Cultura y las Artes/Instituto Nacional de Bellas Artes, 1993). All subsequent references to this catalog are indicated by page numbers in parentheses.

13. This piece was in the Mexico City exhibit but did not appear in the catalog.

5

Primitive Borders

Cultural Identity and Ethnic Cleansing in the Dominican Republic

FERNANDO VALERIO-HOLGUÍN

TRANSLATED BY SCOTT COOPER

Haiti in the Dominican Primitivist Discourse

Dominican primitivist discourse with respect to Haiti is as old as the foundation of the Dominican nation itself. However, it was not until the 1930s that this discourse emerged with much greater force; by then it served as justification for one of the most abominable and incomprehensible acts in Dominican and Latin American history: the massacre of Haitian nationals in 1937. Over a period of several days, members of the Dominican army murdered and decapitated thousands of Haitians on the border between the two countries. Dictator Rafael Leonidas Trujillo's extreme nationalism found the perfect pretext for this slaughter in the alleged "primitivization" of the Dominican border region.

In her book *Gone Primitive*, Marianna Torgovnick defines primitivism as an ensemble of diverse and contradictory tropes that construct a grammar and a vocabulary with reference to the Other.[1] These tropes, which consist of recurrent images and ideas, were crucial in the formation of European cultural identity. Through the use of tropes, as Deborah Root points out, Europeans constructed a vision of the Other as a way of confronting cultural differences and, at the same time, as a justification for the colonization of Asia, Africa, and the Americas.[2]

Since the middle of the nineteenth century, many Dominicans have appropriated European primitivist discourse and reproduced it with respect to the Haitians in order to construct them as the Primitive-Other. This appropriation takes place in the context of a postcolonial imaginary and becomes a metaprimitivism correlating with what Torgovnick calls projection: "Primitives are our untamed selves, our id forces—libidinous, irrational, dangerous."³ Of the binary oppositions good/bad, rational/irrational, civilized/savage, cultural/natural, many Dominicans expel from themselves the second term and project it upon the Haitians as a defense mechanism. A great majority of Dominicans have based their cultural and national identities upon the negation of Haitian culture. In this manner they also construct themselves in the imaginary as that-which-they-are-not.⁴

For many Dominicans, Haitians not only constitute a Primitive-Other but also a Neighbor-Other and an Other-Within. The ensemble of tropes, images, and expressions concerning Haiti that appear in the popular, literary, and academic discourses have been feeding such a construct. My purpose in this essay is to discuss, on the one hand, the Dominican primitivist discourse with respect to the Haitians, a discourse that occupies a privileged place along the border and in the historical justification for the massacre of 1937. On the other hand, I will also address in this context some of the conflicts in Dominican cultural identity.

In his article "Tipología del tema haitiano en la literatura dominicana" (Typology of the Haitian Theme in Dominican Literature), Marcio Veloz Maggiolo studies images and expressions referring to the Haitians since the nineteenth century and makes the following classification: the flattered Haitian, the attacked Haitian, the adulterated Haitian, the pitied Haitian, and the integrated Haitian.⁵ What Veloz Maggiolo calls "typology" is nothing other than the different forms that the tropes of primitivist discourse adopt and that construct the Haitians in a *diversa y contradictoria* (diverse and contradictory) way, as also expressed by Torgovnick and Root. These contradictions are due to the fact that one of the peculiarities of tropes is their ambivalence, which allows them to have different meanings in different contexts.⁶

The diverse forms which primitivist tropes adopt with respect to the Haitians are that Haitians are animals, Haitians are cannibals, Haitians are savages, Haitians are violent, Haitians are thieves, Haitians are close to nature, and Haitians are promiscuous and prolific. All these images and ideas are the same as those employed by Europeans to refer not only to Africans and Asians but also to Latin Americans in general and Caribbeans in particular. I would not want to pass up the opportunity to observe the manner in which Dominican primitivist discourse inserts itself into the discourse of the border, so as to produce an imaginary space that I call "the borders of the primitive." Thus, before my central discussion in this essay, I would like to note some issues concerning the Dominican-Haitian border as a crucial framework for understanding the cultural phenomena to be discussed later.⁷

Floating Borders

The border, as a liminal space of articulation (union/separation) between two nations, gives rise to a privileged discourse in which cultural identity is constructed.[8] If the border demarcates the imaginary nation, it also sets itself forth as the limit that must be transgressed. What I call "floating borders"—the absence of precise limits during several centuries, first between two neighboring colonies and afterward between the independent countries of Haiti and the Dominican Republic—constituted a grave problem, since according to various politicians, the Dominican Republic found itself thereby prevented from laying the foundation of its territorial unity as a nation-state. From this standpoint, for some Dominican intellectuals the genocide of 1937 had a positive outcome because it finally fixed the Dominican-Haitian border.[9]

Furthermore, as Norma Iglesias explains, along floating borders there are no fixed categories from a racial, linguistic, or cultural point of view.[10] Border culture is liminal, unstable, and subject to constant changes. Because of this, García Canclini states, "The uncertainty generated by bilingual, bicultural, and binational oscillations finds an equivalent in its relations with history itself."[11] The absence of fixed categories along the border produces an anxiety bound to the uncertainty of cultural identity, since identity prefers stability and the fixity of "essences."

Floating borders are the social space of cultural hybridization. They represent, according to Fernández L'Hoeste, the space in which "identity wildly shifts according to the viewpoint of the beholder."[12] During almost two centuries, the Haitians and the Dominicans of the border regions intermingled and produced a hybrid, floating culture that, paraphrasing Homi Bhabha, is neither Haitian nor Dominican, but Haitian and Dominican at the same time.[13] On both sides of the border occurred what García Canclini calls a "de-territorialization"—a second process of hybridization—defined as "the loss of the 'natural' relationship of culture to geographic and social territories, and, at the same time, certain relative, partial relocalizations of old and new symbolic productions."[14] Those "de-territorializations" and "relocalizations" produced a hybrid (rayana) border culture.[15] The formation process of this (liniera) border culture manifests itself not only in language (patoiñol or espatois, which served as a shibboleth during the massacre) but also in food, religion, and customs.[16] For the Dominican elite, the "new symbolic productions" and the ambivalence of floating borders proved to be intolerable, and as such contributed to the construction of a series of primitivist tropes. The Dominican-Haitian border then became the limit at which "civilization" ends and "primitiveness" begins.

Dominican Cultural Identity and the Borders of the Primitive

The notion of borders I would like to address now does not refer to historical borders or floating borders but to those Guillermo Gómez-Peña alludes to in a recent book and which I call "primitive borders," or the borders internalized by the majority of Dominicans as a way of combating the anxiety caused by certain conflicts of cultural identity. These "primitive borders" that divide the Dominicans from the Haitians are specifically racial and cultural. What Gómez-Peña writes of the Mexican-American relationship could be applied to Haitian-Dominican attitudes: "They are scared of us, the Other, taking over their country, jobs, their neighborhoods."[17] Following Gómez-Peña, one could argue that instead of perceiving the border as what "we share," the majority of Dominicans have internalized it as "that which separates us" from the Haitians. The borders of the primitive then become not the space of cultural negotiation but the limits of the threatening "Africanization" and "corruption of the good customs inherited from Spain." The "primitiveness" of the Haitian people is constructed as an opposition to the heritage received by the Dominicans from Spanish "civilization."

Manuel Arturo Peña Batlle, one of the principal ideologues of the Dominican primitivist discourse, referred extensively to the border in his famous speech at Villa Elías Piña in 1942. Peña Batlle would seem to abrogate his right to speak in the name of the Dominicans when he states that "For Dominicans, the border is an absolutely insurmountable social, ethnic, economic, and religious barrier."[18] Elsewhere in his speech Peña Batlle explains the necessity of this "barrier" of contention: "El Generalísimo Trujillo has known how to see the ancestral defects, the primitivism lacking any possible evolution, which maintains in a pristine, inalterable state the old and negative customs of a large part of our neighbors, precisely that sector which, because of its needs, most maintains itself in contact with the urban centers of our border region."[19] As can be seen from this quote, Peña Batlle considers Trujillo a visionary because he "has known how to see" what other Dominican leaders did not: the imminent threat of those "defective and primitive" beings. However, Peña Batlle is careful not to generalize; he attributes this primitivism not to all Haitians but to the "sector" of workers and peasants who, because of extreme poverty, find themselves obliged to emigrate, and therefore to cross the border. According to the author, the "defects" of these primitive beings are ancestral, derived from African origins, and constitutive of a conspiracy against the "Dominican destiny."[20]

Joaquín Balaguer, who was Chancellor of the Republic at the time of the massacre of 1937, is the author of one of the most racist and anti-Haitian books, *La isla al revés* (The Island Backward).[21] Like other Dominican intellectuals, Balaguer bases his anti-Haitian primitivism in the Dominican Republic's alleged Spanish cultural orientation. His Hispanophilia attains the absurdity of stating that "Santo Domingo . . . is the most Spanish settlement of America"[22] and presenting photographs of white peasant families as prototypes of what he calls the "Dominican race." Like other intellectuals, Balaguer considers that the Haitians constitute a threat of "primitivization" against the Dominican people. In this sense, he stated: "It was always thought that the development of the population of Haiti, which tends to increase rapidly due not only to the ease with which the African race reproduces, but also to the primitive conditions in which the life of the inferior classes unfolds in that neighboring people, constituted a danger for Santo Domingo since the necessity to seek expansion for this mass would force the leaders of that nation to invade Dominican territory, peacefully or violently."[23] Unlike Peña Batlle, Balaguer does not elevate Trujillo to the visionary who "knew how to see" the Haitian primitiveness. Balaguer's argument centers on the trope of proliferation of what he calls the "African race," which he uses as a synonym for the Haitian people. Balaguer does resemble Peña Batlle in that he excludes himself from the primitivist discourse, but only by using the impersonal "It was always thought." Balaguer, too, is careful not to generalize primitivism: what Peña Batlle calls "a great sector of our neighbors," Balaguer refers to as the "inferior classes."

Primitivist discourse with respect to the Haitians has shaped Dominican identity both racially and culturally. The Dominicans do not consider themselves to be black, but "Indians" or mestizos descended from Spaniards and Taino Indians. This myth has its basis in the Dominican Republic's high percentage of mulatto population, which reaches more than 80 percent, whereas Haiti's population is mainly of African descent. The myth of presumed Indian *mestizaje* gained further ground during the first American Occupation (1916–1924), since the Americans, faced with the variety of racial mixes, began to register Dominican citizens in official documents as being "Indian."[24] Moreover, if we remember that the essence of a nation, according to Renan, is found in, among other things, what is "forgotten" (quoted in Anderson, *Imagined Communities*, 6), one could argue that Dominicans have managed to forget that the Tainos were almost totally exterminated toward the beginning of the sixteenth century and that Dominican culture is predominantly neo-African.

Dominican cultural identity emerges as a negation of Haitian culture by means of the primitivization of the "natural" borders. Racial, linguistic, and cultural differences are then erected as "interior borders"—a way of combating the terror and anxiety caused by the instability of "floating borders." Haiti, as the Primitive-Other, the Neighbor-Other, the Other-Within, becomes the primitive unconscious that Dominicans wish to repress, and because of which they have constructed for themselves a racial and cultural imaginary that is quite distant from their social reality.

The conflict and the discourse of the border reached their most decisive point in the genocide of 1937. As Gómez-Peña states with respect to the Mexican-American border, one could say that the Dominican-Haitian border became the sempiternal hemorrhage of "a wound in the middle of a family."[25] During the 1937 massacre, entire families were separated; spouses, siblings, and children of Haitian, Dominican, and Dominican-Haitian origin were murdered. The border literally became a river of blood along the dividing Río Masacre (River Massacre), whose name alludes to a much older historical event, as though it had foreshadowed the slaughter ordered by Trujillo.

The Massacre of 1937: Bloody Festival and National Foundation

In 1927, ten years before the massacre, and three before dictator Rafael Leonidas Trujillo's rise to power, Balaguer spoke on the border issue in the following manner: "The work of greatest civic determination, after the creation of the Republic, is and will be the colonization of the *litoral fronterizo* [sic]. If it is for one single deed that Horacio Vásquez will pass into the book of history with the splendors of immortality, this will be for the colonization of the border regions. That is the work most called upon to give our nationality a life everlasting."[26] The importance of this quote lies in the emphasis that Balaguer places on the "border problem" before Trujillo's rise to power. As much for Peña Batlle as for Balaguer, the survival of the Dominican nation would depend on the solution of this "problem." The imminent solution would occur ten years later with the genocide of more than twenty thousand Haitian, Dominican, and Dominican-Haitian nationals.

Freddy Prestol Castillo, a judge sent to the border town of Montecristi soon after the slaughter, published in 1973 *El Masacre se pasa a pie* (River Massacre Is Crossed on Foot), the only testimonial novel dealing with the genocide of 1937.[27] Prestol Castillo explains in the "Prologue," a sort of metatestimonial text, that the account was written in situ after the slaughter. However, the differences of style and of diacritical marks in the different chapters suggest that the book was written in stages. In this book, Prestol Castillo relates in the first person a "significant experience" to which he was an eyewitness: "Here I am in these lands. I am a mute witness. An accomplice witness."[28] In *El Masacre se pasa a pie,* Prestol Castillo adds some fictitious details and changes some names to "protect" the identity of certain individuals.[29]

Throughout the chapters, the author laments his own cowardice, submission, and silence when faced with the events that had occurred along the border. Despite the mea culpa of the author-narrator, who seeks to create a social realism and win the readers' sympathy with his rhetoric of *humilitas,*[30] Prestol Castillo's own primitivist vision with respect to the Haitians differs little from those of Balaguer and Peña Batlle. Although constructed with more rhetorical elaboration and less scientific pretension than those of the other two authors, the primitivist tropes utilized by Prestol Castillo dehumanize the Haitians and assimilate them into nature, in opposition to Dominican "civilization": "The Haitian is the traveler of the night. And the best guide is the breeze. The Haitians' nostrils seem to squeeze the breeze so it will tell them where the corrals are, denounced by the smell of manure, in the night. The map of theft operates in the night while the breeze is an accomplice. An alphabet of smells, read by this primitive race."[31] That which Balaguer calls the "African race" is Prestol Castillo's "primitive race." The latter, however, generalizes this primitiveness to all Haitians by means of the nationality synecdoche "the Haitian." For all three authors there is no difference between Haitian, black, African, and primitive.

The genocide of 1937 was not the individual and sole decision of the fascist dictator Trujillo, as the author-narrator of *El Masacre se pasa a pie* suggests; it was also the result of the historical conflicts between the two nations, justified by the anti-Haitian primitivist discourse of the elite and of the majority of Dominicans. However, it must be recognized that, after all, Trujillo's extreme nationalism and personal agenda served as a catalyst for these events.[32] The massacre of 1937 constitutes the most important event in the formation of the foundational myth of the "Patria Nueva" (New Fatherland). Peña Batlle confirms its establishment when in a speech he states that "The New Fatherland is present more than anywhere else in the new borders."[33]

The foundation of the Dominican nation required, however, a human sacrifice in the form of a sacred feast. In *El Masacre se pasa a pie,* the slaughter is represented as the primitive myth of a bloody celebration. The massacre is referred to as a "murderous feast" or a "red harvest"[34]—"The patrol with 'orders,' drunk on rum and blood, is unforgiving."[35] During several days, soldiers and conscripts, drunk and armed with machetes, decapitated thousands of Haitians in one of the most execrable genocides in Latin America during the twentieth century.

The massacre, as a "tragic festival,"[36] refers back to the mythic celebration studied by Mircea Eliade in *The Sacred and the Profane.* Eliade, who has written on the religions and symbols of "primitive" cultures, refers to "celebration" as a sacred time: "A celebration always occurs in original Time. And it is precisely this reintegration of original and sacred Time which differentiates human behavior during the celebration from the behavior before or after. . . . In other terms, they 'exit' their historical time—that is, the time constituted by the sum of profane, personal and interpersonal events—and connect with primordial time, which is always the same, which belongs to Eternity."[37] One of the tropes of primitivism indicated by Deborah Root consists in the purported atemporality of events occurring in non-Western societies.[38] During the massacre the author-narrator says: "In the tavern, there is no time. There is no limit in this land for alcohol or for death."[39]

Like Peña Batlle, Prestol Castillo represents Trujillo as instilled with a messianism that places him in a sacred (ahistorical) time. The participants in the bloody celebration approach Trujillo as if he were a god: "The Captain drinks, as if toasting for the God of the Court, the idol of the slaughter," and "The reservists remained silent, amazed by this impetuous scene. It was like the apparition and disappearance of a deity."[40] The dictator's megalomania became so extreme that he identified himself with God under the motto *Dios y Trujillo* (God and Trujillo). With the restoration of this sacred time, Trujillo succeeds in returning to a primordial moment, that of the slaughter of Jaragua, at the beginning of the sixteenth century, during which the Spanish governor, Nicolás de Ovando, ordered the murder of thousands of Taino Indians. Ovando, who justified the genocide on the legal grounds of an alleged rebellion of that region's Indians, imposed himself definitively on the island of Hispaniola in order to found a historical time. In the same manner, Trujillo succeeded in founding his own historical time, the Era of Trujillo and the era of the "New Fatherland" for all Dominicans.[41]

Conclusion: Our Primitive Neighbors

The Dominican-Haitian border has constituted the social space par excellence of the Dominican primitivist discourse with respect to the Haitians. It is also the space of construction of Dominican cultural identity in opposition to the Haitian. The massacre of 1937 was the culmination of the anti-Haitian primitivist discourse, inscribed within the exacerbated nationalism of Trujillo and the anxiety over conflicts of cultural identity experienced by the majority of Dominicans. With this massacre, Trujillo succeeded in reestablishing the Dominican people's imaginary Hispanism and in "cleansing" the nation of such impure elements as the religion, language, and customs of our neighbors, the Primitives.[42]

By means of the bloody festival, Trujillo also denied his own Haitian—and by extension "black," African, and primitive—personal ancestry, in order to imagine himself as a Dominican; that is to say, as a descendant of Spaniards.[43] The discourse of anti-Haitian primitivism served as an intellectual justification for the dehumanization, enslavement, and genocide of the Haitian people, set forth as a historical necessity for the foundation of the "Patria Nueva" of which Trujillo was God and Father. Primitivist discourse with regard to Haiti and the ensemble of tropes that facilitate its articulation are still present in the Dominican social imaginary. Newspaper headlines and speeches by some politicians and high-ranking members of the armed forces during patriotic events evince not only its presence but also its vitality. During the 1996 elections, opposition parties mounted a racist campaign against José Francisco Peña-Gómez, the presidential candidate of the Dominican Revolutionary Party (PRD), in which emphasis was placed on his Haitian origins and on an alleged agreement that this candidate had reached with the United States for establishing Haitian refugee camps on Dominican soil if he were elected. He was also accused of wanting to reunite both sides of the island into a single state. The image of a Dominican-Haitian integration horrified many Dominicans, no doubt scared by the ghost of Haitian "primitiveness." We are about to reach a new millennium, yet Dominican cultural identity still depends on the rejection of its neighbors, the "primitives."[44]

Notes

1. Marianna Torgovnick, *Gone Primitive* (Chicago: University of Chicago Press, 1990), 8.

2. Deborah Root, *Cannibal Culture* (Boulder, CO: Westview Press, 1996), 34. Tropes are rhetorical figures that organize images, concepts, and symbols. Paraphrasing Root, the notions of savage, cannibal, dumb, animal, decadent, inferior, lustful, and violent are tropes of primitivism. Root also distinguishes between stereotypes and tropes. Unlike stereotypes, tropes can be ambivalent, contradictory and very difficult to deconstruct.

3. Torgovnick, *Gone Primitive*, 8.

4. According to Benedict Anderson, a nation is imagined "because the members of even the smallest nation will never know most of their fellow-members, meet them or even hear of them, yet in the minds of each lives the image of their communion." Benedict Anderson, *Imagined Communities* (London: Verso, 1996), 6.

5. Marcio Veloz Maggiolo, *Sobre cultura dominicana . . . y otras culturas* (Santo Domingo: Editora Alfa y Omega, 1977), 94.

6. Root, *Cannibal Culture*, 34.

7. The border conflict between Haiti and the Dominican Republic is a colonial legacy that has its origin in the Treaty of Ryswick of 1697, in which Spain ceded the western third of the island of Hispaniola to France. For the first time, the island was divided in two: Saint Domingue (in the west) and Santo Domingo (in the east). For over a century, the two colonies coexisted peacefully, providing for free trade. However, social and economic development was uneven. The French colony was characterized by the massive importation of slaves and intensive exploitation of the plantation economy by a white minority. The Spanish colony, although poorer than its neighbor, experienced a slow economic recovery based on cattle ranching, in which feudal and patriarchal relationships prevailed. The impact of some four thousand immigrants from the Canary Islands, the limited importation of African slaves, the coexistence of whites and blacks (both free and slaves) in the extended work of the ranches, and the absence of strict social regulations resulted in a greater mixing of the races. See Roberto Cassá, *Historia social y económica de la República Dominicana*, vol. 1 (Santo Domingo: Alfa y Omega, 1986), 113–117.

The Treaty of Aranjuez, signed by France and Spain in 1777, fixed the precise boundaries between the two colonies. They later became two independent countries on a single island—one of the few such cases in the world. Border disputes, however, lasted more than a century, during which time various treaties and accords were signed. The Treaty of 1936, signed by Haitian President Stenio Vincent and Dominican President Rafael Leonidas Trujillo, seemed to have put an end to the dispute. However, the traditional discrepancy regarding the border would not be resolved without bloodshed. From its independence in 1844, after twenty-two years of Haitian occupation, the Dominican Republic demanded that the boundaries established by the Treaty of Aranjuez be honored; Haiti laid claim to the lands occupied by its citizens after the various wars had ended. See María Elena Muñoz, *Las relaciones dominico-haitianas: Geopolítica y migración* (Santo Domingo: Alfa y Omega, 1995); Pedro L. San Miguel, *La isla imaginada: Historia, identidad y utopía en La Española* (Santo Domingo: Isla Negra/La Trinitaria, 1996); Bernardo Vega, *Trujillo y Haiti (1930–37)*, vol. 1 (Santo Domingo: Fundación Cultural Dominicana, 1988); Frank Moya Pons, *El pasado dominicano* (Santo Domingo: Editora Corripio, 1986); and Eric Paul Roorda, *The Dictator Next Door: The Good Neighbor Policy and the Trujillo Regime in the Dominican Republic, 1930–1945* (Durham, NC: Duke University Press, 1998). Among the novels that represent the conflict between the Dominican Republic and Haiti, see Ramón Marrero Aristy, *Over* (Ciudad Trujillo: La Opinión, 1939); Jacques Stephen Alexis, *Mi compadre el General Sol* (Santo Domingo: Taller, 1987); and Anthony Lespes, *Las semillas de la ira* (Santo Domingo: Fundación Cultural Dominicana, 1990).

8. Madan Sarup, *Identity, Culture and the Postmodern World* (Athens: University of Georgia Press, 1996), 7.

9. Some intellectuals and politicians, such as Joaquín Balaguer, Julio Ortega Frier, Arturo Logroño, Vicente Tolentino Rojas, Jacinto Peynado, Rafael Estrella Ureña, Manuel A. Peña Batlle, and Max Henríquez Ureña, maintained a racist discourse that justified, in certain ways and at different levels, the 1937 massacre. Obviously, not all of them were equally involved nor had the same position with regard to anti-Haitian discourse. For instance, the case of Max Henríquez Ureña is paradoxical, given that he was the brother of Pedro Henríquez Ureña (see note 29), a silent opponent of Trujillo's dictatorship. See Franklin Franco Pichardo, *Historia del pueblo dominicano*, vol. 2 (Santo Domingo: Ediciones del Instituto del Libro, 1992), 524. Balaguer and Peña Batlle, discussed later, were two of the most bitterly anti-Haitian intellectuals.

10. Norma Iglesias, "The Maquiladora Industry in the US/Mexican Border," presented at the Latino Heritage Month Conference, Allegheny College, October 13, 1997.

11. Néstor García Canclini, *Culturas híbridas: Estrategias para entrar y salir de la modernidad* (Mexico City: Grijalbo, 1989), 299.

12. H. D. Fernández L'Hoeste, "On Cinematographic Narratives of the Mexican-American Border: Cultural Resistance in Robert Rodríguez's Early Production," unpublished paper, 8.

13. Homi Bhabha, "The Commitment to Theory," *New Formations* 4 (1988): 10.

14. García Canclini, *Culturas híbridas*, 288.

15. *Rayano* (from *raya*, "line") is a term applied to children who have one Dominican and one Haitian parent. Accordingly, this term is used in the sense of hybrid culture.

16. The word *liniero* (from *línea*, "line") is used to refer to all the people from northwestern towns of the Dominican Republic and to the products from that region as well. When the Haitians or Dominican-Haitians were stopped by the police, they were asked to pronounce the word *perejil* (parsley). If they said *pelejil*, failing the Spanish pronunciation, they were immediately killed. Also, in the nineteenth century there arose the popular saying *El que sea prieto que hable claro* (Those who are dark-skinned better speak clearly). Thus, certain linguistic features came to determine citizenship.

17. Guillermo Gómez-Peña, *Warrior for Gringostroika* (St. Paul, MN: Graywolf Press, 1993), 47.

18. Manuel A. Peña Batlle, *Política de Trujillo* (Ciudad Trujillo: Impresora Dominicana, 1954), 63. In 1929, Peña Batlle was a judicial adviser to the Dominican committee that signed the new agreement to solve the border conflicts.

19. Ibid., 65.

20. Ibid., 63.

21. Joaquín Balaguer, *La isla al revés: Haití y el destino dominicano* (Santo Domingo: Editora Corripio, 1995). Balaguer, one of the most important Dominican intellectuals, participated in politics for nearly seventy years. In 1927, the twenty-one-year-old Balaguer supported the project of "Dominicanization" of the borders implemented by President Horacio Vásquez (1924–1930). In 1930, he was a member of a group that supported Rafael Estrella Ureña for the presidency. Under Trujillo's regime (1930–1961), Balaguer held various government positions, such as Secretary of Education and Chancellor. From 1957 to 1960, he was the "elected" Vice President of the Dominican Republic. When President Héctor B. Trujillo (the dictator's brother) resigned in 1960, Balaguer became President. After Rafael Trujillo was murdered on May 30, 1961, Balaguer continued in the presidency until he was forced to resign due to popular protests. Balaguer went into exile in 1962. After returning in 1966, he ruled the country like a dictator for three consecutive terms (1966–1978), and later returned for two more (1986–1994). Fraud in the 1994 elections was so evident that Balaguer was again forced to resign the presidency in 1996, allowing for new elections.

22. Ibid., 63.

23. Ibid., 129.

24. Robin Derby, "Teaching Democracy: Citizenship and Civic Education During U.S. Military Occupation of the Dominican Republic, 1916–1924," presented at conference at the American Historical Association Meeting, University of Chicago, December 1994, 4. Pedro de San Miguel explains that the use of the term *indio* (Indian), referring to the mulatto population, had already appeared in Antonio Sánchez Valverde's *Idea del valor de la isla española* (1785). See also Doris Sommer, *One Master for Another: Populism as Patriarchal Rhetoric in Dominican Novels* (Lanham, MD:

University Press of America, 1983). According to Sommer, the word "Indian" is linked to Manuel de Jesús Galván's foundational novel *Enriquillo* (1882), in which blacks are erased to allow for the harmonious mingling of Indians and whites.

25. Gómez-Peña, *Warrior for Gringostroika*, 47.

26. Quoted in Vega, *Trujillo y Haití*, vol. 1, 18.

27. Freddy Prestol Castillo, *El Masacre se pasa a pie* (Santo Domingo: Taller, 1973). In 1937, right before the massacre, Prestol Castillo published an article in the newspaper *Listín Diario* titled "El jefe en Navarrete" (The Chief in Navarrete), in which he praised Trujillo. See Vega, *Trujillo y Haití*, 277.

28. Prestol Castillo, *El Masacre*, 131.

29. Pedro Henríquez Ureña, for example, appears under the pseudonym of Doctor Fradíquez: "A native of this country, but having lived many years abroad, Doctor Fradíquez, wise humanist who featured among the most qualified professors in the United States, Chile and Buenos Aires ..." (143). Prestol Castillo uses Pedro Henríquez Ureña's name as a symbol of dignity and resistance to Trujillo's dictatorship. In Contrast to his brother Max, Don Pedro never supported the dictatorship and lived in exile most of his life. From 1931 to 1933, he accepted the position of General Superintendent of Education in the Dominican Republic, perhaps to avoid reprisals against his family. As a Dominican intellectual, Pedro Henríquez Ureña never employed the anti-Haitian primitivist discourse.

30. H. Lausberg, *Elementos de retórica literaria* (Madrid: Gredos, 1983), 32.

31. Prestol Castillo, *El Masacre*, 75.

32. It is said that Trujillo ordered the massacre while drunk, during a party at the house of Isabel Mayer, procuress and close friend. It is not a coincidence that Isabel Mayer was a well-known landowner from the Dominican-Haitian borderlands. See Joaquín Balaguer, *Memorias de un cortesano de la "Era de Trujillo"* (Santo Domingo: Editora Corripio, 1988), 71–73.

33. Peña Batlle, *Política de Trujillo*, 103. For Peña Batlle, the "new borders" referred to the elimination and/or deportation of Haitians.

34. Prestol Castillo, *El Masacre*, 26–27.

35. Ibid., 34.

36. Ibid., 55.

37. Mircea Eliade, *Lo sagrado y lo profano* (Barcelona: Editorial Labor, 1987), 76–79.

38. Root, *Cannibal Culture*, 37.

39. Prestol Castillo, *El Masacre*, 87.

40. Ibid., 87 and 120. The massacre was also known as the *corte* (cut), since machetes were used to try to cover up the army's participation.

41. The name of the River Massacre, formerly called the Gutopana, was changed following the murder of thirty buccaneers by the Spaniards in 1728 (see Vega, *Trujillo*

y Haití, 364). I think, however, that the 1937 massacre is linked to the Jaragua massacre both because of its dimensions and because the Spaniards too definitively dominated the island after this event. See Cassá, *Historia,* 43.

42. Both Balaguer and Prestol Castillo refer to "ethnic cleansing" in their works. Balaguer says: "There is less merit in building a fatherland than in making of it a clean nation" (*La isla al revés,* 99). In his novel, Prestol Castillo alludes to the massacre as follows: "These were the tricks of the 'historical hygiene' that cleansed the Dominican soil of a parvenu bug" (*El Masacre,* 81).

43. As I said before, some of Trujillo's ancestors were Haitian. His maternal grandmother was Luisa Ercina Chevalier, the daughter of an officer who lived in the Dominican Republic during the Haitian Occupation (1822–1844).

44. The following are examples of recent headlines in Dominican newspapers: "Worrisome Presence of Illegal Haitians," *Hoy,* October 15, 1996, 1; "4 Haitians Rape Woman," *Ultima Hora,* April 30, 1997, 1. On the front page of *El Nacional,* November 3, 1996, there is a picture of a Haitian man kissing a human skull. The caption reads: "Voodoo ritual: A Haitian possessed by a spirit kisses a human skull yesterday in downtown Port-au-Prince, Haiti, during the celebration of All Saints Day." To the left of this picture, there is a smaller one of José Francisco Peña Gómez with the headline: "GOES TO ROMANA. Peña arrives in a private flight." The metonymic association with the "primitive" Haitian "possessed by a spirit" seems designed to discredit the politician. Moreover, the headline "arrives in a private flight" suggests that he is arriving from Haiti instead of from La Romana, a Dominican city. In the online edition of *El Listín Diario* one can read the following headlines: "Inmigration and Repatriation of Haitians Along the Border Turns Explosive" (108, no. 28570, www.listin.com/do); and "The Fatherland Begins at the Border" (n.s. 1, no. 90). The latter report, from 1996, is worth quoting. "With the slogan 'the fatherland begins at the border,' the National Army launched a cultural program last week, in Dajabón, Montecristi, Loma de Cabrera, and Restauración. After February was declared by presidential decree 'Month of the Fatherland,' this military institution started to develop a series of patriotic activities, where . . . the National Anthem was sung with pride [*a viva voz*]. . . . the Civil Governor, Santiago Morel . . . praised this cultural project whose purpose, according to an official press release, is to rescue the purest essence of Dominicanhood." The slogan "the fatherland begins at the border" reminds us of Peña Batlle's words almost fifty years earlier. The singing of the anthem *a viva voz* and the rescuing of the "purest essence of Dominicanhood" in these frontier towns constitute a metonymic allusion to the cultural threat posed by the Haitian neighbors, to which is added the presence of the Army and the reference to Peña Batlle, historically one of our most fervently anti-Haitian intellectuals.

6

Dialectics of Archaism and Modernity

Technique and Primitivism in Angel Rama's
Transculturación narrativa en América Latina.

JOSÉ EDUARDO GONZÁLEZ

Primitivism in Angel Rama's critical writings must be seen, above all, as related to the notion of the *archaic*.[1] For Rama, at least during the late 1960s and early 1970s, when he was just beginning to develop his view of Spanish American *modernismo* as resulting from particular socioeconomic circumstances, the archaic represents anything that is not modern. Primitive elements are part of the archaic in a very general sense, insofar as they represent a premodern period. When he published *Rubén Darío y el modernismo* in 1970 (the culmination of his research since the mid-1960s), the term "archaism" had only negative connotations in his texts, and "modern" (as in "modern technology" and "modern literary techniques") became the positive term in this opposition. Thus, what I intend to do in the first pages of this essay is, on the one hand, to reconstruct Rama's transition from a negative view of nonmodern elements in literature and society[2] to a positive one and, on the other hand, attempt to understand how originally opposite poles were later found compatible: the archaic, primitive, or premodern became part of the modern and even made possible the advent of modernization. In later analyzing Rama's theory of transculturation, we will see that he presents a solution for Latin America's modernization not by eliminating archaic elements nor merely incorporating them into modernity, but by using them to achieve modernization. Yet, in trying to incorporate the primitive or archaic, to find a place and function for it in the structure of his thought, Rama unfortunately adopts the prejudices and misconceptions propagated by Western primitivist discourse. The importance of denouncing such a discourse as the basis of Rama's transculturation cannot be overstated, given the enormous prestige and influence that his theory has gained since the 1980s.

In Rama's book on Darío, however, there is still a consistent rejection of anything premodern. After commenting on the specialization of labor as one of the principal effects of modernization and explaining that during Darío's time the Latin American writer was confined to his literary field, Rama points out that the *modernistas* realized that in order to compete in the literary market, they had to create "products as complex and elaborated as the industrial artifacts that [were] beginning to arrive from Europe [in the late nineteenth and early twentieth centuries]."[3] This modernization or "technification" of literature, as Rama calls it, apparently had to exclude the archaic. Thus, for example, Darío's central problem in *Azul*, Rama argues, is that while his prose already shows a new, modern style, his poetry is still following outdated models, lacking any of the daring innovations present in his short stories. Rama saw in Darío's use of elements from old Spanish literature the presence of "archaisms [that] explain the slow change of his poetic production."[4] The Nicaraguan poet was able to achieve artistic success only when he decided to apply in his poetry the modern writing techniques with which he was experimenting in his narrative texts.

Rama later modified his position, and in subsequent studies he talked about the "positive" contributions that premodern elements bring to literary modernization. As for his interpretation of the evolution of Darío's poetry, in an article published years later, "El poeta frente a la modernidad," Rama finally recognized the importance of "archaisms" for the emergence of modernista poetry. Darío's great achievement, he conceded, "was not only the difficult incorporation of foreign rhythms, poetic patterns, topics, new systems of metaphors and adjectives, and grammatical structures," which form the core of the modernization of writing introduced in this period, "but [also] rescuing a tradition of poetry in Spanish to which writers had been contributing for over a millennium, but that being generally unknown in the twentieth century, had become almost as foreign [to Latin Americans] as French poetry was."[5]

The change in Rama's critical thinking between the mid-1960s and early 1970s, which allowed him to accept the premodern and not see it as a threat to his dream of a modern Latin America, represents an important moment in the evolution of his theories. Ultimately, this transformation is inextricably related to the development of his theory of literary transculturation, insofar as this concept entails a combination of modern and premodern

elements. In the case of narrative transculturation, the premodern manifests itself through elements that are even more "archaic" than those Rama
identified in Darío's work: artistic components that he could only describe
as primitive.

Is it possible to determine when this change in Rama's discourse began,
the moment when he found a place and a function for the premodern within
his view of literary modernity? Perhaps it is possible to point to 1971 as the
most important year with respect to this transformation; and specifically to
his essay "Dialectics of Modernity in José Martí," in which the Cuban writer—
whose work Rama initially saw as belonging to the prehistory of modernismo
and whose poetry, he thought, was a reflection of the premodern colonial
world, the "anachronistic Spanish Empire"[6]—is analyzed as the first Latin
American modern writer. This change of interpretation forced Rama to justify the presence of premodern elements in Martí (such as his Romantic
conception of history,[7] or the recourse to traditional topics and other strategies employed by Martí to resist the incorporation of Latin American literature into the world market).[8] This essay defends the position that if Martí's
work registers those archaisms, it is because this is a necessary strategy employed by the Cuban poet to establish a communication with other subjects
in the Latin American region where he was born, and who were still in a
premodern stage of development. Martí's situation was that of a "man standing in between two different epochs" (31). The fact that Martí resorted to
"archaic elements" is seen as a temporary solution that eventually allowed
him to achieve an understanding of modernity as a combination of both
regional and universal elements in his writings (167). However, the final objective of Latin American artistic works, it must be clear, is to achieve a complete modernization, "because this is the appropriate solution to the problem of survival" (163). "Martí does not defend folklore nor the presence of
archaic and unproductive Spanish traditions," explains Rama, "everything
must perish so that a new art can be born" (163).

For the first time, Rama leaves open in his discourse the possibility of
accepting premodern elements as part of modernity, with the hope that they
will be eradicated in the future (both in society and in literature). Yet, a few
months after having read his essay on Martí in Puerto Rico, another of his
articles sparked a controversy with Mario Vargas Llosa. Using the Uruguayan
magazine *Marcha* as the stage for the debate, Rama attacked the "archaic"
critical apparatus employed by the Peruvian writer in his then recent book
on García Márquez, *Historia de un deicidio.* This was of course a new ver-

sion—now within the realm of literary criticism—of the conflict between the modern (or the application of instrumental reason to the field of intellectual production) and the premodern. In this series of articles, Rama reiterated the importance of modern literary techniques in order to refute the commonplace notion that the origin of the work of art is "inspiration" and not hard work. Accordingly, it is not inspiration (or the idea of writing to "exorcise one's own demons" that Vargas Llosa was trying to defend), but rather the use of the most advanced techniques available to a writer in a particular historical situation (in other words, the modernization or "technification" of writing), that will allow a Latin American author to create a literary product useful to his or her society. Rama argued that Vargas Llosa's notion of literary production belonged to the nineteenth century and was no longer adequate to satisfy the demands of the urban middle class and some proletarian sectors in Latin America that were calling for important social changes. Those changes, Rama claimed, found their intellectual counterpart "in a writer whose capacity for rationalization is greater than that of writers from previous literary epochs."[9] This suggests that political and artistic progress go hand in hand, and that a writer who employs archaic techniques will not be able to respond adequately to the social transformations taking place in Latin America.

Rama's theoretical model in this exchange with Vargas Llosa was Walter Benjamin's writings about the modernization of artistic techniques, especially his essay "The Author as Producer." The central topic of this essay was the well-known debate about whether the main function of a literary text is to present a progressive political position or, on the contrary, that the most important standard of value should be its artistic quality. Benjamin proposed a "technical" solution to this old question: it is the literary technique that determines the value of a work. The fact that a writer uses the most advanced techniques guarantees that both the aesthetic quality of the text and its political relevance are of the same high level: "technical progress is for the author as producer the foundation of his political progress."[10] Since literature is an art that has not been affected by external technological changes to the extent that, for example, cinema[11] has (perhaps the only external change of consequence for literature was the invention of the printing press), it is literary technique which determines "the function the work has within the literary relations of production of its time."[12] Benjamin equated the most advanced techniques with the most revolutionary ones; that is, techniques which awaken a critical attitude in the public. This does not mean that the political function of art is subordinated to technique, but that technical progress becomes a way of producing socially and politically relevant works. The use of revolutionary writing techniques guarantees both the aesthetic and the political value of a text. Adopting a critical position similar to Benjamin's, Rama's discourse during the early 1970s privileged rationalization of the literary text, modernization of writing techniques, over any other aspect of artistic creation, including the author's ideology, which is assigned a secondary place. Thus, in Vargas Llosa's case, despite his "nineteenth-century" ideas as a critic, his literary output (like that of Darío) acquired political relevance as a result of the advanced writing techniques he employed as a novelist.

A truly positive view of premodern cultural elements on Rama's part finally took shape with his theory of narrative transculturation, in which modern artistic characteristics are intertwined with the Latin American primitive. For Rama, narrative transculturation constitutes a bringing up to date of the cultural heritage bequeathed to Latin America by Indian and African groups, or of any other cultural element that could be identified as belonging to Latin American traditional cultures.[13] In other words, it is a modernization of the characteristics that are usually associated with Latin America's cultural difference. But in order to revitalize these regional cultures, it is necessary for the author to go back to "original sources." Out of this process, explained Rama, "may result an intensification of some components of the traditional cultural structure that seems to emerge from levels even more primitive than the ones commonly recognized" (31). Rama's theory—his application of Cuban anthropologist Fernando Ortiz's concept of "transculturation" to the specific field of Latin American narrative—has been widely analyzed and studied. What I want to suggest here is that the inner structure of this theory, its origin and function within Rama's discourse, can be appropriately understood only in relation to primitivism.

Two components of Rama's discourse should be emphasized insofar as they affect the formulation of his theory: first, his view of Anglo-American modernism or the Avant-garde (he did not make any distinction between them) as the representation of the irrational in the arts; second, the essentially "technical" character of his theory of narrative transculturation. For Rama, modernism and the Avant-garde were part of a general "irrationalist European movement" (49) that supposedly influenced all fields of intellectual activity, including philosophy and politics. Thus understood, Expressionism, Surrealism, and even Futurism belong to the artistic "movement" whose main characteristic was the rejection of rational thought.[14] This explains why for Rama the "highest point" of this artistic movement was Dadaism. It is interesting that in his interpretation of modernism, Rama does not accord a privileged place to artistic primitivism (and the well-known interest that many Avant-garde artists showed in primitive cultures), as one would expect, given the many points of contact that it has with his transculturation project. The primitivism practiced by many modernist and Avant-garde artists is seemingly, for Rama, only another manifestation of the irrationalist tendency in Anglo-European thought of the late nineteenth and early twentieth centuries.

To this irrationalist tendency Rama links the interest expressed by the anthropologist for the primitive mind. He is careful to point out that the thinking process of the primitive mind should not be equated with myth. The use of mythology by Latin American writers to represent the Latin American primitive is criticized by Rama because through myth they merely return to Reason: "When Enlightenment turns into myth, as a result of the predominance of irrationalism in the twentieth century, the original transformation of myth into Enlightenment is recovered" (52). The reference here is of course to Theodor Adorno and Max Horkheimer's *Dialectic of Enlightenment,* in which myth is seen as the origin of a process of rationalization that later produced a reification of society and the emergence of fascism. In Rama's judgment, contemporary writers' recourse to myth as a device that allows them to understand reality and to structure their texts is still part of "bourgeois" realism and, like the latter, shows a blind belief in rational discourse. Rama's association of mythology with the "rational" allows him to exclude from his theory of narrative transculturation authors such as Carpentier and Asturias, who were very interested in the representation of the Latin American primitive, simply because they employ mythology to give form to their writings. He even goes so far as to associate Carpentier's and Asturias's aesthetics with that of Borges, whose work for Rama seems to be the best example of the use of myth with rational purposes.

Hence, Rama emphatically rejects critical interpretations of Juan Rulfo's *Pedro Páramo* that focus on the Mexican writer's alleged use of Greek mythology. Rama explains that without doubt Greek myths are "alluded to—or, even better, distorted—in Rulfo's fictions, but the meaning of Rulfo's texts does not come from them . . . it emerges from an unknown cultural background in which modes of knowledge are clumsily used" (54). The reference to the "clumsiness" of cognitive abilities found in Rulfo's characters and narrators reveals the type of primitivism that Rama endorses as an example of transculturation. He is not interested in the depiction of the primitive exterior of societies or characters, nor even in the use of cultural aspects associated with a primitive world (myth, for example), but in the representation of "primitive thought," that is, the prerational or counter-rational process that precedes the creation of a (rational) mythology. Rama's well-known argument is that it was the direct influence of Anglo-European Avant-garde movements (and their interest in the irrational) that originally led the *transculturadores* to explore prerational cognitive processes: "As rational or logical discourse is challenged, there is a return [among Latin American writers] to their regionalist roots, and this leads to an examination of the cultural forms employed by traditional subjects" (52).

Curiously, the attack on modern logic that one can perceive in Avant-garde works, and that Latin American transculturadores employ as a point of departure for their own cultural projects, constitutes at the same time the "most advanced" stage of development of literature at that time; that is, its modernity. In other words, the modern or Avant-garde formal experiments (that so greatly resemble primitive mental processes) are possible because of the artists' awareness of having several artistic techniques available and being able to create new ones. This, in turn, is the result of a high degree of rationalization applied to the literary text, a consequence of the modernization of writing.[15] The ideological contradictions of this combination of premodern elements with advanced techniques of writing can be understood when one takes a closer look at Rama's notion of "primitive mind" and sees that it harbors many of the same prejudices commonly associated with Western primitivist discourse.

Since its very beginning, the discourse of primitivism has been composed of two different and contrasting views. Depending on the ideology of the subject employing the discourse, primitive cultures can be either degraded or exalted, represented as an inferior or a superior cultural stage. The first of these versions sees primitive societies as an archaic stage, already overcome by Western civilization, where one can still find all the unharnessed barbaric forces—sexual, political, or cultural—that must be controlled in order to form a civilized society. But, above all, this kind of primitivism is understood as the result of Westerners' desire to have a negative pole against which their own identity can be defined. On the other hand, "positive" primitivism—which in the end is equally negative in its perception and appropriation of its object of study—refers to the version of this discourse that seeks in the primitive that which the West has lost: "innocence, authenticity, natural rhythms, ties to the earth, a religious sensibility, and the stability of collective traditions in the face of, and as an alternative to, chaotic, sterile modernity."[16] This "positive" view of primitivism is the one that in the twentieth century has often been appropriated by the very cultures which were originally its object of study. The main purpose of this appropriation was to create an identity different from the one being imposed by the West.[17]

This version of primitivism is dangerous not only because it is a Western fantasy of a society without any of the modern problems, but also because it reproduces within its discourse, without intending to, the same view of Western superiority that we saw in the "negative" version, and that it originally was trying to avoid. We are reminded of this by Sally Price in her *Primitive Art in Civilized Places* when she discusses the supposed "anonymity" and "atemporality" (ahistoricity) of primitive art. The apparent anonymity of primitive artifacts is a consequence of the critics' belief that these works of art do not reflect the individual personality of their creators, but the traditions or values of the entire community they come from. Since it is not the product of an individual but that of a community, the "primitive" work of art represents a view of the world that has not been affected by the atomization and compartmentalization of modern society. Individualism—and by association the modern economic system that has given it a privileged place—appears as a modern characteristic whose presence cannot be conceived as part of primitive social formations. To this popular and pseudoscientific idea of the primitive artist as communal creator one can associate the notions of atemporality or ahistoricity of the primitive cultural tradition. Not only is the primitive artifact communal, but its anonymous features represent a tradition that has not changed or has changed very little throughout history. The absence of a concept of historical change frees these cultures from the frenetic obsession with time, the superficial changes in artistic trends, and the constant mutation and instability of modern social formations. Primitive art, in contrast, expresses eternal truths about the universe and man.

If, on the one hand, these ideas about primitive art exalt primitivism and denounce the negative effects of modernity, on the other hand they are not the result of careful studies of this art but a reflection of what the West *wants* to see in it. There are not only psychological reasons fostering this perception of primitive art and resisting change in it, but economic ones as well (e.g., the art collector for whom "once you learn who made an object, it ceases to be primitive art,"[18] and therefore loses its market value). Thus, the Western subject refuses to see the importance of the personality of an author for the production of art in other cultures, even though he has no problem accepting it in his own, as Bill Holm has pointed out in reference to some North American Indian artists:

> Northwest Coast Indian artists, like "primitive artists" of other cultures, have been largely anonymous in our time. Moreover, when modern man, a product of a society which puts great emphasis on names, fame, and individual accomplishment, looks at a collection of masks or other works of art from such exotic cultures, he is unlikely to visualize an individual human creator behind each piece. Seldom will he be helped toward personalizing the faceless "primitive artist" by the labels he might read. Work might be identified as "Northwest Coast," "Alaska," or "British Columbia Coast." At best a tribal identification might be made, although the likelihood of its being inaccurate is considerable. The idea that each object represents the creative activity of a specific human personality who lived and worked at a particular time and place, whose artistic career had a beginning, a development, and an end, and whose work influenced and was influenced by the work of other artists is not at all likely to come to mind.[19]

Richard and Sally Price's investigations of Maroon art in Surinam provide another example. The Maroons form a community whose origins go back to a group of runaway African slaves who, in a unique case in Latin America, re-created the way of life of western Africa in the South American jungle. The Prices have shown that even though they have no museums, written history, or any other formal system of handing down a body of oral historical traditions from one generation to the next, Maroon artists are conscious of the artistic tradition within which they work.[20] Just as a Western artist is easily able to recognize Cézanne's style and its importance for the history of Western art, so the artists belonging to this community in Surinam have no difficulty identifying the original works of specific artists (and the fake ones, too) and knowing by name who introduced a stylistic or technical innovation (and approximately when the change took place). There is nothing more foreign to their concept of artistic tradition than the ideas about "communal" and "atemporal" art that the West attributes to primitive production.[21]

It is as part of an attempt to attach positive characteristics to primitivism that one may understand the idea of "primitive mental processes" which Rama utilizes, and which he turns into the cornerstone of his theory of narrative transculturation. His version of the primitive mind is derived in great part from the early writings of Lucien Lévy-Bruhl, whose ideas, even though they were strongly criticized from the very beginning, have exerted an enormous influence on popular (mis)conceptions about primitive thought. Lévy-Bruhl defines the primitive mind as one whose mode of understanding causative relations is completely foreign to Western thought. Accordingly, the primitive mind is indifferent to logic and prefers "mystical" explanations based on invisible connections among the objects that surround us. Events are explained as the result of natural affinities between objects, affinities that from a Westerner's point of view are illogical.

Among the criticisms leveled against Lévy-Bruhl, one that is well known comes from Evans-Pritchard's studies on African magic, especially his 1937 book *Witchcraft, Oracles and Magic Among the Azande*. In his analysis of these practices, this anthropologist concludes that from the Azande's point of view, magic provides logical explanations of certain events occurring around them. Since they do not have any other type of explanations with which to contrast their beliefs, they are unable to see beyond the explanations provided by their paradigm. However, they employ this paradigm as logically as the West uses its own: "Within this web [of belief]," explains Gluckman, summarizing Evans-Pritchard's theory, "the African may reason as logically as we do within the web of scientific thought."[22]

A different kind of criticism has been expressed by Claude Lévi-Strauss and by Rodney Needham. They point out the impossibility of distinguishing between a primitive structure of thought and a modern one, since both utilize similar strategies for reasoning, such as binary oppositions.[23] More recently, Gilbert Lewis has attacked the excessive attention paid to religion and magic by anthropologists trying to differentiate between the primitive mind and the modern.

> [It is odd] that religion and magic rather than economics or politics, for example, should be the usual field in anthropology for comparisons of rationality. In economic and political activities, arguments, decisions and plans are made with explicit purposes in view and entail conscious calculation: these are not necessarily so evident in religion and magic, where motives may be complex and elusive. Surely it is tendentious to compare religious practice in one society with science

or technology in another as a way of assessing the relative place each gives to reason in its affairs; but something like that has often been done when the religious or magical beliefs of people in nonliterate societies are contrasted, implicitly or explicitly, with some general idea of scientific reasoning in industrial societies. Like should be compared with like: religion in one society with religion in the other.[24]

This tendency to analyze only the "logic" of religious beliefs and magic in primitive societies has led anthropologists to ignore other aspects of life in those communities which, when taken into consideration, reveal a very different perspective, incompatible with popular notions about the primitive mind. This is the case, for example, in the use of "common sense" as described by Lewis:

> Although we rarely bother to pay as much attention to the evidence of common sense—of careful observation and logical deduction in daily life—as we do such matters as witchcraft and sorcery, the evidence is there to see in the conduct of practical affairs and subsistence. Kalahari Bushmen make detailed observations of the habitats and behavior of animals; Nigerian farmers exercise effective pest control of grasshoppers through their knowledge of the insect's breeding habits; the Mende of Sierra Leone select varieties of rice on the basis of trial-and-error tests of crop yields: these and other examples provide unequivocal testimony to the use of experiment and deductive reasoning by African subsistence producers.[25]

In *Transculturación narrativa en América Latina,* Rama does not undertake any criticism of Lévy-Bruhl. He accepts the popular view that either locates the primitive subjects in a prerational stage of development or suggests that they employ a non-Western logic. Moreover, his position is a combination of both ideas: for him the fact that the primitive mind precedes the modern automatically frames it as a *different* kind of reason, forgotten or no longer available to Western thought. As we will see later, this view is less the result of poor research by the Uruguayan critic than of the need to accept unquestioningly this version of the primitive mind because his own theory of narrative transculturation depends heavily on it.

Like the concepts of "communal" and "atemporal" art, the notion of a possible "non-Western logic" serves the purpose of establishing a positive view of primitivism, since it attributes to primitive thought cognitive abilities that the West has lost or forgotten: a certain freedom for associating ideas, a nonlineal notion of time, closeness to the natural world, the ability to generate myths, and, in sum, a greater artistic capacity in contrast to the "scientific" tendency of the modern mind. In this case, as in the examples of anonymity and atemporality, the celebration of the positive aspects of the primitive mind hides the desire to deny those societies designated as primitive the characteristics that we have no problem attributing to Western societies. For example, it is necessary to remember that the modernity Rama sees as the future of Latin America is a consequence of the application of instrumental reason to the Western world. To deny primitive groups the access to this type of reason and the notions of causality associated with it, is to deny the possibility that without Western influence they should ever reach the achievements of modernity. It is also a way of explaining social and economic underdevelopment.

A similar subordination of the primitive to the modern can be seen in the combination of the "advanced" artistic techniques of the Avant-garde and the primitive material that Rama identifies in the texts produced by the transculturadores. The re-creation of the primitive mode of thinking in these texts acquires its value not in itself, but in relation to the literary techniques produced by modern mental processes. It is true that the "prerational" literary style of the transculturadores is presented as a Latin American response to Avant-garde techniques; that is to say, instead of merely copying "foreign" techniques, these writers find local equivalents for them. Thus, as an alternative to the fragmentation of the "stream of consciousness" in Joyce or Virginia Woolf, the Brazilian Guimarães Rosa uses a "discursive monologue," and instead of the juxtaposition of narrative fragments present in John Dos Passos's prose, Rulfo employs the "scattered narration" *(discurrir dispersivo)* of the Mexican countryfolk (44). And even though these solutions are preferable to the use of narrative structures imported from Europe, it is obvious that their value comes from the fact that they are similar to the Avant-garde models they are supposedly replacing. In other words, the primitive modes of narrative organization acquire their prestige because of their connection with Avant-garde techniques.

The technical nature of Rama's theory of transcultured narrative has been too often ignored, yet it is precisely in this aspect of the theory that many of its problems can be found: the kind of primitivist discourse Rama is interested in is not the usual one that talks about cyclical notions of time, communion with nature, or the links between the natural and the supernatural, but one that, in employing primitive modes of narration, can achieve the level of technical development of modernist Anglo-European texts. The relationship between primitive and modern in the theory of narrative transculturation is similar to what occurs when a museum, in its desire to promote a primitive art exhibition, advertises an African mask next to a painting by Picasso, asking the viewers to try to distinguish the "primitive" from the "modern." The traditional relationship between the original and the copy has been inverted here: "In a sense, Picasso's image is cast in the role of the 'original,' with the African mask representing a startlingly close second-best whose status depends on its affinity to a recognized masterpiece."[26]

As we have seen, technical progress occupies a privileged position in Rama's view of Latin American literature. Even though in *Transculturación narrativa* he was no longer arguing, as in his essay on Martí, that it is absolutely necessary to eliminate archaic elements in order to achieve modernization, the modern, represented by advanced writing techniques, remains the artistic horizon which helps determine the value of the transculturation project. Thanks to these techniques, transcultured texts could offer their readers the same value that Darío and other modernista writers, in Rama's view, were already producing, though at a more advanced level: literary products whose elaboration is as complex as the First World's industrial artifacts being imported into Latin America. The association technique/technology is not an irrelevant one, since for Rama it is in the cultural sphere, specifically in literature, that Latin America will first achieve the level of development which at this moment she can only dream of having in the economic sphere.

Rama saw the main purpose of narrative transculturation in the need to achieve an advanced level of writing technique. In a way, he was appropriating and rewriting the ideas about technical progress that he discovered in Walter Benjamin's "The Writer as a Producer." As I mentioned earlier, the influence of the German critic on Rama's thought can be perceived in his writings on Darío during the 1960s, and continued to play an important role in the later stages of his critical work.[27] I would like to suggest that Rama's theory of transculturation is to a certain extent the result of his rethinking of Benjamin's ideas from a Latin American point of view. Among other things, a consequence of this Latin American perspective is that he was forced to find a place and a function for premodern elements within modernity instead of simply desiring their elimination.

Rama summarizes his ideas about the "author as producer" in his 1981 article "La tecnificación narrativa" (The Technification of Narrative). The essay contrasts the fates of literary techniques and industrial technology in Latin America. Even though Rama is careful to point out that he does not see literature as a mere reflection of social reality, he says that what has happened with modern narrative techniques in particular is similar to what occurred in Latin America with the technology of the industrial era. In both cases, techniques created under specific circumstances have been transported to "peripheral" countries. This analogy allows him to compare the development in the use of techniques in literature with the changing models for economic development in Latin America. Rama points out that toward the end of the nineteenth century, both capital and technology in Latin Amrican economies were coming, and were being controlled, from the outside, with Latin American countries providing only the raw materials. During World War II, the economy changed to one of import substitution, in which peripheral societies were for the first time controlling the technology (which was still coming from First World countries); and they started to create products that, though lower in quality, began to replace foreign ones. For a limited time the import substitution model created the illusion that the periphery could achieve the same level of development as the most advanced countries. However, economic and political failures during the 1970s showed that it was not enough to bring technology from outside.

In the field of literature (especially since Darío's modernismo), writers were also importing "foreign" techniques and applying them to local "materials," but with very different results. During the 1960s, Latin American literature achieved an enormous artistic and commercial success that for Rama was linked to an innovative appropriation of the most advanced writing techniques. For Rama that kind of success was, more than anything, proof that Latin American literature had achieved a level of development comparable with that of First World literature. How was it possible to achieve at the cultural level something that had been impossible to create in other spheres of Latin American society, specifically at the economic level? Rama suggests a possible answer to this question: "Science and technology, needing a highly developed infrastructure, tend to be concentrated [in First World nations], something that may not apply to literature, which because of its handicraft nature can be linked to archaic modes of production, while at the same time—because it is also a product of the modern era—[it] cannot avoid being influenced by the global circulation of techniques."[28]

The literary field is not an area of human production that depends on the economic or technological development of the society where the writer resides. Put another way, it is precisely because of the "archaic" methods required to produce literature that a Latin American writer can "import" the most advanced techniques in his or her field without being constrained by economic expense. The modernization of literature (in contrast to that of society) is not limited by the lack of capital. From this point of view, the archaic mode of production ascribed to literature is relevant *only* because it allows the creation of modern literary products in a not-so-modern Third World. In the end, it is due to its modernity, to the use of modern literary techniques, that Latin American literature achieves for Rama the same level as that produced in the Anglo-European world. This is a characteristic turn in Rama's writings, one that I have chosen to call the dialectics of archaism and modernity: the first term (local/primitive/archaic) always finds its meaning and function in the realization of the second (modernization/ technification of society/literature). In his theory of narrative transculturation the same dialectical movement can be detected in the combination of a "primitive" Latin American mind with Avant-garde writing techniques. In other words, thanks to primitivism, literary modernity is possible in Latin America.

Rama's reading of the book *Antes o mundo não existia)* (The World Did Not Exist Before), written by two Desâna Indians, Umúsin Panlõn Kumu and Tomalãn Kenhíri, and translated into Portuguese by anthropologist Berta Ribeiro, provides another example of how he sees the need to subordinate the primitive aspects of Latin America to modernity (represented in this case by a Western notion of literature). One could argue that in this example it is necessary to speak about the primitive and not primitivism (understood as *re-creation* of the primitive), since the authors are members of the primitive society they are describing. But Rama finds many similarities between what is taking place in this book and the transculturation process that he discovered in the writings of Rulfo or García Márquez. Like these *transculturadores*, the Desâna Indians attempt to "recover a mythic view of a culture and inscribe it into a contemporary society completely foreign to them." Even more important is the fact that the authors already have an awareness of the written text *(una conciencia del libro)* that does not exist in their native culture. For example, they want to retain their copyright, and their main purpose in writing the book is to help preserve their community's traditions. They hope that in the future this book can be read by the younger generations of their tribe (83). The mere fact that they are employing a Western form of writing turns their "primitive" creation into primitivism.

Most of Rama's analysis of this book, to which he devotes a good number of pages in *Transculturación narrativa,* compares the means of communication in a modern and a "primitive" society. Rama observes that our means of communication, especially writing, "are inferior to the ones traditionally employed in archaic societies" (86). A text employing a scientific language, for example, is incapable of "translating the plurality of connotations and symbols" of indigenous ceremonies (88). That is why these texts that originate in the Indian community are closer to literature, which has a greater capacity for connotation, than to scientific discourse. There is of course nothing original in these statements. What is interesting about this analysis is that almost immediately after praising the higher artistic qualities of indigenous discourse, Rama suggests a "modification of our concept of literature" (89) so that it becomes possible to include oral "literatures" like the one created by these two Desâna Indians. To accept oral traditions as literature would not be anything new, he explains, since throughout the centuries, literary texts have been able to appropriate discourses coming from other fields. Latin American literature in the twentieth century, for example, has been able to incorporate the "chronicles of conquest and colonization," and, from very early on, it accepted the "indigenous religious and historical discourses (i.e., *Popol Vuh, Chilam Balam*) because of their prestige as foundational texts" (89). Premodern "texts" are thus not only preserved but also updated, modernized. Literature is defined in these pages as a field that can contain all other discourses. Obviously, the idea of incorporating oral or "archaic" sources into Latin American literature in no way represents a challenge to our concept of literature, as Rama suggests. On the contrary, it supports that concept.

> Indian literary products belonging to the current of cultural resistance mark the limits of Latin American literature because they represent cultural Otherness like no other type of linguistic communication. For the same reason, they assign a new function to literature, which now has the task of integrating these discourses within a homogeneous framework. Literature has served multiple functions within the [Latin American] continent ... and in the same way it founded Westernization during the Colonial period, and nationality after Independence,

it can just as well found cultural messages in this century, by lending them the homogeneity of its discourse. (94)

It is difficult not to notice that primitive or archaic discourses seem to introduce a fragmentation that Rama wishes to eliminate by incorporating them into a modern notion of literature. It is not, as he argues, a way of giving the Other a voice, but a way of silencing it. The dissemination of discourse provoked by the presence of the primitive must be controlled in order to produce modern literature. In his theory of transculturation Rama was no doubt trying to correct a mistake he made earlier in his career when he gave a negative meaning to the primitive elements present in Latin American culture, but in attempting to give them a "positive" function within his critical framework, he once again subordinates them to modernity.

Notes

1. The term "primitivism" originally was linked to "archaism," from which it later detached itself. Goldwater, for example, employs the adjective "archaic" to talk about the first European conceptions of primitive art, which included Oriental art; Robert Goldwater, *Primitivism in Modern Art* (New York: Vintage, 1967), xxii. As Torgovnick explains, the definition of primitive art became narrower in the twentieth century: "*Primitive* originally referred to painters before the Renaissance; then it broadened to include all early art—ancient, courtly (Chinese or Aztec, for example), and tribal. By the 1920s, the ancient and courtly had been removed from the category of the primitive, which from then on referred exclusively to 'tribal' art"; Marianna Torgovnick, *Gone Primitive* (Chicago: University of Chicago Press, 1990), 19.

2. In an early essay on the effects of modernization on modernismo, Rama talks about a social organization that Darío considered "archaic": literary academies. "In the Age of Patronage, writers used to get together and form academies because that helped them to improve their social status and possibly their financial situation . . . but that does not make sense nor does it have any value in the new society. In a modern society there is only room for unions that can protect economic interests and create an economic structure to facilitate intellectual production . . . Darío did not despise these archaic institutions—'may God save us from the academies'— because of his *modernista* aesthetics, but because they were anachronistic organizations in a new age"; Rama, *Los poetas modernistas en el mercado económico* (Montevideo: Facultad de Humanidades y Ciencias de la Universidad de Montevideo, 1967), 10.

3. Angel Rama, *Rubén Darío y el modernismo. (Circunstancia socieconómica de un arte latinoamericano)* (Caracas: Biblioteca Central de Venezuela, 1970), 47.

4. Ibid., 91.

5. Angel Rama, "El poeta frente a la modernidad," in his *Literatura y clase social* (Mexico City: Folios, 1983), 91.

6. Rama, *Darío*, 46.

7. Maribel Ortiz, "La modernidad conflictiva: Angel Rama y el estudio de la literatura latinoamericana" (Ph.D. diss., State University of New York-Stony Brook, 1993), 113–118.

8. Angel Rama, "La dialéctica de la modernidad en José Martí," in Ivan A. Schulman et al., *Estudios martianos* (Río Piedras, PR: Editorial Universitaria, 1974), 163. All subsequent citations of this work refer to this edition. Page numbers are indicated parenthetically in the text.

9. Angel Rama and Mario Vargas Llosa, *García Márquez y la problemática de la novela* (Buenos Aires: Corregidor, 1973), 65.

10. Walter Benjamin, "The Author as Producer," in his *Reflections* (New York: Harcourt Brace Jovanovich, 1978), 230.

11. For more on cinema, technique/technology, and the political function of art, see also Benjamin's essay "The Work of Art in the Age of Mechanical Reproduction," in his *Illuminations* (New York: Schocken, 1986), 219–253.

12. Benjamin, "Author," 222.

13. Angel Rama, *Transculturación narrativa en América Latina* (Mexico City: Siglo XXI, 1982), 29–30. All subsequent citations of this work refer to this edition. Page numbers are indicated parenthetically in the text.

14. In a recent book, David Graver defines modernism in a very similar way: "[Modernism] defines itself in opposition to the ideology of modernization. Whereas the Enlightenment hailed the discoveries of science, the rule of reason, and ideals of individual freedom associated with the rising bourgeoisie, and aided in establishing the ideology of that class, modernism casts a critical eye on all these aspects of the modern era as well as on the dominant class of which it is a cultural product"; Graver, *The Aesthetics of Disturbance: Art in Avant-Garde Drama* (Ann Arbor: University of Michigan Press, 1995), 18. In Rama's case his view of the Avant-garde seems to come from his readings of Adorno and Lukács. See Rama, *Transculturación*, 49.

15. See Peter Bürger, *Theory of the Avant-garde* (Minneapolis: University of Minnesota Press, 1984).

16. Amy Fass Emery, *The Anthropological Imagination in Latin American Literature* (Columbia: University of Missouri Press, 1996), 4.

17. In the introduction to a recent collection of articles about primitivism, Elazar Barkan and Ronald Bush mention that there is still the need for further study of some of the "peripheral" problems related to primitivist discourse, such as "the deliberate adoption of primitivist practices in the West by members of a victimized

group to increase their relative cultural visibility and significance, as in the case of the Harlem Renaissance"; Barkan and Bush, eds., *Prehistories of the Future: The Primitivist Project and the Culture of Modernism* (Stanford, CA: Stanford University Press, 1995), 13. That the editors consider the appropriation of primitivism to create an alternative identity to be a secondary phenomenon underscores one of the major problems with this collection and with other recent studies on the topic: the exclusion (or lack of knowledge) of primitivism's influence on intellectuals, artists, and writers from "peripheral" countries.

18. Quoted in Sally Price, *Primitive Art in Civilized Places* (Chicago: University of Chicago Press, 1989), 103.

19. Bill Holm, "The Art of Willie Seaweed: A Kwakiutl Master," in Miles Richardson, ed., *The Human Mirror* (Baton Rouge: Louisiana State University, 1974), 60. Quoted in Price, *Primitive Art,* 65.

20. Price, *Primitive Art,* 111.

21. Ibid., 108–123.

22. M. Gluckman, "The Logic of African Science and Witchcraft," in Max Marwick, ed., *Witchcraft and Sorcery* (Harmondsworth: Penguin, 1970), 327. Quoted in Raul Pertierra, *Lévy-Bruhl and Modes of Thought: A Re-Appraisal* (Amsterdam: Universiteit van Amsterdam, 1984), 16.

23. For a summary of the criticism against Lévy-Bruhl's theories, see Pertierra, *Lévy-Bruhl,* 11–22. Although Pertierra wants to defend Lévy-Bruhl, he is less interested in proving that Lévy-Bruhl was right than in suggesting that the issues raised by his work (the possibility of a different kind of logic) be taken seriously.

24. Gilbert Lewis, "Magic, Religion and the Rationality of Belief," in Tim Ingold, ed., *Companion Encyclopedia of Anthropology: Humanity, Culture and Social Life* (New York: Routledge, 1994), 563–564.

25. Ibid., 575.

26. Price, *Primitive Art,* 96.

27. Jesús Díaz Caballero, *Angel Rama o la crítica de la transculturación* (Lima: Lluvia, 1991), 18; and Jorge Ruffinelli, "Rama, Marcha y la crítica literaria en los años 60s," *Nuevo Texto Crítico* 7, no. 14–15 (1994–1995): 55.

28. Angel Rama, "La tecnificación narrativa," *La novela en América Latina: Panoramas 1920–1980* (Bogotá: Procultura, 1982), 314.

scending order in which primitivism increasingly loses its ethical and ideological content, approaching a purely formal and almost cold preoccupation with technique, at the boundary of the artificial and "corrupt"—to use a primitivist term for what departs from the state of nature. Thus, a purely aesthetic primitivism can have only a precarious, ephemeral existence, on the verge of becoming suspect of artificiality, or succumbing to its opposite, a victim of its own sophistication. This would ultimately be a central dilemma for the whole Avant-garde enterprise, exposed a generation later by Existentialist critics overly preoccupied with a new vital theme: authenticity. Such was the starting point for James Baird's 1956 study of Herman Melville and American primitivism, and for his distinction between an "academic" (studied, contrived) and an "authentic" (more spontaneous and intuitive—or should we say "more primitive"?) brand of primitivism.[4]

Suffice it to say that chronological, cultural, and aesthetic primitivisms are theoretical entities never to be found in isolation or "pure" state. Whenever one is encountered in practice, its cousins will not be far off; such that applying one to a work, an author, a movement, or a period is truly to speak of a relative tendency, a predominance, but not necessarily an exclusion. Furthermore, each of these tendencies may be expressed through nearly opposing tastes: "idyllic or soft" primitivism idealizes Arcadian serenity, rustic simplicity, balanced beauty, and pastoral innocence; "morbid or hard" primitivism values the grotesque, monstrous, animalistic—but liberating—force of primitive forms.[5] This darker side of primitivism has always exerted a strange fascination, but in modern times it is through Surrealism and other by-products of psychoanalysis that the notion of recuperating our repressed primitive instincts has acquired a new prestige. From Freud to Lacan, psychoanalysis seeks to uncover in early childhood the primitive substrate of modern man. Similarly, classical anthropology had pointed out primitive vestiges and atavisms as the psychological foundations of modern values and social institutions.

Thus, we might also posit a contrast in focus: between a "psychological" primitivism whose field of inquiry is the individual (representing the species), particularly in childhood, and an "ethnological" primitivism, oriented toward the communal and the culturally specific. This idea that the modern psyche somehow harbors the primitive or encompasses it, as it were, as part of its patrimony, suggests an absorption of the Other into the same, an act of cultural cannibalism, and ultimately another way of proclaiming the "universality" of modern Western man. Unable to find a suitable ethnological

7

Narrative Primitivism

Theory and Practice in Latin America

ERIK CAMAYD-FREIXAS

In one of the few essays devoted to primitivism in narrative, Michael Bell suggests that any attempt to define this term should proceed with a cautious respect for its natural untidiness, without imposing too rigid a theoretical grid. Robert Goldwater points out that there are as many definitions as artists who fit the description. Nevertheless, says Bell following Wittgenstein, to deny a phenomenon's existence because of its diffuseness would be as absurd as claiming that the light of a lamp is not real because it lacks definite borders.[1]

It might be helpful to consider that primitivism is not a unified concept, but rather a family of concepts. Lovejoy and Boas posit two main types: "chronological" primitivism is a philosophy of history that places humanity's golden age at the origins, views history as decline, and considers any renovation a recuperation; "cultural" primitivism is an ideology, a cultural attitude, civilized man's dissatisfaction with the outcome of civilization, the belief that a more natural, simple, even rustic life, such as that of existing rural, exotic, or tribal groups, offers greater freedom, happiness, moral plenitude, or harmony with nature.[2] While this distinction might be sufficient for a study of classical antiquity such as concerned its original proponents, the study of modernist primitivism since the Avant-garde requires the recognition of a more purely "aesthetic" brand of primitivism. Paul Gauguin, who so rejected Parisian society that he took refuge in Tahiti, may be considered the last true icon of cultural primitivism, but according to Goldwater, such a romantic attitude is abandoned by the urban primitives of the Avant-garde, for whom aesthetic aspects are separate from vital ones. Goldwater points out three tendencies in modern artistic primitivism: "vital-romantic" in Gauguin and the Fauves, "emotional" in the Expressionists, and "intellectual or formal" in the Cubists and Surrealists.[3] It is worth noting the debasis within its own culture, modern Western primitivism has developed substantially along psychological lines. Conversely, for much of Latin America, the ensuing transculturation of European primitivism since the Avant-garde is characterized by a shift from a psychoanalytic (individual and universalist) to an anthropological (collective and regionalist) outlook. This shift responded to a desire for *finding* Latin American identity in a non-Western cultural substrate or otherwise *founding* an identity based on difference, a cultural project spurred after World War I and the Mexican Revolution by the coincidental rise of Africanist ethnology and pre-Columbian archaeology.

Having noted the porous and relative nature of cultural frontiers, I will focus this work on those aspects of primitivism which seem to me most pervasive and relevant within the broader spectrum of modern Latin American narrative: the aesthetic, the morbid, and the ethnological. Insofar as it remains a modified Western loan, this concept of primitivism provides an angle from which to reconsider the meaning of a regional or continental identity and its "autochthonous expression," together with such ideologemes as Magical Realism, syncretism, transculturation, and hybridity, which have shaped the Latin American discourse of difference.

Since Andrés Bello's neoclassic *Allocution to Poesy,* the desire for cultural emancipation is stated as a rejection of the "cultured" Europe and search for the "primitive" America: *Tiempo es que dejes ya la culta Europa que tu nativa rustiquez desama, y dirijas el vuelo a donde te abre el mundo de Colón su grande escena . . . do viste aun su primitivo traje la tierra* ('Tis time you leave behind the cultured Europe that your native rusticity disdains, and aim your flight where Columbus's world unfolds for you the grandeur of its scenery . . . where the land is shrouded still in her primitive gown).[6] Underlying this idea of the *landscape* as the source of regional culture is a concept of the primitive essence of America inspired by Humboldt's geographical determinism. "Cultures are born out of their maternal landscape"—Spengler would later insist—"from their manner of feeling and relating to space; [this is] the primary symbol out of which each culture's entire language of forms is to be derived."[7] The romantic and ornamental "sentiment of the landscape" would be transformed by Naturalism into a telluric, monumental, and grotesque presence manifested in the broad cycle of novels of the Amazonian jungle. Works like *Infierno verde* (Green Inferno, 1908), *La vorágine* (*The Vortex,* 1924), and *Canaima* (1934) nourished the myth of "primitive" America with the primeval monstrosity of its savage scenery.

"Academic" primitivism (neoclassic, Romantic, or *modernista*) had to yield to the new claims of authenticity. In the ontology of the landscape the human dimension was missing. The rise of ethnology in those decades demanded a more genuinely anthropological approach. Nativism, *negrismo, indigenismo,* and *mundonovismo* ("New World" regionalism), rejected as provincial by the heirs of the cosmopolitan Avant-garde, led nevertheless, after World War II, to the universalizing regional style of Magical Realism. Consolidating this new narrative style, Alejo Carpentier supplied the primitive landscape with its missing human element by adding history and cultural syncretism to the literary fabric of Latin American identity; Miguel Angel Asturias and Juan Rulfo experimented with rural and indigenous language in order to find an American voice; and Gabriel García Márquez, with his playfully carnivalesque style, brought together primitivist stylization and sophisticated narrative technique into a Magical Realism that was increasingly being considered a distinct form of Latin American expression. In 1956, Venezuelan writer Arturo Uslar Pietri had affirmed that "Creole literature always has a primitive flavor not only because of its rigid stylization, but also by virtue of the abundant presence of magical elements, the penchant for the mythical and the symbolic, and the predominance of intuition."[8]

Once again the growing emphasis on stylization and technique would cause Carpentier's literary myth about "the American marvelous-real" to degenerate into a new aestheticism, a deliberate primitivism that García Márquez would take to the verge of caricature and parody. The "Latin American expression" had proved to be mostly a primitivism of form. Then, when postmodernity began to doubt the authority of the ethnographer—let alone the novelist—to represent the primitive Other, ethnotestimonial narratives became popular for filling the vacant role of satisfying an urban reader avid for the spectacle of the aboriginal. Given that here the "primitive" subject does not directly speak for himself or herself, but is recorded, edited, and transcribed by a Westernized intellectual, the Latin American testimonial narrative, as Miguel Barnet—one of its initiators—admits, continues to be "another way of making literature."[9]

In theorizing narrative primitivism, I will focus on the Magical Realist cycle, since it is there that primitivism acquired its fullest technical development. Although I will be primarily concerned with its formal aspects, it should be noted that these always have an ideological dimension. After the Mexican Revolution and World War I, the ideologues of Latin American identity, disillusioned with the old ideal of European civilization, ceased to look for the roots of that identity in Europe, and sought instead to assert its difference, which they found in the primitive substrate (Afro-Indian or archaic-Christian) on the fringe of the modern cities. The morbid primitivism of the Avant-garde contributed to the revaluation of that "primitive" America, disdained a generation earlier by Positivism. The structural study of myth made it possible for authors to use it as a tool of sociopolitical analysis. Primitive stylization became a mode of cultural interpretation, essentializing perhaps, but certainly more daring and often more meaningful than the documentary specificity of testimonial narrative. In Magical Realism, the mythical becomes an *allegory*[10] of Latin American reality and a vehicle for the anthropological interpretation of history; the latter had also been a hallmark of the "essays of national interpretation," from Ezequiel Martínez Estrada's *X-Ray of the Pampa* (1933) to Octavio Paz's *The Labyrinth of Solitude* (1950).

Their debt to the Avant-garde notwithstanding, Latin American artists tended to distrust Parisian primitivism in comparison with the "authentic" mythical reality they thought to have experienced at home. According to Renato Poggioli, the European Avant-garde failed in its attempt to express the "modern marvelous." The naive cult of machines led them to see technology through the eyes of a child or savage in order to falsely reduce it to magic, to a ludicrous animism that saw in machines not a source of energy but a source of life, not a practical potential but a mystical one.[11] The trick of looking at modern life through primitive eyes became ephemeral. The figure of the artist as an urban savage became a caricature once the epoch ceased to be amazed by it, hence to support it. In retrospect, Gauguin had evinced an admirable wisdom when he chose to be an amateur ethnologist in Tahiti rather than a professional aborigine on the Île de La Cité. Carpentier, who was one of the first to denounce the Surrealist *merveilleux,* found a solution in the change of scenery: it was simply more credible to look for the primitive in America, and with modern eyes, than to feign being possessed by a counterfeiting vision. In the end he was right: even the amazement that the Avant-garde sought in the "miracles" of science—affected and absurd in Paris—became possible, with inverse efficacy, in Macondo.

The influence of the Avant-garde was most substantial in matters of artistic form, but its most accomplished primitivism was that of the plastic arts and, to a lesser extent, music—limited models that did not provide the key for a *narrative* primitivism. Ethnography—including ancient texts, the chronicles of the Indies, travelogues, and other sources of classical anthropology—supplied an essential context. As anatomy is to sculpture, so ethnography became the basis for the narrative approach to the "great village," as Latin America was often called. In *One Hundred Years of Solitude,* imaginary ethnography serves an important poetic function: it organizes and rounds out the characterization of Macondo, not as a place but as a culture. The method consists in defining "the village" in terms of the typical categories of classical anthropology, and outlining its history, from foundation to destruction by outside forces, as a set of rites of passage. It is not difficult, either, to see the ethnographer in Melquíades, that universal foreigner who comes every year to live among the villagers, in order to write a *treatise* (the novel itself) that seeks to relate their particular deeds to universal myths and patterns.

In that function of the Latin American novel as what I have called "imaginary ethnography," a conventional image of the primitive is constructed, a sort of pastiche or simulacrum corresponding to a mixture of beliefs and myths which do not necessarily belong to any single, particular culture. The concept of everyday reality, which is always a matter of social convention, is transcultured: from the bourgeois pragmatism present in the traditional realist novel to the primitivizing mystification of daily life adopted by the new novel as its given, normal reality. Where, then, is the proclaimed "authenticity" of the Latin American expression? The reader may reach his or her own conclusions. Nevertheless, I believe it would be fair to indicate that these authors start from a vast and often direct knowledge of the local folklore on which their novels are based, but even so, it is a knowledge exogenous to the mentality they intend to depict. The author, educated (as are his readers) mostly in the Western tradition, depends on conventionalities of the primitive, on a popular idea of the archaic, shared by his readers, and thus necessary to construct and transmit the idea of a culturally alien fictional world; in this case, that of the *internal otherness* of Latin American culture.

The description of that semiosis, of that "text" of habitual primitive conventions which gives meaning and coherence to the novels' peculiar and often supernatural events, will be the focus of my inquiry. Initially, I supposed that a comparison of the novels against ethnographic accounts of diverse tribes would at least be an interesting exercise; but soon the similarities proved so numerous and compelling that I could no longer read those novels again with the same naivete as before. Narrative technique seemed in fact to be a set of conventions derived from the archaic *episteme* or worldview. The conventionalized representation of the primitive is a subject that has never been studied directly and that remains to be abstracted. My consideration of it is based primarily on a semiotic reading of anthropology, seeking in this case an *aesthetic* relevance for the Latin American novel. I will focus my discussion on four novels: Alejo Carpentier's *The Kingdom of This World* (1949), Miguel Angel Asturias's *Men of Maize* (1949), Juan Rulfo's *Pedro Páramo* (1955), and Gabriel García Márquez's *One Hundred Years of Solitude* (1967). I believe, however, that the abstract of primitive conventions which I now provisionally propose may be useful beyond narrative as well, in the study of other modes and media for aesthetic primitivism.

The archaic perspective could well be indigenous (*Men of Maize* and *The Kingdom of This World*) or provincial (*Pedro Páramo* and *One Hundred Years of Solitude*). Nevertheless, the hyperbolic tendency of primitivism assimilates the provincial to the indigenous. Thus, there is not a true distinction in styles among these novels: the folkloric and the tribal, the provincial and the indigenous, all sharing at the same level this text of primitive epistemic conventions. Now, if traditional realism operated according to "modern" Western conventions, such as linear or chronological time, the chain of cause and effect, the regularity of nature, the continuity of personal identities, the autonomy of the individual, and so forth, which conventions inform primitivism in narrative?

Tradition as a Supreme Norm

The individual in primitive societies must act in accordance with tradition, or his transgressing actions could trigger calamities upon the whole group.[12] Every culture exhibits a complex network of correspondences between violations of customs or taboos and specific consequences. Preconnections of this type are so strong that the transgressors despair of escaping consequences that have not yet ensued, and hurl themselves to their fulfillment. The individual is so much a part of the group that a vengeance can be satisfied upon the killer himself, or upon any member of his clan, and executed by any relative of the victim. All members of the group are responsible for the debt of any single one of them.[13] In Rulfo's Comala, everyone is condemned by the original sin of the patriarch; in Macondo, the incest taboo dooms the whole Buendía lineage to one hundred years of solitude; in *The Kingdom of This World,* the force of African mythical tradition inspires political rebellion; and in *Men of Maize,* the violation (taboo) of the corn (totem) unleashes the curse of the sorcerers, making the culprits rush blindly to their own punishment. This exaggerated presence of tradition also informs short stories like "La cuesta de las comadres" and "El hombre" by Juan Rulfo, or the short novel *Chronicle of a Death Foretold* by García Márquez, whose characters kill without passion, driven by a blind notion of family duty, where tradition becomes synonymous with destiny and fatalism.

And what about those characters created by Rulfo, clinging forever to a miserable land only because it is there that they have buried their dead? As with primitive tribes, ancestor worship is more important than individual survival. A character in *El llano en llamas* abandons his plot defeated, but only because he carries on his back neither food nor cattle, but his father's remains—an ancient and powerful Virgilian image of Aeneas painfully abandoning Troy with the wreck of his father on his shoulders, his son held by one hand and, by the other, the statuettes of his primitive household gods. Rulfo's characters are hieratical figures invested with a fatalistic stoicism before the overwhelming burden of tradition, of ancient transgressions and inherited sins. Likewise, in Macondo, ancestral memory accumulates upon the last of the Aurelianos: " . . . in that flash of lucidity he came to the reckoning that he was unable to withstand the overwhelming weight of so much past upon his soul."[14] Indirectly, the burden of tradition becomes a commentary on the (Colonial) history of Latin America.

The Mythical Conception of Time

Time for primitive man does not flow in a straight line but follows natural, liturgical, or ritual cycles, such that men who live today meaningfully repeat the archetypal, transcendental actions of their mythical ancestors, and associate their present reality with a primeval age.[15] For that reason, the circularity which governs these narratives' temporal structure should not be considered a mere aesthetic whim, but understood within the generalized primitivist optic that affords them their consistency. It has been said that *One Hundred Years of Solitude* does not use historical events for structuring of time; rather, it defines time according to a biblical, genealogical concept.[16] Precisely the genealogy that in the Bible leads directly to the Messiah, in the circular saga of the Buendías ends up in the last child's being born with a pig's tail, a kind of corkscrew that becomes an image of time. The messianic myth distinguishes Judeo-Christian tradition from "primitive" religions in which the gods do not return to redeem, but to demand regenerative sacrifices.

In Christian time, which flows linearly from Creation to Salvation,[17] the coming of the redeeming Messiah is the decisive moment of historical advance, without which it would all be repetition of mythical cycles on to exhaustion. Conversely, the frustration of the messianic myth in the novel accounts for its circularity (and genetic exhaustion): "The history of the family was a clockwork of irreparable repetitions, a turning wheel that would have continued to revolve, had it not been for the progressive and irremediable wear of its axle" (334). If salvation appears linked to procreation, it is because, figuratively, what these novels are actually concerned with is *historical* redemption. The historical redeemer, expected by the Latin American people, is the Liberator, revolutionary or reformer, whom we meet in Gaspar Ilóm and the son who survives him at the end of *Men of Maize,* or in the succession Mackandal-Ti Noel of *The Kingdom of This World.* The presence of the myth underscores the need and hope for historical change; its frustration in *Pedro Páramo* and *One Hundred Years of Solitude* is simply a more bitter form of condemning the same history, deemed to have repeated itself (from colonialism, to independence, to neocolonialism) without substantial alteration.

Curiously, in *One Hundred Years of Solitude,* it is an Amazonian Indian fleeing from her tribe's epidemic who contaminates Macondo with the "fever of insomnia," which in turn leads to the "forgetting" of history (hence, as Santayana would have it, those who ignore history are condemned to repeat it). Macondo is a village that is born, passes, and dies in oblivion, at the margin of history, which devours it. Seduced by the easy boom of the Banana Company, Macondo opted for returning to the (neo)colony, to the Riohacha of its ancestors: a nontranscendental repetition, an incest of history, a pigtail's end, for the family as well as the nation. After the Banana Company's flight, decadence sets in: Macondo's regression to prehistory, to the beginnings, and to dusty nothingness. García Márquez sees the answer neither in the return to the false Arcadia nor in a return to a naive primitive happiness. On the contrary, Macondo's tragedy, from historical oblivion to unconscious, meaningless repetition, is also the tragedy of a backward continent, surprised by history before it had ever ceased to be a village.

In addition to circularity and repetition, structural *fragmentation* or the absence of a logical succession makes events appear as though governed by supernatural forces.[18] With its falsely rudimentary character, fragmentation simultaneously projects an effect of modernity and archaism. A model for Carpentier, Stravinsky's *The Rite of Spring* evokes primitive rhythms through a modernist abolition of the melodic-harmonic sequence.[19] Its compositional analogy with *The Kingdom of This World* becomes clear when one considers that the sequential character of melody has its correlate in the chronological and syntagmatic aspect of narrative. Both works break with those linear aspects of composition, favoring a rhythmical unity where cyclical repetition produces an annulment of time, an impression of timelessness. On the other hand, the connective recourse of *repetition* is the typical constructive procedure of archaic narrative, commonly found, for example, in ancient Mayan texts like the *Popol Vuh* or the *Rabinal Achí,* emulated by Miguel Angel Asturias's formalistic primitivism. The structure in *Men of Maize* reflects that particularity of human deeds which often makes history appear to repeat (variations of) primeval events, each time granting myth a new dimension and broader, more current meanings. One could say that history is ultimately necessary for the (re)interpretation of myths, and vice versa.

The Mystical Notion of Causality

Space for primitive man is a living network of interactive forces. Empirical causality is constantly contaminated by a mystical one. An omen, such as the flight of a bird, is not only the announcement of an event to come but also, at the same time, its cause. The stability of nature is undermined at every moment by the willful forces of magic, natural powers, or the effects of taboo transgressions.[20] The principle that Freud identified as "the omnipotence of thought," the irrational and paranoid belief that a mere thought or wish might carry actual consequences or precipitate a destiny, is another instance of this.[21] The concept of mystical causality dismantles the chain of cause and effect that ruled in rationalist fashion over the traditional realist plot. In *One Hundred Years of Solitude,* mystical causality, blended with omens and premonitions, becomes a structural device with Melquíades's "prophecies." On the other hand, omens in Rulfo serve stylistic rather than structural purposes: "A mockingbird crossed close to the ground and groaned, imitating the moan of a child" (65); near the death of Susana San Juan, the author writes: "The oil inside the lamp sputtered and the flame made its flickering ever weaker. Soon it would be extinguished" (105); "The sky was full of stars, fat ones, swollen from so much night. The moon had come out a while and then had left . . . sad . . . disfigured . . . to hide behind the hills" (109).[22] His is a literary primitivism that blends a delicately poetic sense with a simple, popular language, a rural vocabulary, and, particularly, an appeal to an order of semantic and causal relationships peculiar to archaic mentalities.

The Vitalist and Animistic Vision

All beings, animated or not, are considered to have a "soul" and the potential for intervening in human affairs as carriers of universal forces.[23] *One Hundred Years of Solitude* transforms this animism into a defamiliarizing and carnivalesque technique as the gypsies introduce a magnet into the village: "Everybody was amazed to see pots, pans, tongs, and braziers tumble down from their places and beams creak from the desperation of the nails and screws trying to emerge. . . . 'Things have life of their own,' the gypsy proclaimed with a harsh accent. 'It's simply a matter of waking up their souls.'"[24] Animism reveres everything telluric with respect and fear. Imposing places or those exhibiting extraordinary natural beauty are often contemplated as sacred totemic centers, temples, or concrete expressions of universal forces. Such is the hallucinatory animism represented in El Tembladero, the volcanic sinkhole that swallows up the soldiers in *Men of Maize*. Images of animism, of anthropomorphic and zoomorphic atavism— that is, of the main conceptual elements of primitivist expression—surface in the telluric language of the novel: *lloro de barranco* (11), *silencio de enredadera* (20), *colapso de una voluntad vegetal que ya no quiso resistir más tiempo la embestida del viento* (105), *cadáveres de árboles insepultos* (113), *que enviude todo el hembrerío de cosas que el huracán preña* (115), *el méiz cuesta el sacrificio de la tierra que también es humana* (228).[25]

The Unity of the Natural and the Supernatural

For the primitive, the sense of the sacred is ever present in every activity and every reflection; religion, thought, and life develop within a complete unity between the natural and the supernatural. The frontier between the visible and the invisible worlds, the divine and the profane, the living and the dead ancestors, vanishes. The contact with the supernatural is constant and concrete.[26] This justifies the familiar sense accorded to the supernatural in the novels, particularly in *Pedro Páramo*, where the integrity of the whole fictional world is made possible only within that ideological context whereby the frontier between the living and the dead disappears. Here, the ambiguity of the verbal tenses is one of Rulfo's most subtle techniques: "'Damiana

Cisneros? Aren't you one of them who *lived* at the Media Luna ranch?' 'That is where I *live*'" (37); "'[Susana,] Don Pedro's deceased mother *expects you* to wear her wedding gown'" (43). The unity of the natural and the supernatural makes these categories reversible, interchangeable, a characteristic device in García Márquez, whose characters' equivocal interpretation of ordinary and extraordinary events makes these acquire in their minds an inverse or indiscriminate meaning: they marvel at (seemingly for us) pedestrian occurrences and show utmost indifference before prodigious or supernatural events, which to them appear quotidian and commonplace.

The Unity of the Human and the Telluric

The individual, the collective, and the telluric are interpenetrated. Contrary to modern man, the primitive does not define himself in terms of his *difference* with respect to the rest of creation, but by his "ontological participation" in the substance of other beings. Totemism, recognized by McLennan in 1869, establishes an ontological identity between a human group and the animal or ancestral plant that serves this group as totem. Asturias, an amateur anthropologist, provides an evident example in *nahualism,* which he exploits in his novel under the totemic identity "man-corn" adapted from the *Popol Vuh.*

At a social level, the identity of the human and the telluric is reflected in the novels through the assimilation of history (culture) and nature. Bouckman, in *The Kingdom of This World,* launches a rebellion in the middle of a hurricane by invoking Ogún, as Mackandal had predicted, "in order to unleash the cyclone that would complete the work of man" (33). The figure of Ogún, "Marshal of the storms," deity of war and thunder awakened by the sound of the drums, serves Carpentier's purposes in relating myth to history through an *allegorical* operation that, according to Walter Benjamin, reduces social history (the revolution) to natural history (the cyclone).[27] At the end, Ti Noel watches another storm (intimating a new historical overturn) devastate the last ruins of the old Colonial estate and carry away the last pages of the rationalist *Encyclopedia.* And at the end of *One Hundred Years of Solitude,* the assimilation of social and natural history is given in the telluric tropes of the plagues and the flood, until a "biblical hurricane" destroys the last ruins of Macondo, while the *wind* (read: *time, history*) sweeps the last parchments of Melquíades's manuscript (suggested by the Voltairean *Encyclopedia* in Carpentier's novel).

A determinant in character construction, this assimilation of the human and the telluric also, in a more subtle way, contaminates language. The Bambara from Mali, for example, express themselves in constant comparisons between nature and human life, using the same terminology to describe the parts of the body and the same functions in plants, animals, and humans.[28] Such is Magical Realism's predilection, within its descriptive language, for the zoomorphic caricature of its characters. In *Men of Maize,* zoomorphism prefigures human relationships, assimilating the social to the fatalistic order of nature: "The treekiller ivy is bad. But the corn harvester is worse"(15); "The Indian warrior smells like the animal that protects him" (19); "Mestizo women have an iguana-like dribble that stuns men" (23). Characters are identified by their animal names: (Lice-headed) Piojosa Grande, Cow Manuela, Macho (Stallion) Machojón, Healer-Deer, Coyote Aquino, Goyo Yic the Opossum, Chigüichón Serpent, Venancia Corzantes (Venison Doe). Personalities often bear the signature of the *náhual* (protective animal-self): Machojón is a manly horseman; the Healer is elusive like the deer; the mailman Aquino is as fast as the coyote; Goyo Yic is a seeing blind man like the nocturnal opossum.

According to Sir James Frazer, in magical thought such associations have their basis, their foundation, in the system of similarities of "homeopathic magic." "Animal blood turns vegetal before turning into earth, and that is why one turns green soon in death" (76). For magical thought, everything has its *signature.* "The system of signatures inverts the relationship of the visible with the invisible," Foucault explains. "It is necessary that hidden similarities signal themselves on the surface of things; there must be a visible *mark* for the invisible analogies."[29] " . . . the Healer-Deer of the Seven-Burnings. Well noticed, he had the body of a deer, the head of a deer, the legs of a deer, his tail, his demeanor, his behind. A deer with *seven ash marks above his snout*" (243). Whereas "homeopathic magic" works by similarity, "contagious magic" (Frazer) operates by contiguity, providing another way of associating images and transforming realities by way of similes in the primitivist language of *Men of Maize:*

> The Port Castle prisoners impressed Nicho Aquino, a mountaineer, on all four sides, because he found that by force of being closed up there in the middle of the sea, they were slowly turning into some aquatic beings that were neither man nor fish. The color of their skins, their nails, their hair, the slow movement of their pupils, almost al-

ways fixed, their way of gesturing, of moving their head, of turning, everything was fish-like, even when they showed their teeth in laughter. Only their appearance was human, and their speech, which in some was so tardive that one could say they would open and close their mouths letting off bubbles. (331)

Ontological Fluidity and Transformation

The "spirit" of things does not represent for the primitive an abstract concept opposed to that of "matter," as it is in the Western Platonic tradition, but a *potency* which constantly expresses itself in a concrete manner.[30] Potencies flow through all beings with greater or lesser intensity, resulting in an "ontological fluid" whereby any being may transform into another or shift form at any moment. "To live, for a given individual, is to be involved in a complex network of mystical participations with the other members, dead or alive, of his social group, with the animals and vegetables born of the same soil, with the earth itself, and with the hidden forces that protect the whole ensemble."[31] In the mythical age of the ancestors the vital principle for all beings is transformation. Creation and Origins are always explained via some kind of metamorphosis. In the present age, it is the shaman who maintains this power of transforming and being transformed with the greatest efficacy.

Nahualism in *Men of Maize* and the metamorphoses of Mackandal and Ti Noel in *The Kingdom of This World* represent typical cases of this belief. A less obvious aspect of *ontological fluidity* is the recurrent transformations and "substitutions" of characters that abolish the continuity of personal identities. In *Men of Maize*, María Tecún turns out to be a transformation of Piojosa Grande. All the "tecunas" repeat, ritualistically, the primitive act of Piojosa, who at the beginning *fled* from the slaughter in order to save her son Martín Ilóm. The same occurs with the masculine characters Gaspar Ilóm, Goyo Yic, and Nicho Aquino, all of whom represent variations of the same cosmological principle. Women, always changing and fleeing, symbolize the moon, the rain, and running water; men represent the sun and fire: the union of these opposites engenders the children of the corn.[32] The logic of character behavior based on cosmogony is a primitive device transposed by Asturias from the ancient Mayan texts and calendars.

In *Pedro Páramo,* the fluidity of personal identities results in a web of "substitutions" as yet unexplained by criticism. Miguel, whom Pedro Páramo raises and gives his family name (without questioning if he is actually his son at the moment the boy is delivered to him), replaces Juan, the legitimate heir to all the lands usurped through fraudulent marriage from his mother, Dolores Preciado, whose surname he carries. Juan Preciado arrives with the commission of taking revenge on his father; instead, a man called Abundio, who could (or could not) be the same muleteer, son of the cacique, whom Juan meets when he first arrives at Comala, substitutes for Juan as the killer of his father. It seems as though all the sons of Pedro Páramo were inter-changeable—as if, in effect, they were all one, no matter which. Thus, Juan substitutes for Donis in the bed of his sister, who in turn was a surrogate wife. In his path toward death, Juan Preciado moves from Dolores's care to Eduviges's, to Damiana's, and finally to Dorotea's, every one of them replacing another in their maternal role. Eduviges, who had replaced Dolores in Pedro Páramo's nuptial bed, says to Juan Preciado: "The following year you were born; but not of me, although by a hair it could have been" (21–22). About Eduviges it is said: "She even gave everyone a child. And put him before them for someone to recognize him as his; but no one wanted to do so. She then told them: 'In that case, I am also his father, even though by chance I may have been his mother'" (34). The last of Juan Preciado's mothers is Dorotea, nicknamed La Cuarraca due to her condition as sterile and half-crazy: "She is one who carries a bundle inside her shawl and lulls it, saying it is her pup" (67). Juan Preciado becomes that bundle, a substitute for the child she never had, because both end up buried in the same grave, in the fetal position, as if the tomb were a sterile womb one returns to after death. However, a last substitution plays a joke on Dorotea: "They buried me in your own grave, and I fit very well in the hollow of your arms. Only that it occurs to me that it should be me who cradles you" (65).

All this fluidity of identities, this ontological confusion of the characters, occurs, moreover, within a frame of murmurs and voices, impersonal bundles and shadows, which make themselves felt throughout the novel like an anony-mous chorus of beings consubstantiated in death. Even the voice of Dorotea, so close to Juan Preciado, gets lost in that melting pot of faceless, sexless beings: "'You're right, Doroteo. You do say your name is Doroteo?' 'It's all the same. Even though my name is Dorotea. But it's all the same'" (62). For the sterile Dorotea it's all the same whether she is taken for a man or for a woman; but "it's all the same" also becomes the commentary that annuls all the identities in the novel. It's all the same if Eduviges is the father or mother of a child who belongs to "everyone" and at the same time to no one. It's all the same, any son rather than all the sons, any woman of Pedro Páramo's rather than all the mothers of Juan Preciado, and it's all the same whether the Abundio of the beginning is the same Abundio who kills the patriarch at the end, because in Comala there are no individuals; there is only one voice, one face, one blood, one tribe.

The instability of personal identities (and annulment of their importance), which had acquired a characteristic tenor in Rulfo, returns in *One Hundred Years of Solitude* as the succession of the José Arcadios and Aurelianos. The deliberate confusion of names and identities in tribal fusion feeds the fear of incest, because the repeated characters have lost account of their own origin. A similar procedure, well diffused among primitivist painters, is the "uniformity of facial types."[33] In the paintings by Colombian Fernando Botero, to whom García Márquez is often compared, all the figures show variations of the same face. This uniformity of traits is expressed in the novel by the repeating names and personalities. Contrary to traditional realism, which took pride in the creation of great individualized characters of complex psychology, the primitivist author reduces his characters to one or two distinctive traits—simple, almost childish traits—that often become magnified or intensified. The rest is tribal uniformity.

The Logic of the Concrete

This concept, used by Lévi-Strauss to characterize savage thought, has transcended in a curious way into narrative primitivism.[34] Primitive cultures always express themselves in concrete terms. Their myths explain their origins, beliefs, precepts, and customs, not in a direct manner, but by the representation of concrete situations and the paradigmatic actions of mythical characters. It is a philosophy that proceeds by images. García Márquez turns this conception into a favorite device, a stylistic signature: giving an exaggeratedly concrete and literal sense to what should have had nothing more than a figurative meaning. When in "Eréndira" the objects touched by the young Ulises turn colors, his mother (who is "pure" Indian) affirms: "Those things only happen because of love."[35] The primitive principle of psychic *efficacy,*[36] or the concretion of feelings, is ubiquitous in *One Hundred Years of Solitude:* the ghostly appearance of dead man Prudencio Aguiar is the result of the remorse of Ursula and Arcadio, who killed him; the levitations of Father Nicasio whenever he drinks hot chocolate are a hyperbolic expression of his zeal as a preacher; the assumption of Remedios the Beautiful is the literalization of the moral pretensions for keeping up appearances and saving family honor after the girl elopes; and the raining of flowers is the concretization of universal grief after the death of the patriarch. Nevertheless, the best example is provided by the story "A Very Old Man with Enormous Wings"—an allegory of Man, that being who stands between angel and animal, with the ability for subsuming the most sublime and the most low. Here, popular imagination takes shape in an old man with big and dirty chickenlike wings. The experiment consists in making this figure descend into the daily life of a sleepy Caribbean town where reality turns to carnival: the old man is caged and exhibited as a circus attraction.

The logic of the concrete also governs the characters' reasoning: Ursula's great-great-grandmother was so tortured by nightmares after Drake's attack on Riohacha that her husband finally "built his wife a bedroom without windows so that the pirates of her dream had no way to get in."[37] The steady and daily contact with the supernatural is a given for the primitive in a concrete manner. The Fōn of Dahomey throw bits of food on the floor before eating, calling them "the ancestors' meal." Dishes are not washed until the following day, in case one of the dead, wandering by night, should like to eat the leftovers. They do not sweep in the dark for fear of hitting any of the spirits. That explains why the ghost of Prudencio Aguiar suffers thirst and hunger. According to the logic of the concrete, the ancients buried their dead with their belongings; in Dahomey, it was customary to send messages and presents to the dead ancestors with those who were close to dying; and in Macondo, when Amaranta announces her imminent death, the neighbors bring her letters and errands for their relatives in the other life.

In *Pedro Páramo,* the corporeal presence of the dead and the revived memories of the characters create a space where vivid recollections from the past take shape by erasing the threshold that separates life from death. Thus, the ghost of Dorotea narrates with surprising concreteness her encounter with the *body* of Juan Preciado: "'You want to make me believe that it was the lack of air that killed you, Juan Preciado? I found you in the square. . . . Then we dragged you . . . stiff as die those who die dead with fear. Had there been no air to breathe that night you speak of, we would have lacked the strength to carry you, let alone bury you. And you see, we did'" (62).

The logic of the concrete not only makes this whole universe of wandering souls incarnate, and provides a general consistency for the novel as a whole, but also informs the minutiae of its style, its similes and metaphors, fluctuating between credulous seriousness and skeptical humor: "[Comala] lies between the cinders of the earth, right at the mouth of hell. All I need to tell you is that those who die there, as soon as they arrive in hell they come back for their blanket" (9); "The church's clock marked the hours, one after the other, as though time had shrunk" (19); "'His death caused me much pain,' said Terencio Lubianes. 'My shoulders are still sore.' 'Me too,' said his brother Ubillado. 'Even my bunions have grown larger'" (32–33); "No, it was not possible to calculate the depth of that silence. . . . It was as though the very noise of conscience had ceased" (36); "Can't you see the sin on me? Can't you see those purple stains like from *jiote* that fill me from head to toe?" (55); "It was the murmurs that killed me" (62); "I know how to measure despair, Don Pedro. And that woman carried it by the bushel. I offered her fifty hectoliters of corn to forget the matter; but she turned them down" (68–69); "He never wanted to revive that memory because it brought-on others, as if he broke the burlap of a full sack and then wanted to contain the grain" (71).

In *Men of Maize* linguistic primitivism reverses the visible and the invisible when the simile finds its signature in the logic of the concrete: "Flames shaped like bloodied hands were traced on the air's walls" (119); "The sky is heavy like the water in the cisterns" (128); "The clouds, enormous white oxen" (130); "his heart aching like a horse's stomping" (187); "Last night I measured your sleep, your sleep is too shy for the sorrow you carry around . . . up to your neck is all it reaches, that's it. . . . Your eyes then remain uncovered; and you can't fall asleep, the sleep doesn't reach your eyes, and no matter how you want to stretch the fabric of sleep, which is like a bat's wing . . . you rip it, and the tiredness of lying around creeps into you, as does the urge to go out looking for it" (226).

The Ludic Element

There is an important ludic element in primitive culture that has been lost to the modern. "As a civilization becomes more complex, and the techniques of production and social life itself are more minutely organized, the old cultural silt is gradually buried under stale layers of ideas, systems, doctrines, rules, laws, moralities, and conventions, all of which have lost contact with play. Civilization, we say, has become more serious; now it assigns only a secondary importance to play."[38] The primitive has sacred games as well as utilitarian and profane games. There are no dividing lines among games, rites, and survival activities such as hunting, fishing, agriculture, and the education of children; that is to say, between play and culture.[39] García Márquez, who best perceived the possibilities of this ludic element for narrative primitivism, exploits it in the carnivalesque dimension of his novel. This discovery decisively changes the tone of Magical Realism, opening it to humor and parody.

The Penchant for the Hyperbolical and the Monumental

Primitive man lives a hyperbolic existence within a world of monumental dimensions and countless concealed but omnipresent powers ready to act at any moment. His tales, legends, and myths, nourished by the involuntary exaggeration of generations, increase in measure without ever losing their verisimilitude. For the savage, his mystical sense of causality being much stronger, supposedly, than his logical and empirical sense, almost everything is possible and credible. Myths, notwithstanding their ludicrous enormities, exaggerated proportions, inconsistencies, and variations, do not seem to him, by any means, impossible. Nevertheless, the savage's belief, even before his most sacred myths, is not immune to humor and cannot be separated from the sphere of play. The living myth recognizes no difference between seriousness and play.[40]

José A. Bravo has pointed out the insistent use of exaggeration and its ludic sense in *The Kingdom of This World, Pedro Páramo,* and *One Hundred Years of Solitude,* citing numerous examples that I need not repeat.[41] Yet, I might emphasize that García Márquez is much more prone to hyperbole and literary playfulness than other narrators. More in keeping with postmodern sensibility, humorous play as it occurs in García Márquez is a natural development of the Magical Realist style, a strategy for dealing with aesthetic problems of authority and verisimilitude whose solutions of the "serious" kind had been exhausted in his predecessors.

Deserving special attention, however, is the hyperbolic element of caricature. García Márquez employs it in the traditional, realist manner in characters such as the colonel, the priests, and the Banana Company. However, in Avant-garde painting, caricature acquired a primitivist angle of which *One Hundred Years of Solitude* makes plentiful use as well. Avant-garde painters, particularly Picasso, incorporated caricature in their process of stylization, and perceived its affinity of method with primitive art, given that the "conceptual" nature of both creates hierarchies of representation based more on ideas and feelings than on external appearances.[42] The art of isolating the essential features of a person (or those of a culture or a people, in the case of García Márquez) allows the caricaturist to evoke remarkable similarities even within the most radical artistic deformation. In *One Hundred Years of Solitude,* the similarities with Latin American cultural structures are transformed through the hyperbolic use of primitive forms into an identification by distortion. The forms selected from the primitive lexicon are those which the art of cultural caricature demands. The resultant hyperbole is more festive than grotesque: an affectionate and compassionate caricature of a people.

The Ideal of Sublime Roughness

In *De abstinentia,* the Platonic philosopher Porphyry compares "ancient" Greek statues with the "new" ones in the following manner: "The former, although simple in form, are considered to be divine in nature, while the new ones, having been finished with greater art, may be admired, but no one believes them to have the same divine nature."[43] Primitive works appear to possess a sacred and natural *something* that cannot be re-created at will, something resembling that innate faculty which Schiller ascribed to the "naive" poets in opposition to the cultured and deliberate art of "sentimental" poets. Longinus, in his attributed treatise *On the Sublime,* feels that in contrast to the beautiful, the "sublime" is a way of expression that cannot be obtained at will and that is not a matter of technique: he who possesses the gift of the sublime may abandon the laws of the beautiful; but to try to achieve it deliberately means to fall into the pompous.[44] Edmund Burke, who in 1756 revived this proto-Romantic distinction between the sublime and the beautiful, relates Longinus's "sublime" to primitive and prehistoric artworks such as Stonehenge: "The roughness of the work itself increases the impression of grandiosity, a fact that excludes the idea of artifice and inventiveness; mastery produces another type of effect quite different from this."[45] Thus, *morbid primitivism* is identified throughout the ages with a certain expressive force (the "sublime" or, as Surrealists called it, the "marvelous"), a hyperbolic force issuing from the contact with the natural or the divine, from a feeling of the sacred, the religious, the ritualistic, or, otherwise, the forbidden and transgressive.

The "real-marvelous" in Carpentier is precisely an attempt to capture that ideal of art, not as creation but as a discovery of nature untouched by the human hand; the ideal of recuperating ritual in its prereflexive state, uncorrupted by a self-conscious and disbelieving civilization.[46] For Carpentier, the "real-marvelous" is not accessible to technique and artifice; the author's task is to be a mere discoverer and chronicler of hidden realities, not a creator of fictions and falsehoods. Asturias, on the other hand, pursues "sublime roughness" in language itself, in the force of a natural, spontaneous expression, which Fernando Alegría described as a "monstrous beauty."[47] From the Gothic cathedral's chiaroscuro of the rain forest canopy in *Men of Maize,* tentative beings emerge, still confused in their identities, made up of "ontological fluidity" and "mystical participations," like simulacra just emerged from the primeval broth, or from the world of genesis depicted in the *Popol Vuh* (I:2). Meanwhile, García Márquez seeks the tone of the townsfolk, countrified storyteller of his "grandmother's tales," in order to shun any ostentation of means and conceal his sophisticated technique and his mastery.[48] But it is Rulfo who most closely approaches that ideal, declaring himself a purely "amateur" writer, and entirely suppressing the modern narrator to let his characters speak, in a novel that appears to narrate itself.

Pedro Páramo could well have been an anonymous work. The characters cannot find their identities because the author, too, has left Comala and subtracted himself from the story; what is left is an inexplicable and enigmatic tale whose clues have been lost to unfathomable elisions and silences of death, to a laconic and incomplete language that tells things only halfway. This aspect of unfinished work, of a broken labyrinth whose communicating pieces have been lost to an irretrievable past, a sort of archaeological ruins; of incomplete fragments reassembled into an apparent chaos that almost succeeds in concealing all its mastery, virtuosity, or deliberation, almost succeeds in entirely hiding the mallet, the chisel, the very hand of the artist—all this is the ideal of "sublime roughness," a feeling of the natural and the divine conveyed by primitive sculpture: "stones in a *páramo;*" the anonymous monument of Comala, the Mexican Stonehenge; the monoliths of Easter Island; the incomprehensible Atlantes of Tula, a work of monumental and reverential roughness, where mastery and ornament, as much as facile exegesis, would be the violation of a mystery and a sacrilegious transgression against the gods. *Pedro Páramo,* like no other modern work, approaches that boundary where the distinction between primitiv*ism* and the primitive begins to vanish.

During the rest of his life Juan Rulfo carefully cultivated this myth that others erected around his work. First, he cultivated it with the thirty-year silence that followed the publication of *Pedro Páramo.* He became the zeal-

ous curator of his small oeuvre: a "magnificent, poetic and monstrous" image of a people, according to Ruffinelli.[49] The myth of *Pedro Páramo* to which
I refer is that of the book which could never be duplicated, equaled, or deliberately created, not even by its own author, because it is not the offspring
of art, precept, or mastery, but of nature itself. To cite Schiller in his Romantic and timeless concept of naive or primitive poetry, we are concerned with
a work and a poet that "hardly belong any more in this artificial age . . .
hardly are they possible in it . . . save preserved, by a happy star, from the
influence of the times, which would mutilate their genius. Never will society
produce such poets; but in society still they will appear at times, at intervals,
rather as strangers who surprise, or as ill-trained children of nature, who
irritate. . . . Critics, as normal constables of art, detest such poets as subverters
of rules or of limits."[50] In keeping with this myth, Rulfo was to renounce his
role as artist in order to adopt that of "witness and guardian of nature"
(Schiller) and, therefore, of his own oeuvre—a position which subtly resembles Carpentier's myth of the artist as mere "discoverer of realities." This
mission as a guardian was fulfilled by Rulfo in 1983, when he edited a collection of critical essays about his work, significantly entitled *Para cuando yo
me ausente* (For When I Am Gone).[51]

Rulfo's desire, as that of any author, was to save his book from the same
reductionist grid he so carefully avoided when writing it, a wish that must
be respected by any reading of the work. Nevertheless, the myth of the
unclassifiable and alien work that does not belong to its time disintegrates
the moment that book exists and is read. The reading, the reception of a
work, despite all its singularities, cannot but put that work into circulation
and dialogue with other works of its time; and it is in that dialogue that
literary concepts are renewed, sometimes with a broader, more open spirit.
A subverter of rules or of limits, Rulfo expands those margins, but, in my
opinion, does not break them.

Conclusion: Primitivism as Aesthetic Utopia

From the elements cited, which conform the *text* of habitual primitive conventions, a poetic is derived, a coherent manner of configuring a novel's
fictional universe out of the sentiment of the archaic. This intent acquires a
subversive character at the political and cultural levels. The dominant discourse of the metropolis, which believes itself to be the arbiter of culture, a
pragmatic and rationalist discourse that has its sphere of influence in the

modern urban centers in and out of Latin America, is replaced with the discourses of rural marginality and of the cultural and racial periphery. Nonetheless, even in these discourses, traces of the old Western ethnocentrism survive, as Torgovnick suggests.[52] The very concept of "primitive" belongs to the discourse of the metropolis and designates the "other": what the metropolis is not, that which is not recognized as adjusted to "this" day and age, and whose mere existence is "marvelous," precisely because it is seen as aberrant. To some it is but a deviation that confirms the hegemonic norm.

Others have seen in narrative primitivism a glorification of underdevelopment or a hidden desire for perpetuating cultural inequality in order to exploit it for literary purposes. I believe that what really exists is a reaction, a compensation, a disappointment with the project of Latin American development, and, from this point, an attempt to shift that scale of values which perceives "inequality" where perhaps there is only *difference.* Primitivism can also be read as a defiant celebration of that difference, a vision that replaces the unattainable social utopia with an aesthetic utopia: "primitive" America, a privileged continent where it is still possible to sublimate in the novel all the social desires that history has frustrated.

Notes

1. Michael Bell, *Primitivism* (London: Methuen, 1972).

2. Arthur O. Lovejoy and George Boas, *A Documentary History of Primitivism and Related Ideas in Antiquity* (1935; Baltimore: Johns Hopkins Univrsity Press, 1997).

3. Robert Goldwater, *Primitivism in Modern Art* (1938; New York: Vintage, 1986).

4. James Baird, *Ishmael* (Baltimore: Johns Hopkins University Press, 1956).

5. Ernst H. Gombrich, "Il gusto dei primitivi," *Memorie dell'Istituto italiano per gli studi filosofici* 11 (1985): 7–34.

6. Andrés Bello, *Poesía* (Santiago de Chile: Nascimiento, 1930). All translations, unless otherwise noted, are mine.

7. Oswald Spengler, *La decadencia de Occidente,* vol. 1 (Madrid: Espasa-Calpe, 1923), 229.

8. Arturo Uslar Pietri, *Las nubes* (Santiago de Chile: Editorial Universitaria, 1956), 73.

9. Miguel Barnet, *Biografía de un cimarrón* (Buenos Aires: Centro Editor de América Latina, 1977).

10. On the relation between allegory and primitivism, see Angus Fletcher, "Allegorical Causation: Magic and Ritual Forms," in his *Allegory: The Theory of a Sym-*

bolic Mode (Ithaca, NY: Cornell University Press, 1964), 181–219; and Erik Camayd-Freixas, *Realismo mágico y primitivismo* (Lanham, MD: University Press of America, 1998).

11. Renato Poggioli, *The Theory of the Avant-garde* (Cambridge, MA: Belknap/Harvard University Press, 1968).

12. Bronislav Malinowski, *Magic, Science and Religion* (London: Souvenir Press, 1982), 74.

13. Lucien Lévy-Bruhl, *La Mentalité primitive* (1922; Paris: Retz-CEPL, 1976), 259, 383.

14. Gabriel García Márquez, *Cien años de soledad* (1967; Buenos Aires: Sudamericana, 1977), 349. My translation. In subsequent quotations the parenthetical page number in the text refers to this edition.

15. See Mircea Eliade, *Cosmos and History: The Myth of the Eternal Return* (New York: Harper & Row, 1959) and *The Sacred and the Profane* (New York: Harcourt Brace Jovanovich, 1959); as well as Lucien Lévy-Bruhl, *Primitive Mythology* (1935; St. Lucia: University of Queensland Press, 1983), 34.

16. Suzanne Jill Levine, "Lo real maravilloso: De Carpentier a García Márquez," *Eco* 20 (1970): 574.

17. See Eliade, *Cosmos and History.*

18. Emil Volek, "Análisis e interpretación de *El reino de este mundo* de Alejo Carpentier," *Unión* (Havana) 1 (1969): 99.

19. Theodor W. Adorno, *Philosophy of Modern Music* (New York: Seabury Press, 1973), 154.

20. See Lévy-Bruhl, *La Mentalité primitive;* Sir James Frazer, *The Golden Bough* (1890; New York: Mentor, 1964); and Folco Quilici, *Primitive Societies* (New York: Collins, 1972), 79–84.

21. Sigmund Freud, *The Basic Writings* (New York: Random House, 1938), 865.

22. Juan Rulfo, *Pedro Páramo* (1955; Mexico City: Fondo de Cultura Económica, 1973). These and subsequent parenthetical page numbers refer to this edition; translations are mine.

23. Animism was first outlined by E. B. Tylor; see his *Primitive Culture* (London: J. Murray, 1871).

24. Gabriel García Márquez, *One Hundred Years of Solitude*, trans. Gregory Rabassa (New York: Avon Books, 1971), 11.

25. "A ravine's whimper" (11); "an ivy's silence" (20); "the collapse of a vegetal will that would no longer resist the charging of the wind" (105); "the unburied corpses of the trees" (113); "let all the femaleship of things the hurricane impregnates become widowed" (115); "corn costs the sacrifice of the earth, which is human, too" (228). Miguel Angel Asturias, *Hombres de maíz* (1949; Madrid: Alianza Editorial, 1981). Translations are mine.

26. See Tylor, *Primitive Culture;* Lévy-Bruhl, *La Mentalité primitive;* and Quilici, *Primitive Societies.* See also Roger Caillois, *Man and the Sacred* (New York: Free Press, 1959).

27. See Walter Benjamin, "Allegory and Trauerspiel," in his *The Origin of German Tragic Drama* (1928; London: NLB, 1992), 159–235.

28. Quilici, *Primitive Societies,* 47.

29. Michel Foucault, *Las palabras y las cosas* (Mexico City: Siglo XXI, 1982), 35.

30. See Janheinz Jahn, *Muntu: An Outline of Neo-African Culture* (London: Faber and Faber, 1961).

31. Lévy-Bruhl, *La Mentalité primitive,* 408.

32. René Prieto, *Miguel Angel Asturias' Archaeology of Return* (New York: Cambridge University Press, 1993).

33. See Goldwater, *Primitivism in Modern Art;* and Roger Shattuck, *The Banquet Years: The Origins of the Avant Garde in France, 1885 to World War I* (New York: Vintage, 1968).

34. See Claude Lévi-Strauss, "The Science of the Concrete," in his *The Savage Mind* (London: Weidenfeld and Nicolson, 1974).

35. Gabriel García Márquez, *La increíble y triste historia de la cándida Eréndira y de su abuela desalmada: Siete cuentos* (Buenos Aires: Sudamericana, 1976), 132.

36. See Ernst Cassirer, *The Philosophy of Symbolic Forms,* vol.2 (New Haven, CT: Manheim, 1955), 157.

37. García Márquez, *One Hundred Years,* 27.

38. Johan Huizinga, *Homo Ludens* (Boston: Routledge and Kegan Paul, 1980), 75.

39. See also Quilici, *Primitive Societies.*

40. Huizinga, *Homo Ludens,* 129.

41. José Antonio Bravo, *Lo real maravilloso en la narrativa latinoamericana actual* (Lima: Editoriales Unidas, 1978).

42. William Rubin, ed., *Primitivism in 20th Century Art,* vol. 1 (New York: Museum of Modern Art, 1984), 284.

43. Cited in Gombrich, "Il gusto dei primitivi," 16.

44. Cassius Longinus, *On the Sublime,* trans. W. R. Roberts (Cambridge: Cambridge University Press, 1899).

45. Edmund Burke, *Enquiry into the Origin of Our Ideas on the Sublime and Beautiful* (London: J. Dodsley, 1757). Cited in Gombrich, "Il gusto dei primitivi," 18.

46. Alejo Carpentier expressed these ideas in his prologue to the 1949 edition of *The Kingdom of This World,* and in various articles of that time. An updated version of his prologue is available in English as Alejo Carpentier, "On the Marvelous Real in America," in Lois Parkinson Zamora and Wendy B. Faris, eds., *Magical Realism: Theory, History, Community* (Durham, NC: Duke University Press, 1995), 75–88.

47. Fernando Alegría, "Miguel Angel Asturias, novelista del viejo y del nuevo

mundo," in his *Literatura y revolución* (Mexico City: Fondo de Cultura Económica, 1971).

48. See Ricardo Gullón, *García Márquez o el olvidado arte de contar* (Madrid: Taurus, 1970).

49. Jorge Ruffinelli, "Juan Rulfo," in Juan Rulfo, ed., *Para cuando yo me ausente* (Mexico City: Grijalbo, 1983), 35–72; 47.

50. Friedrich von Schiller, "On Naïve and Sentimental Poetry" (1795), in his *Essays* (London: G. Bell and Sons, 1875).

51. Rulfo, *Para cuando yo me ausente.*

52. See Marianna Torgovnick, *Gone Primitive* (Chicago: University of Chicago Press, 1990).

8

Narrating the Other

Julio Cortázar's "Axolotl" as Ethnographic Allegory

R. LANE KAUFFMANN

I s it possible to represent alterity without reifying, colonizing, or preempting it? In the diverse modes of ideology-critique prevalent at the end of the twentieth century, the Other is often invoked as though it were an amulet to ward off a host of ideological evils—humanism, sexism, monologism, and the proliferating "centrisms" (Euro-, ethno-, anthropo-, phallo-, logo-) —considered endemic to Western thought and society. But it has always been easier to invoke alterity than to depict or commune with the Other in a nonpreemptive way. This is particularly evident in ethnography, that genre of writing about other cultures which provides the empirical basis of cultural anthropology. Looking back at sixteenth-century writers Bartolomé de Las Casas and Michel de Montaigne as early modern forerunners, we see that the intent to rescue foreign cultures from the depredations of European conquest and colonization was part of the ethnographic project from its beginnings.[1] And yet, as Todorov noted in *The Conquest of America,* even sympathetic accounts of alterity have tended to deny "the existence of a human substance truly other, something capable of being not merely an imperfect state of oneself."[2] Has it not always been at least a tacit aim of European ethnography to capture and domesticate the Other in the web of writing—to present the Other as a trophy of sorts to the reader of ethnographies?

Such are the tough questions addressed to ethnography—indeed, to all forms of cross-cultural representation—by contemporary criticism. James Clifford has described this general crisis or "dispersion" of ethnographic authority brought on by the "breakup and redistribution of colonial power" since midcentury, and by the "echoes" of that process in social and cultural theory. Borrowing a term from literary theorist Mikhail Bakhtin, Clifford characterized the postcolonial intellectual climate as one of global heteroglossia: "people interpret others, and themselves, in a bewildering diversity of idioms. . . . This ambiguous, multivocal world makes it increasingly hard to conceive of human diversity as inscribed in bounded, independent cultures. Difference is an effect of inventive syncretism." Since Western anthropology, in self-critical recoil from its earlier links to colonialism, can no longer claim privileged access to knowledge about others, "it has become necessary to imagine a world of generalized ethnography."[3] Geertz put it more colorfully: "We are all natives now, and everybody else not immediately one of us is an exotic."[4] It seems fairly clear that we have not yet emerged from this "heteroglossic" situation, which is roughly coextensive with what we have come to know as postmodernity. Whereas telecommunications and computerization have exponentially accelerated global communication, new ethnic wars and emigration trends have exacerbated national and cultural tensions, making issues of cross-cultural representation more urgent than ever.

It may be useful to recall Clifford's summary of anthropologists' experimentation with new modes of knowing and writing about others, in their efforts to shore up the authority of their representations. Of the four main paradigms of ethnographic authority that Clifford discerns in twentieth-century ethnography—experiential, hermeneutic, dialogical, and polyphonic—the first dominated anthropology between 1920 and 1960. It corresponds to the rise of the academic anthropologist, who comes to know another culture through intensive fieldwork (using the method of "participant observation"), then writes up an authoritative, synthetic account—a mode that became normalized as the standard genre of ethnographic writing. This "experiential" paradigm, with its generally "realist" representational strategy, established a scientific norm in relation to which the next three paradigms came to be defined. In the 1960s, the interpretive or "hermeneutic" paradigm questioned the presumption of an immediate experience of others, instead likening cultural understanding to the reading of texts. Even while interpreting cultures as texts, however, its mainstream practitioners continued to follow a realist or mimetic strategy, construing other cultures as something "out there," to be portrayed and interpreted by the ethnographer. Sometime around 1970—to follow Clifford—a still more significant shift occurred, which may be said to mark the beginning of anthropology's principal response to the postcolonial "crisis" of ethnographic authority and representation: "It becomes necessary to conceive of ethnography not as the experience and interpretation of a circumscribed 'other' reality, but instead as a constructive negotiation involving at least two ... conscious, politically significant subjects. Paradigms of experience and interpretation give way to discursive paradigms of dialogue and polyphony."[5]

My rationale for reading a literary text through the prism of ethnography, a genre usually classified among the social sciences, is an overdetermined one. First, Cortázar's "Axolotl"[6] has the ambiguous ontological status of a fiction that purports at one level to be an ethnographic document: the record of an encounter between the European narrator and a remote foreign culture. Second, it seems to me that the story registers and explores, in its problematic constitution of the "other," the crisis of authority which besets ethnography and contemporary cross-cultural representation in general. Third, Cortázar's narrative practice in "Axolotl" displays an "inventive syncretism" that not only foreshadows the paradigm shift and discursive forms of recent ethnography, but also serves as an emblem of that broader transdisciplinary trend which Kreiswirth has called the "narrativist turn" in the contemporary human sciences.[7]

Theorists as diverse as Hayden White, Jean-François Lyotard, Fredric Jameson, Paul Ricoeur, Richard Rorty, F. R. Ankersmit, and Michel de Certeau have devoted much attention in recent decades to the nature and functions of narrative as a cultural practice, especially to its central place among the deep rhetorical structures and strategies that inform the cultural disciplines. In his influential "report on knowledge" in the late 1970s, Lyotard remarked the "return of narrative" in the officially non-narrative discourse of contemporary science. The postmodern condition—which Lyotard defines as a general loss of faith in "master narratives"—is accompanied by a proliferation of "little" or "local" narratives. In traditional cultures (and in Western venues where storytelling and other modes of "narrative knowledge" flourish as everyday practices), "little narratives" embody common knowledge, and thus are self-legitimating. When the scientific validation of knowledge is at issue, however, these contingent micronarratives play a different role: they displace and complicate, even when they are intended to bolster, the legitimation strategies of postmodern science.[8] With their "nontotalizable discursive energies" (Kreiswirth's words), micronarratives are, as David Carroll puts it, "the form that discourse takes to express diversity and unresolved conflict and, thus, resist homogenization."[9]

Clifford, too, points out the narrative character of cultural representations, "the stories built into the representational process itself," which make ethnographic texts "inescapably allegorical."[10] The "inventive syncretism" that

he notes in cross-cultural representation often takes the form of storytelling—
that is, a strategy of allegorization—in social-scientific and critical discourses.
As investigations of alterity become methodologically more self-conscious,
and more receptive to the multiple perspectives and practices involved in
representing cultural "others," the investigator's implicit task becomes no
longer simply to describe a thematized Other, but to give a plausible account of the Other's construction by the investigator's own and by neighboring disciplines. Disciplinary and generic crossovers, and allegories to relate them, are engendered in the process. Michel de Certeau's study of
"heterologies" shows how the disciplines of historiography, ethnography,
and psychoanalysis, each of which claims an access to scientific "truth" about
"real" Others, have defined their objects and pursuits in relation not only to
one another but also to once-banished "fictive" discourses, which shadow
those sciences as their repressed disciplinary "others."[11] Small wonder that
ethnographers, historians, and psychoanalysts have learned to practice a form
of literary criticism, while critics have felt obliged to take up the intellectual
habits of those neighboring disciplines.

There are distinguished precedents for reading Cortázar's "Axolotl" in
the light of such cross-disciplinary allegorization. In *The Repeating Island,*
Antonio Benítez-Rojo detects in histories and novels a "secret wish to exchange places, which brings about an unforeseen kind of coexistence between the two discourses . . . traveling separately but crossing each other at
their respective nodes of desire." He invokes "Axolotl" as an analogue of this
"unforeseen coexistence," or cross-disciplinary romance, of fiction and historiography.[12] Roger Bartra's *The Cage of Melancholy* combines literary, historical, and ethnographic discourses in its critique of myths of Mexican identity. Not unlike the "contrapunteo" of Cuban anthropologist Fernando Ortiz
(analyzed in Benítez-Rojo's study), Bartra's study takes the contrapuntal,
"polyphonic" form of a fugue: its even-numbered chapters provide historical analysis of the cultural mythology behind Mexican nationalism, while
the odd-numbered chapters (or "vignettes") explore, in a more ironic mode,
the formation of what Bartra dubs "the canon of the axolotl"—a set of stereotypes that function as a sociobiological metaphor of Mexican national
identity. The vignettes are initiated by, and structured around, a parodic
transformation of Cortázar's "Axolotl." Drawing on ludic strategies of
postmodern fiction, Bartra uses Cortázar's tale as an allegorical device in
performing his demythologizing anatomy of Mexican political culture.[13]

The human narrator of "Axolotl," an anonymous Parisian and frequent visitor to the animals exhibited at the Jardin des Plantes, decides one day to vary his routine and to visit the aquarium instead. There he becomes fascinated with the *axolotls* (Nahuatl for *ajolotes,* protosalamanders of Mexican origin). Obsessed, the narrator returns daily to visit them, until one day he undergoes a metempsychosis (transmigration). He finds himself "with my human mind intact, buried alive in an axolotl, condemned to move lucidly among unconscious creatures." The story's opening lines relate this transmigration from human to salamander in a matter-of-fact tone: "There was a time when I thought a great deal about the axolotls. I used to go and see them in the aquarium of the Jardin des Plantes and stay for hours watching them, observing their immobility, their faint movements. Now I am an axolotl."

That statement at once frames the story's action and establishes the complex autodiegetic nature of the narration. The narrator is not only a character in the story; he is also somehow both "subject" and "object" of the transformation, speaking both as human and as axolotl. Immediately following that framing statement, the narrative voice assumes its original human identity, and proceeds to recount analeptically (in flashback mode) the story of how the transformation occurred. Thereafter, up to the moment of transmigration, the narrative first person is linked mainly to the human narrator prior to the metempsychosis, while the third person refers to the axolotls. There are important exceptions, however: at several empathetic moments, while describing the lamentable plight of the axolotls in the aquarium, the narrator slips into the first person plural, clearly identifying with, and speaking as one of, the salamanders: "I saw the diminutive toes poise lightly on the moss. It's that we don't like moving around much, and the tank is so cramped . . . time is less noticeable if we stay quiet." The curious zigzagging (or counterpoint) of narrative voice between human and axolotl continues up to the key moment of transmigration, at which point the flashback rejoins the narrative present. From then on, the first person corresponds to the salamander, the third person now (as in the opening lines) referring to the human being who, estranged from his former obsession, returns only rarely, and with diminishing interest, to visit the axolotls. The closing lines, about which I will have more to say shortly, confirm this separation or estrangement, even as they create the story's central enigma: "And in this final solitude to which he no longer comes, I console myself by thinking that perhaps he is going to write a story about us, that, believing he's making up a story, he's going to write all this about axolotls."

There can be little doubt that the instability of the narrator's identity—the oscillation of narrative voice between human and axolotl—is the key to the story's uncanny effect. Marta E. Sánchez sees in Cortázar's artful handling of pronouns and other deictic "shifters" not only the central narrative device of the story, but also the advent of a new type of fantastic literature, one not apparent to Todorov in his structural study of that genre.[14] In the fantastic mode of the nineteenth century, which based its "linear" narrative style on the mimetic conventions of realism, the reader typically wavered between "natural" and "supernatural" explanations for an anomalous event. In the newer, twentieth-century mode, which Sánchez calls the "modern fantastic," the reader's hesitation (the defining feature of the fantastic genre, according to Todorov) operates not at the level of the events narrated (the "story"), but rather at the level of "discourse," which registers the act of narration itself. In the "modern fantastic" represented by "Axolotl," the reader's hermeneutic challenge is no longer to figure out what has happened or how it happened, but rather to discern who or what is narrating the events. "Who is the subject of the discourse? The man or the axolotl? Or is it both?"[15] While Sánchez admirably clarified the narrative mechanism of Cortázar's story, much remains to be said about the narrative constitution of the "other" in the tale. By reading "Axolotl" as an allegory of Western ethnographic discourse, I hope to glean its philosophical and political implications more fully. The tale may be seen, on the one hand, as the paranoid expression of a European bad conscience toward the conquered and colonized peoples of Latin America. On the other hand, it stands as a parable of Western philosophical anthropology and ethnographic discourse, inasmuch as it calls into question the categories by which Western thought defines human (and nonhuman) beings—thus raising the possibility of a different, non-ethnocentric way of relating to Others.

From the first moment of the encounter, the human narrator claims, retrospectively, "I knew that we were linked, that something indefinitely lost and distant kept pulling us together." How is one to interpret this affinity? Perhaps one does well to resist the biographical fallacy of equating narrator and author, but it would be regrettably naive, in this case, to ignore the circumstances of the story's production. Cortázar, born in Belgium and raised in Argentina, moved to Paris in 1951, at age thirty-seven, and lived there until his death in 1984. By the mid-1950s, when "Axolotl" appeared, the political conscience of this Argentinean-European was awakening to the anticolonial struggles in Algeria and Cuba, although he did not discover and affirm his "true condition as a Latin American," nor his solidarity with socialism and the Cuban revolution, until the early 1960s.[16] In this context, it seems significant that the axolotls are described as having "Aztec" features, that they are amphibious and nomadic (some species are found in Africa), that they are biologically a permanently "larval" form, locked in a perpetual state of arrested development; that they have been exploited and consumed (like cod-liver oil) for their presumed therapeutic value; and that the specimens in this story are captives in a Parisian aquarium, objects of curiosity for idle Europeans.

Awareness of this web of symbolic associations should enable an ideologically richer reading of the tale. I will propose, and then proceed to explore, an interpretive hypothesis with both psychoanalytical and political dimensions. Suppose that the story serves as an imaginative resolution of a guilt complex with a collective, historical basis: the guilty conscience—or perhaps, following Fredric Jameson, I should say the guilty *unconscious*—of Europeans with regard to the formerly colonized peoples of the Americas.[17] It is a guilt complex that Cortázar himself must have experienced in a complicated way, given his problematic identity—at once double (European and Argentinean roots) and divided (cultural identification with Europe versus an awakening political identification with Latin America).

The axolotls represent, in the present allegorical reading, not Latin America as a political or cultural entity, nor the author's biographical link to a particular nation, but rather the autochthonous, precolonial element of the "new world": the indigenous tribes and cultures that were ravaged or colonized by Europeans. This autochthonous element, as symbolically important as it is "indefinitely lost and distant," appears to the author's European imagination as an exotic archetype: an Aztec avatar, in the totemic guise of the axolotl, or salamander.[18] A rigorous psychoanalytical study of the tale would focus on the complementary mechanisms of projection, identification, transference, and idealization as they operate in the paranoid discourse of the narrator. The human narrator's initial reaction to the axolotls is that of a reticent voyeur who shrinks before their piercing gaze. The salamanders "pressed their heads against the glass, looking with their eyes of gold at whoever came near them. Disconcerted, almost ashamed, I felt it a lewdness to be peering at these silent and immobile figures heaped at the bottom of the tank." The observer, who once watched from a safe and dominant position, now feels watched in turn—a theme that recalls Sartre's essay, "Orphée noir," in which European man feels himself penetrated by the returning gaze of the African colonized: "Because whites have for three thousand years en-joyed the privilege of seeing without being seen. . . . But there are no more domesticated eyes: there are only wild and free gazes, which judge our land."[19]

It is the eyes of the axolotl that "speak" to the human observer of "the presence of a different life, of an other way of looking." The narrator under-goes a process of empathetic interpretation, detecting in the salamander's eyes "a metamorphosis which did not succeed in revoking a mysterious hu-manity." At first the narrator denies that this discovery is a case of anthropopathic projection, yet his own words seem to confirm such a diag-nosis, in a passage that indeed foreshadows his own destiny: "I imagined them conscious, slaves of their bodies, condemned infinitely to an abysmal silence, to a hopeless reflection." The paranoid basis of this intuition is sug-gested in the following passage:

> The axolotls were like witnesses of something, and at times like hor-rible judges. I felt ignoble in front of them; there was such a terrifying purity in those transparent eyes. They were larvas, but larva means disguise, and also phantom. Behind those Aztec faces, devoid of ex-pression yet evincing an implacable cruelty, what semblance was await-ing its hour? I was afraid of them. . . . Every fiber of my body reached toward that stifled pain, that rigid torture at the bottom of the tank. They were lying in wait for something, a remote kingdom destroyed, an age of liberty when the world had belonged to the axolotls.

The axolotl is thus construed as an Aztec avatar whose present suffering in the aquarium reminds the human narrator of the historical crimes com-mitted by his European forebears, the conquistadors. This accounts in part for the narrator's ambivalent wavering between pity and fear, idealization and guilt. The most revealing example of paranoid interpretation is the "can-nibalism of gold" that the narrator discerns in the axolotls' gaze. "'You eat them alive with your eyes,' the guard said, laughing; he probably thought I was a little cracked. What he didn't notice was that it was they devouring me slowly with their eyes, in a cannibalism of gold." The axolotls' eyes function as mirrors that reflect back to the narrator the aurivorous gaze of his ances-tors. It is as though the axolotls were avenging themselves, through this "can-nibalism of gold," for the abuses committed upon the Aztecs by the conquis-tadors. Note the exact symmetry of the symbolic retribution: gold, the prime motive for those historical crimes, now appears inscribed, in a strange but appropriate metonymic reversal, in the implacable gaze that accuses and threatens to "devour" the narrator. As Melanie Klein observed, paranoia is by no means incompatible with idealization of the feared object.[20]

The human narrator of "Axolotl" perceives in the salamanders at once "implacable cruelty" and "a terrifying purity." Despite feeling himself "judged" and "devoured" by the axolotls, he attributes to them an idyllic past, an "age of liberty, when the world had belonged" to them. Here one may discern a phantasmagoric variant of two related European myths: that of the noble savage and that of the precolonial past as a lost paradise. The imaginary transmigration of the narrator's human consciousness into the axolotl would have the expiatory function of assuaging the protagonist's vicarious guilt— the guilty unconscious of European man about his colonial past.

It is significant that the only evident channel of "communication" between the human and the salamander is the visual medium of the gaze.[21] It would be neither original nor an exaggeration to say that from Plato onward, sight has provided the metaphorical basis of Western ontology: the world and other beings are constructed by visual analogies. In "Axolotl," the narrator visually objectifies the salamanders before identifying with them. After the first encounter, he heads for the library to look up a few basic facts about the axolotls in a dictionary ("larval stage . . . of a species of salamander . . . genus *Ambystoma*"), but he declines to consult "specialized works," in favor of direct experience. The next day, he returns to the aquarium and begins to study the specimens by close observation. He counts them, giving meticulous descriptions of their physical features and lethargic movement. "Mentally I isolated one, situated on the right and somewhat apart from the others, to study it better." This corresponds, in ethnographic research, to the "fieldwork" phase, when the investigator immerses herself in the empirical particulars of the culture studied. For traditional ethnography, vision warrants the observer's firsthand perception of the Other, and thereby the scientific veracity of the ethnographic account.[22] Despite the narrator's own rhetoric of investigation, however, it becomes evident that his descriptions of the salamanders are closer to fetishism than to neutral description. The central rhetorical device of the story is *hypotyposis,* the attempt to bring an idea to life through the development of a vivid image, as though to convince the reader of the immediate presence of the phenomenon described.

The encounter with the Other depicted in this story is curiously one-sided: the axolotl is the passive recipient of the human narrator's interpreting gaze. The salamander seems not even to notice the presence of the human being who importunes it: "It was useless to tap with my finger on the glass directly in front of their faces: they never showed the least reaction." This apparent lack of reciprocity does not discourage the narrator. On the contrary, he interprets the axolotls' taciturnity as a will to tranquillity, along the lines of Stoic apathy or Epicurean *ataraxia* (which has its rough oriental counterpart in the Buddhist nirvana): "Obscurely I seemed to understand their secret will, to abolish space and time with an indifferent immobility." Next Cortázar's narrator employs a stratagem dear to Western rationalism— Descartes's methodical doubt—to persuade himself that his intuitions are correct, and not mere "mythology." "In vain I tried to prove to myself that my own sensibility was projecting a nonexistent consciousness onto the axolotls. They and I knew." The very suffering he ascribes to them—that of remaining "conscious, slaves of their bodies, infinitely condemned to an abysmal silence, to a hopeless reflection"—presupposes the Cartesian dualism of mind and body (or "intelligent" and "corporeal nature"). A recurring nightmare in Western literature, this imagined plight is yet another symptom of anthropocentric projection.[23]

To take a final example of the projection at work in this story: "Their blind gaze, the diminutive golden pupil, at once expressionless and yet terribly lucid, went through me like a message: 'Save us, save us.'" It seems more likely that the human narrator invents the other's will to be saved in order to rationalize his own salvaging intentions, not unlike missionaries and colonizers throughout Latin America who sincerely thought they perceived the same supplicatory message on indigenous faces. The prototype of this "benign" ethnocentric gaze is that of the good Fray Bartolomé de Las Casas, who detected in natives a primitive or "wild" Christianity, a predisposition and desire for conversion.[24] It is ironic that the human narrator's gaze, which is assumed to be a reliable instrument of observation, turns out to be a vehicle of self-hypnosis. The eyes of the axolotl, which seemed to invite access to a "diaphanous interior mystery," function as a mirror that only reflects back the stereotyping human gaze (in a way reminiscent of Lacan's "mirror stage" of ego development).[25] And the aquarium glass, ostensibly a transparent medium of discovery, is actually the cage that frames and encloses the captive Other.

The predicament of the narrator at the end of the story does not bode well for the Western ethnographic project of grasping the other through close observation and description. For a fleeting moment after the "transmigration," the exiled narrator is face-to-face with his former human self: "Outside, my face came close to the glass again, I saw my mouth, my lips compressed with the effort of understanding the axolotls. I was an axolotl now and I knew instantly that no understanding was possible." One might read this as a tacit acknowledgment of the Other's "difference": the axolotl's consciousness is posited as real and unique, but impenetrable. That inference is soon contradicted, however, when the narrator, speaking as an axolotl, denies that axolotls think differently from humans: "I am an axolotl for good now, and if I think like a man, it's only because every axolotl thinks like a man behind his rosy stone semblance." The only difference acknowledged by the axolotl-narrator is one of location: "He was outside the aquarium, his thinking was a thinking outside the aquarium . . . what used to be his obsession is now an axolotl, foreign to his human life." This reduction of difference to the binary spatial opposition (inside/outside), along with the axolotl-narrator's recourse to psychoanalytic terminology ("his obsession"), seem to support the interpretation of the transmigration as an instance of projective identification. Far from being transformed by communication or exchange with the axolotl, the human subject occupies the latter's place, acting as self-appointed spokesman for the mute creatures. The narrator's "discovery" that all axolotls "think like humans" reveals the limit of the anthropocentric imagination, its incapacity to conceive of a subjectivity radically different from itself.[26]

Only the final sentence of the story, quoted earlier, offers a remote hope of breaching this anthropocentric solipsism: "And in this final solitude to which he no longer comes, I console myself by thinking that perhaps he is going to write a story about us, that, believing he's making up a story, he's going to write all this about axolotls." This narrative *mise en abîme* raises the eerie possibility that it is the axolotl after all, and not the human being, who controls the narration. This is how Marta E. Sánchez views the matter: "[Our] first reaction is to assume that man 'speaks' the axolotl: they are his subject matter and objects. The real case, however, is that the axolotl 'speaks' man. Our traditional notion of 'man as narrator' is undermined."[27] Sánchez infers that the ambiguity over the identity of the narrator (human or axolotl?) in the story reflects a genuine power struggle and reversal of control over the narrative voice. This politically optimistic reading would have the virtue of offering an account, however implausible, of the axolotl's accession to language. Fancying that he is simply "making up a story," the human visitor to the aquarium (the implied author) would in effect operate as unwitting scribe, or ethnostenographer, to the axolotls, who (perhaps telepathically) dictate the text we are reading to the mesmerized author.

Sánchez detects in the axolotl-narrator's final "consolation" an echo of the Hegelian dialectic of master and slave, especially that decisive moment in which the slave challenges the master and affirms his own autonomy. This revolt could also be dubbed the Caliban effect, alluding to the savage in Shakespeare's *The Tempest* who appropriates human language for the purpose of denouncing his masters.[28] But in the scenarios of Hegel and Shakespeare, the slave had language, whereas no one taught the axolotl to speak. As Gayatri Spivak has argued, European intellectuals tend to constitute the colonial subaltern as "the Other of Europe," "the Self's shadow," a pseudosubject who, qua Western construct, "cannot speak."[29] The fantastic suggestion of the axolotls' autonomy that flashes at the end of the story is therefore illusory: the human consciousness which projects an imaginary subjectivity onto the axolotl continues to speak for it to the end. If the axolotl "speaks man," or causes him to speak, it is only insofar as the human subject, first and constitutively, "speaks" the Other—that is, preempts the axolotl and speaks for it.

An analogy from traditional Western ontology may be found in Husserl's transcendental phenomenology. In Husserl's theory of intersubjectivity, the "other" is always an "intentional modification" of the transcendental ego, a noematic object for the subject that construes it; to that extent it remains dependent on that subject.[30] The politically optimistic interpretation (according to which the story's "undermining" of the convention of stable narrative identity is no mere literary device, but the result of the axolotls' genuine bid for autonomy) forgets that the perennial Western ontological hierarchies—subject over object, self over other, human over animal, mind over body—are not overturned, but faithfully replicated, in the story. How little "consoling" it is, then, to suppose that the European author, instead of being always master of language and writing, should for once play scribe to the otherwise mute and physically primitive axolotls—whose only "self-determination" would be the dubious honor of smuggling themselves in as the thematic object, and illusory subject, of discourse.

The anthropocentrism of the human narrator in "Axolotl" has its counterpart in the ethnocentrism of ethnographic discourse, a discourse characterized by Stephen Tyler as "the endorphin of culture, an intertextual practice which, by means of an allegorizing identity, anaesthetizes us to the other's difference."[31] Taken as an allegory of ethnographic practice, "Axolotl" illustrates the occlusion of the Other's difference in at least two crucial ways: historical and communicative. With regard to the first, Johannes Fabian has shown how anthropological discourse typically distances its others (whether construed as "primitive," "savage," or "developing") by relegating them "allochronically" to temporal enclaves within a mythical narrative of Western progress. This amounts to a denial of the other's status as a human "coeval" who intersubjectively shares the same world and time as oneself.[32] The "Other" evoked in Cortázar's story is not the surviving indigenous cultures of Mexico or Central America, but the pre-Columbian Aztecs of half a millennium ago—scarcely candidates for participation in a dialogue of coevals, however sympathetically viewed. It is therefore tempting to see in "Axolotl" an instance of "ethnographic pastoral," which Clifford deems a subgenre of "salvage, or redemptive, ethnography." Drawing on the ethnographic topoi of the "vanishing primitive" and "the end of traditional society," the "allegory of salvage"—the pretense that "the other is lost, disintegrating in time and space, but saved in the text"—is, according to Clifford, "built into the conception and practice of ethnography as a process of writing, specifically of textualization." The scientific and moral authority presumed by salvage ethnography rests on the problematic assumption that "the other society is weak and 'needs' to be represented by an outsider (and that what matters is its past, not its present or future)"—and that the ethnographer is thereby "custodian of an essence, unimpeachable witness to an authenticity."[33]

Also adumbrated in "Axolotl" is an occlusion of the Other in the communicative sense. Just as the narrator speaks ventriloquistically for the axolotls, so the ethnographer speaks preemptively for the natives, interpreting their exotic secrets in the neutral language of science, which presupposes the universality of the translated experience. Even ethnographers with "dialogical" intentions tend to recuperate and manipulate the native's voice, recording and exploiting it as "data" and "evidence" to support their theories and conclusions.[34] Interposed between ethnographer and native is the former's implicit claim to translate otherness, to represent the Other in transparent terms for the true interlocutor, the reader of ethnographies, who nevertheless remains outside the ethnographic encounter. In Clifford's words, "Whatever else an ethnography does, it translates experience into text."[35] This instrumental mediation undermines any possibility of genuine dialogue in Martin Buber's sense—an authentic reciprocity between a self and another, an "I" and a "You"—and ensures that, whatever the pronouns employed by the ethnographer, the reader encounters the native only in the "third person," as an "It," an alien, depersonalized entity.[36] Like the narrator of "Axolotl," the ethnographer speaks *of* the Other but not *to* her, thus precluding the mutuality of real dialogue. In the monologue of traditional ethnography, writes Tyler, "the basso of the ethnographer still speaks for the falsetto of the native. There is not yet in ethnography an effacement of the enunciating subject, of an authorial presence."[37]

Does such an effacement find its literary anticipation in the final sentence of "Axolotl," which makes the narrator's identity at least formally undecidable? This haunting ambiguity is precisely what opens the tale up to allegorical interpretation in the first place, while rendering unanswerable any question as to the story's ultimate meaning or message. We have seen how "Axolotl" recalls many of the essentializing strategies of traditional ethnography, which, as Clifford and Tyler have noted, tended to usurp the voices of real Others while concealing the fabricated nature of its own constructions. May we dismiss the story, then, as a discredited piece of colonialist fiction, whose sympathetic appropriation of the Aztec salamander would have the function of assuaging the guilty conscience of postcolonial Europe, while in effect reinforcing a colonialist ideology of European superiority?[38] It would be easy enough to find "Eurocentric" statements by Cortázar himself to back up an anticolonial criticism of the story. When Evelyn Picón Garfield asked the author in an interview whether the narrator's transmigration into the axolotl was (allegedly like John Keats's empathetic identification with the nightingale of his ode) "for the purpose of experiencing the existence of the other," Cortázar demurred. "What strikes me as terrible in 'Axolotl,'" he replied, "is the total injustice of what occurs, because that man is condemned to the horrible destiny of remaining imprisoned in an axolotl, simply because he is fascinated with the [axolotl's] mysterious life."[39] So much for reaching out to oppressed others!

But my reading of the story is not based on the author's intention or interpretation—and it would be absurd to take the quoted comment as an adequate statement of either—but on the "political unconscious" one sees at work in the story's own narrative logic. What is remarkable about the story, in my view, is the way it both sets up a Eurocentric allegory about encountering the Other, and yet seems to invite an ironic deconstruction of that allegory. The lucid irony with which Cortázar follows his parable through to its grim implications is close to the postmodern spirit of contemporary anthropological critics like Bartra, Clifford, and Tyler.[40] The predicament of the narrator after the transmigration—trapped and incommunicado in the Other's primitive body, "condemned to move lucidly among unconscious creatures"—can stand allegorically for the failure of the Western ethnographic project to know the Other through intense "participant observation" and textual description.

Cortázar evidently wrote "Axolotl" in the early 1950s, in Paris. The painful progress of European decolonization, and its cultural reverberations, would have been fully perceptible to the author, who worked as a part-time translator for UNESCO. His ambiguous existential status as both "insider" and "outsider," a Latin American intellectual who made his home in a European capital, could hardly have left him insensitive to anticolonial struggles under way in Latin America. As late as 1967 he defended, against critics on the Latin American left, the "global" intellectual vision that his European residence supposedly made possible.[41] The "experiential" paradigm (with its "realist" inclination) that was still dominant in ethnography when Cortázar wrote "Axolotl"—the paradigm of intensive contact with the Other in fieldwork, distilled in the authoritative ethnographic account—came soon enough under the withering gaze of postcolonial criticism. Michel Leiris had remarked in 1950 that European ethnographers, however liberal their intentions, had always been "part of the game" of colonialism.[42]

It is not implausible, in this context, to see in "Axolotl" an allegorical adumbration of the impending crisis of authority in ethnographic representation, nor to view the story's narrative ambiguity as a foreshadowing of the antirealist or "modernist"[43] discursive experiments tried out by ethnographers in subsequent decades—experiments that assume the dispersion of univocal authority and the critique of stable identities, whether of natives or ethnographers. In particular, the tale's uncanny ending anticipates the experiments in "polyphonic" or "plural" authorship discussed by Clifford in his survey of ethnographic paradigms. Whatever their generic differences—and my emphasis here on analogies is not meant to blur or deny such differences—both "Axolotl" and those later experiments put monological authorship into question by foregrounding the problematic status of their own discourse, pointedly obliging readers to ask "who is speaking." In Cortázar's story no less than in experimental ethnography, "difference"—the textual production of alterity—is very much an effect of "inventive syncretism," a rhetorical collocation of voices and perspectives once opposed. Clifford acknowledges that "the authoritative stance of 'giving voice' to the other is not fully transcended" in those ethnographic experiments"[44]—nor is that stance fully transcended in Cortázar's "Axolotl." That partial failure does not invalidate the legitimate ethical impulse to know and acknowledge "others" in their historical reality, an urge which motivates many literary and ethnographic allegories of alterity.[45] My allegorical reading of "Axolotl" suggests how difficult it remains to separate the urge to know cultural others from our deeper need to reinvent them—to explore, through fiction, our imaginary relations (affective, libidinal, or ideological) with those others. It offers another lesson as well: that those who would venture to meet the Other in authenticity must first leave behind the security and comfort of their own ontological baggage.

Notes

Dedicated to Fredric Jameson. The present essay is a revised and expanded translation of my "Julio Cortázar y la apropiación del Otro," *INTI: Revista de Literatura Hispánica* 22–23 (1985–1986): 317–326. It grew out of readings and discussions of ethnographic criticism in the mid-1980s with my colleagues Tullio Maranhão, Stephen Tyler, Steven G. Crowell, and Michael M. J. Fischer, to whom I am indebted. My thanks also to Erik Camayd-Freixas and Maarten Van Delden for careful readings and useful suggestions on this revised version.

1. James Clifford discusses the persistent "redemptive" or "salvage" motif of ethnography in "On Ethnographic Allegory," in James Clifford and George E. Marcus, eds., *Writing Culture: The Poetics and Politics of Ethnography* (Berkeley: University of California Press, 1986), 112–115.

2. Tzvetan Todorov, *The Conquest of America: The Question of the Other,* trans. Richard Howard (New York: Harper & Row, 1985), 42. Edward Said studied the ideological functions of Eurocentric representations of a different "Other" in *Orientalism* (New York: Vintage Books, 1979).

3. James Clifford, "On Ethnographic Authority," in his *The Predicament of Culture: Twentieth-Century Literature, Ethnography, and Art* (Cambridge, MA: Harvard University Press, 1988), 22–23.

4. Clifford Geertz, "The Way We Think Now: Toward an Ethnography of Modern Thought," in his *Local Knowledge: Further Essays in Interpretive Anthropology* (New York: Basic Books, 1983), 151.

5. Clifford, "On Ethnographic Authority," 24–31, 37–54, esp. 30–31, 41, 53. One should underscore Clifford's caveats that these four paradigms are "ad hoc inventions and cannot be seen in terms of a systematic analysis of postcolonial representation" (23), and that they are "available to all writers of ethnographic texts, Western and non-Western. None is obsolete, none pure" (53–54). He also notes the persistence of the method of participant observation: "Though variously understood, and now disputed in many quarters, this method remains the chief distinguishing feature of professional anthropology. Its complex subjectivity is routinely reproduced in the

writing and reading of ethnographies" (34). On experimental trends in ethnography—as a response to a perceived "crisis of representation"—see George E. Marcus and Michael M. J. Fischer, *Anthropology as Cultural Critique: An Experimental Moment in the Human Sciences* (Chicago: University of Chicago Press, 1986), 40–44, 68–76.

6. His short story "Axolotl" first appeared in *Buenos Aires Literaria* 3 (1954), and next in *Final del juego* (Mexico City: Los Presentes, 1956). English quotations are from Cortázar's *The End of the Game and Other Stories,* trans. Paul Blackburn (New York: Harper & Row, 1978), 3–9; given the brevity of the text, page numbers are not indicated. I have in a few instances modified Blackburn's translation for nuance or emphasis. The original text is readily available in several editions: I have relied on *Final del juego* (Madrid: Alfaguara, 1982), 151–157.

7. Martin Kreiswirth, "Tell Me a Story: The Narrativist Turn in the Human Sciences," in Martin Kreiswirth and Thomas Carmichael, eds., *Constructive Criticism: The Human Sciences in the Age of Theory* (Toronto: University of Toronto Press, 1995), 61–87.

8. Jean-François Lyotard, *The Postmodern Condition: A Report on Knowledge,* trans. Geoff Bennington and Brian Massumi (Minneapolis: University of Minnesota Press, 1984), 18–37.

9. David Carroll, quoted in Kreiswirth, "Tell Me a Story," 71.

10. Clifford, "On Ethnographic Allegory," 98–100. I shall try to forestall confusion and unintended associations by using "allegory" here to mean a narrative with an extended figurative or analogical meaning, accessible through interpretation.

11. Michel de Certeau, *Heterologies: Discourse on the Other,* trans. Brian Massumi (Minneapolis: University of Minnesota Press, 1986). See, for example, "The Freudian Novel: History and Literature," 17–34, and "History: Science and Fiction," 199–221. Hayden White's work, such as *The Content of the Form: Narrative Discourse and Historical Representation* (Baltimore: Johns Hopkins University Press, 1987), has played a crucial role in illuminating the narrative and rhetorical strategies of historiography.

12. Antonio Benítez-Rojo, *The Repeating Island: The Caribbean and the Postmodern Perspective,* trans. James E. Maraniss (Durham, NC: Duke University Press, 1996), 261.

13. Roger Bartra, *The Cage of Melancholy: Identity and Metamorphosis in the Mexican Character,* trans. Christopher J. Hall (New Brunswick, NJ: Rutgers University Press, 1992), 8–9.

14. Marta Sánchez, "A View from Inside the Fishbowl: Julio Cortázar's 'Axolotl,'" in George E. Slusser, Eric S. Rabkin, and Robert Scholes, eds., *Bridges to Fantasy* (Carbondale: Southern Illinois University Press, 1982), 38–50. See Tzvetan Todorov, *The Fantastic: A Structural Approach to a Literary Genre,* trans. Richard Howard (Ithaca, NY: Cornell University Press, 1975).

15. Sánchez, "Inside the Fishbowl," 41–42. Sánchez sees Cortázar's linguistic experimentation as a radical subversion of the mimetic norms of realism: "Cortázar's fantastic breaks down the security of the [narrating] subject" (40).

16. Cortázar, "Carta a Roberto Fernández Retamar (sobre 'situación del intelectual latinoamericano')," in his *Obra crítica*, vol. 3, ed. Saul Sosnoski (Madrid: Santillana, 1994), 31–43. This letter, published in Cuba in 1967, summarizes the writer's political evolution.

17. Fredric Jameson, *The Political Unconscious: Narrative as a Socially Symbolic Act* (Ithaca, NY: Cornell University Press, 1981). Jameson's postulate of a "political unconscious" at work in narratives lends allegorical force to his Marxist hermeneutics.

18. The axolotl's "symbolic potential" as an exotic metaphor of Mexican identity was noticed by André Breton, who claimed the animal as part of Surrealism's "coat of arms" (Bartra, *Cage of Melancholy*, 8). Cortázar had strong links to Surrealism, and probably knew of Breton's heraldic gambit.

19. Jean-Paul Sartre, "Orphée noir," in Léopold Sédar Senghor, ed., *Anthologie de la nouvelle poésie nègre et malgache de langue française* (Paris: Presses Universitaires de France, 1977), ix–x (my translation).

20. Klein's views are cited in Jean Laplanche and J. B. Pontalis, *Vocabulaire de la psychanalyse* (Paris: Presses Universitaires de France, 1981), 186–187, 318–319.

21. Sánchez, "Inside the Fishbowl," 45.

22. On the visualist bias of Western science, and of anthropology in particular, see Johannes Fabian, *Time and the Other: How Anthropology Makes Its Object* (New York: Columbia University Press, 1983), 105–141; and Stephen A. Tyler, "Ethnography, Intertextuality, and the End of Description," *American Journal of Semiotics* 3, no. 4 (1985): 85.

23. René Descartes, *Discourse on Method and Meditations on First Philosophy*, trans. Donald A. Cress (Indianapolis: Hackett, 1980), 18–19. Michel de Montaigne had drawn a similar mind-body distinction in conjuring his own worst nightmare, one not unlike the plight of Cortázar's narrator: "I can imagine no state so horrible and unbearable as to have my soul alive and afflicted, without means to express itself." *The Complete Essays of Montaigne*, trans. Donald Frame (Stanford, CA: Stanford University Press, 1981), vol. 2, pt.6, 270.

24. Todorov, *Conquest of America*, 163–164.

25. Evelyn Picón Garfield, *Cortázar por Cortázar* (Mexico City: Editora Veracruzana, 1981), 94. When Picón Garfield suggested in an interview with Cortázar that the human narrator of "Axolotl" "is hypnotized by his own idea of what the animals are," the author responded, "Exactly." However, Cortázar's interpretive remarks on "Axolotl" in this interview differ in crucial respects from my interpretation. Concerning the function of the mirror in specular projection, see Jacques Lacan,

"The Mirror Stage as Formative of the Function of the I," in his *Écrits,* trans. Alan Sheridan (New York: Norton, 1977), 1–7.

26. Roger Bartra points out that "the axolotl as metaphor makes reference to a classical anthropological theme, on which Claude Lévi-Strauss has reflected: namely, the 'savage mind,' dealing with the sensitive properties of the animal kingdom as if they were elements of a message" (*Cage of Melancholy,* 8). Lévi-Strauss's *The Savage Mind* (Chicago: University of Chicago Press, 1966) interpreted the thought of primitive tribes as local variants of universal human cognitive functions. Todorov discusses the relation between conferrals of "identity" and assimilation of the Other in *Conquest of America,* 42–44, 247–249. Clifford reminds us that "the ability of the ethnographer to inhabit indigenous minds is always in doubt. Indeed this is a permanent unresolved problem of ethnographic method" ("Ethnographic Authority" 47). In this respect, "Axolotl" reads almost like a parody of interpretive ethnography (Clifford's "hermeneutic" paradigm), whose main injunction, in Geertz's formulation, was "to see things from the native's point of view" (*Local Knowledge,* 56). Geertz argued that since ethnographers cannot get inside the minds of their informants, they must instead be content to construe and interpret their "symbol systems"(70).

27. Sánchez, "Inside the Fishbowl," 48.

28. See Marta E. Sánchez, "Caliban: The New Latin American Protagonist of the Tempest," *Diacritics* (Spring 1976): 54–61; and Wolfgang Bader, "Von der Allegorie zum Kolonialstück: zur produktiven Rezeption von Shakespeares *Tempest* in Europa, Amerika und Afrika," *Poetica* 15, no. 3–4(1983): 247–288.

29. Gayatri Spivak, "Can the Subaltern Speak?," in Bill Ashcroft, Gareth Griffins, and Helen Tiffin, eds., *The Post-Colonial Studies Reader* (London: Routledge, 1995), 24–28.

30. Edmund Husserl, *Cartesian Meditations: An Introduction to Phenomenology,* trans. Dorothy Cairns (The Hague: Martinus Nijhoff, 1973), 114–116. See also Michael Theunissen, *The Other: Studies in the Social Ontology of Husserl, Heidegger, Sartre, and Buber,* trans. Christopher Macann (Cambridge, MA: MIT Press, 1986), 151–152.

31. Tyler, "Ethnography, Intertextuality, and the End of Description," 95.

32. Fabian, *Time and the Other,* 37–104.

33. Clifford, "Ethnographic Allegory," 112–114.

34. Tyler, "Ethnography, Intertextuality, and the End of Description," 93. For a discussion of "Axolotl" as a dialogical experiment, see R. Lane Kauffmann, "The Other in Question: Dialogical Experiments in Montaigne, Kafka, and Cortázar," in Tullio Maranhão, ed., *The Interpretation of Dialogue* (Chicago: University of Chicago Press, 1990), 157–194. The section on Cortázar presents, in dialogue form, some of the arguments elaborated here.

35. Clifford, "Ethnographic Allegory," 115.

36. Martin Buber, *I and Thou,* trans. Walter Kaufmann (New York: Scribner's, 1970). See commentary by Theunissen, *The Other,* 295–300.

37. Tyler, "Ethnography, Intertextuality, and the End of Description," 95.

38. Abdul R. JanMohamed argues, in "The Economy of Manichean Allegory," in Ashcroft et al., eds., *The Post-Colonial Studies Reader,* that the ideological function of much colonialist fiction is to "justify the moral authority of the colonizer and—by positing the inferiority of the native as a metaphysical fact—to mask the pleasure the colonizer derives from that authority" (23).

39. Cortázar, quoted in Picón Garfield, *Cortázar por Cortázar,* 93–94.

40. Neil Larsen suggests, in "Cortázar and Postmodernity: New Interpretive Liabilities"—his contribution to the valuable recent collection, Carlos J. Alonso, ed., *Julio Cortázar: New Readings* (Cambridge: Cambridge University Press, 1998)—that Cortázar's fiction appears dated to postmodern readers, in part because his "thinking remains entrapped in Eurocentrism" (69). Larsen argues that in the story "Apocalypse at Solentiname," Cortázar (with "allegorical cleverness") "thematizes his own 'authenticity' problem" in relation to an "ethnographic fetish"—the reification of cultural stereotypes or "ethnoscapes" in the search for a "true" and "authentic" Latin American culture—from which neither Cortázar's cosmopolitan perspective nor the regionalist one of his critic, José María Arguedas, manages entirely to escape. According to Larsen, the postmodern "ideology of reading" that considers Cortázar passé moves away from the utopian spirit of the "canonical decolonization" associated with the Latin American "boom," suspecting now that such utopianism "concealed a certain overdetermining drive to recolonize Latin America (and the third world generally) through a subtle 'voicing-over' of the 'subaltern'" (66). In one sense, my reading of "Axolotl" could be said to exemplify that suspicion. Yet, in another sense, I believe that, in showing how the story anticipates ethnographic developments that are motivated by a similar critical suspicion, my argument tends to corroborate Carlos J. Alonso's astute observation, in his introduction to the volume cited above, that Cortázar's "shifting and questioning of the ground on which the ideological and philosophical category of identity rests aligns him more closely with the critique of that enterprise of ontological definition which is the hallmark . . . of post-Boom literary production," and with "the philosophical preoccupations that have characterized the poststructuralist period as a whole: the exploration of the subject as problematically inscribed in language and the understanding of literature as a discourse whose existence discloses the precarious foundation of the other discourses with which it shares a social and cultural space" (13–14).

41. Cortázar, "Carta a Fernández Retamar," 35.

42. Michel Leiris, "The Ethnographer Faced with Colonialism," in his *Brisées: Broken Branches,* trans. Lydia Davis (San Francisco: North Point Press, 1989), 113.

43. Sánchez's distinction between the "realist" narrative conventions of the nineteenth-century fantastic mode studied by Todorov, and the nonlinear, "modernist" narrative techniques of "Axolotl" ("Inside the Fishbowl," 40) parallels the distinction drawn by Marcus and Fischer between "realist" and "modernist" ethnographies

(*Anthropology as Cultural Critique,* 14, 25, 67–73). The periodization is of course different: the ethnographic "modernist" experiments began well after the middle of the twentieth century, whereas literary modernism began over half a century earlier.

44. Clifford, "Ethnographic Authority," 51.

45. The ethical dimension of representations of alterity leads one to the work of philosopher Emmanuel Levinas, and to wonder what a "Levinasian" reading of Cortázar's story might yield. The narrator's empathetic transformation would seem at first to be an ethical response to the "face" of the Other. The problem with such an interpretation is the doubtful authenticity of the "other" in "Axolotl." In his *Totality and Infinity,* trans. Alphonso Lingis (Pittsburgh: Duquesne University Press, 1969), Levinas wrote, "The face with which the other turns to me is not reabsorbed in a representation of the face. To hear his destitution which cries out for justice is not to represent an image to oneself, but is to posit oneself as responsible" (215). In "Axolotl," as noted earlier, no authentication through "hearing," no modality beyond the visual, is posited.

9

Jungle Fever

Primitivism in Environmentalism: Rómulo Gallegos's *Canaima* and the Romance of the Jungle

JORGE MARCONE

This essay interprets the "return" to Nature and "primitive" life exemplified by Marcos Vargas, protagonist of Rómulo Gallegos's *Canaima* (1935),[1] within two contexts: the Spanish American romance of the jungle and the primitivist ideology of contemporary environmentalism. Marcos Vargas's "return" to Nature is peculiar within that corpus of Spanish American fiction traditionally referred to as *la novela de la selva* (romance of the jungle). His voyage into the wilderness finds its fuller meaning when compared with other exemplary adventures of this genre. Yet, my main concern will be to read *Canaima* also in dialogue with critiques of contemporary environmentalism. My returning gaze upon this 1935 classic, then, is not merely nostalgic. This turn-of-the-millennium reading does more than rescue the novel's currency. I suggest that it shows *Canaima* as a text which prefigures, but also subverts, current ideological debates on primitivism and development.

An educator who was later president of Venezuela, Gallegos is evidently concerned with development in its many facets. In *Canaima*, he embarks on an intimate struggle to mold the clay of a "natural man," Marcos Vargas, but the character's essential freedom bursts through the ideological molds imposed upon him and tacitly rebels against the author's best civilizing designs. Gallegos's intimate struggle with the contradictions of his own country and culture produces a hero whose "savage" return to Nature and oblique primitivism can be seen as a radical alternative to development, an alternative even to current "green development theory" and its often tendentious programs for "sustainable development."

The Myth of "Primitive Ecological Wisdom" and the Critique of "Sustainable Development"

"Environmentalism" refers to a concern for actively protecting the environment from the harmful effects of human activities, particularly those emanating from industrial society. It is a search for alternatives to industrial societies as much as their cultural product. This concern, as Kay Milton reminds us in *Environmentalism and Cultural Theory,*[2] is usually expressed in a variety of ways: through support for organizations dedicated to environmental protection, government policies aimed at decreasing pollution or conserving wildlife, "green" parties and political reforms of land use, the purchase of goods claimed to be environmentally sensitive, and so on. Such activism, in the long run, is also a search for alternative forms of social organization, as well as of moral and spiritual values about the environment. In this search, however, the environmentalism of industrial society projects the solutions to its problems onto other peoples, while reasserting the conviction that industrialism is responsible for humanity's alienation from nature. Environmentalists frequently point to some non-industrial society as a model for "sustainability." In these cases, "the spiritual ties between some non-industrial peoples and their land are contrasted with the way in which industrial society turns land into a commercial good, whose value is assessed in terms of what it can produce. These kinds of contrast have contributed to the impression, widespread among environmentalists in industrial societies, that non-industrial peoples live in harmony with nature whereas industrial processes work against natural ones. This impression is expressed in the contention that it is industrialism that is the root cause of environmental problems."[3]

The myth of primitive ecological wisdom outlined above is often reinforced by the politics of the environmentalist struggle. Contemporary environmentalism in areas outside industrial society is largely about the conservation of wilderness. Diversity becomes the most highly valued of nature's characteristics, seen as a source of spiritual and economic benefit to humans. The greatest possible variety of life is considered beneficial to the process of evolution, to which human beings and all other life forms are assumed to owe their existence. "Primitive" cultures are believed to be always more inclined than the industrial world to preserve wilderness and not damage the environment.[4] The politics of nature conservation, therefore, usually becomes one with the struggle for the preservation of cultural diversity.

Over the years, environmentalist organizations have grown increasingly involved in indigenous rights movements as long as these peoples are perceived, rightly or not, as defenders of nature.[5]

The problem with this myth of primitive ecological wisdom, as Milton rightly argues, is that it is held dogmatically. It assumes that primitives always embody alternatives which are genuinely benign toward the environment. Since alienation from nature is considered a consequence of industrial development, primitives must be seen as bearers of an essential human condition lost to the modern world. The myth of primitive ecological wisdom is, indeed, a version of the Western myth of the "noble savage." Paradoxically, this celebration of the primitive rarely translates into empowerment for the "primitive" peoples who have been affected by development or other modernization processes. It usually works the opposite way. Milton informs us that primitivism favors those who simply look more genuinely "primitive" or "natural." It also prefers peoples living in ecosystems considered a priority (like the rain forest), and privileges "natives" over immigrants. Recent Amazonian indigenous movements, like the struggle of the Kayapo in Brazil, have shown that, eventually, primitivism will backfire.[6] The celebration of "primitive" difference sooner or later becomes an obstacle for people trying to bring positive changes into their lives by asserting their rights as, for instance, women or citizens.

"Sustainable development" (SD) is currently the largest environmentalist initiative worldwide. It is development theory's response to, or co-optation of, postmodernist and environmentalist critiques of development. According to W. M. Adams, SD was launched in the 1980s and 1990s, following the report of the World Commission on Environment and Development (1987) and the United Nations Conference on Environment and Development in Rio de Janeiro (1992).[7] Since then, SD has clearly been part of the agenda for multilateral relations in the Americas. It was at center stage during the 1994 Presidential Summit of the Americas in Miami. The Miami Summit's Declaration of Principles, for instance, calls for democracy, free trade, and sustainable development as the foundations for prosperity. Furthermore, there is a chapter on SD in the Summit's Plan of Action, focused on sustainable uses of energy, protection of biodiversity, and pollution prevention. The Miami Summit's proposals were further developed two years later in Santa Cruz, Bolivia, at the OAS Summit of the Americas on Sustainable Development. Finally, SD was showcased once more in the 1998 Presidential Summit in Santiago de Chile. Again there was a long process of consultation with

civil society and organizations throughout the hemisphere for drawing up
the Summit's agenda, resulting in SD being ranked next to the Free Trade
Agreement of the Americas. This is no coincidence. In all these documents
SD is presented as an alternative path for regional and global integration, as
well as for promoting democratization.[8]

"Sustainable development" echoes postmodernism's rejection of modernity in favor of a broader pluricultural range of styles, techniques, and voices,
including the rejection of unitary theories of progress and scientific rationality, and the hierarchy between "high" and "low" culture. Although the
influence of such arguments should not be exaggerated, Katy Gardner and
David Lewis suggest that development theory has reached a profound im-
passe, and that this is partly a result of postmodern tendencies. On the one
hand, during the 1980s it was increasingly argued that the age of the "grand
narrative" was largely over. Indeed, "sustainable development" challenges
Western notions of "progress" and "evolution" present in theories of modernization as much as in dependency theory. Gardner and Lewis understand
that the problems of the Third World, the awareness of the colonial roots of
discourses of progress, the primacy of localized experience, and the emphasis on diversity ended up undermining any attempt at theoretical generali-
zation. By the 1990s neither modernization nor dependency theory had survived intact as a viable paradigm for understanding change and
transformation, or global inequality and poverty, once the polarities of the
Cold War became obsolete. More concretely, SD rejects the implications or
consequences of policies of industrialization, such as major changes in modes
of production, capital expansion, large investments in technology, major
infrastructure projects, urbanization, and consumerism. It also acknowledges the failure of "trickle-down economics" to eradicate poverty, illiteracy, and marginality, as much as it recognizes that any radical change imposed from above is presently unfeasible.

As an alternative, SD advocates more participation in policy-making and
implementation processes. "Participation" means, in this context, the greater
involvement of "beneficiaries" in deciding the type of development projects they need, and how they are run. "Development project," in turn, means
the intervention aimed at promoting social change, usually by, or with the
support of, an outside agency for a finite period. The ultimate goal is, of
course, to replace colonialism, centralization, or dependency with policies
that empower the people to solve their problems or achieve positive changes

in their lives by asserting their rights. In this context, "sustainability" means the desire by planners and agencies to avoid creating projects whose success depends on continued support, as much as it means the desire to ensure renewal of natural resources. In the same manner, SD expects to include the cultural differences of its "beneficiaries," which requires questioning the authority implicit in oppositions such as "primitive/civilized." Indeed, SD has come to recognize that indigenous or local knowledge is not an obstacle to development, but a source for it.

Sustainable development, however, is not a concept from which clear policies have been derived. On the contrary, it should be understood as a site for open discussions on development alternatives that carry some of the most problematic features of development. Like previous development models, it can be seen as an outcome of capitalism's current expansion and crisis, and as a result of new scientific advances and social theories.[9] SD has been accused, for instance, of being simply a "greening" of global capitalism.[10] In the Americas, the regional free-trade agenda has associated itself with the sustainable development movement, as the last two OAS Presidential Summits have shown. Prospecting for biotechnology industries, for instance, has become one of the fastest-growing businesses in Latin America. The incorporation of indigenous or local knowledge is no less problematic. First, it does not make SD any less technocentrist or supportive of a utilitarian view of science.[11] Second, the recording, storage, and circulation of indigenous knowledge on sustainable practices have already raised concerns regarding ownership and copyright issues. Although SD challenges the hierarchy between the "civilized" and the "primitive," it does not subvert the authority of the opposition itself, nor the relationship of power between "primitive" peoples and the primitivist subject who celebrates them. The celebration of the local and/or the indigenous may presuppose the otherness of peoples being classified as such, even though it is very likely that these peoples have already lived in contact with industrial societies or gone through at least two waves of development projects. Another risk in the celebration of local and/or indigenous cultures is that it implies that such peoples are "legitimate" inhabitants with greater rights than newcomers, much as we protect "native" species of a given ecosystem from "foreign" ones. All of these concerns associated with SD point to the fact that, after all, it is another initiative predicated by Europe, the United States, and international agencies as a self-serving solution for the rest of the world.

Marcos Vargas's primitivism in *Canaima* takes ecological primitivism in contemporary environmentalism to its extreme implications. Initially, Vargas's primitivism seems to be moving along with contemporary environmentalism. It first denounces the annihilation of indigenous cultures by the modernization process taking place in the Venezuelan Guayana. Second, Vargas's primitivism increasingly appears to be a sure path toward the foundation of a nationalistic development alternative rooted in the region's nature and cultures. Eventually, however, Vargas's primitivism evolves into a critique of modernity and development, even more radical than those of contemporary environmentalism and sustainable development. We can recognize, in Marcos Vargas's journey into the jungle, environmentalism's fascination with indigenous cultures and their respect for nature as the foundation of their wisdom. We can also recognize throughout *Canaima* the language of the opposition "primitive/civilized" that prefers the "native" to the "immigrant" and the "acculturated." Nevertheless, the text eventually loses its utopian quality, and replaces it with a primitivism no longer concerned with reversing humanity's alienation from nature but driven by a desire for alienation from humanity.

The idea of "sustainable development" shows some affinity with the discourses of modernity and nature in the *novela de la tierra* and the *novela de la selva*. The former proposed a development alternative that ended up failing in the latter: the aspiration to root an autochthonous version of modernity in Latin American nature and in the values of the peoples who populated its wilderness.[12] Arguably, the *novela de la selva*, or at least Marcos Vargas in *Canaima*, becomes a rejection of the entire paradigm; from a search for development alternatives to an incursion into "alternatives to development." The utopia of a modern Latin America, free from the problems created by the processes of modernization, is put on hold. The romances of the jungle face the eternal dilemma of how to insert the jungle and its "primitive" peoples into a cosmopolitan and/or national modernity. However, as we will follow in Gallegos's *Canaima*, these books also voice a desire to break with the Western world and search for an alternative lifestyle that will re-create the conditions before the conquest of America. In the Spanish American romance of the jungle, the failure of the protagonist's "return" to Nature is also the failure of the possibility of an alternative modernization. That is, as soon as the hero's "return" appears to be successful, it proves incompatible with the search for an alternative modernity.

The "Return" to Nature and the Spanish American Romance of the Jungle

There are only a few protagonists in the Spanish American romance of the jungle who, like Marcos Vargas, intentionally disappear into the forest. In fact, the opposite is more common: usually the protagonists are successful in resisting the temptation to remain in the forest, and even return to the city to enjoy the success derived from writing about their adventure. The objective of the "return" to Nature is actually the return home, not the journey itself. Marcos Vargas, like Saúl Zuratas ("Mascarita") in Mario Vargas Llosa's *El hablador* (1987; *The Storyteller*),[13] unexpectedly turns away from unique opportunities for securing his personal and family financial situation. Zuratas rejects a fellowship that would allow him to study in France and earn a graduate degree in anthropology. He disappears for decades until the novel's narrator believes that he has found him living among the Machiguenga Indians in the Peruvian Amazon, as one of their last storytellers. Vargas, on the other hand, always drawn toward the jungle, gives up the transportation business that his mentor, Manuel Ladera, had passed on to him, in order to pursue a life of adventure in the forests of the Orinoco River. After Manuel Ladera's death at the hands of the criminal Cholo Parima, Vargas again rejects the opportunity, and responsibility, of becoming manager of Ladera's properties, despite the fact that this decision jeopardizes the survival of Ladera's family. Once more, after having successfully managed José Vellorini's rubber-tapping grove for a year, Vargas turns down a permanent position that would have brought him, and his mother, a much-needed fortune. Throughout the years preceding their final and surprising move, both Saúl Zuratas and Marcos Vargas learn indigenous languages and the secrets of the forest from their informants. Vargas, for instance, learns how to roam for days in the forest without a guide. One night, inexplicably, he runs madly through the forest during a storm, holding in his arms a little monkey he had rescued from drowning in a flood. Another afternoon, he sits for hours by the trees near a river, until his companions see only a tree in the same place where Marcos is sitting. Finally, neither Marcos nor Saúl ever returns to civilization; both join indigenous tribes.

The motivation for such a move in *Canaima* is not clear, however. It is quite unexpected in a novel where Gallegos seems to be setting up his character as the Man of Action with a vision of progress that could eventually lead Guayana into modernity. Although troubled by his past, Marcos Vargas is not running away from justice, unlike another infamous character of the Spanish American romance of the jungle, Arturo Cova, the protagonist of Colombian José Eustasio Rivera's *La vorágine* (1924; *The Vortex*).[14] In fact, justice had exonerated Vargas of any criminal responsibility in the death of Cholo Parima, the dark character who killed Vargas's older brother as well as his mentor and partner Manuel Ladera. Also unlike Cova, Vargas does not get lost in the jungle while trying to rescue his kidnapped fiancée. On the contrary, in the provincial city of Upata, Vargas leaves behind Aracelis Vellorini, Ladera's goddaughter, and his passport to the provincial upper class of the Venezuelan Guyana.

Unlike the anonymous protagonist of *Los pasos perdidos* (1953; *The Lost Steps*),[15] by the Cuban Alejo Carpentier, Marcos Vargas is not attempting to "regenerate" himself, through contact with the wilderness, from a postwar disillusionment with Western civilization. Guayana has been generous to Vargas, more generous than Ciudad Bolívar, the Orinoco River port where he spent his childhood. The jungle, too, is generous to Vargas. While administering José Vellorini's latex farm, Vargas matches his improvement of the rubber tappers' subhuman working and living conditions, with influence over the Indians (who provide him with the necessary knowledge of the forest) and a small fortune in rubber. Vargas's success in the *caucherías,* or rubber-tapping farms, contrasts with the misfortunes of other such entrepreneurs in the short stories of the Uruguayan Horacio Quiroga, set in Misiones, a tropical province of northern Argentina.[16] Quiroga's stories are populated by foreigners who have embarked on unwise industrial ventures and by pioneers dedicated to small-scale agriculture. His characters are always threatened by the wilderness and isolation that surround them.

Marcos Vargas does not need to run away from civilization. He does not need to look in the jungle for financial opportunities or personal self-fulfillment. In fact, by entering the jungle, Vargas turns down the responsibility of becoming the leader that his mentor, Manuel Ladera, would have liked him to become. Ladera saw in Marcos the potential leader who would take Guayana into modernity by means of a nationalistic capitalism. Ladera's understanding of progress called for a focus on agricultural development that would reestablish the population's ties with the land. This development alternative is opposed, on the one hand, to the underdevelopment of the Ardavines and other caudillos (local strongmen), as well as to the ambiguous "creolization" and progress brought by foreign investors such as the Vellorinis. Marcos Vargas is not looking among the Indians for the spiritual

balance lacking in modern society, nor does he ever find it. Indeed, his ex-
pectations of the jungle are always about adventure, danger, and survival.
Such was the allure in the stories told by the *purgueros* (rubber tappers)
coming back from the jungle, which Vargas heard in his native Ciudad Bolívar.
It was in Ciudad Bolívar that he first met Ponchopire, the indigenous cacique who later in the novel welcomes Marcos to live among his tribe.

Despite his fascination with Ponchopire's people, Marcos never becomes
a full member of the tribe. Meanwhile, in *The Storyteller*, Saúl Zuratas, nicknamed Mascarita, becomes the last of the Machiguenga *habladores*, the institution that had been holding together this nation of seminomadic peoples
through times of adversity. Once in this position, however, Mascarita manages to impose his own primitivist and environmentalist agenda onto the
storyteller's function. While the Machiguenga are adapting to, and strug-
gling with, the processes of modernization and cultural contact taking place
in the Peruvian Amazon, Mascarita preaches resistance to the white outsid-
ers' influence, especially the missionaries', and demands secrecy about his
existence. Marcos holds some messianic aspirations. After experiencing firsthand the exploitation and cultural degradation to which white "civilized"
people had subjected the Indians, he finally entertains the idea of becoming
the leader who would take "his" people into a liberating modernity. As with
his previous promise of leadership, however, Vargas runs away from this
one. Vargas's liberating modernity and Zuratas's "archaic utopia" (as Mario
Vargas Llosa has called similar projects on other occasions) propose alternative futures for indigenous populations confronted with the expansion
and processes of modernization. Both proposals—that of a mentored adaptation to modernity and that of a postmodern cultural resistance to modernity—are challenged not only by the strength of the modernizing process
but also by processes of transculturation, hybridization, and globalization
already at work in the region. Although each is looking for a solution to the
"modern/primitive" dichotomy, both positions are actually blind to the collapse of such categories. The collapse is registered in the texts, but it is understood by neither the protagonists nor the narrators.

Marcos Vargas's "Return" to Nature and Contemporary Environmentalism

Although Marcos Vargas's "return" to Nature has its own peculiarities in
relation to the *novela de la selva*, overall it illustrates the struggle of two

different forces affecting the lives of individual characters as well as the social configuration of Amazonia. I will refer to the first of these forces as the
"return" to Nature and to the second as "jungle fever" (or, as the Spanish
American romance of the jungle would have it, *el mal de la selva*).

The first concept refers to the attempt, by many characters in the *novela
de la selva* and in the Spanish American regional novel overall, to root modernization in the autochthonous cultures and nature, instead of following
Western, cosmopolitan, and urban models. The "return" to Nature, therefore, is necessary for building a Latin American version of modernity that
balances the capitalist drive for profit with moral values learned in the interaction with nature, while integrating modern science and technology with
the arcane mysteries of the forest and its peoples. The Spanish American
regional novel is a modern response to the experience of modernity as lived
out in rural areas, but especially, too, as experienced in the Latin American
city. Surely, the desire to live and work in the Amazonian frontier originates
in the frustration with urban life and/or the failure of "civilization" to ac-
commodate individual or collective self-fulfillment projects.

Thus, the "return" to Nature in regional and jungle novels shares many
ideologemes with contemporary environmentalism. It posits a search for
alternative forms of social organization and new moral and spiritual values.
It shares SD's aspiration to imagine environmentally sound alternatives for
economic growth. Each responds in its own time to the expansion and crisis
of capitalism, the appeal of new scientific and technological advances, and
the influence of new social theories. The Spanish American regional novel is
also inclined toward the more genuinely "primitive"- or "natural"-looking
peoples in ecosystems considered a priority (e.g., the pampa, the llano, the
Andes), and to "natives" over immigrants or foreigners (e.g., Marcos Vargas,
born in Guayana, over the Vellorini brothers and other immigrants from
Caracas). Despite the conviction that global capitalism, urbanism, and industrialism are responsible for humanity's alienation from nature, global
poverty, and inequality, these novels ironically illustrate that the utopian
celebration of "primitive" wisdom rarely translates into empowerment for
the peoples whose cultures are being celebrated. Yet, similarities aside, the
novela de la selva, and particularly *Canaima,* will end up taking the "return"
to Nature far beyond the primitivism in contemporary environmentalism.

"Jungle fever" (*el mal de la selva*) refers to the alleged force that subverts
and/or sabotages modernity in general, and particularly the indispensable
"return" to Nature sought by development alternatives. In the *novela de la*

selva this harmonious "return" fails miserably as it succumbs to the Amazonian wilderness. The protagonist of *The Lost Steps,* in spite of having found in the jungle the inspiration for a musical score that would recapture the origins of music, abandons the forest because he needs more paper to continue his work. When he attempts to return to the forest, he can no longer find his way back, because the rising river has flooded every familiar landmark. This hostility of Nature toward those who want to reintegrate is common in other fictions. Many characters die in the forest or get lost and are "devoured" by the jungle. Although in very different circumstances, Arturo Cova in *The Vortex,* Marcos Vargas, and Saúl Zuratas are all "possessed" by the jungle. They become victims of *el mal de la selva,* the jungle madness that drives men into the woods, corrupts women, and interferes with, or diverts from, the building of an alternative utopia. The jungle is presented as an ecologically hostile "Green Hell," but arguably this hostility defends the forest: first, from civilization's violence upon nature and, more interestingly, from modernity's desires and fantasies about Nature.

"The adventurers' Guayana, unfinished world"—*Canaima* begins with a panoramic view of the Venezuelan Guayana as a region in a state of barbarism. The processes of modernization that had taken place in other parts of the country have not been finished in this region. On the other hand, the indigenous peoples have fallen into a barbaric state as a consequence of their exploitation by the whites. They have become degenerated or acculturated races that are only a shadow of their own past, even exiles in their own lands. Underlying the narrator's account of what has happened in Guayana is the Western opposition between "savage" and "civilized." While the fascination with "primitive" life has taken hold, the arrival of modernity is not under discussion in the novel, at least initially. As Anthony Pagden explains with reference to Diderot: "The savage, placeless and also timeless, may be, then, the only truly happy man. But Diderot recognized that civil society is a state that awaits us all. In the end, the kind of happiness the savage enjoys is simply not our human lot. But, or so Diderot seems to imply, no real life savage ever did resist the civilizing process."[17]

Thus, if we agree with Diderot that all civilized peoples have been savages and, if left to their natural impulses, all savage peoples are destined to become civilized, then we might conclude that bringing Guayana into civilization may be a very unwise thing to do. Nevertheless, in *Canaima* civilization is needed precisely in order to protect indigenous peoples from further exploitation and cultural degeneration. This argument, Pagden explains, was already formulated in Diderot's reflections about "savages" in America: "If nearly three hundred years after their 'discovery' the Indians of America remained in a state of near imbecility—and Diderot had largely been persuaded by de Pauw that they had done so—then this was because of the tyrannies to which they had been subjected since their lands were invaded."[18]

I have resorted to Pagden's reading of Diderot because it helps to illuminate the opposition "savage/civilized" in a point that has been obscured in Latin American intellectual primitivism. Although interchangeable in everyday language, "primitive" and "savage" are not interchangeable with "barbarian" in Diderot, nor in *Canaima*:

> There, in effect, were those Guaraúnos in full barbarism, if not totally savage, like all Venezuelan natives who under the regime of the *encomienda* or the Mission could not but lose the vigor and freshness of the genuine condition, subjected like unconscious *braceros* to a work that was alien to their needs, whose human meaning could not be made to reach them, and whose technique, when there was one, was never given them. (143)

In Diderot's terms, the barbaric conditions in Guayana have been created by traveler/colonists seeking to fulfill ambitions for which their native land offered no opportunities. By traveling through space for five hundred years, these colonists, in Diderot's view, have gone backward in time from civility to savagery. But this "corrupted natural man" is not the free and innocent "savage" who inhabits the land. This gold-thirsty "domestic tiger who has returned to the jungle" is for Diderot the "new barbarian."[19]

In light of this distinction among the "savage," the "barbarian," and the "civilized," one can argue that Latin American intellectual primitivism, while posing as "the returning gaze of the colonized" (see the Introduction to this volume), in fact attempts to erase the stigma of barbarism from modern Latin America. Even when called "savage" or "primitive," the Spanish and Portuguese colonial societies, as well as later the Latin American national states, have been charged with that barbarism, or degeneration of civilization which, among other things, has corrupted the American "savage" who captured the imagination of the West. Primitivism in Rivera, Gallegos, and Vargas Llosa conforms to Diderot's fascination with the "savage," his condemnation of the "new barbarian," and the acceptance of civilization.

Gallegos rearticulates an argument that Rivera put forth in *The Vortex*, and that Vargas Llosa in turn recasts in *The Storyteller* and elsewhere. All three authors seem to agree that the victimization of indigenous peoples is not a result of modernity but rather of its lack. By "modernity," in this case, I mean the normalizing practices of the modern state: the effort to produce and reproduce disciplined citizens and governable subjects. Certainly, it is not the underdevelopment of the "primitive" that justifies the struggle for civilization. After all, one can argue with Michael Watts that the desire for accumulation, central to modern society, has meaning only in a world where "primitive economies" have no desire of their own: "the modern (and developed) require the non-modern (and underdeveloped)."[20] It is the lawless, barbaric, and even unnatural conditions into which Guayana has fallen that justify and legitimize the battle for modernity in the Orinoco Valley.

In the course of the first twelve chapters of *Canaima,* Gallegos struggles to bring Marcos Vargas from his barbarian background in the streets of Ciudad Bolívar, and his obsession with the jungle, to a kind of midway station between the savagery of the Guayanan adventurer and the civility of Manuel Ladera or his intellectual friend, Gabriel Ureña. It is Ureña, Vargas's friend from Caracas, who understands Vargas's preference for the jungle and rejection of opportunities. He reprehends him in this manner toward the end of the novel:

> With a few words that you told me in Upata upon your return from Guarampín [where Vargas had encountered the worst and most "barbaric" capitalism], I understood that you had found the full measure of yourself and a glimmer of the work to which you should be devoted. You have witnessed iniquity and even suffered it upon your own self; you have the generous impulse necessary to dedicate yourself to combating it; you can (let me put it this way) pick up the message of the voice that clamors in the desert; and all you are missing is the intellectual training. Read a bit. Cultivate yourself. Civilize that barbaric force within you. Study the problems of this land and take on that disposition which is your duty to take. When life gives talents—and you have them, I repeat—it also gives responsibilities along with them. This people expect everything from one man, the Virile Man, as they say today, and you, why not?, you can be that Messiah. (170–171)

Despite this admonition, Marcos Vargas again refuses to take responsibility in the development of Guayana, and after a couple of days he disappears again into the jungle. By the end of the novel, Guayana is not only the "unfinished" but also the "frustrated" world. It has become even poorer and more miserable than at the beginning: its natural resources are exhausted, the economy is in ruins, and the region is still isolated from the rest of the country. At the end, the only thing left is the promise of another messianic figure: the son Marcos had in the jungle with Aymara, his partner in Ponchopire's tribe.

Marcos Vargas's "return" to Nature has shown its true face as "jungle fever." In a way, his journey into the wild was a return home, since that is the life of adventure and violence he had dreamed of for years. Apparently, no opportunities or responsibilities were stronger than the desires and fantasies he nurtured on the piers of Ciudad Bolívar. It would be a mistake, however, to think that Vargas has become another victim of the wrong environment. His adventurous life in search of a fortune quickly earned and spent is not simply a case of Guayana's barbarism. There is something more about Vargas's journey. Something that the opposition "savage/civilized" cannot explicitly formulate, but that links *Canaima* to primitivism in modern art.[21] On the banks of the Guarampín River, Vargas met the mysterious Count Giaffaro, who can speak only in a manner reminiscent of avant-garde poetry: "already that mind had lost the habit of discursive thought, acquiring in turn that of submersion into integral intuitions which could not be expressed, except at best, as Indians did, with a single word amid spaces of silence which surround it with an aura of meanings that are merely suggested" (124).

Marcos Vargas's adventurous life is a modern reaction to the barbarism of Guayana as much as to the development alternatives for which the narrator tries unsuccessfully to recruit him. His decision to remain in the jungle is motivated by a specific disillusionment with the "lies" of civilization, the lifestyle of the bourgeoisie, and capitalism's injustices: "But now he understood that the Ardavines were not the only evil, that that whole world was rotten with iniquity, even himself, who in the Guarampín enterprise had substituted the Cuyubini's whip for the easy treatment that produced more while costing less" (135). His "return" to Nature, however, goes beyond a dissatisfaction with the complexities of civilization, or the belief that a more natural and elementary life would offer greater freedom and moral plenitude. Instead of countering humanity's alienation from nature, his "return" actively pursues the alienation from humanity:

> The obsession with observing it at every moment, unable to take his eyes off the invariable spectacle of one tree and another, all identical,

all towering, all motionless, all silent! . . . The obsession with penetrating through them, wandering like an elf, slowly, silently, as one who grows. Of leaving completely, from among men and beyond himself, until losing all memory that he was once a man, and standing under the sunlight that pours from the cauldron where the life that is to replace the fallen giant boils. . . . And one day, abandoning himself to the allure of the green abyss, he disappeared into the forest, recklessly. (136–137)

The opportunity to return to the universal essence of his humanity takes him beyond the human condition he has always known:

The deepest roots of his being dug into the tempestuous soil; the clash of bloods inside his veins was still a storm; the innermost essence of his spirit participated in the nature of the irascible elements, and amid the awesome spectacle the satanic earth now offered him, he found himself, a cosmic man, devoid of history, reintegrated into the initial step at the edge of the creational abyss. (151)

In *Canaima,* Marcos Vargas's desertion from the ranks of development and environmentalism is not a case of desperate fall into barbarism, as ideologues would have us believe. His "jungle fever" is simply a modern subject's response to the processes of modernization and to development policies. Some features of his response, or the conditions that elicit it, are comparable to current postdevelopment positions. Certainly, I am not arguing that Vargas anticipates postdevelopment as it has been proposed in current postmodern and/or poststructural critiques of development. But I do not hesitate to recognize his "jungle fever" as a postdevelopment position. Indeed, Vargas's attitude rejects the alleged "natural" need to develop. The very limitations of his options, though, invite us to consider the possibility of a more radical democratization of modernization processes, unless we are willing to accept that there are no alternatives to development.

Notes

1. Rómulo Gallegos, *Canaima* (1935; Madrid: Archivos, 1991). All quotations will refer to this edition. Translations are by Erik Camayd-Freixas.

2. Kay Milton, *Environmentalism and Cultural Theory. Exploring the Role of Anthropology in Environmental Discourse* (London: Routledge, 1996).

3. Ibid., 29.

4. See Milton, *Environmentalism*. See also Katy Gardner and David Lewis, *Anthropology, Development and the Post-Modern Challenge* (London: Pluto Press, 1996).

5. See Susanna Hecht and Alexander Cockburn, *The Fate of the Forest: Developers, Destroyers and Defenders of the Amazon* (London: Verso, 1990).

6. See *Amazon Journal,* dir. Geoffrey O'Connor New York: Realis Pictures, 1995. Videocassette.

7. W. M. Adams, "Green Development Theory: Environmentalism and Sustainable Development," in Jonathan Crush, ed., *Power of Development* (London: Routledge, 1995), 87–99.

8. See Organización de Estados Americanos, *Declaración de principios* and *Plan de acción* (Miami: Cumbre de las Américas, 1994), www.americasnet.net/indexdocs/spa/1505.html & 719.html; *Proyecto de declaración de Santa Cruz de la Sierra* and *Proyecto de plan de acción para el desarrollo sostenible de las Américas* Santa Cruz, Bolivia: Summit of the Americas on Sustainable Development, November 26, 1996, http://environment.harvard.edu/cumbre/eng/fdec-es.html & pl-so000.html, Harvard Environmental Resources On-Line Archive.

9. Michael Cowen and Robert Shenton, "The Invention of Development," in Crush, *Power of Development,* 27–43.

10. Arturo Escobar, "Imagining a Post-Development Era," in Crush, *Power of Development,* 211–227.

11. See Adams, "Green Development Theory."

12. Carlos Alonso, *The Spanish American Regional Novel: Modernity and Autochthony* (Cambridge: Cambridge University Press, 1990).

13. Mario Vargas Llosa, *El hablador* (Barcelona: Seix Barral, 1987).

14. José Eustasio Rivera, *La vorágine* (1924), ed. Monserrat Ordóñez (Madrid: Cátedra, 1990).

15. Alejo Carpentier, *Los pasos perdidos* (1953), ed. Roberto González Echevarría (Madrid: Cátedra, 1985).

16. Horacio Quiroga, *Cuentos, 1917–1935* (Madrid: Cátedra, 1991).

17. Anthony Pagden, *European Encounters with the New World* (New Haven, CT: Yale University Press, 1994), 153.

18. Ibid.

19. Ibid., 158–161.

20. Michael Watts, "'A New Deal of Emotions': Theory and Practice and the Crisis of Development," in Crush, *Power of Development,* 44–62; 61.

21. See James McFarlane, "The Mind of Modernism," in Malcolm Bradbury and James McFarlane, eds., *Modernism, 1890–1930* (New York: Penguin, 1978), 71–93.

10

Primitivism and Cultural Production

Future's Memory: Native Peoples' Voices in Latin American Society

IVETE LARA CAMARGOS WALTY

In this time of postmodernism, postcolonialism, and multiculturalism, it is necessary to analyze the role of native peoples in the constitution of Latin American societies. Despite the process of decimation and their survival only as marginalized social segments, native peoples have traversed literature and history, making it possible for an alternative sociopolitical model to persist. Drawing from the book *Histórias de maloca antigamente* (Old-Time Meetinghouse Stories) by the Brazilian Indian Pichuvy Cinta Larga, a native of the state of Rondônia, this essay aims to reflect on native peoples' cultural production, which is taken as primitive. *Histórias de maloca antigamente* is made up of oral stories, in broken Portuguese, transcribed from tape recordings. In this book, an illiterate man tells the story of his people so that it can be published and read in the society in which he lives: white man's society.

The central issue is thus the written/oral dichotomy, which in turn reproduces other dichotomies arising from the difference in relationships mediated by violence—between indigenous and so-called civilized society, self and other, colonizer and colonized—even though these dichotomies have come to be relativized. Bearing in mind the relationship between written and oral language, this essay intends to investigate the construction of Pichuvy's narrative and the worldview it expresses, in order to reflect on the writer's place in the context of his traversing different cultures, times, and spaces.

Pichuvy's words show this traversing movement when he explicitly defines the function of storytelling as one of cultural resistance, of maintaining a link between epochs and generations: "I'm alive, I tell many story. This I do is what my people did, my people told stories. And many times I said that Indians have to remember what it was like in the past, such as the old told us, and old people told us many stories. That's why I tell many story so."[1]

That function of cultural resistance is also expressed by another Brazilian Indian, Ailton Krenac: "Western intellectuals write books, make films, give lectures, teach at universities. In our indigenous tradition, an intellectual does not have so many institutional responsibilities, and so diverse. But (s)he has a permanent responsibility, which is to be among his/her people, narrating in his/her story, with his/her group, family, and clan, the permanent meaning of that cultural heritage."[2] Krenac adequately voices his concern about the intellectual's place in Latin American society, comparing him/her with the Indian who would play a similar role in an indigenous society.

Like Krenac, I am deeply concerned with that issue and have focused on it in my Ph.D. dissertation, "Narrative and Social Imaginary,"[3] which analyzes Pichuvy Cinta Larga's book. Pichuvy is one of those Indian "intellectuals" who has the function of telling his people their stories, the stories of the Cinta Larga people in the northern Brazilian state of Rondônia. Made up of two parts, *Histórias de maloca antigamente* presents stories that take place before and after the Indians' contact with the white colonizer, thus preserving the remains of one culture in the midst of another.

Words create what they name. Pichuvy Cinta Larga's text actualizes the cosmogonic myth in that it repeats the act of creation through words. Like Ngurá, his god, who makes things appear through words, Pichuvy molds a world through the spoken word. Thanks to memory, tradition and creation are united. On an island where orality is preserved as a space of exchange, experience and memory transmission, like knowledge inscribed on a body, Pichuvy takes his people's word and makes it individual in order to allow it to survive collectively. Under the threat of the written word—a metaphor for a different society, colonizing and ethnocidal—it is necessary to preserve the oral word, and the only way to do this, paradoxically, is through writing, crystallizing speech and making it a prisoner of the written code. Being powerless in his illiteracy, and in an attempt to make his word survive, Pichuvy hands his word to those who had previously silenced it.

In a study of illiterate peoples' biographies, Philippe Lejeune keenly noticed that when you *give* the word to those who are voiceless, you are actually *taking* their word.[4] Lejeune points to the ambiguity present in all ethnological attempts: the act that anchors and preserves an "oral" society's memory is the very act that alienates and reifies it. Paul Zumthor shows the link between orality and the collective constitution of medieval society, in which communication took place *in praesentia.*[5] In that context the interpreter assumed the role of an author; there was no concept of copyright. Dialogue took place even if only one party had the floor. For Zumthor, the supremacy of phonetic writing, mainly since the introduction of the printing press, may be taken as a sign of a change involving man's detachment from himself and from his body. Public life's theatricality declines, spaces turn private, and a rift grows between the visual/tactile sensorial registers and life's perception, as well as between science and the arts. Cultural activities become more diversified in the functions they fulfill, the subjects who practice them, and the public they target. Division of labor takes place, and positions become more specialized. The idea of the text's fixedness comes into being. There is a consolidation of the notion of author linked to the idea of authority, owner of a text, owner of knowledge. This is why change, variation, permanent reconsideration of old themes, the recourse to the authority of a nonwritten tradition, and the indisputable predominance of oral communication are all restricted to the poor, to marginalized areas linked nowadays to popular culture (for "high" culture these same traits have become intolerable).

Like other Brazilian indigenous peoples, the Cinta Larga can be located in that marginal space where orality is alive and active. One wonders, then, whether orality and primitivism could exist side by side in a space threatened by extinction. In this sense, the first part of Pichuvy's text is worth examining, in order to see how orality markers appear in the construction of a mythical narrative where worldview is implicit. This contrasts with the second part of the book, which deals with the time after the appearance of the white man. Language differences between the two parts are worth noting.

Word in Action

In the first part of Pichuvy's book, paratactically constructed stories end and start again, like the cycle of life. The most frequently used verbs are to be born, to germinate, to begin, to go out, to call, to name, to talk, to speak, to do, to create, to hatch, to walk, to live, to know, to appear, to turn (in the sense of becoming), to copulate. The verb "to make" and its correlates become relevant. The ideas of creation, fecundation, transformation, and living predominate. Everything is action. Death, when it occurs, is reversible. Animals, plants, and Indians die but are reborn: *Todo o tempo tinha arco com flechinha pra, quando osso virar índio, matar onça* (At all times there was bow with wee arrows ready to kill jaguars at the moment when bones turned into Indians) (60).

The book's second part deals mainly with sterility. Death leads to an irreversible apocalypse, to total extermination; never to renewing chaos. The verbs often used there include to kill, to catch a cold, to sneeze, to cry, to complain, to shoot arrows, to cut, to burn, to spoil, to finish, to lose, to overturn, to divide, to restrict. Stories have an end, as people come to an end: *Aí morreu morreu morreu morreu morreu morreu, aí cabou* (And there Indian died died died died died died, there it was all over) (106).

The characters/agents of the first part are supernatural elements, animals, plants, and men. They all have the word. This can be seen in the constant use of dialogue signaled by frequent verbs of saying: —*É verdade!—falou. É verdade! Acredita comigo! É verdade!—ele falou. Vocês credita que eu fala?—primo falou* ("It's true!" he said. "It's true! Believe me! It's true!" he said. "You don't believe what I say?" cousin said) (37–38).

The ideas of sharing and collective life prevail. Possessive pronouns, for example, are few. These are used only when referring to family members—my grandpa, my father, my mother, my brother—or when it is necessary to assert his people's identity—my language, our land. The idea of property is present only in relation to the land; this, however, is collectively owned—"our" land, never "my" land.

The book's second part is predominantly narrative. There are fewer dialogues and the only characters are men, both white and Indian. Are they subjects or objects of the historical process? The collective subject of the first part gives way to an individual subject in the second. The subject named in terms of species is thus replaced by one named in terms of individuality. The interactive worldview of the first part becomes atomized, signaling a loss of referentiality. Sharing gives way to alienation and lack of information.

Given that the narrator is the same before and after the white man's arrival, the question arises of why there is such a change from one part of the book to the other. The same narrator could make differing statements, but the time in which those statements are produced could not be different. It is worth remembering, however, that mythical narrative suspends profane time and focuses on primordial time, *ab origine.* Thus, even if it is outside its own cultural space, Pichuvy's narrative pluralizes the subject because his word is inhabited by voices coming from different times and spaces. Besides, it is not a single narrator, but a divided one, pluralized in his search for identity.

As narrator, Pichuvy traverses both spaces, along a blurred line between the word of creation and the word of destruction, between the word of fertility—the feast, the singing, the dance—and the word of sterility—the absence of feasts, singing, and dance. From a ludic relationship among gods, animals, and men, in which one mocks the others and is at the same time mocked by them, there is a shift to a relationship between white men and Indians in which there is the threat of deceit. In his attempt to recover his people's identity, the narrator walks a tightrope, trying to balance two types of knowledge and two powers, placing movement, repetition, and reiteration side by side with stasis and crystallization.

The Body-Space

Another fundamental aspect to be noted in the book is its time-space configuration. The concept of boundary or frontier seems adequate to guide this reading. The frontier, characterized by division and impenetrability, obeys the need to demarcate the sacred space within chaos. The mythical procedure of building posts and signs to mark off spaces for the initiated is alive and growing in modern society. In fact, demarcating spaces has to do with power relationships. Material frontiers (wells, walls, hedges) give a concrete form to invisible and more resisting religious, moral, social, and psychic frontiers.

When we first read *Histórias de maloca antigamente,* we notice two different positions concerning frontiers: the white man's and the Indian's. In the first part, even in the pictures drawn by the Indians, we can notice that there are boundaries, but they do not generally prevent the continuity of relationships. In all stories, spaces are interpenetrable: village and forest; earth, air, and water; inside and outside; high and low.

As in all mythical narratives, in the beginning time and space are not differentiated. Through the word, Ngurá organizes chaos:

> *Ngurá fez primeiro mato. Ngurá conversar . . . queria mato . . . falava.*
> *Mato vai aparecer. Vai saindo . . . brotando raiz, folha, espinho, tudo. . . .*
> *Ngurá fez índio e índio ficou morrendo de sol quente. . . . Aí Ngurá falou*

assim:—Então, vou mandar escuro pra dormir. Dia todo não dá pra dormir.

(Ngurá first created forest. Ngurá talk . . . wanted forest . . . talked. Forest will appear. It is already appearing . . . root budding, leaf, thorn, everything. . . . Ngurá created Indian and Indian was dying under the hot sun. . . . So Ngurá said: "So I will send darkness for sleeping. Indian can't sleep at no moment in the day.) (18–19)

Species become differentiated; time and space become organized. There is a primordial difference between gods and men, even though, as we shall see, there is a threshold, an area of intersection of the two. What is relevant to our argument now is that the *maloca* should be seen as an integral part of the forest; that here, culture is an element of nature and vice versa.[6] This is evinced in the great number of metamorphoses. Everything moves and changes constantly.

Daí quando ele porrava cabeça de mulher, daí mulher virou cutia. . . . Aí soprou no buraco, deu besouro tudinho miudinho, tudo voando. . . . Quando ela falou que "esse pedaço de teu carne", ele voando—passarinho, né?—ele foi embora. Ele virou passarinho, né? Passarinho é homem que rancava pedaço.

(And so when he beat on woman's head, woman turn into *cutia* [rodent]. . . . And then he blew into the hole, a beetle came out, wee buggie, flying around. . . . When she said that "this piece of your flesh," it flying—"a birdie, isn't it?"—it went away. It became birdie, didn't it? Birdie is man that gnawed bits of flesh.) (71, 86)

There are many examples like these. A woman turns into an owl; a toad turns into a man; dead people come back to life. The interchange among living beings promotes the interchange of spaces: the bird-woman can stay above the trees; the fish-man lives underwater. Animals, like the *socó* and the *mutum* (types of birds), can live in the maloca, and men can enter them.

Mulher entrou dentro do pescoço de socó. (por isso socó tem pescoço grande, né?). . . . Kaboêp é mulher, né? Escondeu debaixo asa de mutum com medo de coruja achar ela

(Woman got into socó's neck. [That's why socó has a big neck, right?] ... Kaboêp is a woman, isn't she? She hid under a mutum's wing, afraid of owl finding her.) (65)

Likewise, together with the interpenetration of spaces, the pictures repeatedly depict a physical link between man and animal, as if one were an extension of the other.

Conception and pregnancy, involving both animals and humans, gods and plants, are processes that epitomize a single idea: an integrative view of the universe. The body is the house, the world. Sexuality is a mark of life, of renewal. It is present in every segment of nature. It is interesting to notice that the god Cinta Larga was born out of a stone, the world's womb. An uncut and unpolished stone is considered androgynous, thus constituting the perfection of the primordial state. Similarly, the egg is the embryo from which comes life, the first principle for the organization of chaos. The mother stone is circular, similar to a collective maloca. With the stone and the egg is the nut, origin of the Cinta Larga people.

> *Primeiro ele transava o coco de castanha. Coco de castanha tem boca que cabia jibaca dele. Aí zup ficou lá dentro castanha. Gente nasceu dentro de castanha. . . . Agora neto transou fruto. Transava fruto amarelo de kakin. . . . Por isso que tem Cinta Larga Mãm, kakin, kabãn.*

(First he had intercourse with the coconut of the chestnut. The coconut of the chestnut has a mouth to enter his jibaca [penis]. Then zup [sperm] remained inside chestnut. People were born inside chestnut. . . . Now grandson had intercourse with fruit. Had sex with yellow fruit of kakin. . . . That is why there is Cinta Larga *Mãm, kakin,* kabãn [three types of chestnut trees].) (19)

The two vital principles of this people are here united: divinity and sperm. Moreover, the union takes place inside a fruit, a nut. The Cinta Largas' conception of life is thus integrative. Man is vegetable, animal, and mineral. This, however, does not diminish his human identity in the least. We can see a man-nature relationship akin to the one established between the individual and the collective. An individual has his own identity within the group. It is not by chance, then, that malocas host and hosted all the community, who shared them for sleeping, weaving, cooking, or chatting, everyone doing what he or she pleases without bothering the others. The individual is a member of his people, who, in turn, are part of a greater whole that integrates nature and culture. Socioeconomic relationships have a collective character. The land is worked by everybody, and the resulting product belongs to them all: *Não ter isso dividir terra não. Mesma terra, né?* (There is not that, divide the land, no. Same land, isn't it?) (119). Paths are opened through walking. Branches and trunks are cut in order to allow passage, but they soon grow again; similarly, there is a periodic renewal of the tilled land.

> *Não é marcado terra nada. Tem nada! Só caminho—picada, né? Ninguém vai ir lá. Não tem caminho de lá longe não. Só caminho de maloca nossa. Cinta Larga, né? Só Cinta Larga tem caminho. Mas Suruí assim, branco, não ten caminho não, pra ir não.*

> (The land is not demarcated at all. There's nothing! Only road—a trail, right? Nobody is going to go there. There is no road from there. Only the road of our maloca. Cinta Larga, right? Only the Cinta Larga have a road. But Suruí like that, white, have no road, no, not to go.) (119)

There is an identity between the people and their land. The Cinta Larga establish a difference from neighboring peoples like the Suruí, the Gavião, and the Zoró, and fight for their physical and cultural integrity, defending their frontiers. It is evident, however, that individuality and individualism are not confused, as is also the case with solidarity and superiority, power and property. The land is sacred and everything tends to sacredness, since everything is part of the primeval time and space inhabited by the gods. Two figures dwell on the threshold as mediators between gods and men: Pawo and Wãwã, the shaman. Hence, the higher frontier, that between gods and men, allows for openness, thus signaling the paradoxical place where the sacred and the profane interact.[7]

Pawo, the forest's guard, has a vegetable and animal nature; it has power over men and is part of the divine order. Pawo defends the frontiers of Ngurá's world, but seems to traverse both the world of good and that of evil; it can also be the carrier of death. Pawo attracts and seduces through different forms thanks to its capacity for transformation. *Ele brilho brilhando todo pendurado de vagalume. Pequenininho . . . bem baixinho* (35); *Esse bicho é igual gente . . . É gente?* (39); *Não é qualquer um vê não* (40) (It shine shining all full of glowworm. A wee glowworm . . . very tiny; That bug is like people . . . It's people?; It's not everybody who sees it, no). From a sexual point of view, Pawo is an ambiguous figure, sometimes male, sometimes female: *Quando meu primo tava láaaa longe . . . armou rede lá longe, aí Pawo vem deitar com ele.—Mulher Pawo vem deitar com ele* (When my cousin was far, far from here . . . he set hammock far over there, then came Pawo to lie with him—Female Pawo came to lie with him) (43).

Pawo has a power over speech so strong that it can interfere with the speech of others. It sings like birds and speaks like men, and is able to prevent a person from saying what he or she wants to: *Aí ele quer falar: "Pawo quer me matar"—assim ele quer—aí ele falou: "traz fogo pra mim!" . . . O bicho que tá me matando—quer falar assim, né?* (And then it wants to speak: "Pawo wants to kill me"—so it wants—then it spoke: "Bring me fire!" . . . The animal is killing me—wants to speak like that, right?) (43). Pawo changes the words, dominates the Indian by controlling one of its/his most characteristic features: language and the power to play with it and mock it.

Moreover, Pawo owns the hog, an essential figure in Cinta Larga rituals and beliefs. The hog represents the owner of the feast. It is also the enemy; that is why, when there is war, they say they are going to kill hogs. When they eat the hog, they take part in an anthropophagous ritual. They eat the owner of the feast or the enemy. Pawo has the capacity to punish or reward the Indians as well as the power to transform them into hogs: *E daí que Pawo falou:—Agora tem pessoal vai virar porco lugar meu porco* (And then Pawo said: "There's those who will become hogs in the place of my hog") (45). The hog is, then, an ambiguous figure like Pawo, and it has the power of life and death.

Another character who participates in the world of transformed and monstrous nature, seductive but threatening, is Wãwã. It also shares human, divine, and animal natures, playing the role of mediator, as a threshold being. To reach that stage, it must go through an initiation ritual that involves suffering and even death.

> *Vira pajé quando muito doente, depois que bicho ele sonha, muito doido cabeça, fica doido cabeça depois que ele fuma. O Wãwã canta muito, canta muito. . . . Aí Wãwã chama bicho, chama onça, tudo tipo urubu.*

(It turns shaman when it is very ill, after becoming animal it dreams, very crazy head, it gets very crazy head after it smokes. Wãwã sings a lot, sings a lot. . . . Then Wãwã calls an animal, calls jaguar, all type buzzard.) (48)

As shaman, it becomes a sort of non-sense figure, the paradoxical instance of sharing two spaces. It is interesting to note that smoke, used as a purifying element in healing rituals, is the antithesis of mud—water and earth—since it corresponds to air and fire. It is then a mediation between god and man.

> *Daqui terra ele vê. Ele vê outro Wāwā daqui. Wāwā tem aqui no terra, né? Vira fumaça, o pajé vem junto daquela fumacinha, porque Wāwā sempre fuma, né? Jogando fumaça.*

> (From here land it sees. It sees another Wāwā from here. Wāwā is here in land, isn't it? It turns to smoke, the shaman comes together with that smoke, because Wāwā always smokes, right? Throwing out smoke.)(47)

In her work on the Cinta Largas' music, Priscilla Ermel shows how blowing plays a central role in the tribe and is perhaps the strongest unifying element in their cultural expressions. "Blowing transcends the space-time of art and operates in the space-time of the healing made by the *Wāwā*—the shaman."[8] Blowing is further connected to language, which plays a central role in the shaman's work. In fact, the shaman masters several languages: *aí bicho vai conversar com pajé. Só pajé que bicho, árvore, tudo coisa conversa* (47); *Eu sei cantar, eu sei falar de peixe, sei cantar de onça* (49) (and then animal talks to shaman. It is only with the shaman that animal, tree, everything talk; I know how to sing, I know how to speak about fish, I know how to sing about the jaguar"). The healing ritual is also the feast of language: of singing, dancing, communicating with the gods, exercising power over the spirit. This reinforces the paradoxical role of Wāwā, who traverses between sense and non-sense, uniting different times and spaces. Pawo and Wāwā are thus metonymic figures of the Cinta Larga, since they stand for the maximum degree of integration/separation of different spaces; they are the expression of the sacred for denoting the death/birth of the cosmos.

Language is a basic element in this interplay of relationships. If Ngurá created the world through the word, then Indians can master it through the word. Here is an instance of what Tzvetan Todorov calls communication with the world, as opposed to communication merely with man:[9]

> *Aí índio mandou logo o madrugada, né? Chamando ela. Cantava tudo de passarinho, né? Jacu, jacutinga, nambu . . . tudo ele cantava chamando madrugada. Aí madrugada chegou.*

(And then Indian summoned dawn, right? Calling it. He sang everything from birds, right? Jacu, jacutinga, nambu . . . all in himself sang,
calling dawn. And so dawn arrived.) (54)

The Indian's space is never atomized. Everything and everybody in it play
a role in the process of creation, even animals: *Aí aranha botou cipó todo
canto. Pegou tudo árvore de pau, cipó . . . pra lá, né? Aí cipó começando cipó.
Por isso que tem cipó no árvore. Tudo canto cipó tem* (And then the spider
spread vines everywhere. It took all wood trees, vine . . . there, right? And
then vine beginning vine. That's why there's vine on trees. Everywhere there
is vine) (55). Ngurá created the world, but everybody continues his work.
Animals choose their features from a tree and pick the colors they want to
dress up in, as is shown in the story "Popakey." The spider creates the vine,
the worm creates the tree, and so on. Man and woman create objects and
plant species: *Mulher inventou fazer virar taboca, né? Essa taboca eu inventei
pra você matar bicho* (Woman decided to make appear bamboo, right? That
bamboo I invented for you to kill animals) (52).

The Indian's space appears as a spider web, spreading its threads in every
direction, although this web is a product of individual rather than of collective spinning. This is seen in the authorial status of the book: Pichuvy's name
on the cover does not erase the collective nature of the stories. The interplay
between "I" and "we" is a hallmark of the book, since the narrator's voice
expands to incorporate his people's voice. The stories' textual space is a product of his people's experience, a site of interaction and exchange, pleasure
and pain. This relationship of mutual dependence accounts for the fact that
a given story can include another story or parts of it. Not even the stories'
closing formulas prevent them from being continued: *Assim é história pra
nós; Assim que história de Bepuixi foi isso* (And so this is history to us; And so
Bepuixi's story was that) (21, 26).

There is interaction within the textual sphere, as there also is within and
between the geographical, sociopolitical, and existential spaces. There is no
fixed form for the text, since, being oral, it changes every time it is repeated.
In spite of having become a written, fixed text, it still bears marks of the oral
process: *Tem outra história de Pawo assim, sabe?; Então, história de Ngurá
também. Outro Ngurá também que nome Tiriri* (There is another story about
Pawo like this, you know?; So with Ngurá's story, too. Another Ngurá that
also has the name Tiriri) (43, 21).

The book's language can be said to be the space of a feast, of performance as an excess of the word, since the oral language is not associated with a unique voice—God's voice, as phonocentrism would have it—but represents the space of different voices, be they God's and/or the devil's. If language is the site of man's relationship with himself, with others, and with God[10]—a site of appearance and revelation of man's faults and needs, being, as he is, a subject of desire—the Indians' language can be read as a manifestation of this site. The "I" abandons the self to the other/the mirror, saying *Paikinim pa mã, pa mã* (We are here, let us look at each other, let us get to know each other), as the Cinta Larga do in their ritual of greeting.

Here it is worth noticing the parallel with Claude Lévi-Strauss's observations about the savage mind. He states that the main feature of primitive thinking is its being atemporal, since it captures the world simultaneously as a synchronic and diachronic whole.[11] In this sense, the metaphor of the room with fixed mirrors on opposites walls, reflecting one another in an interplay of identity and difference, repeats the mobility of Pichuvy's narrative. Could this be a feature of native peoples' thinking, of the kind of thinking taken as primitive, or a trait of oral cultures, characterized by myths and poetry?

What could be the role of a narrative like that in a world which aims at globalization, without fixed frontiers although, paradoxically, full of fragmentation? In his discussion of the difference between the native peoples' memory and Western memory, Ailton Krenac states that memory kept in boxes is a result of man's incapacity to dream. He concludes:

> For these small human groups—our tribes—which still preserve this legacy from ancient times, this mode of being in the world, it is very important that mankind, which is becoming increasingly westernized, civilized, and technological, recollects that common memory the human being has of the world's creation. Mankind needs to cast a new light on its history; on the history that is preserved in books, museums, dates, since in the recognition of that memory lies a way out for us. If not, we will witness the countdown of that collective memory's extinction, 'till there is only History. And, if I have to choose between History and memory, I had rather preserve the latter.[12]

Regardless of one's acceptance of this distinction between history and memory, it is worth reflecting on how Indians like Pichuvy and Krenac take the written word and make use of Western man's resources to record future's memory. As Paul Klee's angel in Walter Benjamin's metaphor would suggest: the history of Latin American native peoples would be Western man's future.[13]

This is also the message transmitted by shaman Davi Kopenawa Yanomami to anthropologist Bruce Albert:

> This way heaven will end up splitting. Many Yanomami shamans have already died and they will certainly claim vengeance. . . . When shamans die, their assistant spirits, the *hekurabê*, get extremely angry. They see that the white men lead their "fathers," the shamans, to death. The hekurabê will seek revenge, will want to shatter heaven to pieces so that it will fall down onto the earth; they will also make the sun fall down, and when the sun falls down, everything will get dark. When the stars and the moon also fall down, the sky will also get dark. We want to tell all this to the white men, but they refuse to listen. They are different people and do not understand. I think they do not want to listen. They think: "these people are merely lying." That's what they think. But we are not liars. They do not know about this. That is why they think that way.[14]

Pichuvy ought to be a shaman like Davi Yanomami, since he has nobody to whom he can tell what he knows, nobody to speak to about his culture, for they refuse to listen. Paradoxically, Pichuvy tells stories to the people who disregard his people, sharing with them his knowledge. Pichuvy, however, died as a victim of the process he himself denounced in his book: while drunk, and accompanied by two prostitutes, he crashed the Toyota donated by lumber businessmen into a lumber truck coming from his village. On the asphalt there remained the signs of the accident, the marks of future's memory.

It is not by chance, then, that Sepultura, a rock band from the Brazilian state of Minas Gerais, produced a record called *Roots* with the Xavante Indians. This is not a search for our roots as we traditionally understand this concept. Today we are aware of the rhizome, a concept that has made the idea of identity construction more relative and dynamic. The band's record does not represent a naive nostalgia of origins. By incorporating an Indian rhythm into a Western one, the band shows a form of resistance and struggle similar to the songs of Mercedes Sosa or to Mario Vargas Llosa's insertion of oral speech in his novel *The Storyteller,* about the Matchiguenga of the Peruvian Amazon, a people who know that it is necessary to keep on moving and narrating in order for heaven not to fall to pieces: *Vivos y andando, pues. A lo largo del tiempo y a lo ancho del mundo, también* (Alive and moving, then. Throughout time and across the world as well).[15]

It is worth reflecting, then, upon the reasons that lead a world taken as primitive to resist in the midst of a technological world, facing up to massacres, genocide, colonization, in order to preserve its difference and make use of it in a dialogue with a civilization that claims to be unique and homogeneous. Could we not think of the primitive element as a dislocating and subversive force of the instituted order, since from its marginal position the primitive no doubt forces Western civilization to problematize its own stance? In this sense, the primitive could signal a possibility of change, of movement, and of interaction. It is this possibility that stirred Pichuvy to narrate, to record what it was like before: *Eu tô fazendo livro pra nós saber história como é que foi* (I'm making a book for us to know history the way it was) (115). Likewise, Vargas Llosa's narrator states: "Everyone was once something different from what they are now. Something has no doubt happened to everyone that can be told."[16]

Martin Lienhard highlights the relevance of this type of narrative which transcends the boundaries of one culture to move into another that usually disregards and ignores it.[17] In that way, I believe, a voice forces its way into another culture, leaving its mark, even if it is in the form of remains. Ruins, as Benjamin says, are the interaction between past and present. To this I would add my own question: Are they not, then, future's memory?

Notes

1. All translations are mine: "*Eu tô vivo, eu contar muito de história. Assim que eu faço pessoal meu, contava meu pessoal. E muita vez que eu falava que índio tem que lembrar como foi antigamente, como que velho contava pra nós, que velho conta muita história pra nós. Por isso eu conta muita história assim.*" Pichuvy Cinta Larga, *Histórias de maloca antigamente*, ed. Ana Leonel, Leda Leonel, and Ivete Walty (Belo Horizonte: SEGRAC, 1989), 16. All citations of this work refer to this edition. Page numbers are indicated parenthetically in the text.

2. Ailton Krenac, "Antes, o mundo não existia," in *Tempo e história*, ed. A. Novaes (São Paulo: Companhia das Letras, 1994), 201–204; 201. My translation.

3. Ivete Walty, "Narrativa e imaginário social: Uma leitura de 'Histórias de maloca antigamente' de Pichuvy Cinta Larga" (Ph.D. dissertation, University of São Paulo, 1991).

4. Philippe Lejeune, *Je est un autre: L'Autobiographie de la littérature aux médias* (Paris: Seuil, 1980).

5. Paul Zumthor, *La Lettre et la voix. De la Littérature médiévale* (Paris: Seuil, 1987).

6. The maloca is the Cinta Largas' meetinghouse, their assembly, and by extension their village, their tribe, their culture.

7. See Mircea Eliade, *The Sacred and the Profane: The Nature of Religion* (New York: Harcourt Brace Jovanovich, 1959).

8. Priscilla Ermel, "O sentido mítico do som. Ressonâncias estéticas da música tribal Cinta Larga" (M.A. thesis, Pontifícia Universidade Católica, São Paulo, 1988), 103.

9. Tzvetan Todorov, *The Conquest of America: The Question of the Other,* trans. Richard Howard (New York: Harper & Row, 1984).

10. See Zumthor, *La Lettre et la voix,* 147.

11. Claude Lévi-Strauss, *The Savage Mind* (Chicago: University of Chicago Press, 1966).

12. Krenac, "Antes, o mundo não existia," 204.

13. Walter Benjamin, "Sobre o conceito de história," in his *Magia e técnica, arte e política,* trans. Sérgio P. Rouanet (São Paulo: Brasiliense, 1987), 222–232.

14. Quoted in Laymert Garcia dos Santos, "O tempo mítico hoje," in *Tempo e história,* ed. A. Novaes (São Paulo: Companhia das Letras, 1994), 191, 200.

15. Mario Vargas Llosa, *El hablador* (Barcelona: Seix Barral, 1997), 192.

16. Ibid., 189.

17. Martin Lienhard, "La percepción de las prácticas 'textuales' amerindias: Apuntes para un debate interdisciplinario," in *América Latina: Palavra, literatura e cultura,* ed. Ana Pizarro (São Paulo: Memorial, 1995), 169–185.

11

Primitive Bodies in Latin American Cinema

Nicolás Echevarría's *Cabeza de Vaca*

LUIS FERNANDO RESTREPO

Cabeza de Vaca (1991), the first feature film by ethnographic film direc-tor Nicolás Echevarría, reworks *Naufragios*, the 1542 chronicle of Span-ish explorer Alvar Núñez Cabeza de Vaca.[1] In the film, Latin America's vio-lent colonization is strategically disavowed by highlighting one intercultural experience as "exemplary": Alvar Núñez's journey. Through a cathartic, "gone native" narrative the film invites the spectator to condemn the colonization and revalue native culture. Through its shaman-hero the film produces an emotional pact between the modern and the tribal. Its pathos, however, can exist only as long as the Amerindian world is envisioned as a primitive, van-ishing world. As in Roland Joffe's *The Mission* (1986) or Kevin Costner's *Dances with Wolves* (1990), tribal societies are viewed through the nostalgic lens of a high-tech primitivism.[2] In this ideological entrapment, native sur-vival, resistance, and cultural negotiations are basically suppressed.

In this essay I will focus on *Cabeza de Vaca*'s process of inscribing Amerindians in the realm of the primitive. The film primitivizes the Other in several ways. Its main theme is the hero's discovery of his primitive Other. Also, the Other is turned "primitive" through a film language that focuses on the body, the site of Otherness par excellence. Amerindian bodies are turned into rich, exotic, and erotic textures that can be gazed at (consumed) by the metropolitan spectator. In addition, the monstrous and savage vision of the Other emerges through the figures of Mala Cosa ("Evil Thing") and the Amazons. First, a brief summary of the film's narrative and some gen-eral comments on its adaptation of the sixteenth-century chronicle are in order.

Cabeza de Vaca's narrative structure is rather conventional, as Joanne Hershfield has noted.[3] It consists of a prologue, the main narrative, and an epilogue that circles back to the opening moment. The narrative starts in 1536, at a Spanish camp in Culiacán, northern Mexico. The camera closes in on Alvar Núñez and his companions. They are seminaked. Their lacerated faces and bodies suggest that they have endured the wilderness—the typical image of the castaway. Alvar Núñez then retells his journey. The main narrative, recounted as an act of memory, shows Alvar Núñez Cabeza de Vaca and the few survivors of Pánfilo de Narváez's expedition adrift somewhere near the western coast of Florida. They reach shore and are soon captured by Indians. Alvar Núñez is given to a shaman as a slave/apprentice. He learns to cure and even to resuscitate. He sets forth on a pilgrimage across the land, passing through several villages. In this journey he is followed by other survivors of the expedition and an increasing number of Indians, who hold him in high esteem as a shaman-priest. His success lasts until he reaches the Spanish camps, where his powers cannot stop the destruction generated by the Conquest. In the epilogue, after returning to the opening scene, the narrative develops a bit further, enough for Alvar Núñez to witness the death and enslavement of his Amerindian friends. The film centers on the hero's loss rather than on the Indians' suffering, and it closes with an allegory that suggests a complete/uncontested colonization: several Indians carry a huge cross, as European martial music is played, toward a black, cloudy horizon.

In general, Echevarría's film follows Alvar Núñez's criticism of the then current method of military colonization. In his chronicle, Alvar Núñez advocated a softer, paternalistic colonization. This is expressly addressed in the last chapters of the chronicle. There, Alvar Núñez stresses that he managed to "pacify" a native population unsuccessfully colonized by force. The hero of the sixteenth-century text, however, conforms for the most part to Western rationality and Christian orthodoxy. The film, in contrast, attempts to go beyond this narrowly centered subject by offering a vision of the fascinating world that Alvar Núñez may have encountered.

Yet, the film suppresses key parts of the chronicle, the early and final chapters. What is worth questioning here is not its fidelity to an "original." First, because the film expressly states that it is *inspired* by the chronicle. Second, because adapting is always a complex process that involves interpretation, transformation, and intersections.[4] The crucial point is the ideological implications of the choices made in the adaptation.

The omission of the early chapters suppresses colonial violence and

Amerindian resistance. The film starts at chapter 10 of the chronicle. Adrift at sea, the Spaniards are experiencing a misfortune with no known cause. They are presented as victims. An Aristotelian strategy inciting pity is at work here: someone "like us" has fallen into misfortune. The nine chapters omitted, however, focus not on a few helpless Spaniards but on a full expedition involving five ships and six hundred men. These early chapters tell of several raids in which Alvar Núñez took part. Crops and villages were looted; women and children were held hostage (98). Had the film included these passages, it would have been extremely difficult to portray the Spaniards as victims.

In both chronicle and film, Amerindian responses to the invaders are structurally coded within a main narrative focused on a white man's journey. The chronicle, however, registers planned and strategic native resistance (94, 96, 100, 101). This is suppressed in the film. Amerindians do attack the Spaniards, but this is presented from the Spaniards' point of view. No natives are shown, only arrows that appear from the wilderness. A wide-angle lens gives the sense of an encroaching landscape, and the camera rotates, stressing the vulnerability of the Spaniards. Consequently, Indian resistance is presented as unprovoked, irrational violence.

The omission of the last chapters may be more than an individual blind spot. Rolena Adorno has rightly argued that scholarship on the *Naufragios* has devoted too much attention to Alvar Núñez's "miracles," overlooking their meaning within the whole narrative.[5] In the chronicle Alvar Núñez presents his project of consensual colonization in the final chapters.

Considering current scholarship on Colonial Latin America, Echevarría's film does not offer a radically different view of the colonization. It simply reflects a growing concern for a less Eurocentric vision of the Encounter. Its production is part of a multinational diffusionist project galvanized around the quincentennial celebration of the Discovery. The film was a coproduction of state and international agencies, including the Mexican Film Institute (IMCINE), Spanish Television, the Spanish Quincentennial Commission, American Playhouse, Channel Four Television (England), the José Revueltas Cooperative, and the state governments of Nayarit and Coahuila. Hershfield further explores this wider historical context of the film throughout her article. However, we have yet to see a comprehensive study that examines Latin American cinema's vision of the Other from decade to decade, from the then censored 1920s Bolivian films *Corazón aymara* (Aymara Heart), *Profesía del lago* (The Prophecy of the Lake), and *Wara Wara* (The Stars)—or the controversial 1928 Brazilian film *Abaporu* (The One Who Eats), which advocated cultural cannibalism as a response to imperialism—to the New Latin American Cinema and beyond: Jorge Sanjinés's 1968 *Yawar mallku* (Blood of the Condor), Nelson Pereira Dos Santos's *Como era gostoso o meu frances* (How Tasty Was My Little Frenchman), and more recent productions such as Paul Leduc's 1992 *Barroco* (Baroque).[6]

Film Narrative and Its Secrets

In popular narratives, words do not seem to get in the way of the story. Likewise, in film, the camera's movements, cuts, and so on offer the impression of a story that simply unfolds naturally by itself. Frank Kermode argues that there are two intertwined processes in narrative: one that seeks to follow the story (sequence) and another that seeks to develop the text's secrets (decoding, interpreting).[7] These two processes may be at odds with one another. It seems that too much scrutiny disrupts sequence. A story's success may depend on "underreading" and acceptance of the narrator's authority. Narrative secrets may not contribute much to the plot. However, they may be more revealing and interesting than the story itself. This may be the case with *Cabeza de Vaca,* whose powerful film language cannot be reduced to sequence.

Reading secrets in film is somehow different from reading them in texts. Seymour Chatman has noted that in order to prevent disrupting the story flow, narrative texts tend to offer few details and leave much to be filled in by the reader.[8] Lengthy descriptions slow down the story. Film, in contrast, can provide a considerable number of details without interrupting the story. This plenitude of visual details in film narrative, however, tends to be suppressed by the film itself. We are not allowed enough time to dwell on the details. Some films' overabundance of visual details may be too much for the story line to support. This may be the case for some sequences in *Cabeza de Vaca* that depict Amerindians and their villages. How should this unresolved tension between sequence and secrets be approached? Or, in Kermode's suggestive question: "What is the critic to say when confronted with the evidence of debauch committed behind the back of authority?"[9] In *Cabeza de Vaca* the rich representations of Amerindian bodies are "narrative secrets" that betray the story which the film is seeking to tell.

The Primitive Self

Cabeza de Vaca's main narrative presents a white man's return to his "primitive" self as a critique of colonization. This idealized primitivism seems to originate from the vantage point of "civilization and its discontents," as Hayden White argues: "Primitivism simply invites men to be themselves, to give vent to their original, natural, but subsequently repressed desires, to throw off the restraints of civilization and thereby enter into a kingdom that is *naturally* theirs."[10] This return to the primitive self can be examined in at least three aspects of the film: the "ship of fools" sequence, the shaman figure, and the topos of dance.

THE SHIP OF FOOLS

In the opening sequence, a soldier approaching Alvar Núñez comments, "It must have been hard living with savages." In response, Alvar Núñez laughs hysterically as the screen fades out into the story of his journey. As Hershfield notes, his laughter situates the story as an act of memory by a madman.[11] The narrative starts at a liminal point between madness and reason. This liminality is presented through the Western topos of the "ship of fools." It situates the hero on a journey to the other side of Renaissance reason, to the inner, savage self.

The second sequence begins the main narrative: Alvar Núñez and other survivors of Narváez's expedition are drifting on rafts, fighting each other like madmen (see figure 11.1). A laughing, delirious man ironically proclaims, "*Qué asamblea, señores! Cuánta gracia y dulzura! Y nuestras vestiduras, regias! del oro de Indias! . . . Qué asamblea señores!*" (A great gathering, gentlemen! Such grace and sweetness! Dressed as monarchs, with gold from the Indies! . . . A great gathering, gentlemen!). Looking at the rafts, he says, "*Esta es toda la España que nos queda. Nuestros barcos son España, ¿dónde están esos barcos?*" (Spain is only this for us. Our ships are Spain. Where are those ships?) The loss of the ships represents a material and symbolic rupture with "civilization." This rupture is expressed by the captain of the expedition, Narváez. He refuses to help Alvar and his party, as well as to take any responsibility, proclaiming that from then on, it is every man for himself.

The image of the ship of fools has been associated with madness since the Middle Ages. It was a benign, liberating image of madness. This image changed during the Renaissance, the time of Alvar Núñez Cabeza de Vaca. Madness became reason's Other, a process that Michel Foucault has dis-

FIGURE 11.1. A "ship of fools." Opening scenes of *Cabeza de Vaca.*

cussed in *Madness and Civilization.* Textual representations of the ship of fools from the Renaissance cease to envision its voyage as liberating. Rather, they represent a dangerous, unrestrained desire. For Erasmus, "madness is the punishment of a disorderly and useless science."[12] In contrast, representations of the ship of fools—like the drawings of Hieronymus Bosch (ca. 1450–1516)—offer an image that stirs imagination and desire.

Our question here is which image of madness is presented in *Cabeza de Vaca* and what its relationship is to the film's main narrative. In another film on the colonization of the Americas, the ship of fools represents a return to a chaotic, violent nature. Werner Herzog's *Aguirre: The Wrath of God* tells the story of Lope de Aguirre's insurrection and search for El Dorado. Unrestrained desire leads to a catastrophic end. The final scene is revealing. All Spaniards but Lope de Aguirre have died or have been killed. Monkeys (nature) have invaded the raft. The camera circles the raft, suggesting the cyclical movement of nature. Here, a return to nature represents the failure of the rational project of modernity. In contrast, *Cabeza de Vaca*'s ship of fools sequence has an important narrative function: it frees the hero from social restraint. But how far will he dare to go? That is, how liberating is this journey?

This story has much in common with many Western novels and films that deploy a mythic narrative in remote colonial regions (Africa, the Amazon) where no white man has been. Slavoj Zizek discusses three examples: *King Solomon's Mines,* the story of a powerful black empire; *She,* the tale of a mysterious and beautiful black woman; and *Tarzan,* an account of a man who lives in complete harmony with nature. The important element here, Zizek argues, is the effect of these mythic spaces: "The fantasy-space is therefore strictly secondary, it 'gives body,' materializes a certain limit, or, more precisely, it changes the *impossible* into the *prohibited.*"[13] In *Cabeza de Vaca* the fantasy-space opened by the ship of fools sequence presents a possible, though forbidden, world that delimits the (Lacanian) symbolic order. Through the shaman theme, which I will examine next, the hero's experiences transcend Western rationality and religious orthodoxy. But, surprisingly, the core of the restrained modern subject is kept in place. Narcissistic desire (Narváez), cannibalism (Esquivel), gender-role inversion (the savage women), and homoerotic desire (for the young Amerindian Ariano) are condemned and/or suppressed.

THE SHAMAN

It is not difficult to see that Echevarría's ethnographic filmmaking has left its trace in *Cabeza de Vaca.* Public rituals, shamanism, and ritual consumption of hallucinogens are some of the themes of his early productions, such as *Judea: Semana Santa entre los coras* (Judea: Holy Week Among the Coras, 1973), *Kikure-Tame: La peregrinación del peyote entre los Huicholes* (Kikure-Tame: The Huicholes' Peyote Pilgrimage, 1977), *María Sabina, mujer espíritu* (María Sabina, Spirit Woman, 1978), *Tesguinalda: Semana Santa Tarahumara* (Tesguinalda: Tarahumara Holy Week, 1979), *El niño Fidencio: Tramaturgo de Espinazo* (Fidencio: Healer from Espinazo, 1981).[14]

In *Cabeza de Vaca* the shaman sequences are very powerful. Alvar Núñez becomes a shaman, curing many natives and earning high prestige. How are we to "read" these shamanistic practices? Given how little we know about the North American cultures that Alvar Núñez encountered in the sixteenth century, they can hardly be read as ethnographic reconstructions of native practices.[15] A more reasonable approach is to understand the shaman theme as a central element of the film narrative. The film's main theme is a story of intercultural exchanges, as the filmmaker confirmed in a TV interview with Alejandro Pelayo.[16] Alvar Núñez incorporates native and Christian signs and symbols—prayers, gourds, and the cross—into his healing practices. The shaman figure works, then, as a metaphor for transculturation. This inscribes the film in a long Latin American debate on the cultural identity of the past and present peoples of the Americas. But these cultural exchanges are represented in a way that primitivizes the Other. Alvar Núñez becoming a shaman is presented as a "return" to a primitive self. Enslaved and humiliated by his Amerindian captors, he breaks down. This scene is presented as a regression: Alvar Núñez collapses and assumes the fetal position. His speech collapses, too. At first, he states his name, title, and origin, but he soon loses coherence, singing, crying, and babbling. Although this regression serves to liberate the hero from the restraints placed on the individual by Spanish society, it primitivizes native cultures, which are thus assumed to be at an infant or early stage in relation to European civilization.

WHITE MAN CAN'T DANCE: THE PICTURESQUE AND THE ETHNOGRAPHIC CAMERA

Modern anthropology's interest in primitive body movements, photography, and cinema can be seen as early as the work of Félix-Louis Regnault. At the 1895 Paris Ethnographic Exposition, Regnault studied West African performers through chronophotography, a series of consecutive photographs. This is, according to Fatimah Tobing Rony, the beginning of ethnographic film: "Regnault believed that by filming the movements—walking, running, climbing, jumping—of West Africans, and comparing them with films of the movements of Europeans, one could establish a typology of the races. Human history could be read in locomotion."[17] However, ethnographic attention to primitive body movements can be traced to an earlier period: the travel writing related to the scientific expeditions of the late eighteenth and early nineteenth centuries. The travelogue—as, later, the twentieth-century ethnographic cinema did—sought the picturesque. This was not the ideal, the sublime, nor the beautiful, but those visual elements which by virtue of their roughness, lighting, irregular form, and even sound left an impression in the mind of the observer. Landscapes, ruins, native peoples, and their rituals were by this process inscribed in the realm of memory, thus in a still past.[18] Among those rituals which are the focus of this romantic primitivism are native dances.

Dance in Western society is associated with leisure, the opposite to the realm of work—white man can't dance, he must work. For the urban, working spectator, film codifies native rituals as dance or spectacle: a primitive world desired, created through the powerful image/sound machine. This can be seen in Latin American films like Carlos Diegues's *Quilombo* as well as in *Cabeza de Vaca*. *Quilombo* presents the seventeenth-century Maroon society through its dances. Colorful and adorned bodies fill the screen. The choreography is clearly designed with the cinematic frame in mind. In *Cabeza de Vaca* the camera also presents native cultures through dance scenes. The village of savage women, which will be discussed below, is presented during a dance-ritual. Also, in one of the villages visited, Alvar Núñez and his party encounter a funeral march. Native people dressed in black walk mournfully to the pace of a drum and a high-pitched flute toward a smoke-filled background. Both the music and the image evoke pain and despair.

Dance is part of the film's main theme, shamanism. The sequence in which Alvar Núñez becomes a shaman is a clear example. He saves a dying Indian. His healing practices are accompanied by movements and sounds that are, at first, somewhat arrhythmic. Soon they become increasingly rhythmic and euphoric. The natives, observing from the hut rooftop, start to bang sticks to accompany Alvar Núñez's movement: this guy can dance! The camera at one point assumes Alvar Núñez's point of view and rotates 360 degrees. Echevarría's camera work is at its best here. The Western, self-restrained subject is liberated through this ritual healing dance. However, this subversive act depends on a vision of the Other as psychically primitive. Tribal rituals have been turned into dance/spectacle, an object for metropolitan consumption.

Primitive Bodies

Cabeza de Vaca uses very little spoken language (or Amerindian "mock" languages—in the interview cited earlier, Echevarría states that the Indian "words" in the film were invented). Yet its visual narrative tells us a complete and comprehensible story. One element that makes this possible is the body. In this film we see it represented in multiple ways: buried, tortured, burned, wounded, killed, healed, decorated, mourned, resuscitated. What meanings are embodied here? How are they turned into text and texture?

In *Cabeza de Vaca* we are confronted (or complicit?) with camera work that gazes at native bodies, rich in decorations and ornaments, turning them into text and texture for consumption by the metropolitan spectator. Instead of inscribing them as historical subjects, they are gazed upon as objects of desire/power/knowledge.

The first shot of indigenous cultures, for example, is a close-up of a woman's face exotically decorated with feathers and leaves. Next, a master shot allows us to see her, and other Indians dressed like her, eating and speaking an unrecognizable language. None looks directly at the camera. From a safe distance we can gaze freely at their bodies. As a result, the indigenous culture is turned into an object to be viewed, while the gaze, the image-making technology, and the ethnographic representation itself are *naturalized*. Only once are we confronted with the gaze of the Amerindians. Right after Cabeza de Vaca's collapse, we have a close-up of a young shaman's face. It seems that from this point on, the camera invites us to see Cabeza de Vaca's journey through the Other's eyes. But such critical gestures are not the norm in this film. For the most part, the film narrative allows us to passively consume its images. Hershfield argues that the film narrative is strategically fragmented to dissolve the illusion of reality.[19] The narrative breaks can also be seen as episodes or "chapters" of Cabeza de Vaca's journey through some five Indian villages, which are loosely tied together.

Colonial iconography is reproduced in *Cabeza de Vaca* without critical distance. The film's art director, José Luis Aguilar, stated in the TV interview with Alejandro Pelayo that the indigenous costumes were based on the copperplate engravings of Theodore De Bry, the author of the thirteen-volume *The Great Voyages* (1590–1634). These widely circulated images of Amerindians have been described as a "bricolage." De Bry offers us a "sort of Tower of Babel of Amerindian peoples."[20] From his workshop in Europe, he produced detailed illustrations based on multiple sketches and narrative descriptions of the New World. The engravings mix elements of different cultures: physical types, ornaments, hairstyles, and so on. Old illustrations are separated from their original context and employed in new arrangements. As a result, it is common to find, for example, the Arawak in Inca garb, or an illustration of Cuzco that includes drawings of the Aztec jugglers brought back to Europe by Hernán Cortez. *Cabeza de Vaca* is, then, a new "bricolage" where the numerous elements that represent Amerindian cultures tell us more about ourselves than about our Others. As in Debry, the juxtaposition is far from chaotic: "[European] perception of cultural differences and of social and political relations becomes clearer when seen through a complex symbolism of the human body, whether alive and healthy, dismembered, or monstrous, and of the foods exchanged, prepared, or eaten by Amerindians and Europeans."[21]

If such is the case in *Cabeza de Vaca*, what meanings are bestowed on the monstrous, textured, adorned bodies it presents? To answer this question I will concentrate on the figure of Mala Cosa (Evil Thing), the village of "savage" women, and the "Amerindian brother."

FIGURE 11.2. Mala Cosa/Evil Thing: The Other as monstrous.

MALA COSA/EVIL THING

The film figure of Mala Cosa (fig. 11.2) is quite different from that rendered in the text, although each plays an important role in its narrative structure. In the *Naufragios,* this figure validates the colonization and Christianity: the Christian soldier, Alvar Núñez, defeats a pagan sorcerer and liberates the Indians from the forces of evil.[22] In the film, Mala Cosa appears first as a feared, cruel being. Later, however, he is cast as more human when he cries upon Cabeza de Vaca's departure. In narrative terms, Mala Cosa is an important figure because he initiates Cabeza de Vaca, the man, into shamanism and the indigenous world. However, it is problematic that Mala Cosa's abnormality (he is a midget without arms or legs) should embody the "Otherness" of Amerindian cultures. Confined to the realm of the monstrous, the magical, and the emotional, Mala Cosa becomes an emblematic figure for ethnographic imagination. Feared and desired, it is a figure through which colonial violence can be safely brought to language. In his monologue, the film's Alvar Núñez exclaims: "*¿Dios, qué hago aquí en esta tierra? . . . Esclavo de granujas y de este ser monstruoso, Mala Cosa. Ríete, Ríete! En mi país te habrían empalado*" (God, what am I doing here in this land? . . . Enslaved by morons and this monstrous being, Mala Cosa. Laugh, Laugh! In my country they would have impaled you).

FIGURE 11.3. The village of "savage" women.

THE VILLAGE OF "SAVAGE" WOMEN

After leaving Mala Cosa, Cabeza de Vaca wanders through the desert (the trial by suffering of the Christian hagiographic tradition) and arrives at a village where several women have captured the remaining soldiers of Narváez's expedition. The women are engaged in a euphoric ceremony accompanied by music, cries, and excessive consumption of a beverage (fig. 11.3). Several issues are raised by this sequence: the figure of the savage woman, the colonial gaze, cannibalism in colonial discourse, and the importance of this sequence within the film narrative as a whole.

The first shot of the village is preceded by Alvar Núñez's cry of "*¡Dios mío!*" (My God!) in "off." This utterance is striking because it is preceded by a speechless desert sequence. It is significant because Alvar Núñez's expression morally distances the spectator from the images that follow. The camera focuses on a fat woman dressed in a leopard's hide. Her arms are painted blue, and we see her gulping a beverage. The obesity and the excessive consumption of beverage suggest an uncontrolled sexual desire. The animal hide and the painted arms convey an ambivalent body: fierce and erotic at the same time. She is an object of desire and of horror. This ambivalent figure is quite common in the colonial imaginary, known under various names and belonging to different periods and literary traditions: the Amazons, the *vagina dentata*, the femme fatale. In colonial discourse, it is a disturbing figure because it undermines the sexual matrix (phallocentrism) that presupposes and justifies colonization, since colonial discourse represents the land as a virgin, feminine space, waiting to be penetrated.[23]

But the Amazon or the femme fatale is much more than a figure of feared role inversion. This figure's violence and power expose the epistemological trauma of colonial discourse—its desire, and inability, to know everything. The anxiety generated by this failure is, in turn, expressed through a figure "not entirely legible, predictable, or manageable." Sexual discourse, as Doane argues, becomes not only the locus of what can and cannot be known, but also of what can and cannot be possessed. This figure disrupts the basis of patriarchal order, decentering the active/passive axis of the gendered subject: "[the femme fatale] is an ambivalent figure because she is not the subject of power but its *carrier.* Indeed, if the *femme fatale* over represents the body it is because she is attributed with a body which is itself given agency independently of consciousness. In a sense, she has power *despite herself.*"[24]

Through rapid-paced movements, music, cries, absence of language, and abrupt cuts, *Cabeza de Vaca* portrays these native women as "fatal"—with power but without conscience. What role do these irrational, violent figures play in the film's narrative? What closure do they demand? The eventual destruction of these figures is paramount in *Cabeza de Vaca* because through this act, the hero-shaman emerges as a rational, autonomous, and self-restrained subject. If this figure expresses the anxiety of the dissolution of male identity (uncontrollable desires, loss of subjectivity and conscience), its elimination restores it. In a colonial context, the destruction of this figure plays another role: it justifies European intervention and the restoration of order.

One particular prop used in this sequence represents the restoration of colonial/patriarchal order. It is a long, phallic-shaped staff carried by the woman who commands the ritual. It resembles the one described in another colonial narrative about cannibalism—Hans Staden's captivity in Brazil during the 1500s, retold in Nelson Pereira Dos Santos's film *How Tasty Was My Little Frenchman* (1971).[25] It is also depicted in one of Debry's engravings. It is not surprising, then, to see that with this staff the savage women kill Esquivel, the Spanish survivor who ate other members of the expedition. In the confusion that is created later in the sequence, Esteban, the black man, "restores" order. Perhaps the choice of a black man is not gratuitous here. In the colonial imaginary, black bodies are often oversexualized. Esteban takes the staff and kills the savage woman who had just stabbed a young

Indian from another village (who later becomes Cabeza de Vaca's "brother"). The reappropriation of this staff signals the restitution of the phallic order, a *poetic justice* that restores the symbolic order (in a Lacanian sense).

The second important element in this fragment is the colonial gaze. The camera's perspective is conformed by a gendered, one-directional view. The colonial gaze here is phallo-ethnocentric. It is the bodies of the Others that are the main object of inquiry or visual pleasure. This fantasy can be sustained only as long as the objects of the erotic gaze remain passive. If they act as a subject, however, they are seen as monstrous, then destroyed.[26] In the climax of the ritual in progress, three women with their legs painted blue come out of small tents. The camera objectifies them, focusing only on their legs. Other strategies of colonial discourse turn them into erotic objects: the unveiling of the mysterious, unknown, or desired, and the trope of abundance.[27] Moving erotically, the first pair of legs exits a tent (unveiling) and is joined by two other pairs of similarly textured legs—signaling an abundance or excess of sexual gratification. In the next shot, we see the face of a woman who is carrying a torch in her hand. As a subject, the indigenous body is turned monstrous. At this point, arrows appear from all directions and destroy the village of "savage women."

The third important element in the sequence of the "savage women" is the update of what happened to the rest of the Narváez expedition. Lost and without food, those Spaniards had begun to eat each other until only one was left: Esquivel, an overweight Spaniard who laughs obnoxiously as he retells the story. Peter Mason mentions that one of the reasons why cannibalism was condemned by medieval and Renaissance European culture was its being associated with the lack of sexual control.[28] The term *vagina dentata*, for example, reveals how sexual and oral desires are intertwined. Here, Esquivel's obesity, cannibalism, and disrespect tell a story of lack of social restraint. Most important, it is a story framed by a story of unbridled sexuality (the "savage women"). The two stories are ambiguously separated because we never know for sure if the "savage women" are cannibals or not—we do see, however, the building of fires below large cauldrons next to the Spanish prisoners. These two stories set the hero-shaman on the "right" side. In other words, he is presented as a self-restrained, gendered subject. The hero-shaman has successfully endured the trial by temptation.

In *Cabeza de Vaca,* cannibalism becomes a metaphor for the self-destruction of the body politic, of the rule of Law. It is through the human body that the disastrous story of Narváez's expedition is told. Now it is read as a

result of misfortunes caused not by external forces but by an internal, uncontrolled force: desire. The bottom line is that unrestrained desire destroys/
devours nations—Spanish (Narváez's expedition) and native (the village of
"savage women"). This is hardly a proposal that breaks with the tenets of a
rational, autonomous modern subjectivity. In this respect, what Brazilian
director Pereira Dos Santos does with cannibalism in *How Tasty Was My
Little Frenchman* is, in my view, a more thought-provoking proposal. For
him and other Brazilians of the Movimento Antropófago (Cannibal Movement) of the 1920s and the Cinema Novo of the 1960s and 1970s, cannibalism is a metaphor that describes the savage "nature" of modern, capitalistic
society. Joaquim Pedro de Andrade, a contemporary of Pereira Dos Santos,
explains it quite vividly: "Every consumer is reducible, in the last analysis, to
cannibalism. The present work relationships, as well as the relationships
between people—social, political, and economic—are basically cannibalistic."[29] If for Echevarría the unrestrained individual destroys nations, for
Andrade and Pereira Dos Santos the nation (status quo) devours the individual.

The fourth important element of the "savage women" sequence in *Cabeza
de Vaca* is its place within the film narrative. First of all, the story is preceded
by Cabeza de Vaca's pilgrimage through the desert. As in the sixteenth-century text, this represents a journey of spiritual cleansing.[30] The arid landscape strengthens the hero's will to face future trials (the "savage women").
His arrival in their village is thus framed as the struggle between Virtue and
Sin. Since the "savage women" are destroyed, Virtue prevails: from this point
on, Cabeza de Vaca and the other Spaniards are *followed* by the Amerindians.
This consensual domination is expressed through the brotherly love between
Cabeza de Vaca and a young Amerindian, Ariano.

Those Melodramatic Moments: Mexican Cinema
and the Amerindian Brother

Family and love relationships have been two themes used by colonial discourse in the Americas. In film, the paternalistic Jesuits of *The Mission* and
the love story in *Dances with Wolves* are recent examples. Along the same
line, the disastrous journey in Werner Herzog's *Aguirre, the Wrath of God*
was doomed, perhaps because of Lope de Aguirre's incestuous desire for his
daughter. In *Cabeza de Vaca*, a brotherly love articulates an idealized colonial relationship. Ariano, the young Indian man, was introduced in the "savage women" sequence. One of the women wounds him near the heart—the

symbolism couldn't be clearer. Cabeza de Vaca decides to save him. For this he has to cut open the Amerindian's body and extract the arrowhead embedded in his chest. Alvar Núñez succeeds, and from then on, the young Amerindian follows him (consensual domination) until they come close to a Spanish camp. The opening of the Indian body is followed by the opening of the native body politic. After the successful operation, Cabeza de Vaca and his party are well received in the boy's village. Everyone cheers their arrival. Half-naked women approach the Spaniards and offer them baskets of food: an offer that suggests the offering of the body (and body politic), as in Debry's engravings or the Tahitian figures of Gauguin.[31] This welcome is followed by a utopic vision of colonial relationships: around a warm campfire, Esteban sings African songs to indigenous children, and the Spaniards sleep peacefully, embraced by Amerindian women. This utopian vision is a nostalgic rendering of a world seen as completely lost (in the end, Ariano dies). As in *The Mission,* the entire story stresses the European hero's impotence to "save" Amerindian cultures.[32]

This story is quite revealing of the film's ultimate affirmation of a self-restrained, gendered hero. A homoerotic desire seems to run through it, although it is suppressed. This is suggested by John Kraniauskas, who comments on the passage in which Alvar Núñez resuscitates an Amerindian woman:

> It becomes a central event in the process of cementing an alliance between Cabeza de Vaca and the young Indian Chief Ariano. The event is so staged and gendered in a particular sexual fashion now that the intended audience is not the Imperial Crown but an unknown middle-class one. Cabeza de Vaca resuscitates an apparently dead and naked Indian woman by blowing all over her body to rid it of evil spirits. This act of eroticized shamanism consolidates the alliance between Alvar and Ariano. The Indian woman, however, subsequently drops out of view. And Ariano is soon killed at the melodramatic end of the film when "civilization" reappears. The culture industry leaves its trace insofar as it transforms the essentially mournful or tragic materials of the Chronicle into a melodrama of failed male cross-cultural bonding.[33]

Cabeza de Vaca's melodramatic plot is made possible by reducing Amerindian culture to individual characters. Ariano seems to become the metonym of

Amerindian society. Also, the story invites the spectator to identify with the white man's suffering. The pathos of the story is Alvar Núñez's suffering for the death of Ariano, not Amerindian suffering.

The melodramatic element in *Cabeza de Vaca* as a trace of the industry highlighted by Kraniauskas is essential for understanding the film in its own historical context; that is, its relationship with Latin American cinema, particularly Mexican cinema and its golden age, the age of *Allá en el rancho grande* (Over on the Big Ranch, 1936) and *María Candelaria* (1943). During roughly two decades (1935–1955), Mexican cinema became not only Mexico's third largest industry, but also a recognized medium of national self expression.[34] During this era, the works of director Emilio Fernández, "El Indio," and cinematographer Gabriel Figueroa established an image of "Mexicanness" that left its trace on the country's cinema and national imagination for many decades. The landscape was coded as "national" through several thematic and formal procedures: emblematic plants such as the maguey and oblique perspectives that offered impressive images of the land, the horizon, and the sky.[35] In *Cabeza de Vaca* the desert landscapes and smoky horizons are significant elements for coding the past in a national and Latin American film language, although in a subtler way than the poetics of Fernández and Figueroa's films of the golden age of Mexican cinema. Although it is not the topic of this article, examining filmmaking in Mexico since the golden age may be equally important for understanding Echevarría's cinematography. For example, I find a strong resemblance between Luis Buñuel's *Simón del desierto* (Simon of the Desert, 1965) and *Cabeza de Vaca*. Buñuel's desert landscapes (Figueroa was the photographer for this film) are, as in *Cabeza de Vaca*, morally coded spaces. The coarse "Dreyerian" faces, the midget farmer, and the trials by temptation of Buñuel's work all seem to be echoed by Echevarría's film. Buñuel's morbid satire, however, contrasts with *Cabeza de Vaca*'s somber tone.

To sum up, Nicolás Echevarría's *Cabeza de Vaca* tells a powerful and moving tale in which the modern and the tribal worlds collide. Seeking to overcome the Eurocentric vision of the colonization of the Americas, the film focuses on the intercultural practices of an "exemplary" man, Alvar Núñez Cabeza de Vaca, who discovers and embraces a tribal world. This modern look at a tribal world is nonetheless realized through a nostalgic lens that derives its power (pathos) from the suppression of the Other's historical reality (Amerindian resistance and endurance). The film's circular narrative structure seems to underscore this ideological entrapment. The metropolitan spectator's desire for the tribal world emerges from its (imagined) absence. The film, thus, actualizes and mediates a desire for a remote, unrecoverable, primitive world. This comes as no surprise, considering that film has been known precisely for this aspect since the Lumiere brothers: its unprecedented ability to render in captivating images worlds we dream of, while apparently dissolving our complex neocolonial world.

Notes

1. Alvar Núñez Cabeza de Vaca, *Naufragios* (Madrid: Cátedra, 1989).

2. See Jean Franco, "High-Tech Primitivism: The Representation of Tribal Societies in Feature Films," in *Mediating Two Worlds,* ed. John King and Ana López (London: British Film Institute, 1993), 81–94. Renato Rosaldo illustrates how an idealized primitive society is used as a stable referent for modern metropolitan identity without the complexities of the present in "Imperialist Nostalgia," *Representations* 26 (1989): 107–122. Regarding the image of tribal societies in the United States, see Robert Baird, "Going Indian: In and Around *Dances with Wolves,*" *Michigan Academician* 25 (1993): 133–146.

3. Joanne Hershfield, "Assimilation and Identification in Nicolás Echevarría's *Cabeza de Vaca,*" *Wide Angle* 16, no. 3 (1995): 13.

4. Dudley Andrew, *Concepts in Film Theory* (New York: Oxford University Press, 1984), 96–106.

5. Rolena Adorno, "The Negotiation of Fear in Cabeza de Vaca's *Naufragios,*" *New World Encounters,* ed. Stephen Greenblatt (Berkeley: University of California Press, 1993), 48–84. See also Jacques Lafaye, "Les miracles d'Alvar Núñez Cabeza de Vaca (1527–36)," *Bulletin hispanique* 64 (1962): 2–28; Enrique Pupo-Walker, "Pesquisas para una nueva lectura de los *Naufragios* de Alvar Núñez Cabeza de Vaca," *Revista Iberoamericana* 140 (1987): 517–539, and "Los *Naufragios* de Alvar Núñez Cabeza de Vaca: Notas sobre la relevancia antropológica," *Revista de Indias* 47, no. 181 (1987): 755–776; Maureen Ahern, "The Cross and the Gourd: The Appropriation of Ritual Signs in the *Relaciones* of Alvar Núñez Cabeza de Vaca and Fray Marcos de Niza," in *Early Images of the Americas,* ed. Jerry M. Williams and Robert E. Lewis (Tucson: University of Arizona Press, 1993), 215–244.

6. For a general view of Latin American cinema, see John King, *Magical Reels: A History of Cinema in Latin America* (London: Verso, 1990).

7. Frank Kermode, "Secrets and Narrative Sequence," in *On Narrative,* ed. W. J. T. Mitchell (Chicago: University of Chicago Press, 1981), 82–84.

8. Seymour Chatman, "What Novels Can Do that Films Can't (and Vice Versa)," in Mitchell, *On Narrative*, 117–136.

9. Kermode, "Secrets and Narrative Sequence," 87.

10. Hayden White, *Tropics of Discourse: Essays in Cultural Criticism* (Baltimore: Johns Hopkins University Press, 1978), 171.

11. Hershfield, "Assimilation and Identification," 13.

12. Michel Foucault, *Madness and Civilization: A History of Insanity in the Age of Reason*, trans. Richard Howard (New York: Vintage, 1988), 25.

13. Slavoj Zizek, "How to Give Body to a Deadlock?" in *Thinking Bodies*, ed. Juliet Flower MacCanell and Laura Zakarin (Stanford, CA: Stanford University Press, 1994), 63–77.

14. For a complete listing of Echevarría's works, see Joaquim Romaguera, *Diccionario filmográfico universal*, vol. 1, *Directores de España, Portugal y Latinoamérica* (Barcelona: Laertes, 1994).

15. Cabeza de Vaca spent most of those eight years on the coast of Texas, among the Coahuiltecans and Karankawas. According to Campbell and Newcomb, besides Cabeza de Vaca's chronicle, we do not have much information about these cultures in the sixteenth century. T. N. Campbell, "Coahuiltecans and Their Neighbors," in *Handbook of North American Indians*, ed. Alfonso Ortiz, vol. 10 (Washington, DC: Smithsonian Institution Press, 1983), 334; and W. Newcomb, "Karankawa," in ibid., 359.

16. "Cabeza de Vaca," in Mexican TV series *Los que hacen nuestro cine* (n.d.). Distributed by Latin American Video Archives (LAVA).

17. Fatimah Tobing Rony, *Race, Cinema, and Ethnographic Spectacle* (Durham, NC: Duke University Press, 1996), 14.

18. Ibid., 79–80.

19. Hershfield, "Assimilation and Identification," 13.

20. See Bernadette Bucher, *Icon and Conquest: A Structural Analysis of the Illustrations of De Bry's "Great Voyages,"* trans. Basia Miller Gulati (Chicago: University of Chicago Press, 1981), 17–18.

21. Ibid., xvi.

22. Mala Cosa appears in chapter XXII of the *Naufragios*. It is a story in which body and dismemberment are highly symbolic. According to the chronicle, he often came to indigenous villages and selected, apparently at random, someone to be operated on: he made several cuts on his/her body, extracted his/her bowels, severed his/her arms and then proceeded to replace them. Since the Amerindians feared Mala Cosa, Cabeza de Vaca promised to protect them from such an evil thing. For a more detailed discussion of this topic, see Rolena Adorno, "Cómo leer a 'Mala Cosa': mitos caballerescos y amerindios en los *Naufragios* de Cabeza de Vaca," in *Crítica y descolonización: El sujeto colonial en la cultura latinoamericana*, ed. Beatriz González

Stephan and Lucía Helena Costigan (Caracas: Universidad Simón Bolívar, 1992), 87–107.

23. Peter Mason, "Portrayal and Betrayal: The Colonial Gaze in Seventeenth Century Brazil," *Culture and History* 6 (1989): 59.

24. See Mary Ann Doane, *Femmes Fatales: Feminism, Film Theory, Psychoanalysis* (New York: Routledge, 1991), 1–2.

25. See also Richard Peña, "How Tasty Was My Little Frenchman," in *Brazilian Cinema*, ed. Randal Johnson and Robert Stam (East Brunswick, NJ: Associated University Presses, 1982), 191–199.

26. See Mason, "Portrayal and Betrayal," 59.

27. David Spurr, *The Rhetoric of Empire* (Durham, NC: Duke University Press, 1993), 174–175.

28. Peter Mason, *Deconstructing America: Representations of the Other* (New York: Routledge, 1990), 56.

29 J. Pedro de Andrade, "Cannibalism and Self-Cannibalism," in Johnson and Stam, *Brazilian Cinema,* 82–83.

30. Pupo-Walker, "Pesquisas," 528.

31. Bucher, *Icon and Conquest,* 65; Peter Brooks, *Body Work: Objects of Desire in Modern Narrative* (Cambridge, MA: Harvard University Press, 1993), 194.

32. Franco, "High-Tech Primitivism," 85.

33. John Kraniauskas, "Cabeza de Vaca," *Travesia (Journal of Latin American Cultural Studies)* 1, no. 2 (1992): 113–122. Quote from 120–121.

34. Charles Ramírez Berg, "The Cinematic Invention of Mexico: The Poetics and Politics of the Fernández-Figueroa Style," in *The Mexican Cinema Project,* ed. Chon Noriega and Steven Ricci (Los Angeles: UCLA Film and Television Archive, 1994), 13.

35. According to Ramírez Berg (ibid., 19–23), Fernández and Figueroa, who worked on some thirteen films together, drew from different visual traditions, including the popular art of the Mexican engraver Guadalupe Posada and the depth composition of Eisenstein, Greg Tolland, Orson Welles, and others, to render an oblique perspective counter to the hegemonic perspective of Hollywood films.

12

Subliminal Body

Shamanism, Ancient Theater, and Ethnodrama

GABRIEL WEISZ

This text comes out of the void because it deals with an unformed world in dramaturgical discourse. The world of the "Indians" or of the "Natives"—one can see that naming has become problematical—is depicted in dramaturgy only to create a melodramatic setting to promote nationalistic projects, or else to discuss how the unjust treatment of Indians demonstrates the inadequacy of various governments. However, little if anything is mentioned about shamanistic tradition, its intrinsic cultural and social value, and its dramaturgical potential. It seems that this has been a forgotten land of mind for most playwrights, as though part of a general atmosphere of cultural denial. The Indians are there, but most people prefer to place their human presence inside an invisible bubble.

Part of the untold story is inhabited by marginal female figures. Women who belong to various ethnic groups throughout the Mexican territory are the most repressed and ignored. Within shamanistic lore, however, these women are central; they abandon a silent identity and have access to a highly participatory one. Women shamans are endowed with power and command respect within the community. A new dramaturgy, an alternative field of character representation, could undoubtedly come forth if these female voices were heard. Yet, driven out by poverty, the woman shaman becomes a servant in the city, losing her culture, dignity, and strength.

Part of my aim is to connect the healing performance of women shamans in Mexico with the ancient dramaturgical role of women in the origins of Greek theater rituals. If we recall the mythical manifestations of female performers during the Dionysian festivities, we can appreciate the critical role played by women in ancient ritual performance, before the paternalistic development of classical theater.

In exploring the tension between body and voice, and other characteristics in theater and shamanistic performance, I have also chosen to look at the play *María Antonia,* by Eugenio Hernández, which addresses the magical world of Cuban Santería. Thus I have deliberately sought to cut across cultural boundaries in configuring a discourse on ethnodrama. Moreover, as a representative piece of Afro-Cuban theater, *María Antonia* seems to escape from the above-mentioned shortcomings of *indigenista* theater; nevertheless, the special demands of dramaturgy, as well as the play's marked preference for creating spectacular dramaturgical effects, end by overshadowing an otherwise suggestive shamanistic discourse.

My theoretical discussion, then, will center on performance and hinge upon three instances: the woman's role in ancient Greek theater, the construction of a female character in a modern Afro-Cuban play, and the "real-life" healing performances of Indian women shamans in Mexico. These instances will illustrate the problems and possibilities of a body-centered (as opposed to logocentric) dramaturgy, which may serve to redirect and authenticate (the often superficial) primitivism in modern theater.

A powerful theoretical tool for theater studies stems from the strategies used in performance criticism, while a relatively new and related dimension is born with the introduction of a research area where theater and anthropology converge. Acknowledging this field, I want to mention the role played by ethnodrama. I coined the term *ethnodrama* as a noetic approach to ritual phenomena. Ethnology addresses the problem of ethnic performative forms that do not correspond exclusively to the kind of performance that defines Western theater. In the context of ethnodrama, drama is conceived as a text whose final destination is action. Shamanistic events are eloquent examples of ethnodramatic performance; a text incorporating space, the body, and the supernatural is written during healing ceremonies. In this way a different concept of dramaturgy in action enters the sacred precinct of the written text in our cultures. In contrast, performance criticism selects the text of a play as a script to be worked in performance. The need to perform plays is framed by a method. This analytical method redefines a written text: through a historical framework it activates the performance idioms of the past and present.

Dramatic critical literature depends heavily on Aristotelian poetics, or a dramatic *logos* prejudiced against the stage idioms of theater. Aristotle considered "spectacle" as "the least artistic [part], and connected least with the art of poetry." Later, it was considered a truism that "The production of spectacular effects depends more on the art of the stage machinist than of the poet."[1] A more recent trend is for exponents of New Criticism to insist on subordinating performance idioms to the verbal elements of the text. These critical modalities tend to derogate the basic attributes of performance and to decipher plays as somewhat complex poems. In performance criticism the text is exposed to actors and then worked by the visual and temporal demands of a play performed for an audience.

Ethnodramatic analysis, in turn, is not as focused on the operative elements of theater as performance criticism. Ethnodrama explores a variety of body techniques that provide performance with a ritual structure. This analytical activity is not restricted to the dramatic and performable attributes that belong to the theater. Our field of study deals with a diversification of drama to include phenomena, such as shamanistic performances, that are very different from theatrical events.

Many performance researchers apply the same terminology to theater and shamanistic performances. I think that each entity has specific dramaturgical strategies, and they should not all be regarded as one and the same. Greek theater inherited most of its performance idioms from Dionysian rituals and Aristotelian poetics. Shamanistic performances are conformed by ritual and conceptual backgrounds directed to the manifestation and healing of magical bodies. Once our field is made clear, we can focus our attention on a few specular projections of women characters in Greek mythology, then move on to some examples of women's roles in ethnic theater and shamanism.

To explain specular projections we will throw a quick glance at Lacan's mirror-stage theory. Lacan observed that before the infant has reached the age of eighteen months, it is able to recognize itself in the mirror. The infant visualizes a gestalt or body image located in the world and yet distinct from itself. The image of a corporeal integration is achieved, separated by an "I" concept that provides a space where the self is able to create itself. The specular image designates a way in which humans recognize and create themselves through the image of others.[2]

Specular theory suggests the composition of an intrinsic nature. For the present purposes we can imagine the creation of an intrinsic text organized around an inner character; this entity could be the source for specular projections in mythology. Thus the maenads, women followers of Dionysus, at the pitch of a sacred ecstasy seized animals and devoured them. It was believed that by consuming the animals, the maenads incorporated both the god and the creatures' power within themselves. Following specular theory, it might be said that a sacred Dionysian gestalt was achieved by the maenads. Ecstasy was defined as a trance state "in which the soul, quitting the body, [saw] visions."[3] By means of this Dionysian gestalt, the maenads experienced an ecstatic specular projection that provided an integration of a magical body. The shamanistic traits of Dionysus appear not only in the legendary dismemberment theme but also in his shape-shifter attributes and the trance dance rituals related to Dionysianism. Dionysus Eleutherus was a shaman-istic god believed to posses apotropaic and curative powers; but the intro-duction of his image to the psyche could be the cause of disease.[4] The god was associated with vines, ivy, and bulls, and sometimes he was called "the god of the tree"; he and his maenads were clad in fawn skins. The maenads wore human masks.

The participation of women in Dionysian myths and rituals generated the basic elements for performance and character formation in Greek the-ater. During the Dionysia, festivals in which dramatic performances took place, women had vanished from the scene and male dramatists prevailed. One can wonder how these dramatists took over to implement a patriarchal appropriation of the theater, soon turning ritual behavior into an aesthetic and rationalistic frame of the logos. Two modalities of cognition seem to emerge.

We are confronted with a basic difference between symbolic and body cognition. The symbolic order is where reason, the conscious mind, logic, analysis, and writing are construed; in body cognition, the heavily meta-phoric, sensual, and affectionate persist. Likewise, we may envisage drama as belonging to a symbolic order or to a realm of body cognition where shamanism and ethnodrama are found. Body cognition is also linked to what in contemporary terms Hélène Cixous has called *écriture féminine,* a textual place where bodily energies and the voices of the unconscious emerge. Artaud, according to Derrida, thought about a kind of theater where "visibility is not a performance staged by the *parole* [voice] of the master. [It is] Repre-sentation as self-representation of the visible and the purity of the sensi-tive."[5] In this way Artaud broke the ground for a body dramaturgy closely related to Cixous's *écriture féminine.* However, this *écriture* has not yet been incorporated within the discursive parameters of a contemporary drama-turgy that deals with ritual practice. It appears that the body dramaturgy of shamanistic lore is denied by the textual dramaturgy of theater.

Before giving full attention to shamanistic performances and ethnodrama proper, some considerations must be set aside in the realm of the symbolic order of drama. For this purpose, I have selected Eugenio Hernández's *María Antonia,* written in 1964, because of the ritual contextualization of Cuban Santería.[6] Santería is a religious amalgamation of African Yoruba healing cults and Spanish Catholicism. The supernatural powers of the Yoruba gods were transferred to certain Catholic saints by virtue of their symbolic or iconic affinity.

Hernández's plot can be summarized as the following. María Antonia is a strong female who wants to establish a longstanding relationship with Julián. After he wins a boxing match, Julián's future seems to offer better opportunities than before. María Antonia poisons Julián, afraid that the successful young boxer will abandon her. This basically simple plot may be misleading, since at critical moments in the play Santería ritual invocations provide the text with an encoded semantic system. For the time being, a few ideas on specific aspects of dramaturgical and ritual discourse should be laid out.

Although the play does not lack interesting ritual aspects, it cannot escape from a good deal of problematizing, mainly through the construction of femaleness and maleness that often falls into every conceivable macho cliche. A disabling of the macho/master discourse would have fruitfully challenged the self-legitimizing positions held by all the male characters. At any rate, a set of subjective issues is introduced in the play to reinforce a recuperative enterprise of the Santería (culturally specific) magical discourse. Later, this discourse becomes reshaped within the dramaturgical milieu, in order to interweave theatrical and ritual elements. The culture-specific dimension of the Santería terminology supports an autonomous dramaturgical language. Nevertheless, throughout the play the Santería performative body is subjugated to the symbolic logos of the theatrical master discourse.

The first scene deploys playwright Eugenio Hernández's tactics to integrate magical shamanistic elements in his dramaturgical structure in an ornamental fashion. Madrina, María Antonia's godmother, invokes magical help to free her goddaughter from an evil entity. As spectators, we do not know that María Antonia has murdered Julián. This adds to a paradoxical atmosphere that helps to enhance a ritual setting for the play as a whole. The godmother asks for the intervention of Oshún, patroness of rivers and goddess of love. Elegguá, the one who opens and closes doors, is also summoned, because he is able to open destiny's trap. Shangó sends thunderbolts and personifies virility. The last to be invoked is Yemayá, a goddess who controls maternity and womanhood. Shortly afterward, in what seems a rather cryptic statement, Madrina begs the *babalao* (shaman) to assist her and thus prevent "the separation of the head from the body." Such was the fate of Saint Barbara, invested in Santería with the supernatural powers of Shangó. Saint Barbara—historically a Christian princess who lived in the fourth century—was beheaded by her father. Instantly he was struck down by a bolt of lightning. The association between the male principle or thunderbolt and the female characteristics of Saint Barbara come together. In addition, we observe the association of Shangó and Saint Barbara in María Antonia's character. Yet María Antonia is too far gone to enjoy the healing advantages of Santería. She despises the shaman's restorative powers and is blind to the evil spirit that has taken hold of her. Later she is murdered by a jealous boyfriend. The denial of Shangó's male powers along with the female ones has tragic consequences. The murderous boyfriend thrusts a knife into María Antonia's vagina, killing her in her sexual femaleness.

This limited account shows how the play operates at different semantic and cultural levels, as well as adding a few examples of the complex intertextuality that flows between Santería and the characters in *María Antonia*.

Since dramaturgical structures provide a certain kind of knowing, we could affirm that an epistemology of conflict leads to a tendency for dramatic action to be solved in a specific way. If ritual discourse is subjected to dramaturgical structures, will there not be a need to appropriate and capture otherness so as to make it conform to an epistemology of conflict? The problem with this subjection is that it acts as an instrument which requires equating, within a dramaturgical nomenclature, what remains unequal to its purpose. This is what I meant earlier by the subjugation of ritual to a theatrical master discourse.

However, is this not, at a broader cultural and historical level, the very problem implicit in a whole Christian power system assimilating the divine attributes of the Yoruba pantheon, as occurs in Santería? These and other questions must be raised while discussing any strategy to challenge the multiple articulations of a master discourse, appropriation, and subjugation. It was through the colonization process that Catholicism and Spanish were introduced to Cuba; these were the main devices in the construction of the master's logos. Moreover, after indigenous culture was obliterated and Africans were imported through the slave trade, the colonizer's strategy consisted in keeping black male societies isolated in order to prevent the unification of the dreaded African ethnic groups. However, in the late eighteenth century a revolutionary slave movement fighting against captivity and promoting the restoration of human dignity broke out. The movement, which culminated in the Escalera Conspiracy, was denounced in 1843, and the colonial authorities unleashed a terrible repression against all African cults. It was not until 1880 that the abolition of slavery was approved by the government. But even by 1870, African religious cults were tolerated. During the late nineteenth century, in the secret male Society of the Abakuá, Andrés Petit and Pedro Nkisi brought together African and Catholic religious elements. Thus, a slow process of resignification, affecting both traditions, took place. Later, Lorenzo Samá worked another merging process with Latúa, a black Yoruba woman. They wove a liturgical body known as the Regla de Ocha (Rule of Ocha) or Santería.

Perhaps the most important aspect of Santería, within the theoretical narrative that concerns us, is that language merges with herbs, plants, roots, and flowers. The *santero* shaman is able to cure practically any disease. This herbalism is closely related to the *orishas* (gods or goddesses), since roots, flowers, trees, and plants belong to them, and thus the right protocol, asking for their permission, must be performed before using any of the plants that they inhabit. A somatic dramaturgy involving the santero's spells, a conversation with supernatural herbal spirits, and the patient, seems to define Santería as a shamanistic performance dedicated to the body.

In order to amplify this concept, we will shift our attention to another domain of somatic dramaturgy in shamanistic performances, this time within Indian tradition. Body cognition in pre-Hispanic Mexican shamanism combines myth, performance, and healing. During Colonial times the Yappan myth was very popular among the Indians. This was a creation myth in which, according to Náhuatl tradition, animals were still human. The myth, as told by a native, was first recorded by Hernando Ruíz de Alarcón in a 1692 treatise.[7] The legend describes the life of Yappan, a man who aspired to attain perfection. Yappan abandons his wife and dedicates his life to penitence. The goddess Xochiquetzal wants to prevent Yappan from receiving the gift of sublime transformation, the reward of the gods for his penitence. Xochiquetzal seduces him, an enemy cuts off Yappan's head, and the gods turn him into a headless scorpion. He is later immortalized as Colotl, the scorpion constellation, beautifully depicted in the *Codex Tro-Cortesiano*.

The shaman who treated a scorpion's bite had to be a woman or a male of the *sexe-renversé,* in order to incarnate the magical powers of the goddess Xochiquetzal. The wound was rubbed with *piciete,* a kind of tobacco believed to have healing properties. As the shaman suctioned the wound, s/he exclaimed: "Come here most pious Yappan, the one with the curved tip; where have you wounded us?" Then s/he covered the person with a *huipil* (mantle) and tied a ribbon around the injured part, after which s/he embraced and caressed the patient.[8] The purpose of all these activities was to simulate the legendary intercourse between the goddess and Yappan. This kind of ritual performance invokes a healing function and addresses both the legendary deities and the body. (The term "performance" has been defined as "Variously called actions, events, . . . pieces, things, the works present in physical activities, ordinary bodily functions and other usual and unusual manifestations of physicality.")[9] Thus we could think of a healing performance as a space where unusual and magical manifestations of physicality take place.

I have already indicated the rationalistic frame of the logos. Another dimension of the term is available among Mazatec shamans, for whom hallucinogenic mushrooms are known as the Word. The late Mazatec shaman María Sabina explained once that it was through the voice of the mushrooms that she was instructed: "María Sabina, this is the Book of Knowledge. This is the Book of Language. All that is written within is for you. The Book is yours; take it and work with it."[10] María Sabina contacted an invisible book in a subjective performance that endowed her with shamanistic knowledge. Mushrooms take on humanlike attributes and are called *santitos* (little saints). These characters advised María Sabina on the healing procedures required to cure her patients. This is why I referred to a subjective performance.

Another eloquent example of shamanistic subjective performances comes to mind when reviewing the magical activities of Pachita, a woman shaman who worked in Mexico City until her death a couple of years ago. She received in her body the spirit of Cuauhtémoc, a notorious Aztec king who ruled just before the Spaniards invaded Tenochtitlan (later known as Mexico City). Pachita explained that as she fell into a trance, brother Cuauhtémoc's spirit spoke through her body. While in a trance, and with the spirit occupying her body, she was able to see into her patient's anatomy and thus arrive at a proper diagnosis. In certain cases the patient was subjected to a shamanistic surgical intervention. The operation took place in a darkish room, because, Pachita said, "Human organs do not tolerate intense light and might even be damaged." She used a kitchen knife to extirpate the deficient organ. Some people gossiped about a medical friend who provided Pachita with human organs and bones; others suggested that dog and stag vertebrae were used.[11]

What must be pointed out at this stage is the presence of an inner voice, somewhat similar to the voice or voices that engage the dramatist's mental space when he is creating dialogue in a play—but it is different, due to the fact that the voice comes from an inner presence. Also pertinent are the procedures through which a surgical performance occurs. Organs materialize in a magical way; the operation appears as convincing as those performed in a hospital. Once more we find those "unusual manifestations of physicality" identified with performance. At another level, we must not ignore the process by which the body is redefined. The body is a *text* that has undergone cultural patterning. The shaman and her patients believe in the healing power that stems from the body and from those supernatural forces acting against illnesses. Shamanistic performances do not depend on a certain entertainment value devised for an audience; instead, they operate on numerous healing therapies. Let us imagine a circumstance in which the information of an organ deteriorates because of the noise or interference produced by illness. To this we might add that the body is suffering from a disorder in its somatic information or text. In this scenario the shaman is in charge of modifying the somatic text to restore health.

A more detailed appraisal of our own behavior, somatic texts, and their cultural patterning is introduced by Kristeva's notion of the symbolic function:

> By symbolic function we mean a system of signs (first rhythmic and intonational difference, then signifier/signified) which are organized into logico-syntactic structures whose aim is to accredit social communication as exchange purified of pleasure.

Given this frame of the symbolic, she explains:

> The symbolic order functions in our monotheistic West by means of a *system of kinship* that involves transmission of the name of the father and a rigorous prohibition of incest; and a *system of speech* that involves an increasingly logical, simple, positive, and 'scientific' form of communication, that is stripped of all stylistic, rhythmic, and 'poetic' ambiguities.[12]

The symbolic order defines a logocentric blueprint of our somatic constitution in contrast to the "rhythmic and intonational differences" prevalent in shamanistic invocations. The system of kinship is the manner in which our culture writes the body over a system of speech that patterns our communicational monotheism. Once these systems have been enunciated, we come to terms with the differences between body-cognitive writing and symbolic writing.

The Christian logos tradition that dissolves the polytheistic attributes of the Yoruba pantheon, such as in *María Antonia*'s setting for Santería, seems to illustrate such monotheistic communication patterns. However, theater is—in a manner of speaking—also "monotheistic" in the sense that it has an ingrown dramaturgical logos that excludes body dramaturgy. I suspect this is the reason why somatic writing fails to appear, especially in *María Antonia*. If, say, the writer had been as careful with the shamanistic discourse as with the dramaturgical logos imperative, another symbolic dimension of writing would have nourished his play.

To end this paper, I would like to make a brief allusion to Cixous's *écriture féminine* as a possible frame of reference for a future somatic dramaturgy:

> When we read a text, we are either read by the text or we are in the text. Either we tame a text, we ride on it, we roll over it, or we are swallowed up by it. . . . There are thousands of possible relations to a text, and if we are in a nondefensive, nonresisting relationship, we are carried off by the text."[13]

It might be, however, that somatic dramaturgy will have to sprout from a certain autobiographical somatic model provided by the Indians themselves. This dramaturgy is now very much alive in ritual tradition, but much remains to be learned before we cannibalize this tradition into our writing machines. It must be stressed that "writing," in the shamanistic setting, is quite different from that other kind of writing which we associate with novels, poems, and theater. The shamanistic tradition used, and still works with, a certain kind of inscription performed on the body. As the body is "written," it enunciates a meaningful constellation—what Western cultures are now trying to revive.

Notes

1. Aristotle, *Poetics*, in *Criticism: The Major Statements*, ed. Charles Kaplan and William Anderson (New York: St. Martin's Press, 1986). Kaplan's book is quoted in "Performance Criticism," in *Encyclopedia of Contemporary Literary Theory*, ed. Irena R. Makaryk (Toronto: University of Toronto Press, 1993).

2. See Jacques Lacan, *Écrits: A Selection*, trans. Alan Sheridan (New York: W. W. Norton, 1977).

3. "Ecstasy," in *The Oxford Classical Dictionary*, ed. M. Cary et al. (Oxford: Clarendon Press, 1966).

4. A most interesting approach to the shamanistic attributes of Dionysus is researched by Ernest Theodore Kirby, *Ur-Drama: The Origins of Theater* (New York: New York University Press, 1975). I also consulted Steven Lonsdale, *Animals and the Origins of Dance* (New York: Thames and Hudson, 1982).

5. Jacques Derrida, "Le Théâtre de la cruaté et la clôture de la représentation." in his *L'Ecriture et la différence* (Paris: Seuil, 1967), 349.

6. Eugenio Hernández, *María Antonia: Teatro* (Havana: Letras Cubanas, 1989).

7. Hernando Ruíz de Alarcón, "Tratado de las supersticiones de los naturales de esta Nueva España," in his *Tratado de las idolatrías, supersticiones, dioses, ritos, hechicerías y otras costumbres gentilicias de las razas aborígenes de México*, 2nd ed. (Mexico City: Ediciones Fuente Cultural, 1953).

8. This material is found in Gonzalo Aguirre Beltrán, "Medicina indígena," in his *Medicina y magia* (Mexico City: Instituto Nacional Indigenista, 1963). Alarcón is quoted in Beltrán, 53.

9. Sharp, quoted in Bruce Barber, "Indexing: Conditionalism and Its Heretical Equivalents," in *Performance by Artists*, ed. A. A. Bronson and Peggy Gale (Toronto: Art Metropole, 1979), 192.

10. María Sabina, *Vida de María Sabina la sabia de los hongos*, ed. Alvaro Estrada, 3rd ed. (Mexico City: Siglo XXI, 1980), 56.

11. See Lilian Scheffler, "Especialistas: Pachita," in her *Magia y brujería en México* (Mexico City: Panorama Editorial, 1983).

12. Julia Kristeva, "About Chinese Women," in *The Kristeva Reader*, ed. Toril Moi (New York: Columbia University Press, 1986), 150–151.

13. Hélène Cixous, "'Sunday Before Falling Asleep': A Primal Scene," in *Reading with Clarice Lispector*, ed. and trans. Verena Andermatt Conley (Minneapolis: University of Minnesota Press, 1990), 3.

13

Primitivist Construction of Identity in the Work of Frida Kahlo

WENDY B. FARIS

The force of Frida Kahlo's painting depends both for its evocative power and for its individual design and detailing on a fully developed and pervasive primitivism. Given Kahlo's tendency to portray herself repeatedly in her works, her primitivism constitutes an intensely focused construction of identity. Furthermore, her original success, as well as the recent immense enthusiasm for her work, attests to the continuing significance of primitivism as a psychic and aesthetic program, despite postmodern critiques of the cultural appropriation that it involves.

Kahlo's primitivism forms one strand of many artistic traditions that converge in her aesthetics, the other central ones being European Surrealism and New World Baroque, especially Christian ex-votos. Like Alejo Carpentier, who as Amaryll Chanady has shown in a discussion of Carpentier's "*real maravilloso americano*," positions himself with respect to Surrealism so as to "territorialize the imaginary," Kahlo uses an American primitivism to construct an identity that distinguishes her from the European Surrealist matrix that threatened to overwhelm her even while it promoted her.[1]

Because primitivism is so pervasive in Kahlo's work, it is useful to divide it into three interrelated categories: a natural primitivism, in which she connects herself to the earth; a cultural primitivism, in which she links herself to Mexico's indigenous past; and a psychological primitivism, in which she allows herself to regress emotionally—to replay basic childhood scenarios. These primitivisms are primarily thematic, but Kahlo's painting, like that of Henri Rousseau, who may have influenced her, is also formally primitivist in that it eschews linear perspective and illusionist lighting.[2]

FIGURE 13.1. Frida Kahlo, *Self-Portrait with Braid* (1941). (Oil on canvas, 51 cm X 38 cm; © 2000. Reproduction authorized by the Instituto Nacional de Belles Artes y Literatura and by Banco de México, Trustee of the Diego Rivera and Frida Kahlo Museums, Av. 5 de Mayo No. 2, Col. Centro, 06059, México, D.F.)

Kahlo's representations of herself in nature and her move toward pre-Columbian culture provide links to a primitivistically conceived cosmos that includes both natural forms and pre-Columbian images. In *My Nurse and I* Kahlo portrays herself as sucking nourishment from a breast resembling a flower, held in the lap of a large woman with a face that resembles a pre-Columbian obsidian mask. It projects a sense of impassive calm that counteracts the teardrops in the sky rather than an intimate connection between mother and child. The strength of the nurse figure, a combination of nature and indigenous culture, literally nourishes Kahlo's artistic self in the face of personal deprivation.

This is, however, not a traditionally soft, motherly primitivism, but rather a hard if ultimately empowering one, which allows Kahlo to mature—perhaps prematurely and incompletely in some domains—into her artistic self. The awkwardness of that artistic maturity, conjoined with a certain psychological childishness, is suggested by the adult head on the child's body. Thus, in addition to the natural and cultural primitivism here, the psychological variety is clearly in evidence in the figure of the nursing child. The portrait suggests that while Kahlo's personal hunger for intimacy and affection may have remained perpetually unsatisfied, her artistic self found nourishment at the breast of Mexico's indigenous and natural forms.[3] Kahlo may look unresponsive here, but perhaps her impassive face is the face of Kahlo the mature artist, identified with the similarly impassive face of the nurse figure, now distinct from, although also forever related to, the only partially nourished child.

Kahlo survived and flourished as an artist because she was able to substitute this harsh but enabling hard primitivism, which inspired her art, for the mutuality of the softer variety. In *Self-Portrait with Monkeys* and other works, the paintings are structured around Kahlo's connection to the plant and animal world but her self is not subordinated to it. On the contrary, the characteristically frontal view suggests that she commands it while drawing strength from it. Another painting, *The Earth Herself* (or *Two Nudes in a Jungle*), was painted in the same year as *The Two Fridas*, for which it might be seen as a kind of primitivistic, earth-centered, and less pain-ridden remedy: the sturdy twisted vines sheltering the two women replace the thin, blood-red line of heartfelt pain connecting the two Fridas.

In addition to connecting herself to the earth symbolically, Kahlo frequently binds herself to it contiguously. In linguistic terms, she is visually creating a poetic language as Roman Jakobson described it, shifting her discourse from an axis of similarity to one of contiguity.[4] That strategy, which places her body in close proximity to nature and its products, emphasizes the drawing of strength and inner nourishment from the earth. That distinction between similarity and contiguity has its parallel in the domain of magic, appropriate here because in her repeated self-portraits Kahlo is in some sense serving as her own shamaness, the paintings enacting a kind of curing ceremony. In terms of magic, she is moving from sympathetic magic, which operates according to a symbolic similarity of images, to contagious magic, which operates according to the principle of contiguity. Rather than casting a spell on an object that resembles the person the magician wishes to affect, she employs something that was formerly a part of the person—hair, fingernails, a piece of clothing.

In keeping with this sense of magical contiguity, Kahlo in many of her self-portraits is literally linked to vegetation. Over and over again, this weaving of self into nature takes place, constructing her identity by making her literally a child of nature. At one level, as a woman and an artist, she deconstructs her social persona and reestablishes herself as a primitive being before the advent of culture, so that she may start her personal growth from ground and jungle zero, as it were. In the relatively late painting *Roots,*

Kahlo replaces her inner organs with the sturdy stems of a healthy-looking plant whose root source, while not specified, seems to be both her own head region and the earth behind it, identifying her mind with a natural source of life. The smaller lines resembling blood vessels are painted on top of the leaves and stems, and seem to lie on the surface of Kahlo's dress rather than entering her body; that the green stems are inside her body while these minuscule blood vessels are outside it seems to tie her particularly closely to plants, almost suggesting—primitivistically—her participation in a prehuman life force.[5]

Kahlo's sense of herself not only as inextricably bound to Diego Rivera but also as an elemental being connected to life processes appears in this imagining of her relationship to him: "I'm not just your—mother—I am the embryo, the germ, the first cell which—potentially—engendered him—I am *him* from the most primitive . . . and the most ancient cells, that with time became *him*."[6] Even though this diary entry comes just after Kahlo expresses her wish to give all her health and youth to Diego, it also suggests how her primitivistic vision—both biological and aesthetic—enabled Kahlo to reconfigure her fragile identity in relation to the overpowering Diego. A similar sense of cosmic connectedness, this time in relation to a prehistoric Earth, emerges from a description of Diego, who stands "invincibly on the earth like an antediluvian being from which emerges, from the waist up, an example of future humanity, distant from us by two or three thousand years."[7]

In two paintings, Kahlo's hair or body seems to be joined to leaves. In *Diego in My Thoughts,* a web of lively lines twines out from the leaves on Kahlo's headdress and covers the canvas. Although on close inspection the lines can be seen to emerge from the tips of the leaves, their dark color and place of origin next to Kahlo's head mean that they are easily mistaken for, and finally conflated with, her hair. Diego may be consciously on her mind, but flowers and leaves are growing to and from her body, which thereby participates in a vital force that may partially counteract his. Similarly, in *Self-Portrait with Braid,* while it is eventually possible to attach stems to leaves in naturalistic fashion, one's initial impression of the left-hand stem is that it might well emerge from or lead into Kahlo's chest—as if she were magically continuous with plant life.[8]

In several instances, nature is Kahlo's source of personal adornment. In *Self-Portrait with Bonito,* Kahlo wears no jewelry, and the parrot is the one who is called pretty, but the foliage is adorned with a major butterfly and minor caterpillars, and as in several other paintings, a small parrot perches on her shoulder. She has no need of artificial jewelry: nature adorns her and she it. In *Self-Portrait with Thorn Necklace,* Kahlo connects herself meaningfully with her suffering and takes symbolic action to alleviate it through a natural form and an indigenous amulet. She is further imbricated in nature by the fact that both her hair decorations and those of the foliage behind her are butterflies. The thorn necklace, commonly associated with Christ's pain, is extended from a circular crown to a more natural and diffuse shape, and the Christian symbol of the dove has become a hummingbird. Thus the Christian iconology of suffering is mitigated by a primitivist aesthetics of healing.

Kahlo's fondness for heavy stone jewelry is another natural element in her contagious magic. Often, she wore one or more strands of undecorated pierced and rounded stones.[9] In form and material those necklaces come as close as possible to unmediated physical contact with Mexico's ancient past and the earth: she wears stones that weigh her down to the earth which nourishes and heals her.[10] This aspect of Kahlo's construction of her identity illustrates Jung's idea that stone can represent the self to itself. If we take photographs as evidence, Kahlo seems to have favored this type of jewelry in her younger years, when she was constructing her identity. She was able to contact this source of strength even though such objects also participated in the artificially created and politically co-opted construction of national identity. A similar feeling of intense personal connection to nature, which I wish to argue goes beyond a purely fashionable primitivism (although it is not entirely separate from such a fashion), emerges from a photo of Kahlo in a boat; she is wearing a necklace of stonelike beads, and looking intently into the river, in which her hand is immersed.[11] The stone jewelry contrasts with a later statement (in her diary) in which she asks why she needs her feet (one of which is about to be amputated, along with her leg) if she has wings with which to fly. In her youth, she used stones to ground her and to construct her individual identity; as her death nears, she affirms a different reality, that of the bodiless spirit which can fly beyond the earth.

In a primitivist discourse similar to Kahlo's, which implicitly conflates the female body and the earth, Susan Griffin articulates an earth-centered healing process similar to the one that Kahlo instinctively pictured for herself. She, too, uses the stone as a grounding weight, repeating it as an anchoring motif: "*The stone dropped in water.* Space that knows her. . . . Space where she weaves. Where she builds the house of her culture. Where her breast is a self-reflection. This space which she paints. . . . *The stone dropped in the water."*[12] In exposing the common commercial appropriation of bodies and trees, Griffin's contemporary poetic discourse on women and nature theorizes the process in which Kahlo also participated in a more instinctive way. Griffin juxtaposes the categorization of paper for manufacture with the characteristics of clerks in offices: "For paper (Does she catch on easily?) Spruce, southern Yellow Pine, Hemlock (Learns very rapidly, catches on easily, learns without difficulty). For toothpicks, White Birch (needs repeated instructions, dull)."[13]

Both Griffin's and Kahlo's texts, like Georgia O'Keeffe's, open a space in which the earth's commodification can be deconstructed and turned toward other ends, drawing strength from the identity of the female body and nature. The Cuban artist Ana Mendieta exemplifies a similar impulse toward bodily identification with the earth, although she enacts it in a style completely different from Kahlo's. In contrast to Kahlo's intricate imbrications of body and nature or her elaborate self-costuming, Mendieta imprints her nude form baldly on the earth. Kahlo embroiders, as it were; Mendieta plants.

Even when the connection between Kahlo's body and nature is not contiguous, it is often visually symbolic. In *Self-Portrait with Monkey,* the hair on the monkey's arm reaching across Kahlo's chest and Kahlo's own hair are extremely similar, and the monkey has a ribbon tying its hair on top of its head that matches the ribbon decoration on top of Kahlo's head. Similarly, in *Self-Portrait with Monkey and Parrot,* the yellowish bromeliads to the side of Kahlo's head closely resemble in both color and form the ribbons in her hair. In *Self-Portrait with Braid,* Kahlo goes a step further, painting herself as the exotic flower emerging from leaves, an exaggerated form of a Tehuana headdress like a crown on her head, suggesting her elevation to the stature of nature goddess.[14] In contrast to these reconstructed primitivist (and often indigenist natural) selves, Kahlo has represented her shattered corporeal self in the form of Western culture in *The Broken Column,* where a shattered Ionic column replaces Kahlo's spine.[15] The column is in no way either contiguously or metaphorically connected to the unusually barren land behind the figure.

Naturaleza viva, in which roots sprout from some of the fruits, is an explicit primitivization of the still life convention. Just as Kahlo reconstructs her own bodily health by wearing connections between her body and the earth, such as birds, flowers, and leaves, so here she reconnects these fruits to their roots. Like all primitivism, Kahlo's is largely a fantasy, a nostalgia for what is perceived as a more elemental experience of the natural world, of cultures that live closer to it than does the primitivist's contemporary society, or, in the personal realm, of early childhood. But in addition to being regressive, this primitivism is also progressive. Focusing on Kahlo's still lifes, Salomon Grimberg theorizes that they represent moments of regression, of "desperate hunger for life," which stemmed from disrupted feeding experiences. Even if that speculation were true, there is another compensatory process at work here. Kahlo's primitivist self-reconstruction focuses not on the European form of the still life but on the indigenist connection to the living land. That compensatory fantasy influences even this last painting. And in naming it *Naturaleza viva,* she verbally reconfigures the tradition of the still life *(Naturaleza muerta),* reaffirming her appropriation of the life-giving force of nature. Even if we retain Grimberg's characterization of the "fiercely ingrown roots [which] shape the title of the work and convey the impression of pulsating tension," that fierceness and tension represent not only infantile neurosis but also elemental strength and self-healing power.[16]

These paintings suggest that try as she might to embody the victim of patriarchal culture as represented by Diego, and even taking into account her very real sufferings of love and the body, Kahlo's strong identification with a feminized nature works against that identity and helps her to construct a complementary one. Thus, in feminist terms, Kahlo's work provides an especially compelling example of the dynamics between victim feminism and power feminism.[17] In *Thinking of Death,* the conventionalized skull and bones are well contained in the medallion—and in her mind—while the foliage provides a verdant backdrop and perhaps even a living alternative for the medallion. The colors are similar, although the foliage is clearly greener, suggesting its greater vitality. This intimate terrestrial enracination distinguishes Kahlo's work from that of many European Surrealists, one of whose characteristic forms was the collage, an embodiment of artificiality and rootlessness. This strong, indigenous earth-centered power, which results from the use of nature in conjunction with indigenous culture, and from the contagious magical connecting of the body with nature, effectively recovers a time before. In Simone de Beauvoir's words: "In woman dressed and adorned, nature is present but under restraint, by human will remolded nearer to man's desire."[18] At the same time, however, Kahlo elaborately dressed and adorned herself for Diego in just the way that de Beauvoir describes.

For these personal reasons, in addition to aesthetic considerations, a primary icon within Kahlo's cultural primitivism is native dress, a topic that has been much discussed.[19] Kahlo's Tehuana dresses are also primitivistic in the public context of the history of urban culture: in harmony with Kahlo's home barrio of Coyoacán, which retains an atmosphere similar to that of a village within Mexico City even today, they reconstruct indigenous Mexican village culture both materially and symbolically. Strangely enough, in *Self-Portrait on the Borderline Between Mexico and the United States,* a painting that might be seen as the exception which proves the rule, Kahlo, caught in a moment of possible vacillation in the creation of her primitivist identity, has painted herself not in her Tehuana dress but in a rather uncharacteristically demure and frilly pink one, complete with lacy white fingerless gloves, and placed herself on a mechanized pedestal (attached to a generator), unconnected to anything around her. The dress, together with the plants that exist outside of their native soil (although still rooted), and their American mechanical counterparts (including the genrator, an industrial light, and other elements of a factory), neither of them linked to Kahlo, suggest her feelings of deracination.[20]

Although Rivera championed Kahlo's Tehuana mode of dress and the fashionable nativist primitivism that it represented, Kahlo's appropriation of the mode and its cultural connotations not only ties her to Rivera by conforming herself to his design for her, but also enables her to construct her own identity as a Mexican woman by partially assuming the spirit of the strong women of the isthmus of Tehuantepec, "the undefeated counterparts to the despised 'Chingada,'" who were reported to "run the markets, handle fiscal matters, and dominate the men."[21] Frida's adoption of the dress thus represented solidarity with Mexican indigenous traditions unconquered by colonial and male rule, so that it "asserted both a feminist and an anti-colonialist position."[22] While the dynamics of Kahlo's relations with Rivera as she constructed her identity throughout her life are of course extremely complex, and even though her adoption of a primitivist ideology (with clothing to match) was greatly influenced by him, the enthusiasm with which Kahlo created her own female kind of primitivism enabled her to achieve a certain (limited) independence from Rivera.

The success of Kahlo's hard primitivism associated with this form of dress can be seen in *Itzcuinctli Dog with Me,* in which Kahlo appears calm and majestic. As in the facial self-portraits, she is clearly the dominant presence in the picture, a powerful Tehuana in the company of her animal familiar, which is colored to match her. The mood is somber and resigned rather than joyful, but it is not tormented. A mere touch of the virginal blue indicates that La Dolorosa—Our Lady of Sorrows—is in retreat.

However, the process of identification with the strong Tehuanas was certainly not complete; much of Kahlo's work projects a dynamic quality that can be seen as an ongoing cultural conversation between La Dolorosa and La Tehuana.[23] That conversation is exemplified in many ways. It can be overheard in the conjunction of her last painting of herself as a martyr with her last words that she awaits her departure joyfully, hoping never to return. And in the juxtaposition of two necklaces she wears: the thorns that embody her suffering in the 1940 *Self-Portrait Dedicated to Dr. Eloesser,* painted in the ex-voto style that typically commemorates bloody Christian sufferings and miracles, and the simple stone beads that connect her solidly to the earth and indigenous culture in the 1933 *Portrait with Jade Necklace.*[24] In *The Love Embrace of the Universe, the Earth (Mexico), Diego, Me, and Señor Xolotl,* Kahlo's Tehuana dress aids her in creating her chosen family in its own primitivist painted scenario, though it is once again overlaid with echoes of the suffering Virgin—note the tears in her eyes as she holds a child/Diego on her lap. Kahlo herself again is held here, as in *My Nurse and I,* not by a soft, motherly presence but by a strong, indigenous figure with a face like an obsidian mask, who forms part of a hard but ultimately nourishing primitivistic environment.

Kahlo's connection to the land partially counteracts and grounds (but never abolishes) the decorative impulse embodied in costumes, which were elaborate packaging that "camouflaged her pain for herself and others," an artwork that Hayden Herrera compares to a piñata, "a fragile vessel decorated with frills and ruffles, filled with sweets and surprises, but destined to be smashed"; knowledge of its imminent destruction made "its bright beauty all the more poignant."[25] Perhaps indigenous primitivism lends Kahlo the support to overcome the Spanish tradition of the *vanitas,* which tended to undermine affirmative female self-portraiture through showing the vanity of earthly beauty by painting women in the company of skulls. As Eli Bartra points out, Kahlo's "Mexicanidad is precisely the fusion, the unity of the indigenous and the European."[26] This duality, and others in her work, such as the conversation between La Tehuana and La Dolorosa, and the sense of a divided self, may be, as Robin Richmond suggests, another primitivistic element in her work, a persistence of the dualities that characterized Aztec culture, the most evident being the oscillation between the opposing gods Quetzalcoatl and Tezcatlipoca.[27]

Kahlo's extreme physical suffering, allied to her particular psychology, and her sense of her own striking beauty, lead her to fetishize her body, painting it repeatedly: sometimes clothed, sometimes not, often making it into a primitivist idol. Her affinity for the camera, attested by the many photographs of her in which she is clearly a willing model, documents and contributes to this self-idolization. Thus her primitivism is a narcissistic primitivism tempered by cosmic references. Within this personal system, the Tehuana dress becomes a kind of totem or fetish representing the self. In the realm of corporeal symbology, even when her body is in shreds, the dress remains relatively intact. And in several instances, such as *My Dress Hangs Here* and *Memory,* it hangs not on her but for her, an expression of a self unencumbered by a mutilated body, a self that is playing an elaborate game of hide-and-seek with its public, a game aided by the donning of various primitivist guises. That she paints the dress bodiless suggests an implicit awareness of its value as a commodification of the female body, but an awareness which coexists with a willingness to adopt that very commodity fetishism for the purposes of self-fashioning.

Significantly, in *Memory,* in which Kahlo wears European clothes and has a hole where her heart would be, a Tehuana dress hangs beside her, intact, while Kahlo is not. A schoolgirl's blouse and skirt hang on the other side of Kahlo, and each empty outfit extends an actual arm toward her, but it is the Tehuana arm that links with the sleeve of the jacket Kahlo wears, and a pole projects from the waist of the Tehuana dress through the hole in Kahlo's chest. That pole, on whose end a small angel sits, could be held by an arm projecting from the Tehuana dress's other armhole. It is as if the spirit of the dress were keeping Kahlo company and consoling her for what she has lost, even while reminding her of an integrity she has constructed with it. It balances the schoolgirl's outfit with its arm reaching toward her and the large heart that bleeds into the ground on the other side of Kahlo, as if proposing the identity of the mature and strong Tehuana woman to replace that of the diminutive schoolgirl with the broken heart. Kahlo may have temporarily discarded the dress, but in addition to its literal connection to her via its arm, and despite the suffering recorded in the painting by her tears and her bloody heart, and the lack of volition indicated by her armlessness, it also retains part of her identity, and the possibility of new growth and vitality in the plantlike curves of its skirt. The latter contrast with the flat and comparatively lifeless surface of the skirt she is wearing.

Part of the painting's formal balance derives from the correspondence between the deep red heart from which blood flows into the greenish brown earth and the dark red blouse connected to Kahlo by a blood vessel. That analogy implicitly identifies a central part of her physical and emotional self with the dress. However, here again, the conversation between La Tehuana and La Dolorosa continues. As Grimberg points out, the painting virtually duplicates Saint Teresa of Avila's description of her transverberation, in which her heart is pierced by divine love, a reference he takes to refer to her identity as a martyr to Rivera's love, a European-style martyrdom that is counter-acted by the native Tehuana's strength in the face of adversity.[28]

Similarly, in *My Dress Hangs Here,* the coherence and integrity of the Tehuana costume centers and partially counteracts the visual multiplicity, perhaps even the cacophony, of modernity.[29] And five years later, Kahlo wears a Tehuana dress in *Remembrance of an Open Wound,* in which she seems to have at least partially conquered her suffering and put it behind her.[30] Thus, these dresses remain until the end not only the physical camouflage of a deformed body (the length of the skirts hiding her maimed and ultimately amputated leg) but also a source of psychic support. A reversal of exterior and interior, ostensibly a covering, they are perhaps even more essentially an infrastructure, a kind of exoskeleton. In this creation of a primitivism of dress, Kahlo achieves something of a female redefinition of male modernist primitivism by dignifying the decorative.

As we have been seeing, Kahlo's focus on herself is virtually unparalleled in the history of early twentieth-century painting.[31] In this context, in addition to the natural and cultural primitivisms represented by her use of nature and the Tehuana dress, Kahlo's repeated self-portraits constitute a particular kind of psychological primitivism, a regression to Lacan's mirror stage, a period in which the child first recognizes her own image, and is enthralled with it. This period eventually allows her to develop as a separate individual before its ending, which "inaugurates . . . the dialectic that will henceforth link the I to socially elaborated situations."[32] The repeated return to clearly recognizable self-portraiture reconstructs a mirror stage that is also an enabling narcissism—a return to the child, *la niña Frida* (a child name that she, Diego, and their friends perpetuated), before her disastrous bus accident, and even earlier, before the accident (or the polio, depending on the story) that damaged her left foot. Most important, perhaps, it reestablishes a time before her meeting with Diego, which, as she said, was the most traumatic "accident" in her life, and before she had to take responsibility for herself. It compensated for her subsequent injuries by allowing her to enjoy this stage, "in which the *I* is precipitated in a primordial form, before it is objectified in the dialectic of identification with the other, and before language restores to it, in the universal, its function as subject."[33]

Such a reconstruction posits a different and undamaged self in the attractively primitivized heads Kahlo depicts. In contrast to many of her other pictures, in which she shows herself in relation to others, these heads are painted alone, in an unusual number, and often with the use of an actual mirror. Even within Kahlo's distinguished body of work, these heads stand out. They are especially masterfully designed, with a fully achieved visual coherence and integrity.[34] In repeatedly using her face, with its distinctive traits, Kahlo differentiates herself from other Surrealist embodiments of woman as primarily corporeal—one of the earliest and more notorious being Breton's headless female torso floating down the Seine.[35] In these portraits, Kahlo seems to allow herself an almost infantile and yet formalized narcissism, which is why the mirror stage seems the appropriate psychoanalytical time frame in which to view them. Luckily for my argument here, in her *Self-Portrait with Loose Hair* she includes a legend in the scroll at the bottom of the painting, which documents her "mirror stage" of composition, noting that she painted herself *con la imagen del espejo* (as reflected in a mirror) and, almost as if to suggest her momentary regressions to infancy in such portraits, identifies Coyoacán as the place of her birth.[36] Painting self-portraits with the aid of a mirror is common enough, but the number of Kahlo's similar portraits—virtually constituting a series—many of which used this technique, is unusually large.[37]

Kahlo's own reflection is so powerfully enthralling to her in these portraits that occasionally even the huge Diego is reduced (in *Diego in My Thoughts* and *Diego and I*) to a miniature engraved on her forehead. Perhaps these paintings that include a miniaturized Diego serve as intermediate substitute self objects, leading (though not necessarily chronologically) to the portraits of her alone. As Lacan describes them, self objects are "relationships that mimic the ones we had—or wish we had had—in infancy," and that we imbue with responsibility for our sense of wholeness.[38] This role was usually played in her mind by Rivera, but since he was so often emotionally unavailable to her, Kahlo used her art for this purpose, prolonging the mirror stage, the staging of the self so it becomes a self object.

These facial portraits construct Kahlo's identity as a primitivist work of art. Their formal hieratic composition duplicates the quality of constructed identity Lacan also discerns in the mirror stage: "a drama whose internal

thrust is precipitated from insufficiency to anticipation—and which manu-
factures for the subject, caught up in the lure of spatial identification, the
succession of *phantasies* that extends from a fragmented body-image to a
form of its totality that I shall call orthopaedic—and, lastly, to the assumption of the armor of an alienating identity, which will mark with its rigid
structure the subject's entire mental development."[39] That drama seems un-
cannily like the one Kahlo stages in her self-portraits generally, even down
to the orthopedic dimension, and especially in these heads. Even the last
stage, as Lacan articulates it, seems to picture the way in which Kahlo's primitivistic self-costuming constructs a somewhat static identity. On another
level, however, because they are the work of her own hand, these self-portraits lessen the alienating identity normally experienced by the developing
individual. Moreover, these pictures, with their leafy backgrounds, and totem animals, usually monkeys and parrots, create a sense of intimate immensity, bringing the jungle into the private world of the portrait, again
connecting Kahlo to the cosmos. In Lacan's terms, the "function of the mirror-stage . . . is to establish a relation between the organism and its reality," a
reality that for Kahlo was intimately connected to nature and to pre-
Columbian Mexico."[40]

As commentators have repeatedly remarked, these portraits are in many
ways masked performances of a fragile self that through them gains in consistency.[41] In Grimberg's interpretation of Kahlo's need to create self objects,
these portraits are an especially good example of her "insatiable need for
mirroring, for the positive regard she needed to achieve a sense of wholeness."[42] As has often been noticed recently, however, a woman's self-portrait
carries certain cultural inconsistencies with it. Thus these paintings, like
Kahlo's creation of her actual decorated body, are designed to please both
male and female audiences; they are the object of both Rivera's objectifying
and her own self-constructing gazes.[43] Since in Mexico, especially, masking
is, among other things, a primitivizing act, Kahlo's primitivism also helps
her to negotiate the boundary between male and female gazes.

As if implicitly recognizing the ultimate insufficiency of this narcissistic
stage, which inevitably "projects the formation of the individual into history" and, in contrast to these heads, which seem to be examples of the reconstructed self's "jubilant assumption of his specular image by the child at
the *infans* stage," the repeated paintings of suffering or mutilated bodies,
usually—though not always explicitly—her own (e.g., *Henry Ford Hospital,
My Birth, A Few Small Nips, Memory, The Two Fridas, What the Water Gave*

Me, The Broken Column, Without Hope, Tree of Hope, and *The Little Deer),* serve a different and complementary function. They help Kahlo to come to terms with the physical and emotional pain she experienced, and to document that process, as ex-votos document miraculous and often painful events.[44] Significantly, in these paintings, the body Kahlo paints tends to be less contiguously connected to the natural world, as if acknowledging her growth out of the primordially mirrored self, but also her unwillingness to abandon it. They are less primitivist, more constructive of a hybrid identity.

One of them, *My Birth,* is, as Sarah Lowe points out, a "radical adaptation of the established depiction of the goddess Tlazolteotl."[45] Thus in addition to providing her with Tehuana dresses to camouflage her pain, Kahlo's cultural primitivism also occasionally provided her with vehicles that enabled her to confront it. Whether we consider Kahlo's portraits as repeated depictions of a relatively coherent (-ly evolving) self (as in the stylized heads) or as a disjunctive set of constantly transforming versions of a destabilized self (as in many of the other full-length canvases), the nature and arts of pre-Columbian and indigenous Mexico are important props in that drama of self-fashioning.[46]

An investigation of Kahlo's work as a primitivist construction of identity suggests that she sensed—correctly—that the newly valorized art of indigenous Mexico, together with its natural forms, could provide her with a psychologically supportive and visually seductive source of images for the narratives of her own life that she wished to create. Although Kahlo's primitivism was more cultural than that of O'Keeffe, and similar to that of Cather in her portrayal of both Southwestern indigenous culture and landscape, the partial erasure of Colonial culture that Kahlo's primitivism represented, somewhat like the spare desert landscapes for Cather and O'Keeffe, enabled her to create her own artistic identity. And with regard to Kahlo's sexual identity, that partial erasure may have cleared a space in which sexual as well as artistic identities could be reforged and realigned. Again like Cather, this imperative often carried with it a certain destabilizing of traditional gender configurations, which included strong and sexually charged relationships with other women.[47]

In this primitivist construction of her identity, then, Kahlo refocuses the artist's gaze through the eyes of a self-constructed and self-worshiping nature goddess in the body and on the canvas.[48] In this project, she adopts the self-primitivizing impulse of post-Revolution *mexicanidad,* itself a prime example of primitivist construction of identity that has lasted almost a century, to create an individually restorative and distinctive aesthetic.[49]

Notes

For Nancy and Judith

1. See Amaryll Chanady, "The Territorialization of the Imaginary in Latin America: Self-Affirmation and Resistance to Metropolitan Paradigms," in *Magical Realism: Theory, History, Community,* ed. Lois Parkinson Zamora and Wendy B. Faris (Durham, NC: Duke University Press, 1995), 125–144. Alice Gambrell's discussion of Kahlo as "courtesan" similarly explains how Kahlo engaged with the patriarchy while at the same time sagely crafting her own—marketable—body and canvases within it. See Alice Gambrell, "A Courtesan's Confession: Frida Kahlo and Surrealist Entrepreneurship," in her *Women Intellectuals, Modernism, and Difference* (Cambridge: Cambridge University Press, 1997), 40–73. Gambrell provides a well-informed discussion of Kahlo's complex relations with European Surrealism in the person of André Breton, especially his tendency to appropriate her work. Dawn Ades makes the valid point that Kahlo participated in the Mexican cultural moment of the affirmation of national identity, in contrast to the French Surrealist era, where dissolution of national and personal identities predominated. Ades, "Orbits of the Savage Moon: Surrealism and the Representation of the Female Subject in Mexico and Postwar Paris," in *Mirror Images: Women, Surrealism, and Self-Representation,* ed. Whitney Chadwick (Cambridge, MA: MIT Press, 1998), 107.

2. Sarah M. Lowe makes this point about Kahlo in her *Frida Kahlo* (New York: Universe, 1991), 88.

3. Salomon Grimberg's interpretation does not make this distinction, minimizing the role of such a hard primitivism in Kahlo's development. He sees the picture, which Kahlo apparently considered a companion piece to *My Birth,* as evidence that "she was still working on the issue of attachment to her mother." It may be true that, as he says, "there is no evidence of mutuality: no affectionate cuddling, no holding, no touching," and that "Kahlo lies unresponsive to the nanny's engorged left breast." And certainly this unfinished maternal agenda with its craving for attention may drive her desperate attachment to the older Rivera as a substitute parental figure. I would also want to stress the cosmic relatedness this lack of interpersonal mutuality represents. Salomon Grimberg, *Frida Kahlo* (Dallas: The Meadows Museum, Southern Methodist University, 1989), 9–11. Lowe interprets the image in a more progressive manner, "as a projection into the past that enables Kahlo to formulate a self in the present," and maintains that her full-grown head marks her "as creator of the image." Lowe, *Frida Kahlo,* 48.

4. See Roman Jakobson, "Language in Relation to Other Communication Systems," in his *Selected Writings,* vol. 3 (The Hague: Mouton, 1971), 704.

5. Hayden Herrera quotes a letter in which Kahlo pleads for the government to help Rivera build his Anahuacalli museum, which shows Frida's affinity with the elemental earth of Mexico; she describes Rivera's building in terms that might also apply to many of her own paintings: it "grows in the incredibly beautiful Pedregal landscape like an enormous cactus that looks at the Ajusco, sober and elegant, strong and refined, ancient and perennial; from its entrails of volcanic rock it cries out with voices of centuries and days: Mexico is alive! Like Coatlicue, it contains life and death; like the magnificent terrain on which it is built, it embraces the earth with the firmness of a living and permanent plant." Kahlo, "Retrato de Diego," in *Exposición nacional de homenaje a Diego Rivera* (Mexico City: Instituto Nacional de Bellas Artes, 1977), 11–23; cited in Hayden Herrera, *Frida: A Biography of Frida Kahlo* (New York: Harper & Row, 1983), 313–314 (no original provenance, date, or pages given); and in Raquel Tibol, *Frida Kahlo: An Open Life,* trans. Elinor Randall (Albuquerque: University of New Mexico Press, 1993), 148–149. Herrera also points out that Kahlo includes the rocky landscape of that region in many of her self-portraits, linking herself to "the land Diego loved" in order to feel closer to him. In addition to linking herself with Diego, I would argue, as Herrera also implies, that Kahlo's imbrication in the landscape in this painting "linked her very body with the chain of life"—this time, instead of being nourished by it, as in *My Nurse and I,* serving as the source of its fertility. Herrera, *Frida,* 313–315.

6. Frida Kahlo, *The Diary of Frida Kahlo: An Intimate Portrait* (New York: Abrams, 1995), 57–58 of the diary, translated on 234.

7. From Kahlo, "Retrato de Diego"; cited in Herrera, *Frida,* 124.

8. Grimberg claims that it is in the picture *Frida and the Abortion* that Kahlo "began to forge her unmistakable iconography"; *Frida Kahlo* (New York: Barnes and Noble, 1997), 24. Inasmuch as this lithograph contains the vessel-like entwined connection of figures, which becomes a distinctive part of her style, it is possible that Kahlo's abortions played a part in its development, the connecting vines and blood vessels expressing, in addition to a desire for connection with a nurturing natural world, an attempt to reconnect with her lost children.

9. See, for example, portraits of Kahlo by Manuel Alvarez Bravo, Rivera, and Edward Weston in *Frida Kahlo: The Camera Seduced* (San Francisco: Chronicle Books, 1992), 31, 37, 54, and 104. The Weston photo (from 1930) is particularly striking in this regard; in it, Kahlo wears three strings of heavy stone beads. And in one by Guillermo Dávila (n.d.; 43) two strands of such beads contrast with the light, white Western-style dress Kahlo wears.

10. My interpretation contrasts with Herrera's, for whom, in *Self-Portrait with Braid,* "oppressiveness is reinforced by the heavy choker of pre-Columbian beads." Herrera, *Frida,* 312.

11. *Frida Kahlo: The Camera Seduced,* 44.

12. Susan Griffin, *Woman and Nature: The Roaring Inside Her* (New York: Harper & Row, 1978), 169–170.

13. Ibid., 60.

14. Herrera interprets this portrait as referring primarily to Kahlo's remarriage to Rivera, and stresses its somber tone, the oppressive and threatening nature of "the huge predatory jungle leaves," and the "unruly strands" at the end of Kahlo's braids as the "nerve ends of an anxious psyche" (*Frida,* 311–312). The portrait is certainly not joyous, but I would argue that the bearing is regal; both Kahlo's face and the dramatic composition are calm and majestic rather than frantic. The anxiety is (at least temporarily) managed, aided by a primitivist identification with indigenous and natural worlds.

15. This painting exemplifies the beginning of what Jean Franco sees as Kahlo's characteristic depiction of one of her selves as controlled by science, the other self being dressed as a Tehuana. Jean Franco, *Plotting Women: Gender and Representation in Mexico* (New York: Columbia University Press, 1993), 107.

16. Grimberg, *Frida Kahlo* (1989), 43.

17. For a popular formulation of this feminist dichotomy, see Naomi Wolf, *Fire with Fire: The New Female Power and How It Will Change the 21st Century* (New York: Random House, 1993).

18. Simone de Beauvoir, *The Second Sex,* cited (without a page number) in Griffin, *Woman and Nature,* 169.

19. See Herrera, *Frida,* 109–113: "Frida's Tehuana costume . . . is a primitive animistic approach to clothes that recalls the way a child senses his mother's presence in items of clothing . . . clearly Frida knew this magic power of clothes to substitute for their owner." Franco's observation that "the 'inner' Frida is controlled by modern society far more than the clothed Frida, who often marks her deviation from a norm by defiantly returning the gaze of the viewer," suggests that the clothes she chose were instrumental in her construction of her identity. Franco, *Plotting Women,* 107.

20. Oriana Baddeley interprets this painting as showing "the artist poised between the technological inhumanity of a capitalist North America and the archaic fertility of Mexico." Oriana Baddeley, "'Her Dress Hangs Here': De-Frocking the Kahlo Cult," *Oxford Art Journal* 14, no. 1 (1991): 15.

21. Eli Bartra, *Frida Kahlo: Mujer, ideología, arte* (Barcelona: Icaria, 1994), 77; Herrera, *Frida,* 110. See Rivera's primitivist construction of Frida: "Frida despises mechanisms, and therefore has the resilience with which a primitive organism meets the stronger and always varied experiences of the life about him"; Parker Lesley's transcription of notes from a conversation with Rivera about Kahlo and her work, May 1939; cited in Herrera, *Frida,* 111; Herrera adds that "donning peasant clothing had to do with the fashionable notion that the peasant or the Indian is more earth-

bound and thus more deeply sensual, more 'real' than the urban sophisticate. By wearing native dress, women declared the primacy of their link with nature. The costume was a primitive mask, releasing them from the strictures of bourgeois mores." Ibid.

22. Baddeley emphasizes the cultural identity encoded in Frida's dress in contrast to what she sees as a recent appropriation of Frida and her clothes as an icon of individualistic female suffering and pain. Baddeley, "'Her Dress Hangs Here,'" 12–13.

23. Lowe brings up the issue of the *vanitas* but does not connect it specifically to Kahlo's use of the Tehuana dress.; *Frida Kahlo,* 38.

24. Herrera implicitly acknowledges the emotional management that Kahlo's portraits represent. Here she is speaking about Kahlo's self-portraits after her divorce from Rivera, especially the one dedicated to Dr. Eloesser: "Her elaborate self-mythologizing performance provides psychological distance from what might otherwise be overwhelming grief. Calling perhaps upon the pieties of her Catholic childhood, she turns herself into an icon that she—and others—can worship, thus transcending pain." *Frida,* 283.

25. Ibid., 112–113.

26. Bartra, *Frida Kahlo,* 79.

27. Robin Richmond, *Frida Kahlo in Mexico* (San Francisco: Pomegranate Artbooks, 1994), 34.

28. For a more psychologically negative interpretation of this painting, see Grimberg, *Frida Kahlo* (1989), 20–23.

29. According to Baddeley, "There is no place 'there' for the values the Tehuana dress represents." "'Her Dress Hangs Here,'" 16.

30. See Herrera's discussion of this painting. She maintains that to consider it in relation to the conventional use of the Sacred Heart in Mexico lessens somewhat the grotesqueness, and consequently the personal horror, of the image. *Frida Kahlo,* 188–191.

31. Recent work by photographers such as Cindy Sherman and others suggests that in this self-fetishization and fashioning of identity Kahlo was a prophetic figure in twentieth-century women's aesthetics.

32. Jacques Lacan, *Ecrits: A Selection,* trans. Alan Sheridan (New York: Norton, 1977), 5.

33. Ibid., 2

34. Picasso, with his own sense of design, recognized the quality of Kahlo's head portraits: "Neither Derain nor I nor you are able to paint a head like those of Frida Kahlo"; cited (with no reference) in Margarita Zamora, *Frida Kahlo: The Brush of Anguish,* abridged and trans. Marilyn Sode Smith (San Francisco: Chronicle Books, 1990), 73. I believe that the heads stand out from much of Kahlo's work, and therefore do not fit into Jean Franco's otherwise illuminating characterization of her paint-

ings, which shock because "they reveal the painter's 'inner' life not as spirit but as bodily organs." Franco, *Plotting Women,* 107.

35. The fact that a number of these particular portraits were painted at a time when Kahlo was separated from Rivera and attempting to sell her work in no way diminishes their role in her construction of her identity.

36. As Grimberg notes in citing Kahlo's statement (apparently drawn from an Egyptian creation myth) in her diary, "the one who gives birth to herself," these portraits are formalized self-birthings. Grimberg, "Frida Kahlo: The Self as an End," in Chadwick, *Mirror Images,* 95.

37. It might be objected that this method of mirror painting was particularly attractive to Kahlo because she was increasingly immobilized in bed; yet many of these paintings were done before her movements were seriously impeded.

38. Grimberg, "Frida Kahlo: The Self as an End," 89–90.

39. Lacan, *Ecrits,* 4.

40. Ibid., 5.

41. See Laura Mulvey and Peter Wollen's description of Kahlo's face in her portraits as an "expressionless mask with an unflinching gaze," which is "surrounded by luxuriant growths, accouterments, ornaments and familiars," so that the face is fetishized and serves to construct an "imaginary look of self-regard," which is therefore "feminine, non-male and narcissistic." Such a look displaces the subject from a traumatic childhood "ever-remembered, ever-repeated." Laura Mulvey and Peter Wollen, *Frida Kahlo and Tina Modotti* (London: Whitechapel Art Gallery, 1982), 26.

42. Grimberg, "Frida Kahlo: The Self as an End," 91.

43. As Chadwick points out in her introduction to *Mirror Images: Women, Surrealism, and Self-Representation,* "It is in the nature of the self-portrait to produce the subject as object, but, as Luce Irigaray has noted, the process of objectification that enables the woman to describe herself *as if from outside the body* also implicates her in a masculine dynamics that projects the woman as other: ... 'mirror of male desire, a role, an image, a value, the fetishized woman attempts to locate herself, to affirm her subjectivity within the rectangular space of another fetish—ironically enough, the 'mirror of nature.'" "An Infinite Play of Empty Mirrors: Women, Surrealism, and Self-Representation," 8–9; the quoted passage from Irigaray is from *Between Feminism and Psychoanalysis,* ed. Teresa Brennan (London: Routledge, 1989), 83.

44. Chadwick, "An Infinite Play," 2.

45. Lowe, *Frida Kahlo,* 45.

46. For additional discussion of the various ways in which Kahlo uses native dress to transform herself, creating a changing identity, see Gambrell, "A Courtesan's Confession," 53–54.

47. Chadwick interprets Kahlo's painting *Two Nudes in the Jungle* as alluding to a sexuality based in sameness rather than difference, and of a gentle nature, which

suggests self-pleasuring; "An Infinite Play," 30. Interestingly, however, Chadwick evaluates the presence of nature in this painting as hostile to that pleasuring activity, claiming that "nature's involvement here lends the caress an uneasy flavor." She sees the figures as isolated; vines and trees constitute a "strangling embrace"; and nature is a "brutal witness" to a "gentle caress." Chadwick, *Women Artists and the Surrealist Movement* (London: Thames and Hudson, 1985), 158.

48. That Kahlo's identification with nature and indigenous culture, like post-Revolution Mexico's affinity with pre-Columbian art, was a consciously constructed identity is clear from a statement like this one: "Do you know I've never seen any forests? How is it that I'll be able to paint a forest background with little animals in a *drepa* [Kahlo's version of the slang expression *padre,* meaning "cool," in the sense of "wonderful"] space?" From a letter to Gómez Arias, October 12, 1934; cited in Tibol, *Frida Kahlo,* 68.

49. Carlos Monsiváis maintains that from 1920 to 1950, a period he characterizes as one of institutional consolidation, and that coincides approximately with Kahlo's painting, *mexicanidad* differed substantially from today's "official and commercial product," so that it was especially nourishing for her artistic development. Carlos Monsiváis and Rafael Vásquez Bayod, *Frida Kahlo: Una vida, una obra* (Mexico City: Ediciones Era, 1992), 16.

14

Mi andina y dulce Rita

Women, Indigenism, and the Avant-Garde in César Vallejo

TACE MEGAN HEDRICK

Qué estará haciendo a esta hora mi andina y dulce Rita
de junco y capulí . . .
Dónde estarán sus manos que en actitud contrita
planchaban en las tardes blancuras por venir . . .

(What will she be doing now, my Andean and sweet Rita
of rushes and berries . . .
Where will her hands be which in contrite attitude
ironed future whiteness in the afternoons . . .)
   —Vallejo, *Los heraldos negros* (1918)[1]

Oh . . . mi aquella
lavandera del alma. Qué mañana entrará
satisfecha, capulí de obrería, dichosa
de probar que sí sabe, que sí puede
             ¡COMO NO VA A PODER!
azular y planchar todos los caos.

(And if I knew that she'd come back;
And if I knew that morning she'll come in
to hand me my clean clothes, that
soul-laundress of mine. What morning she'll come in
satisfied, dark berry-worker, proud
to prove that sure she knows, that sure she can
             HOW WILL IT NOT BE POSSIBLE!
bleach and iron every chaos.)
   —Vallejo, *Trilce* (1922)[2]

The fragments above are from César Vallejo's first two collections of poetry, both published before he left Peru for Paris in 1923. Although his second collection, *Trilce,* attracted little critical attention when it was published, it is now regarded as a radical break with earlier Latin American poetics and a pioneering work of the Latin American avant-garde.[3] At first glance these two poems, like the collections themselves, seem essentially unalike, although they share a few elements. The first poem, "Idilios muertos" (Dead Idylls), is the last in a section of *Los heraldos negros* (The Black Heralds; hereafter LHN) entitled "Nostalgias imperiales." This section, in its *modernista*[4] tone, general sonnet structure, and *indigenista*[5] sensibility, seems completely removed from the vanguardist concerns with linguistic experimentation and fragmentation found in the second poem, T6, and generally throughout *Trilce.* In both instances, the references to women's domestic labor seem merely an incidental part of any description of Peruvian provincial life. However, Vallejo's propensity to rewrite and rework previous images and even whole poems for inclusion in *Trilce* suggests that significant links exist, and not just between these two poems.[6]

In fact, the indigenista sensibility of this section of LHN carries over into *Trilce's* particular avant-garde concerns and practices, themselves deployed in part through a certain kind of primitivist discourse. The connections between the *indigenismo* of LHN and the primitivist aspects of *Trilce* can be made clear by a reading of specific images of indigenous and non-indigenous laboring women across these two collections. Often the move from an older artistic practice (such as *modernismo*) to a new, presumably more radical one (such as *vanguardismo*) is presented as a decisive break leaving an unbridgeable gap. However, the move from modernismo to the avant-garde in Vallejo's work can be read in terms of larger, *ongoing* contemporary cultural concerns and assumptions both about women and about the indigenous.[7]

Starting before the turn of the century, both European and Latin American calls for cultural and artistic renovation were often marked by an emphasis on a return to an "originary" or, even sometimes, "primitive" source of creativity. This notion found its counterpart in the idea that it was the female who embodied that primitive *source*—of life and death, of the natural, and of a kind of primeval authenticity.[8] The indigenist section of LHN, "Nostalgias imperiales," shows Vallejo's (re)use of images of indigenous, female, laboring bodies—common in indigenist literature, art, and photography of the time—as a kind of primitive, original source for the avant-garde experimentations with language, content, and form in *Trilce*.

However, the fact that similar assumptions about women prevail in European and Latin American cultures does not necessarily imply a sameness of artistic context, desires, or cultural motivations. Vallejo's representations of women's domestic labor as a more original source of creativity also derived from his own very specific cultural setting: in Andean indigenous and mestizo cultures, women's weaving, spinning, and knotting are of primary importance.[9] Paying attention to Vallejo's imaginings, representations of and assumptions about women, the indigenous, and women's work that underlie both collections allows us to avoid a too facile reading of a series of artistic breaks forming a kind of linear progression from a derivative, indigenista-inflected modernismo to a sophisticated vanguardismo. Instead, we can begin to mark the juxtapositions and superimpositions of at least these three artistic movements, showing the often overlapping, sometimes contradictory, commonly gendered impulses embedded in their various practices and concerns. In turn, connections as well as disjunctions between European and Latin American avant-garde practices should become clearer.

It has become something of a critical truism that avant-garde work is often characterized by a sense of "undoneness," however imparted. Peter Bürger, for instance, maintains that avant-garde languages and practices tend to a "contradictory relationship of heterogeneous elements," yet "[e]ven where the negation of synthesis becomes a structural principle, it must remain possible to conceive however precious a unity."[10] Using Bürger's assumption, I argue that *Trilce* employs a (generally attenuated, sometimes unsuccessful, but always necessary) poetic pulling-together or reweaving or mending of a vanguardist impulse toward undoings. As noted above, this shows itself in *Trilce* by references to the manual labor of domestic tasks, invoking in particular the constructive, cohering aspects of spinning, weaving, and knotting. By association with these domestic gestures, *Trilce* also uses representations of women sewing, mending, ironing, cooking, and serving food. Thus a seemingly *un*modern (even at heart primitivist) gesture toward an (anachronistic) poetics of women's work, while pointing toward the provincial and the indigenous, and away from the more urban aesthetics of Vallejo's European contemporaries, in fact works to motivate and give form to a vanguardist poetic labor. So while *Trilce* bears, and employs, traces of avant-garde artistic practices such as verbal collage, Cubist fragmentation, and typographical experimentations, these are knotted together with the traces of an implicitly gendered indigenist (though not *indigenous*) discourse.

Mítico Aroma de Broncíneos Lotos

The general critical sense about the section "Nostalgias imperiales" has been one of faint embarrassment; the style of these poems tends to be read as derivative, as a young poet's experiment with a modernismo that is already passing out of favor among younger artists, and an indigenismo that is largely read as lacking true literary merit. In addition, certain modernista sensibilities such as "rarefaction, the flaunting of excess . . . a heavily loaded surface of verbal texture" would seem to run counter to the presumed "realist" aesthetics of indigenista writing, which purports to faithfully represent social injustices, and uses simple, rural imagery and indigenous lexicon.[11] However, the call to renovate Latin American writing and intellectual thought, and to make it more American, meant ultimately that even so inward-looking a form as modernismo would have to respond to Americanist concerns. In fact, although Antonio Cornejo Polar argues that indigenista literature was actually silenced during the height of modernismo, indigenist discourse does not disappear, but is manifested *within* the modernismo of the time.[12] In the indigenist-inflected modernismo of "Nostalgias imperiales" Vallejo clearly was following the advice of Manuel González Prada (himself at one time a modernista poet), who in the 1880s "had been the first to recommend that Peruvian art break with Spain and the linguistically conservative Lima spirit, explore Peru's indigenous traditions, seek renewal through popular sources, and search for new forms in other literatures."[13] Even the modernismo of such poets as Julio Herrera y Reissig (an influential poet for Vallejo) became concerned with "Americanist" topics: "Many of the poems from the section 'Nostalgias imperiales' are reminiscent of the sonnets of *Los éxtasis de la montaña*, where Herrera y Reissig creates [Americanist] pastoral scenes and adds symbolist and decadent images. [In Vallejo's poems], the idealized and distant past is now not a classical golden age but a lost indigenous heritage [revealing] a new fusion of *modernismo*'s exotic strains with the more local tone of *mundonovismo* [New World regionalism]"[14]

Despite the strength of Latin American mundonovismo, the back-and-forth movement of intellectual and artistic ideas between Europe (particularly Paris) and Latin America meant also that there were close connections between people and ideas on both continents. One of the shared, though differently motivated and expressed, discourses of the international artistic community from the late nineteenth century onward revolved around the idea that incorporating or representing cultural artifacts from faraway or temporally distant, and therefore simpler, cultures might serve to renovate an artistic and intellectual work that for various political and social reasons had become stultified, degraded, or even immoral.[15] As I mentioned above, the primitivist aspect of much indigenista thought resonated with (although it did not exactly parallel) a primitivist tradition in late nineteenth-century European art. This tradition, as Gill Perry notes, "associated what were perceived as simple lives and societies with purer thoughts and . . . a more direct or purified expression; it exalted peasant and folk culture as evidence of some kind of innate creativity."[16]

Such ideas were inherited, reworked, and modified, not only in European movements such as Cubism and Surrealism, but also in the work of Vallejo's Latin American contemporaries, such as the Peruvian indigenist painter José Sabogal, the European-trained Mexican Cubist and muralist Diego Rivera, and the Mexican artist Frida Kahlo. In Latin American countries with large and unassimilated indigenous populations, like Mexico and Peru, the exaltation of the indigenous as simpler and culturally "purer" collides with, and sometimes is used in the service of, a growing concern about how best to absorb these populations into the nation. In fact, by the turn of the century, largely because of the work of such anthropologists as Franz Boas, Latin American writers on the "Indian problem" were often disclaiming earlier scientific eugenic claims for the genetic inferiority of darker races. However, the difference between indigenous, mixed, and creole populations was still read as a gradation between *culturally* simpler or primitive and culturally advanced or civilized. Interpretations of cultural primitiveness were ambivalent at best; for example, Mexican writer Manuel Gamio's 1916 *Forjando patria* (Forging Homeland) noted that Indians were "backward," their life "archaic," though their culture was also "curious, attractive and original."[17]

Su Blanco Corazón Bravío

In "Nostalgias imperiales," Vallejo's primitivism connects indigenous figures with a "wild," uncultivated, or natural sensibility, in images like "untamed heart," "wild hallelujah," "wild bird," "primitive altar." This sensibility, in turn, is linked with a kind of original innocence and purity, and is attributed particularly to Indian woman and her work. These three things—(Indian) women, a primitive sensibility, and women's manual labor—are often conflated. For example, in the poem "May" a "shepherdess" sings a "wild halellujah" like a "sacred Ruth, pure,/who offers us a wheat stalk of tenderness"; in "Autochthonous Tercet" her "untamed white heart" is also a "spindle," and she is adorned "with pleats of candor." While it is not unusual to see this combination of Judeo-Christian, neoclassical, and Indianist references in modernista poetry, this *Venus pobre* or poor Venus is in remarkable contrast to other (presumably non-Indian) female figures in LHN: Vallejo's exclamation in the poem "Desnudo en barro" (Nude in Clay) that "The tomb is still a woman's sex that attracts man!" captures this collection's recurring anxiety about women's sexuality. His attribution of "candor" and "purity" to the more simple Indian woman echoes a widely shared idea (on both sides of the Atlantic) of (certain kinds of) women as located outside the urban and modern: "located within ... an intimate web of familial relations, more closely linked to nature through her reproductive capacity, woman embodied a sphere of atemporal authenticity."[18] This notion, as Perry notes, is taken up in "the construction of a 'primitive' art [which] often (though not always) involved a *gendered* concept of nature and the natural ... or even the 'essence of a race.'"[19] A close look at "Nostalgias imperiales" shows that the male indigenous figures, for the most part pictured as angry, drunken, resigned, or weeping, are less convenient for a sense of innocence, purity, and nostalgia than are the female figures, who bear implicit connections with the passivity of the animal world and with the earth.

Combined with actual references (including a sprinkling of Quechua words) to a primitive culture, the use of modernismo's twinned feeling-tones of melancholy and a distant exoticism are important in thinking about the ways in which Vallejo reworked and modified a primitive sensibility in *Trilce*. In "Nostalgias imperiales" the sense of melancholy is "blued," echoing the modernista emphasis on this color (and on its appearance in smoke, in the dusk, in the fadings of the sky and clouds). The predominant mood of these poems is a kind of exhausted sadness, a meditative contemplation of a distant and possibly lost time and space that corresponds metaphorically with the evanescent blueness of dusk and smoke, as in "Mayo":

Vierte el humo doméstico en la aurora
su sabor a rastrojo. . . . Delante de la choza
el indio abuelo fuma . . . mítico aroma de broncíneos lotos,
el hilo azul de los alientos rotos!

(Household smoke pours its savor of stubble
into the dawn. . . . In front of the hut
the Indian grandfather smokes . . . mythic aroma of bronzed lotus,
the blue thread of broken breaths!)

The *broncíneos lotos* ("copper" or "bronze" evoking Indian skin color) and
the Indians' *asiática emoción* (Asiatic emotion) are traces of a modernista
exoticism, imposing a sense of distance. Meanwhile the *mómico valle de oro
santo* (mummified valley of sacred gold) and the "Byzantium" that "suffo-
cates" the poet vaguely recall both a classical and a pre-Conquest past.

This modernista concern with the distancing effect of exoticism and with
poetic melancholy and evanescence, rather than jarring with "realistic"
indigenist depictions, dovetails nicely with a widespread imagining of the
Peruvian indigenous population as "sad," "melancholic," and, most important, "nostalgic" for the lost and distant glories of the Inca empire. As Mark
Thurner notes, this largely imaginary indigenism included a "schizophrenic"
nineteenth-century Andean anthropological discourse in which "contemporary Indians had no history, no contemporaneity. They were simply, and
irremediably, hung over . . . [concomitantly, Andean anthropology] has nurtured, and been nurtured by, 20th-century popular and nationalist images
of 'the Andean' as essentially continuous with the precolonial Inca."[20] In
such lines as *La anciana pensativa, cual relieve/de un bloque pre-incaico* (The
pensive old woman, that relief/from a pre-Inca block"), or "Terceto
autóctono"'s *yaraví de sangre que se cuela/en nostalgias de sol por la pupila*
(song of blood that slips in/through the pupil in nostalgias of sunlight),
Vallejo's word pictures of lost glories share, to some extent, a vocabulary and
an attitude with a history of creole imaginings of Peru's indigenous peoples.

The presumed nostalgia (sometimes attributed to the indigenous figure,
sometimes felt by the indigenist writer) for an exoticized "imperial" past of
the Inca, combined with a contemporary "melancholy" for a degraded Indian present, creates a temporal feeling that is important in an Americanist
reading of the conjunctions of modernist and primitivist sensibilities. Ultimately, the "primitive" and exoticist discourses underlying modernismo and
indigenismo, seemingly so different in motivation, are actually marked by a
similar sensibility. As we have seen, they share an exoticized distance, sometimes identified as a distance in geographical space but, for Latin American
creoles and mestizos who lived intimately (though not always lovingly) with

indigenous populations, more often as a doubled distance in cultural time: a degraded, yet still culturally simpler, present alongside a glorious though "primitive" past, those *prehistorias de agua, tiempos viejos* (prehistories of water, old times) of Vallejo's "Terceto autóctono." This double sensibility of degeneration and exoticism fits with the similar sense of women's simultaneous innocence and degradation that runs throughout *LHN*.

For Latin Americans, the mundonovista idea of a renovation in art, literature, and politics was strengthened by a desire to dissociate themselves from perceived dependencies on European (and, increasingly, North American) models of thought and culture, and to create a new and authentically Latin American art. This desire was fed by, and fed on, Latin American vanguard artists' impulse to break with conventional forms of representation. Particularly in countries with a relatively large Indian population, such as Mexico, Guatemala, and Peru, Latin American avant-garde artists found this original source of renovation in the physical and cultural proximity they could claim—and, indeed, often in the intimate relationships they had— with an autochthonous population.[21] The celebration of what Vicky Unruh calls vernacular cultures was effected by "claiming a cultural proximity to the discovered"; thus, Latin American avant-garde practices invoked "Taulipang and Arekuna myths, Andean cosmology, Afro-Cuban ritual, Mesoamerican rites . . . and America's untamed song as prodigious aesthetic resources."[22] Importantly, for American artists, these were claims Europeans could not, by and large, make.

The diffusion of a primitivist indigenism into a less obviously primitivist vanguardism in *Trilce* is by no means a clearly delineated process. Indeed, *Trilce*'s poetry for the most part turns away from the overtly indigenist themes, images, and language of "Nostalgias imperiales." Instead, these themes are mutated into another, closely related, vernacular—that of the provincial and the familial, which for Vallejo was unavoidably intertwined with women and their domestic work as well as with indigenous people, life, and culture. Much has been made (by critics who read Vallejo as a *cholo* or mestizo poet) of the fact that both of his grandmothers were Indian, but I point this out only to reinforce the idea that the cultural circumstances and discourses of Vallejo's life in provincial Peru, intimately bound up with indigenous life, work as a motivating force not only in his early poetry but in his vanguardist experiments as well.

The unevenness of modernization in a country such as Peru meant that local intellectuals and artists often had a different conception of modernity, industrialization, and technology—as well as of the autochthonous or primitive—than did their counterparts in Europe.[23] At the same time, however, Latin American artists such as Vallejo were well aware of the discourses of modern bourgeois rationalization, and like their European counterparts "expressed a profound antipathy toward dominant ideologies and worldviews" and "sought to explode the complacent certainties of bourgeois attitudes" in order to create a radically modern art.[24] But in so doing, they still held traditional assumptions, shared by their more bourgeois contemporaries, about the nature of women and Indians as embodying a primordial "source" from which they might drink deeply of originality and newness.

Azular y Planchar Todos los Caos

Vallejo's "chaos" of language in *Trilce*, its "destructive fragmentation and highly mobile metaphoricity," is considered one of the hallmarks that situate him within the avant-garde.[25] In fact, *Trilce*'s fragmentations, neologisms, and typographical and syntactic experimentations connect with such differing artists as Mallarmé, Apollinaire, Picasso, and Stein, while his colloquial references and indigenist sensibility position him on an early cusp of indigenist avant-garde experimentations by Latin American artists like—to name a few—Peruvian writers Gamaliel Churata, Alejandro Peralta, and Martín Adán, and painter José Sabogal, as well as Nobel laureates like the Guatemalan expatriate Miguel Angel Asturias and the Chilean poet Gabriela Mistral.

The ways in which Vallejo gets from the highly stylized language and imagery of "Nostalgias imperiales" to the punning, "stuttering and disarticulations" of *Trilce* have much to do with what Ortega calls Vallejo's *poética de la tachadura* (poetics of strikeovers), as in the corrections of a manuscript.[26] Many *Trilce* poems are "written over" earlier work, so that the book at certain points resembles a palimpsest where language, images, and tone seep up or bleed through from past work into the present text.

In reading *Trilce*, Julio Ortega makes a link between Vallejo's avant-garde use of language and his evocation of women. Ortega maintains that in Vallejo's poetic "world of objects in movement," the (speaking) subject must begin by unlearning institutionalized discourses and by going back "to the regional landscape, to infancy, to feminine speech."[27] Insofar as the avant-garde work, then, requires some gesture toward coherence, part of the function of *Trilce*'s representations not merely of "feminine speech" but also of women's domestic work is, as I have noted, to provide a structural element for poetic unity. Images of women's domestic labor are appropriated not only in an attempt to restitch the torn and chaotic edges of Vallejo's language, but also, as T6 puts it, to *azular y planchar todos los caos* (bleach and iron every chaos) of Vallejo's poetics.

Denise Arnold maintains that "without understanding weaving, we cannot really understand in any depth Andean culture." Arnold discusses knotting and weaving in terms of their use by Andean indigenous peoples for the ordering of knowledge, as aids in memory, and in the transmission of important narratives; she notes that "the knotted cords called *kipu* in Quechua or *chinu* in Aymara . . . were used in some Andean communities until a generation ago as record-keeping devices," and by the Inca as "the mnemonic basis of tales of the great deeds and genealogies." Discussing the gendered status of weaving in Andean culture, she notes that it, like knotting, "often form[s] . . . a matrixing knowledge, centred on women's bodies. . . . The close relationship between weaving and giving life gives rise to numerous prohibitions on spinning and weaving during pregnancy."[28] Vallejo's readings in indigenist literature, along with his early life in the provincial town of Santiago de Chuco, intimately surrounded by and connected to Indian lives and culture, would have provided him with a vocabulary of images first seen in "Nostalgias imperiales" that, brought into the more personal realm of *Trilce,* forms the matrix for this collection's avant-garde concerns.

A poem late in *Trilce,* T66 or "Dobla el dos de noviembre" (The Second of November Tolls), clearly states a general connection in this book between life, death, and endings, and the gendered spinning out (and, by implication, cutting) of thread first mentioned in sonnet II of "Nostalgias imperiales":

La anciana pensativa, cual relieve
de un bloque pre-incaico, hila que hila;
en sus dedos de Mama el huso leve
la lana gris de su vejez trasquila

(The pensive old woman, that relief
from a pre-Inca block, spins and spins;
in her Mama fingers the light spindle
shears the gray wool of her old age)[29]

Again conflating a neoclassical idea with a pre-Conquest image, the spinning *anciana* refers us imaginatively to the Fates who spun, measured, and
cut off the thread of life. This poem helps to gloss the much more difficult,
but still related, *Trilce* poem "Dobla el dos de noviembre." In this case, mending and knotting gestures, particularly in the second stanza, work to pull
together the poem's attenuated syntax and signification:

> Difuntos, qué bajo cortan vuestros dientes
> abolidos, repasando ciegos nervios,
> sin recordar la dura fibra
> que cantores obreros redondos remiendan
> con cáñamo inacabable, de innumerables nudos
> latientes de encrucijada.
>
> (Dead ones, how low your abolished
> teeth cut, mending blind nerves,
> forgetting the tough fiber
> that simple singing workers repair
> with unending hemp, with innumerable knots
> throbbing with crossroads.)

Addressed to the dead on All Souls' Day, this poem reminds the dead of
their continuing absence and ineffectiveness. In attempting to mend their
"blind nerves," the "abolished teeth" of the dead bite the thread perhaps too
"low" for sucessful mending, having themselves been cut off from the vigor
of the living. The biting and sawing imagery in this poem evokes the pain of
memory (the "other heart" of the speaker himself is being "sawed" by the
dead in the verses that follow). The poem simultaneously works to cut or
bite off that pain by allowing the irruption of the everyday actions of the
living, such as a wagon rolling down the cobbled street:

> Vosotros, difuntos . . . cómo aserrais el otro corazón . . . y la rama del
> presentimiento
> se la muerde un carro que simplemente
> rueda por la calle
>
> (You, dead . . . how you saw up the other heart . . . and the branch of
> presentiment

is bitten by a wagon simply
rolling down the street)

But it is, first, in the use of words such as *repasar* (here "to mend") and *remendar* (also "to mend"), then in the comparison between the threadlike "blind nerves" and the "hard fiber" of the "unending" hemp with its "innumerable throbbing knots," and finally in the confrontation of the ineffective but painful memory of the dead with the living, singing, *redondos* ("rounds" but also, colloquially in the Andes, "stupid" or "simple") workers, that there is a constellation of ideas connecting the motifs of threads, mending, and knotting to a more vibrant though rudimentary life. This vitality, then, is connected directly with the colloquial and the indigenous through the everyday vernacular images of the ropemaking *obreros* and wagons rumbling in the cobbled streets.

Vallejo's general tendency to conflate a "textilic" poetics of knotting and weaving with his concerns and cultural ideas about life and death is underscored by the anxiety manifested over bodily *un*knottings and, concomitantly, linguistic undoings in an earlier poem such as T26, "El verano echa nudo a tres años" (Summer Knots Up Three Years). Here, as in T60, "Es de madera mi paciencia" (Wooden Is My Patience), the displacement of Vallejo's "vise of sex and death"[30] onto this kind of women's work is layered over by associations with the life-giving and death-bound female body itself. This produces its own "knot" of associations between domestic labor, women, and their bodies that, in a poem such as T26, motivates linguistic and formal avant-garde experimentations:

Nudo alvino deshecho, una pierna por allí,
más allá todavía la otra,
      desgajadas,
      péndulas.
Deshecho nudo de lácteas glándulas
de la sinamayera,
bueno para alpacas brillantes,
para abrigo de pluma inservible
[...]
Al calor de una punta
de pobre sesgo ESFORZAFO,

la griega sota de oros tórnase
morena sota de islas,
cobriza sota de lagos
en frente a moribunda alejandría
a cuzco moribundo.

(Whitish undone knot, one leg there,
even further over there the other,
        torn off,
          pendulous.
Undone knot of lacteal glands
of the *sinamayera,*
good for shiny alpacas,
useless for a coat of feathers
[...]
At the heat of one corner
with poor and VIGOROUS profile,
the Greek jack of diamonds turns into
dark-skinned jack of islands,
coppery jack of lakes
facing moribund Alexandria
Cuzco moribund.[31]

An indigenista/modernista sensibility of a lost, exotic time surfaces in this poem's comparison of past but glorious civilizations, in its images of *alpacas brillantes* and *abrigo de pluma,* and in the transformation of the *griega sota de oros* into indigenous *morena* (dark-skinned) and *cobriza* (coppery) figures.

The specific textiles invoked—alpaca, the feathered coat, and *sinamay* (a fine Philippine fabric)—take naturally as their central figure the *sinamayera,* a female vendor of sinamay. In the poem's punning references to pregnancy *(encintados de cárdenas cintas, lácteas glándulas)* and in its naturalizing of selling and textile work as women's work, the physical nature of the female body and its *labor,* in both senses of the word, are underscored and conflated. This recalls but also problematizes such images from "Nostalgias imperiales" as the indigenous "shepherdess" of "sad, heroic wool" whose heart is a spindle, a bundle of hemp or cotton. What has been added to the body of ideas about women and their production is that here the "undoing" of the female figure's body/knot implicitly links the female capacity for (re)production with the engendering of (indigenous) children *ya para qué tristura* (now for what sadness). This literal embodiment of women's work, so important in Vallejo's writing, refers us back to the poem quoted at the beginning of this paper:

El traje que vestí mañana
no lo ha lavado mi lavandera:
lo lavaba en sus venas otilinas,
en el chorro de su corazón
[...]
A hora que no hay quien vaya a las aguas,
en mis falsillas encañona
el lienzo para emplumar
[...]
Y si supiera si ha de volver;
y si supiera qué mañana entrará
a entregarme las ropas lavadas, mi aquella
lavandera del alma. Qué mañana entrará
satisfecha, capulí de obrería, dichosa
de probar que sí sabe, que sí puede
            ¡COMO NO VA A PODER!
azular y planchar todos los caos.

(The suit I wore tomorrow
my laundress hasn't washed it:
she used to wash it in her Otilian veins,
in the stream of her heart
[...]
At an hour when there's no one who goes to the waters,
in my guide-sheet lines she quills
the [writing-]cloth for feathering ...)[32]

As I have been emphasizing, "Nostalgias imperiales" marks the beginning of Vallejo's tendency to make the female body one with its work; this continues in the conflation of Vallejo's real-life lover, Otilia, with her presumed duties as a laundress. The poetic persona's *traje turbio de injusticia* (suit soiled with injustice) used to be washed *en sus venas otilinas,/en el chorro de su corazón;* she is imagined as his *capulí de obrería,* suggesting that "Otilia is the fruit of her own labor."[33] This phrase accomplishes *Trilce*'s emphasis on women's manual labor further by collapsing into one female body the work of different classes of women: Otilia, in real life a middle-class woman of urban Lima, would not go "to the waters" to wash her clothes; this image conjures up instead the figure of the poor mestizo or Indian woman who goes to the site of public washing, quite different from the figure, site, and work of the middle-class woman.[34] The reference to *capulí*, among other things, "colors" the figure of Otilia, placing her closer to the primitivizing ideal of the indigenous woman.

Poem T60, "Es de madera mi paciencia," further glosses the paradoxes inherent in the poetic use of women's domestic gestures. As does T26, T60 posits a female body that, though it brings the speaker into the world, also ultimately exiles the speaker from a childhood (originary, simple, and in this way primitive) imaginary of maternal wholeness; at the same time, the female body and its domestic gestures engender/suture/exile the poetic body to, or into, the merely material world of physical flesh and muffled poetic speech. The loss of wholeness already presaged by the maternal body's unknotting in T26 is here similarly denoted by the lines *te partes y me dejas . . . sin tu nudo de sueños, domingo* (you part and leave me . . . without your knot of dreams, Sunday). This departure of the whole and solid body-knot leaves behind, poetically speaking, nothing but a *sábado de harapos* (Saturday of rags), with nothing to hold it together but *esta horrible sutura/del placer que nos engendra sin querer,/y el placer que nos DestieRRa* ("this horrible suture/of the pleasure that engenders us without meaning to,/and the pleasure that eXXiles us). The feminine suturing together of an always ripped-apart bodily experience, itself paralleled by and manifested through the constant coming apart of the work's language, appears as a motif of sewing in *Trilce*. This sewing gesture is repeated in such poems as T35, "El encuentro con la amada" (The Encounter with the Beloved) where the lover

se interna
entre los cortinajes y ¡oh aguja de mis días
desgarrados! se sienta a la orilla
de una costura, a coserme el costado a su costado, a pegar el botón de esa
camisa

(she hides herself
between the curtains and oh! needle of my ragged
days! she sits on the edge
of a seam, to sew my side to her side, to stick on the button of that shirt).

In keeping with the constant associative connections and tensions between women's productive and reproductive properties, anxiety about and
desire for the lover's body are implicitly directed toward the maternal body
as well. *LHN* poems "Mayo" and "Hojas de ébano" provide some of Vallejo's
most important *Trilce* poems with an entire constellation of vocabulary and
images of a provincial home, connected by association with indigenous life,
whose central figure is that of the mother. "May" evokes the kitchen's smoke
and the evanescence of life: *Vierte el humo doméstico en la aurora. . . . el hilo
azul de los alientos rotos!* (Domestic smoke pours into the dawn. . . . the blue
thread of broken breaths!). In a similar vein, "Ebony Leaves" recalls the doors
of the family house, which, once "youthful," are, now that the poetic persona
has returned, *coágulos de sombra oliendo a olvido* (clots of shadow smelling
of forgetfulness). Yet, the "arms" of the doors welcome him back, prompting
him to ask after a now-dead "Señora"; *aún la veo envueltita en su rebozo* (I
can still see her wrapped up in her little shawl). Such scenes of provincial
melancholy are transformed in particular and important ways into poems
of personal and familial life scattered throughout *Trilce:* in T28, for example,
He almorzado solo ahora, y no he tenido/MADRE (I have eaten alone now,
and I haven't had / a MOTHER), and because of the death of the mother, the
kitchen is "in darkness"; in T65, the speaker desires to return to the family
home: *Madre, me voy mañana a Santiago,/a mojarme en tu bendición y en tu
llanto* (Mother, tomorrow I go to Santiago,/to soak myself in your blessing
and in your tears); and again in T61:

> Esta noche desciendo del caballo,
> ante la puerta de la casa, donde
> me despedí con el cantar del gallo.
> Está cerrada y nadie responde
>
> (Tonight I descend from my horse,
> in front of the door of the house, where
> I took leave with the crow of the rooster.
> It's closed and nobody answers)

Most important, the associative connections found in "Nostalgias imperiales"
between provincial life and the family home are recast in a poem such as

T52, "Y nos levantaremos cuando se nos dé" (And We'll Get Up When We Feel like It):

Los humos de los bohíos ¡ah golfillos
en rama! madrugarían a jugar
a las cometas azulinas, azulantes,
y, apañuscando alfarjes y piedras, nos darían
su estímulo fragante de boñiga,
          para sacarnos
al aire nene que no conoce aún las letras,
a pelearles los hilos

(The smoke from the huts—oh, raw
young ragamuffins!—
would get up early to play
at bluish kites, bluing,
and, crowding crossbeams and stones,
would give us
their dung-fragrant stimulus,
          to get us out
into the baby-air which doesn't even know its letters yet,
to kite-fight with the strings.)[35]

In "May" the too picturesque scene of the simultaneously degraded and exoticized figures of the Indians is distanced, made unreal by the artificial language and style of the poem. In T52, this distance is closed considerably by projecting onto the scene the literally more familiar (for Vallejo) poetic stance of the persona as provincial boy, T61's *niño aldeano* (village boy). Traces of Indianist modernista language still persist, for example in the poem's references to "smoke," to rural fragrances, to the soaring "blueness" of the smoke and its "kites" against the sky. However, the poetic function (to evoke a set scene of rural nostalgia) of the references to the manual work of women in "Nostalgias imperiales"—spinning, sheepherding, gathering wood, shearing wool, gleaning in the fields—is displaced in a poem such as T52 onto domestic but still manual and provincial labor—*la anciana* cleaning out the chamberpots, the maternal figure waking the children and making the country lunch, a "musical lunch" evoking the kitchen clatter of labor-intensive country food. The primitive or simple mood of the penultimate stanza further conflates the laboring maternal figure with that of the laboring indigenous figures in "Nostalgias imperiales":

Otro día querrás pastorear
entre tus huecos onfalóideos
        ávidas cavernas,
        meses nonos,
        mis telones.
  O querrás acompañar a la ancianía
a destapar la toma de un crepúsculo,
para que de día surja
toda el agua que pasa de noche.

(Another day you'll want to pasture
in your omphaloid hollows
        avid caverns,
        ninth months,
        my stage curtains.
  Or you'll want to accompany old woman-age
to uncover the spout of a twilight,
so that by day surges
all the water that passes at night.)[36]

Echoes from "Nostalgias imperiales" in such language as *pastorear,* *ancianía,* and even the oft-repeated term *crepúsculo* (twilight) recall both the "shepherdess" and "the pensive old woman" spinning her own "old age." All these images are implicitly contained, or "pastured," in the maternal space of *tus huecos onfalóideos,* where "omphaloid" recalls the navel, archetypal sign of the maternal connection. In fact, in keeping with Vallejo's propensity to make one word work in several different though related directions, this word also performs more than one associative function: it serves to call attention to the knot, which is literally at the center of every human body, while it also recalls a neoclassical reference to Omphale, queen of Lydia, in whose service Hercules, dressed as a woman, spun wool and performed other "womanly tasks" for three years to appease the gods.

Although the poetic cross-dressing in (pseudo)Indian garb I detect here may seem far-fetched, such a reading resonates with T33, "Si lloviera esta noche" (If It Rained Tonight), a poem in which the persona will himself, "without mother, without lover," attempt to spin his own *fibra védica* (Vedic fiber—a reference to the ancient Hindu sacred texts), his own origins, in a vain effort to go back "a thousand years./Better just a hundred," as though "nothing had happened":

> O sin madre, sin amada, sin porfía
> de agacharme a aguitar al fondo, a puro
> pulso,
> esta noche así, estaría escarmentando
> la fibra védica,
> la lana védica de mi fin final, hilo
> del diantre ...
>   Haga la cuenta de mi vida,
> o haga la cuenta de no haber aún nacido,
> no alcanzaré a librarme.

> (Or without mother, without lover, without the stubbornness at heart
> to crouch down and wait, by main
> strength,
> tonight like this, I would be carding
> the Vedic fiber,
> the Vedic wool of my final finality, devil's
> thread ...
>   Whether I add up my life,
> or add up not having even been born,
> I won't manage to free myself.)[37]

Not only demonstrating the speaker's failure in appropriating what, from "Nostalgias imperiales" onward, has been the exclusive province of women, this poem implicitly posits the feminine as original and moreover indigenous "source" of *masculine* artistic creativity. However, in spite of the speaker's admission of failure to appropriate this source for himself, the very invocation of the absent lover or mother in fact produces this poem, and produces its linguistic sophistication. Thus, while *amada y madre* might be the absent but still primitive and original source of creativity, the *poetic* product is the (male) poet's own. Just as Huyssen notes that in Europe the second half of the nineteenth century saw the "obsessively argued inferiority of woman as artist,"[38] so Latin American artistic notions of creativity's essential masculinity share the same assumptions about women's artistic inferiority, while, at least for Vallejo, the chain of such gendered assumptions about creativity leads his poetic work both toward and away from the unartistic "naturalness" of "women's work."

Buenos con b de Baldío

Christiane von Buelow and Julio Ortega are among the many critics who suggest that Vallejo's poetry, in particular *Trilce,* has some of the same hallmarks of fragmentation as does Cubism. However, it seems to me that it is verbal collage (itself intimately connected with Symbolist, Cubist, and Dada experimentations in typography) which is one of the avant-garde practices most resonant with Vallejo's own appropriations of modernist preoccupations and techniques. Cubism already had something of a literary parallel in writers such as Gertrude Stein. But Vallejo's references to the fabriclike ripped, ragged, unraveled, and wrinkled nature of his bodies and his language, and the gestures throughout *Trilce* toward maternal and feminine labor such as ironing, sewing, and mending, relate his work more closely to the assumptions and activities underpinning such seemingly diverse practices as Picasso's collages and Sonia Delauney's work in fabric, which often included language collage. Delauney worked in the 1920s, for example, with "simultaneous dresses," embroidered or appliquéd with poems by writers such as Blaise Cendrars, so that the movements of the body constantly broke and re-formed the words of the poem. Although while he was still in Peru, Vallejo may not have seen examples of Delauney's work, her experiments with the fabriclike malleability and foldability of language resonate with Vallejo's concern with the materiality and "fabricality" of poetic language and bodies.

It is clear both from the examples given here, and from a more general reading of *Trilce,* that Vallejo posits his text as sharing qualities with its (linguistic) cousin the textile. Again, this is by no means a new idea; what interests me is a reading in which the "textile" nature of Vallejo's avant-garde writing is reconnected with its specifically Andean, indigenist subtext of communication by weaving and knotting. In fact, I would like to go back for a moment to T6, "El traje que vestí mañana" (The Suit I Wore Tomorrow), to illustrate Vallejo's reworking of his earlier indigenist images within *Trilce*'s much more problematized language and textuality. The second stanza contains what are perhaps the most difficult lines of this poem:

A hora que no hay quien vaya a las aguas,
en mis falsillas encañona
el lienzo para emplumar, y todas las cosas
del velador de tánto qué será de mí,
todas no están mías
a mi lado.
                    Quedaron de su propiedad,
fratasadas, selladas con su trigueña bondad.

(At an hour when there's no one who goes to the waters,
in my guide-sheet lines she quills
the [writing-]cloth for feathering, and all the things
on the nightstand from so much what'll-become-of-me,
all are not there mine
at my side.
                    They remained part of her property,
rubbed over, sealed with her dark-skinned goodness.)[39]

The lines *en mis falsillas encañona/el lienzo para emplumar* have been translated by Eshleman as "the linen for feathering/fledges in my underlining"; however, I read *encañona* (to quill or pleat fabric by ironing) as a verb whose subject is "she"; and *falsillas* (lined sheets used as guide underneath blank writing paper) as the pleats that constitute the ordering subtext of *his* poems. Thus, the first three lines can be glossed: "When she is not laundering, she irons pleats underneath my paper to keep my lines straight and makes folds to receive the quills, preparing the cloth to be feathered or the poem to be written." The woman's labor is the source of both the poem's order and its creativity, emanating from behind the page. Thus, the things on the *velador* (nightstand, but also, conceivably, writing table) "remain part of her property." Further, Vallejo punningly connects *cañón* (quill) and *pluma* (feather, pen), *falsilla* and *velador,* not only with tools for writing and the act of writing itself but also with the medium: *lienzo* (linen, canvas, and also the "cloth" on which indigenous peoples recorded their pictograms); finally, Neale-Silva makes the further association of lienzo with Inca feathered textiles.[40] These

text/textile associations make the poem's self-referentiality clear: it is a radically modern exploration of the limits of communicative gestures, couched
in a practice that uses (indigenous) woman as original creative source, and
her labor as a source of order and unity. The always failing gesture toward a
coherence of poetic language uses the simplicity or primitiveness of her work
to drive, to hold together, and, at the same time, to hinder or hold back the
possible success of such a gesture. That is, the speaker depends on the absence and/or futility of domestic labor as, paradoxically, something around
which the poem can build.

A reading that situates the above poems in context with a poem such as
T52, about the safe maternal and domestic space of infancy, will make it
clear that *Trilce* connects its nostalgic sense of a provincial childhood (and
the conflated figures of different women's bodies, classes, and labors which
accompany that sense) not with any sufficiency of language but with those
vanguardist problematics of language which mark this entire collection:

> . . . y en el almuerzo musical,
> cancha reventada, harina con manteca,
> con manteca,
> le tomas el pelo al peón decúbito
> que hoy otra vez olvida dar los buenos días,
> esos sus días, buenos con b de baldío,
> que insisten en salirle al pobre
> por la culata de la v
> dentilabial que vela en el.

> (. . . and at the musical lunch,
> popped roasted corn, flour with lard,
> with lard,
> you tease the decubital worker
> who today again forgets to say *buenos días,*
> those *días* of his, *buenos* with backward b,
> which insist on coming out of the poor guy
> by the butt of the dentilabial
> *v which keeps vigil in him.*[41]

Connected with the impulses back toward a supposedly unmodern, presumably "whole" childhood space that run throughout this collection, poem

T52 is also paradoxically connected through its "dentilabial/v" to Vallejo's vanguardist anxieties about any possible wholeness of poetic language. These anxieties are represented in the image of the slobbering (sexual) female lips and stuttering speech of T9, as well as the toothless mouth of T56, which has lost its speech; further, we see this v-b play in several *Trilce* poems.

Each time, in fact, that the play of this slip between *v* and *b* is introduced in Vallejo's poetry, it serves to evoke a fragile materiality of language, a fragility constantly compromised by a crude, sexualized fleshiness itself often coded as female (Ortega suggests, and I concur, that the letter *v* has female sexual connotations for Vallejo). The deliberate crudeness of the poem's final image, as the peon's *b* stutters out like a kind of verbal fart, instead connects the stuttering language of this collection unmistakably with rural and "primitive" bodies as well as with those material, animal aspects of the body coded as female in other *Trilce* poems. Although—or perhaps because—the above poem professes to evoke a "baby air which doesn't even know its letters," its "primitive" linguistic concerns are the mark of, and form the unmistakable setting for, the book's sophisticated vanguardism, its typographical and syntactic fragmentation, poetic stammerings, and vocalic substitutions.

It is one of the central paradoxes of Vallejo's poetry that his seemingly anachronistic gestures toward a primitive, provincial, and domestic poetics of labor and the female body should generate a vanguardist poetry couched in a sutured-together verbal collage of torn and ragged body parts and fragmented language. Although Jean Franco identifies *Trilce*'s central theme as "the dislodging of the 'I' from the home," and it is true these poems are clearly nostalgic for a lost childhood enclosed by the maternal walls of the house, the speaking subject is never totally dislodged from this space.[42] If the "primitive" and originary nature of women's laboring bodies is at once opposed to and implicated in poetic work, it is largely the tension between these two poles of effort that effects, and is in turn affected by, *Trilce*'s constant poetic breakages, which simultaneously mark the failure of poetic discourse and the beginnings, for Vallejo himself, of a vanguardist poetics.

Notes

1. César Vallejo, *The Black Heralds*, trans. Richard Schaaf and Kathleen Ross (Pittsburgh: Latin American Literary Review Press, 1990) 104. All subsequent translations are mine unless otherwise noted.

2. César Vallejo, *Trilce,* ed. Julio Ortega (Madrid: Cátedra, 1991), 63. All poems in *Trilce* are untitled; instead, they are numbered with Roman numerals. For ease of reference, I will refer to them with the designation T followed by an Arabic numeral (e.g., T6).

3. The Spanish literary magazine *Cervantes* served as one of the vehicles in which young Latin American writers and artists could note European avant-garde trends. Included in the August 1919 issue, for example, around the time that Vallejo was writing or rewriting many *Trilce* poems, were Tristan Tzara's manifesto "DADA 1919" and "Otro manifiesto" by Francis Picabia.

4. *Modernismo* refers to a specifically Latin American literary period (late nineteenth and early twentieth centuries) influenced by, but not always imitative of, French Symbolism.

5. Broadly speaking the literary term *indigenismo* refers to a Latin American genre that, while written by creole or mestizo authors (more or less), sympathetically narrates the plight of indigenous populations. Indigenista texts were not, by and large, written by Indian authors. See Efraín Kristal, *The Andes Viewed from the City: Literary and Political Discourse on the Indian in Peru 1848–1930* (New York: Peter Lang, 1987), 2–3.

6. As Julio Ortega notes, "We know that Vallejo tried to erase explicit evidence of the [original] poem, in a process of revision equivalent to trimming referents" (*Trilce,* 10).

7. For an expansion of this idea, see Rita Felski, *The Gender of Modernity* (Cambridge: Harvard University Press, 1995), 27.

8. For example, Perry notes "a well-established convention within Post-Enlightenment European art and culture . . . in which the rural female was represented as close to nature, as a symbol of the 'natural' peasant life." Charles Harrison, Francis Frascina and Gill Perry, *Primitivism, Cubism, Abstraction: The Early 20th Century* (New Haven, CT: Yale University Press, 1993), 22.

9. Denise Arnold, "Using Ethnography to Unravel Different Kinds of Knowledge in the Andes," *Journal of Latin American Cultural Studies* 6, no. 1 (1997): 33.

10. Peter Bürger, *Theory of the Avant-Garde,* trans. Michael Shaw (Minneapolis: University of Minnesota Press, 1984), 82.

11. Gwen Kirkpatrick, *The Dissonant Legacy of Modernismo: Lugones, Herrera y Reissig, and the Voices of Modern Spanish American Poetry* (Berkeley: University of California Press, 1989), 15. Also, as Kristal points out, the presumed "realism" of indigenista texts accords more with their critics' and readers' ideological standpoints than with verisimilitude (Kristal, *The Andes,* 7).

12. Kristal, *The Andes,* 22.

13. Vicky Unruh, *Latin American Vanguards: The Art of Contentious Encounters* (Berkeley: University of California Press, 1994), 226. Besides González Prada, Peru-

vian modernista José Santos Chocano and vanguardist Alejandro Peralta wrote indigenist-inflected modernista poetry at various times in their careers.

14. Kirkpatrick, *Dissonant Legacy,* 207–211.

15. As Kristal points out, Manuel González Prada led the way in this matter, explaining Peru's defeat by Chile in the War of the Pacific (1879–1883) in two terms that for him were connected: first, the disenfranchisement of Peru's indigenous people, who as a result had no well-developed sense of national identity; and second, in terms of national discourse, the lack of realism and connection to "the country's moral plane" which led journalists and writers to cover up "the weaknesses of political figures rather than pointing to the problems in Peruvian society" (*The Andes,* 124).

16. Harrison et al., *Primitivism, Cubism, Abstraction,* 3, 6.

17. Quoted in Alan Knight, "Racism, Revolution, and *Indigenismo:* Mexico, 1910–1940," in *The Idea of Race in Latin America, 1870–1940,* ed. Richard Graham (Austin: University of Texas Press, 1990), 71–114.

18. Felski, *Gender of Modernity,* 16.

19. Harrison et al., *Primitivism, Cubism, Abstraction,* 27.

20. Mark Thurner, *From Two Republics to One Divided: Contradictions of Postcolonial Nationmaking in Andean Peru* (Durham, NC: Duke University Press, 1997), 12, 15.

21. These countries' concern with their largely nonassimilated indigenous populations was by no means new. According to Kristal (*The Andes,* 1–2), literature which can be called indigenista has been produced in the Andean region—Bolivia, Peru, and Ecuador—at least since the 1840s.

22. Unruh, *Vanguards,* 158, 4.

23. For more on this, see José Cerna-Bazán, *Sujeto a cambio: De las relaciones del texto y la sociedad en la escritura de César Vallejo (1914–1930)* (Lima: Latinoamericana Editores, 1995), 42.

24. Felski, *Gender of Modernity,* 27.

25. Christiane von Buelow, "Vallejo's *Venus de Milo* and the Ruins of Language," *PMLA* 104, no. 1 (1989): 50.

26. See Ortega in *Trilce,* 13–14.

27. Julio Ortega, "La hermenéutica vallejiana y el hablar materno," in *César Vallejo: Obra poética,* ed. Américo Ferrari (Paris: Archivos, 1988), 609, 612.

28. Arnold, "Using Ethnography," 37, 46.

29. *Trilce,* 311.

30. See Clayton Eshleman, Afterword: "Vallejo's Succulent Snack of Unity," *Trilce,* trans. C. Eshleman (New York: Marsilio Publishers, 1992), 243.

31. *Trilce,* 142–143.

32. *Trilce,* 63. See opening page of this essay for the remaining verses.

33. Eshleman, Afterword, 215.

34. Although much has been made of Vallejo's mixed heritage, as Jean Franco points out "in Santiago de Chuco the Vallejo family were certainly not considered either Indian or particlarly humble." Jean Franco, *César Vallejo: The Dialectics of Poetry and Silence* (Cambridge: Cambridge University Press, 1976), 2. When I use terms such as "white," "creole," or "middle class," I am referring to the relative context of Peru, especially urban Lima.

35. *Trilce*, 246–247.

36. Ibid.

37. *Trilce*, 167.

38. Andreas Huyssen, *After the Great Divide: Modernism, Massculture, Postmodernism* (Bloomington: Indiana University Press, 1986), 50.

39. *Trilce*, 63.

40. Quoted in Ortega, ed., *Trilce*, 64–65.

41. *Trilce*, 247.

42. Jean Franco, "La temática: De *Los heraldos negros* a los 'Poemas póstumos,'" in Ferrari, ed., *César Vallejo: Obra poética*, 582.

Selected Bibliography

This selection includes three categories of works: (1) general works on primitivism and its history, or otherwise important for the development of the concept; (2) studies of primitivism in non–Latin American cultures that nevertheless focus on authors of significant influence in Latin America or afford examples relevant for Latin American research; (3) studies that analyze the sources, presence, or effects of primitivism and related ideas in Latin American arts and culture.

Alonso, Carlos. *The Spanish American Regional Novel: Modernity and Autochthony.* Cambridge: Cambridge University Press, 1990.

Araeen, Rasheed. "From Primitivism to Ethnic Arts." *Third Text* 1 (1987): 6–25.

Baird, James. *Ishmael.* Baltimore: Johns Hopkins University Press, 1956.

Barkan, Elazar, and Ronald Bush, eds. *Prehistories of the Future: The Primitivist Project and the Culture of Modernism.* Stanford, CA: Stanford University Press, 1995.

Barker, F., et al., eds. *Europe and Its Others.* Colchester, UK: University of Essex Press, 1985.

Bartra, Roger. *The Cage of Melancholy: Identity and Metamorphosis in the Mexican Character.* New Brunswick, NJ: Rutgers University Press, 1992.

———. *Oficio mexicano.* Mexico City: Grijalbo, 1993.

———. *Wild Men in the Looking Glass: The Mythic Origins of European Otherness.* Ann Arbor: University of Michigan Press, 1994.

———. *The Artificial Savage: Modern Myths of the Wild Man.* Ann Arbor: University of Michigan Press, 1997.

Bell, Michael. *Primitivism.* London: Methuen, 1979.

Benamou, Michel. "Ethnopoetics: A First International Symposium." *Alcheringa: Ethnopoetics* 2, no. 2 (1976). Special issue.

———. "The Concept of Marginality in Ethnopoetics." In *Minority Language and Literature: Retrospective and Perspective,* 150–160. Ed. Dexter Fisher. New York: Modern Language Association, 1977.

Birtwistle, Graham. "On E. H. Gombrich's Contribution to the Study of Primitivism." In *Gombrich on Art and Psychology.* Ed. Richard Woodfield. Manchester, UK: Manchester University Press; New York: St. Martin's Press, 1996.

Blocker, Gene. *The Aesthetics of Primitive Art.* Lanham, MD: University Press of America, 1994.

Boas, Franz. *Primitive Art.* 1927. New York: Dover, 1955.

————. *The Mind of Primitive Man.* 1911. New York: Macmillan, 1965.

Boas, George. *Primitivism and Related Ideas in the Middle Ages.* 1948. Baltimore: Johns Hopkins University Press, 1997.

Bonfil, Guillermo, et al. *Culturas populares y política cultural.* Mexico City: Museo de Culturas Populares/SEP, 1982.

Boon, J. A. *Other Tribes, Other Scribes: Symbolic Anthropology in the Comparative Study of Cultures, Histories, Religions, and Texts.* Cambridge: Cambridge University Press, 1982.

Borges, Jorge Luis. "El arte narrativo y la magia." 1932. In his *Prosa completa.* Barcelona: Bruguera, 1980.

Bravo, Víctor. *Magias y maravillas en el continente literario: Para un deslinde del realismo mágico y lo real maravilloso.* Caracas: La Casa de Bello, 1988.

Brotherston, Gordon. *Book of the Fourth World: Reading the Native Americas Through Their Literature.* New York: Cambridge Univeristy Press, 1992.

Brown, Betty Ann. "El pasado idealizado: La utilización de la imaginería precolombina por Diego Rivera." In *Diego Rivera, retrospectiva,* 149–166. Ed. Ministerio de Cultura. Mexico City: Ministerio de Cultura, 1987.

Burns, Allan F. "Yucatec Mayan Ethnopoetics: The Translation of a Narrative View of Life." *Journal of Mayan Linguistics* 2, no. 1 (1980): 3–12.

Bury, J. B. *The Idea of Progress.* New York: Macmillan, 1932.

Caillois, Roger. *Man and the Sacred.* New York: Free Press, 1959.

Camayd-Freixas, Erik. *Realismo mágico y primitivismo.* Lanham, MD: University Press of America, 1998.

Carpentier, Alejo. "Prólogo." In his *Ecue-Yamba-O!: Novela afro-cubana.* Havana: Editorial Arte y Cultura, 1977.

————. "Prólogo." In his *El reino de este mundo.* 1949. Mexico City: EDHESA, 1980.

Carr, Helen. *Inventing the American Primitive: Politics, Gender, and the Representation of Native American Literary Traditions, 1789–1936.* Cork, Ireland: Cork University Press, 1996.

Cassirer, Ernst. *Language and Myth.* New York: Dover, 1946.

Castillo, Debra A. "Postmodern Indigenism: 'Quetzalcoatl and All That.'" *Modern Fiction Studies* 41 (1995): 35–73.

Certeau, Michel de. *L'Ecriture de l'histoire.* Paris: Gallimard, 1975.

————. *Heterologies: Discourse on the Other.* Minneapolis: University of Minnesota Press, 1986.

Chanady, Amaryll, ed. *Latin American Identity and Constructions of Difference.* Minneapolis: University of Minnesota Press, 1994.

Cheymol, Marc. "Miguel Angel Asturias entre latinidad e indigenismo." In Miguel

Angel Asturias, *Paris 1924–1933: Periodismo y creación literaria*, 844–881. Nanterre, France: ALLCA XX, 1988.

Clifford, James. *The Predicament of Culture: Twentieth-Century Ethnography, Literature and Art.* Cambridge, MA: Harvard Univerity Press, 1988.

———, ed. *Writing Culture: The Poetics and Politics of Ethnography.* Berkeley: University of California Press, 1986.

Coe, Michael D. *The Maya Scribe and His World.* New York: Grolier, 1973.

Connelly, Frances S. "Ruskin's True Griffin: The Relationship of Medievalism to Primitivism and the Formation of an Alternate Aesthetic." *Poetica: An* 39–40 (1994) 179–189.

Dagen, Philippe. *Le Peintre, le poète, le sauvage: Les voies du primitivisme dans l'art français.* Paris: Flammarion, 1998.

DiAntonio, Robert. "Conscious Primitivism in the Poetics of Mario de Andrade." *Mester* 14, no. 1 (1985) 12–19.

Dolgin, Janet L., et al., eds. *Symbolic Anthropology: A Reader in the Study of Symbols and Meaning.* New York: Columbia University Press, 1977.

Elbaum, Henry. "Industrialism vs. Primitivism in the Soviet Russian Literature of the Twenties and the Thirties." *Sociocriticism* 2, no. 1 (1986): 131–171.

Eliade, Mircea. *Cosmos and History: The Myth of the Eternal Return.* New York: Harper & Row, 1959.

———. *The Sacred and The Profane.* New York: Harcourt Brace Jovanovich, 1959.

Emery, Amy Fass. *The Anthropological Imagination in Latin American Literature.* Columbia: University of Missouri Press, 1996.

Fabian, Johannes. *Time and the Other: How Anthropology Makes its Object.* New York: Columbia Univrsity Press, 1983.

Foster, Hal. "'Primitive' Scenes." *Critical Inquiry* 20 (1993): 69–102.

Frazer, Sir James. *The Golden Bough.* 1890. New York: Mentor, 1964.

Freud, Sigmund. "Totem and Taboo." In his *The Basic Writings,* 807-930. New York: Random House, 1938.

Freyre, Gilberto. *The Masters and the Slaves (Casa-grande & senzala): A Study in the Development of Brazilian Civilization.* 1936. Berkeley: University of California Press, 1986.

Frye, Northrop. "Myth, Fiction, and Displacement." *Daedalus* (Summer (1961): 119–137.

———. *Anatomy of Criticism.* 1957. Princeton, NJ: Princeton University Press, 1973.

García Canclini, Néstor. *Hybrid Cultures.* Minneapolis: University of Minnesota Press, 1995.

García Márquez, Gabriel. "Fantasía y creación artística en América Latina y el Caribe." *Texto Crítico* 14 (1979): 3–8.

Goetsch, Paul. "Linguistic Colonialism and Primitivism: The Discovery of Native Languages and Oral Traditions in Eighteenth-Century Travel Books and Novels." *Anglia: Zeitschrift für Englische Philologie* 106, no. 3–4 (1988): 338–359.

Goldwater, Robert. *Primitivism in Modern Art.* 1938. New York: Vintage, 1986.

Gombrich, Ernst H. "Il gusto dei primitivi." *Memorie dell'Istituto italiano per gli studi filosofici* 11 (1985): 7–34.

González Echevarría, Roberto. *Myth and Archive: A theory of Latin American narrative.* Cambridge: Cambridge University Press, 1990.

Graham, Richard, ed. *The Idea of Race in Latin America, 1870–1940.* Austin: University of Texas Press, 1990.

Hall, Edith. *Inventing the Barbarian: Greek Self-Definition Through Tragedy.* Oxford: Clarendon Press, 1991.

Hamlin, William M. *The Image of America in Montaigne, Spenser and Shakespeare: Renaissance Ethnography and Literary Reflection.* Basingstoke, UK: Macmillan, 1995.

Harrison, Charles, Francis Frascina, and Gill Perry. *Primitivism, Cubism, Abstraction: The Early 20th Century.* New Haven, CT: Yale University Press, 1993.

Henighan, Tom. "Shamans, Tribes, and the Sorcerer's Apprentices: Notes on the Discovery of the Primitive in Modern Poetry." *Dalhousie Review* 59, no. 4 (1980): 605–620.

Hiller, Susan, ed. *The Myth of Primitive Art.* London: Routledge, 1991.

Huizinga, Johan. *Homo Ludens.* Boston: Routledge and Kegan Paul, 1980.

Jackson, Kenneth David. "Primitivismo e vanguardia: O 'mau selvagem' do modernismo brasileiro." *Arquivos do Centro cultural português* 23 (1987): 975–982.

Jahn, Janheinz. *Muntu: An Outline of Neo-African Culture.* London: Faber and Faber, 1961.

JanMohamed, Abdul. "Sophisticated Primitivism: The Syncretism of Oral and Literate Modes in Achebe's *Things Fall Apart.*" *Ariel* 15, no. 4 (1984): 19–39.

Jiménez, Reynaldo. "Realidad y mitificación: el narrador niño en *Los ríos profundos.*" *Texto Crítico* 5, no. 14 (1979): 104–116.

Johnson, Lemuel. "El tema negro: The Nature of Primitivism in the Poetry of Luis Palés Matos." In *Blacks in Hispanic Literature: Critical Essays,* 123–135. Ed. Miriam DeCosta. Port Washington, NY: Kennikat Press, 1977.

Jordan, Glenn, ed. *Cultural Politics: Class, Gender, Race, and the Postmodern World.* Oxford: Blackwell, 1995.

King, John, and Ana López, eds. *Mediating Two Worlds: Cinematic Encounters in the Americas.* London: British Film Institute, 1993.

Knapp, James F. "Not Wholeness but Multiplicity: The Primitivism of William Carlos Williams." *Mosaic* 20, no. 1 (1987): 71–81.

Kristal, Efraín. *The Andes Viewed from the City: Literary and Political Discourse on the Indian in Peru, 1848–1930.* New York: Peter Lang, 1987.

Kuper, Adam. *The Invention of Primitive Society.* New York: Routledge, 1988.

Lafaye, Jacques. *Quetzalcóatl and Guadalupe.* Chicago: University of Chicago Press, 1976.

León Hazera, Lydia de. *La novela de la selva hispanoamericana.* Bogotá: Instituto Caro y Cuervo, 1971.

Lévi-Strauss, Claude. *Structural Anthropology.* New York: Doubleday, 1967.

————. *The Savage Mind.* London: Weidenfeld and Nicolson, 1974.

Lévy-Bruhl, Lucien. *La mentalité primitive.* 1922. Paris: Retz-CEPL, 1976.

————. *Primitive Mythology.* 1935. St. Lucia: University of Queensland Press, 1983.

Lienhard, Martin. "El substrato arcaico en *Pedro Páramo:* Quetzacoatl y Tlaloc." In *Juan Rulfo, Toda la obra.* Madrid: Archivos, 1992.

Lipschutz, Alejandro. *Indoamericanismo y el problema racial de las Américas.* Santiago de Chile: Nascimiento, 1944.

Lloyd, Jill. *German Expressionism: Primitivism and Modernity.* New Haven, CT: Yale University Press, 1991.

Long, Charles H. "Primitive/Civilized: The Locus of the Problem." *History of Religions* 20 (1980): 43–61.

Lovejoy, Arthur O., and George Boas. *A Documentary History of Primitivism and Related Ideas in Antiquity.* 1935. Baltimore: Johns Hopkins University Press, 1997.

Madrigal, José A. "El discurso primitivista en las obras de colonización de Lope de Vega." *Círculo: Revista Cultural* 20 (1991): 147–55.

Marouby, Christian. *Utopie et primitivisme.* Paris: Seuil, 1990.

Middleton, J. C. "The Rise of Primitivism and Its Relevance to the Poetry of Expressionism and Dada." In *The Discontinuous Tradition: Studies in German Literature in Honour of Ernest Ludwig Stahl,* 182-203. Ed. Peter F. Ganz. Oxford: Oxford University Press, 1971.

Montaigne, Michel de. "Of Cannibals." In *The Complete Essays of Montaigne.* Trans. Donald Frame. Stanford, CA: Stanford University Press, 1981.

Moody, David. "Peter Brook's Heart of Light: The Discourse of Primitivism in Inter-Cultural Theatre." *Journal of Commonwealth Literature* 29, no. 1 (1994): 93–101.

Morales, Leonidas. "La vorágine: Un viaje al país de los muertos." *Anales de la Universidad de Chile* (1965): 148–170.

Mouralis, Bernard. "Le Concepte de primitif: L'Europe, productrice d'une science des autres." *Notre librairie* 90 (1987): 86–91.

Munro, Thomas. *Evolution in the Arts.* New York: Harry N. Abrams, 1961.

Napier, A. David. *Foreign Bodies: Performance, Art, and Symbolic Anthropology.* Berkeley: University of California Press, 1992.

Newton, Stephen J. *The Politics and Psychoanalysis of Primitivism.* London: Ziggurat Books, 1996.

Nilsson, Nils Ake. "Futurism, Primitivism and the Russian Avant-Garde." *Russian Literature* 8 (1980): 469–482.

Oelschlaeger, Max, ed. *The Wilderness Condition: Essays on Environment and Civilization.* Washington, DC: Island Press, 1992.

Ortiz, Fernando. *Los negros brujos.* 1906. Miami: Universal, 1973.

————. *Cuban Counterpoint, Tobacco and Sugar.* 1940. Durham, NC: Duke University Press, 1995.

Pagden, Anthony. *The Fall of Natural Man: The American Indian and the Origins of Comparative Ethnology.* Cambridge: Cambridge University Press, 1982.

————. *European Encounters with the New World: From Renaissance to Romanticism.* New Haven, CT: Yale University Press, 1994.

Patout, Paulette. "La cultura latinoamericana en París entre 1910 y 1936." In Miguel Angel Asturias, *París, 1924–1933: Periodismo y creación literaria,* 748–757. Nanterre, France: ALLCA XX, 1988.

Paz, Octavio. *The Labyrinth of Solitude.* 1950. London: Penguin, 1990.

Pellón, Gustavo. "Portrait of the Cuban Writer as French Painter: Henri Rousseau, José Lezama Lima's Alter Ego." *Modern Language Notes* 103 (1988): 350–373.

Perera, Hilda. *Idapo: El sincretismo en los cuentos negros de Lydia Cabrera.* Miami: Universal, 1971.

Pérez, Alberto J. "El lector salvaje." *Chasqui* 20, no. 1 (1991): 50–53.

Piccolomini, Manfredi. "Vico, Sorel, and Modern Artistic Primitivism." *New Vico Studies* 4 (1986): 123–130.

Poggioli, Renato. *The Theory of the Avant-garde.* Cambridge, MA: Belknap/Harvard University Press, 1968.

Portilla, Miguel León, ed. *South and Meso-American Native Spirituality: From the Cult of the Feathered Serpent to the Theology of Liberation.* New York: Crossroad, 1993.

Pratt, Mary Louise. *Imperial Eyes: Studies in Travel Writing and Transculturation.* London: Routledge, 1992.

Price, Sally. *Primitive Art in Civilized Places.* Chicago: University of Chicago Press, 1989.

Prieto, René. *Miguel Angel Asturias' Archaeology of Return.* New York: Cambridge University Press, 1993.

Rado, Lisa. "Primitivism, Modernism, and Matriarchy." In her *Modernism, Gender, and Culture: A Cultural Studies Approach,* 283–300. New York: Garland, 1997.

Rama, Angel. *Transculturación narrativa en América Latina.* Mexico City: Siglo XXI, 1982.

Reed, Eugene Elliott. "Herder, Primitivism and the Age of Poetry." *Modern Language Review* 60 (1965): 553–567.

————. *The Civilized vs. Civilization: Primitivism in the Literature of German Pre-Romanticism.* Moscow: University Press of Idaho, 1978.

Revue des sciences humaines 101, no. 3 (1992). Special issue on primitivism.

Rhodes, Collin. *Primitivism and Modern Art.* London: Thames and Hudson, 1994.

Robles, Humberto E. "The First Voyage around the World: From Pigafetta to García Márquez." 1985. In *Gabriel García Márquez*, 183–201. Ed. Harold Bloom. New York: Chelsea House, 1989.

Rosenblat, Angel. *La primera visión de América y otros ensayos.* Caracas: Monte Avila, 1965.

Rubin, William, ed. *Primitivism in 20th Century Art.* 2 vols. New York: Museum of Modern Art, 1984.

Ruiz-Esparza, Jorge. "Desperately Seeking Julio." *Inti: Revista de Literatura Hispánica* 22–23 (1986): 367–378.

Rushing, W. Jackson. *Native American Art and the New York Avant-Garde: A History of Cultural Primitivism.* Austin: University of Texas Press, 1995.

Said, Edward. *Orientalism.* London: Routledge and Kegan Paul, 1978.

Schiffer, Reinhold. "Ethnopoetics: Some Aspects of American Avant-Garde Primitivism." *Dutch Quarterly Review of Anglo-American Letters* 9 (1979): 39–51.

Schiller, Friedrich von. "On Naïve and Sentimental Poetry." 1795. In his *Essays.* London: G. Bell and Sons, 1875.

Servier, Jean. *Historia de la utopía.* Caracas: Monte Avila, 1968.

Shattuck, Roger. *The Banquet Years: The Origins of the Avant Garde in France, 1885 to World War I.* New York: Vintage, 1968.

Sklodowska, Elzbieta. *La parodia en la nueva novela hispanoamericana.* Amsterdam: John Benjamins, 1991.

Sommers, Joseph. "The Indian Oriented Novel in Latin America; New Spirit, New Forms, New Scope." *Journal of Inter-American Studies* 6 (1964): 230–255.

Spengler, Oswald. *The Decline of the West.* 1918, 1921. New York: Knopf, 1996.

Spurr, David. "Myths of Anthropology: Eliot, Joyce, Lévy-Bruhl." *PMLA* 109 (1994): 266–280.

Stanton, Anthony. "Estructuras antropológicas en *Pedro Páramo*." *Nueva Revista de Filología Hispánica* 36, no. 1 (1988): 567–606.

Tedlock, Dennis. "Introduction, Notes, and Comments." In *Popol Vuh.* Trans. Dennis Tedlock. New York: Touchstone, 1996.

Todorov, Tzvetan. *The Conquest of America: The Question of the Other.* New York: Harper & Row, 1984.

Torgovnick, Marianna. *Gone Primitive.* Chicago: University of Chicago Press, 1990.

—————. *Primitive Passions: Men, Women, and the Quest for Ecstasy.* New York: Knopf, 1997.

Tylor, E. B. *Primitive Culture.* London: J. Murray, 1870.

Unruh, Vicky. *Latin American Vanguards: The Art of Contentious Encounters.* Berkeley: University of California Press, 1994.

Uslar Pietri, Arturo. "Lo criollo en la literatura." In his *Las nubes,* 66–79. Santiago de Chile: Editorial Universitaria, 1956.

Van Doren, Charles. *The Idea of Progress.* New York: Frederick A. Praeger, 1967.

Van Wyck, Peter C. *Primitives in the Wilderness: Deep Ecology and the Missing Human Subject.* Albany: State University of New York Press, 1997.

Viart, Dominique. "Un Mausolée pour le Sud: Faulkner et les paradoxes du primitivisme." *Revue des sciences humaines* 101, no. 3 (1992): 197–219.

Virgilio, Carmelo. "Primitivism in Latin American Fiction." In *The Ibero-American Enlightenment,* 243–255. Ed. A. O. Aldridge. Urbana: University of Illinois Press, 1971.

Volek, Emil. "*El hablador* de Vargas Llosa: Del realismo mágico a la post-modernidad." *Cuadernos Hispanoamericanos* 509 (1992): 95–102.

Wasserman, Renata R. M. *Exotic Nations: Literature and Cultural Identity in the United States and Brazil, 1830–1930.* Ithaca, NY: Cornell University Press, 1994.

Webb, Barbara. *Myth and History in Caribbean Fiction: Alejo Carpentier, Wilson Harris and Edouard Glissant.* Amherst: University of Massachusetts Press, 1992.

Zamora, Lois Parkinson. *The Usable Past: The Imagination of History in Recent Fiction of the Americas.* New York: Cambridge University Pess, 1997.

Zamora, Lois Parkinson, and Wendy B. Faris, eds. *Magical Realism: Theory, History, Community.* Durham, NC: Duke University Press, 1995.

About the Contributors

ELI BARTRA is Professor of Cultural Policy and Women's Studies at the Universidad Autónoma Metropolitana–Xochimilco. Her books include *En busca de las diablas. Sobre arte popular y género* (Mexico City: Tava, 1994); *Frida Kahlo: Mujer, ideología, arte* (Barcelona: Icaria, 1994); and edited books on feminism in Mexico. She has been a visiting professor at several universities in the United States, Latin America, and Europe. Her articles on art, ideology, and feminism have appeared in Mexican and international journals, including *Nuevo Texto Crítico, Studies in Latin American Popular Culture,* and *La Jornada Semanal.*

ROGER BARTRA is Professor of Anthropology at the Universidad Nacional Autónoma de México. He is a leading critic of Mexican cultural and political life whose writings extend across cultural studies, social anthropology, ethnology, history, politics, and the arts. A central preoccupation in his research is the dynamics of power and legitimation in state and social strata, and its mediation in cultural production, ideology, and identity. His recent work sheds light upon the role of primitivism in the construction of a myth of nationhood. For his recent books, see the bibliography in this volume.

ERIK CAMAYD-FREIXAS is Assistant Professor of Latin American Literature at Florida International University in Miami. He is the author of *Realismo mágico y primitivismo* (Lanham, MD: University Press of America, 1998). His articles have appeared in *Texto Crítico, Revista de Crítica Literaria Latinoamericana, Canadian Review of Comparative Literature,* and in other journals and volumes. His research focuses on anthropological approaches to Latin American literature: questions of *mestizaje,* hybridity, and identity in cultural studies, narratology, and poetics.

AMARYLL CHANADY is Professor of Comparative Literature at the Université de Montréal. She has published on national identity, cultural otherness, marginalization, multiculturalism, postcolonialism, and Latin American literature and culture. Her articles have appeared in *Sociocriticism, Imprévue, Espace caraïbe, Río de la Plata, Semiotica, Études françaises, Terceira margem,* and other journals and volumes. Her books include *Magical Realism and the Fantastic: Resolved Versus Unresolved Antinomy* (New York: Garland, 1985) and, as editor, *Latin American Identity and Constructions of Difference* (Minneapolis: University of Minnesota Press, 1994). She is now completing a monograph on the construction of collective identity in the Americas.

DELIA ANNUNZIATA COSENTINO is a Ph.D. candidate in art history at UCLA, specializing in Mexican art. She has been an intern at the Fowler Museum and the Sesnon Gallery, and has worked with the Xunantunich Archaeological Project in Belize. Her research interests also include Renaissance and Islamic art. She has been a Fulbright scholar in Mexico and a resident scholar at Dumbarton Oaks.

WENDY B. FARIS is Professor of English and Comparative Literature at the University of Texas in Arlington. She is the author of *Carlos Fuentes* (New York: Frederick Ungar, 1983) and *Labyrinths of Language: Symbolic Landscape and Narrative Design in Modern Fiction* (Baltimore: Johns Hopkins University Press, 1988), and coeditor of *Magical Realism: Theory, History, Community* (Durham, NC: Duke University Press, 1995). Her work in progress includes a book on magical realism as shamanistic narrative and a study of exotic primitivism in Baudelaire, Gauguin, Gide, and Matisse. For the last ten years Dr. Faris has taught on primitivism. She has published numerous articles and contributed to several collective volumes, among them *Modern Latin American Fiction,* ed. Harold Bloom (New York: Chelsea House, 1990) and *Do the Americas Have a Common Literature?,* ed. Gustavo Pérez Firmat (Durham, NC: Duke University Press, 1990).

JOSÉ EDUARDO GONZÁLEZ is Assistant Professor of Latin American Literature at the University of Nebraska–Lincoln. He is the author of *Borges and the Politics of Form* (New York: Garland, 1998). His articles have appeared in *Revista de Crítica Literaria Latinoamericana, Modern Language Notes, Revista de Estudios Hispánicos,* and *Nuevo Texto Crítico.* His work in progress includes a book on the influence of Walter Benjamin and the Frankfurt School on Angel Rama's literary theories, as well as a study on postmodernism and politics in the novels of Carmen Boullosa and Ricardo Piglia.

TACE MEGAN HEDRICK is Assistant Professor of English and Women's Studies at the University of Florida in Gainesville, specializing in Latin American, Latino, and North American Literature. Dr. Hedrick has published in *Latin American Literary Review, Women's History, Iowa Review,* and other journals. She has received several grants and fellowships, among them a Capital College Research Grant and an NEH Study Grant.

R. LANE KAUFFMANN is Associate Professor of Spanish and Chair of Hispanic and Classical Studies at Rice University. His research focuses on the modern European essay, comparative literature, literary theory, philosophy, and semiotics. His articles have appeared in *Diacritics, New American Scholar, Inti, Diogène, Telos, Revista Mexicana de Sociología, Philological Quarterly, Transculture,* and *L'Esprit créateur,* and in several collective volumes. His work in progress includes a book on the modern Spanish essay.

JORGE MARCONE is Associate Professor of Latin American Literature at Rutgers University. He has published *La oralidad escrita* (Lima: Universidad Católica del Perú, 1987) and is working on a monograph titled *El mal de la selva. Amazonía, ecologismo y la novela de la selva.* His articles have appeared in *Hispania, Estudios* (Venezuela), *Monographic Review,* and a special issue of *Hispanic Journal* dedicated to Latin American literature and ecology.

LUIS FERNANDO RESTREPO is Assistant Professor of Latin American Literature at the University of Arkansas in Fayetteville. He specializes in the Colonial period and currently studies the role of epic in colonial societies. His articles have appeared in *Torre de Papel, Revista de la Universidad Pontificia Bolivariana, Aleph, Thesaurus* (Colombia), *Revista de la Universidad Católica* (Peru), and will appear in forthcoming volumes: *History of the Caribbean* (University of Virginia) and *Tomás Carrasquilla* (Southern Colorado State University). Dr. Restrepo has received an NEH group grant for developing interactive software on the encounter of Europeans and Native American cultures of the Mississippi Valley.

FERNANDO VALERIO-HOLGUÍN is Assistant Professor of Latin American Literature at Colorado State University, specializing in Afro-Caribbean literature and literary theory. He studies the Caribbean Diaspora and the representation of the *trujillato* in Dominican narrative. He is the author of *Poética de la frialdad: La narrativa de Virgilio Piñera* (Lanham, MD.: University Press of America, 1997). His articles have appeared in *Revista de Estudios Hispánicos, Chasqui, Latin American Issues, Romance Quarterly,* and *Explicación de Textos Literarios,* among others. His work in progress includes a book on the Dominican novelist Marcio Veloz Maggiolo.

IVETE LARA CAMARGOS WALTY is Professor of Literature at the Pontifícia Universidade Católica de Minas Gerais. Dr. Walty studies the oral literature of the Tupí tribes in Brazil. Her linguistic and literary studies of this material feature among her publications in Brazilian journals and have been presented at conferences in Cuba, Mexico, and the United States. She is coeditor of Pichuvi Cinta Larga's book *Mantere ma kwé tinhin: Histórias de maloca antigamente* (Belo Horizonte: SEGRAC/CIMI, 1988).

GABRIEL WEISZ is Professor of Comparative Literature at the Universidad Nacional Autónoma de México. He has been a lecturer at the University of Medellín, the University of Paris VII, and Washington University. Among his works, *Palacio chamánico* (Mexico City: UNAM, 1994) surveys shamanism in Artaud; *El juego viviente* (Mexico City: Siglo XXI, 1993) studies body, environment, and ritual games; *Tribu del infinito* (Mexico City: Arbol Editorial, 1992) explores mathematical, ethnological, and philosophical models for shamanistic performances; his article "Personificaciones somáticas" (*Revista de Literatura Comparada* [UNAM], 1996) deals with personifications in healing ceremonies and literature; "Mathematics of Introspection" (*Méli-Mélo* [Tokyo], 1989) is an article on pre-Hispanic hieroglyphs and the body; and "Le Cerveau rituel" (*Internationale de l'Imaginaire* [Paris], 1986) is an essay on the biology of ritual events.

Index